I0820121

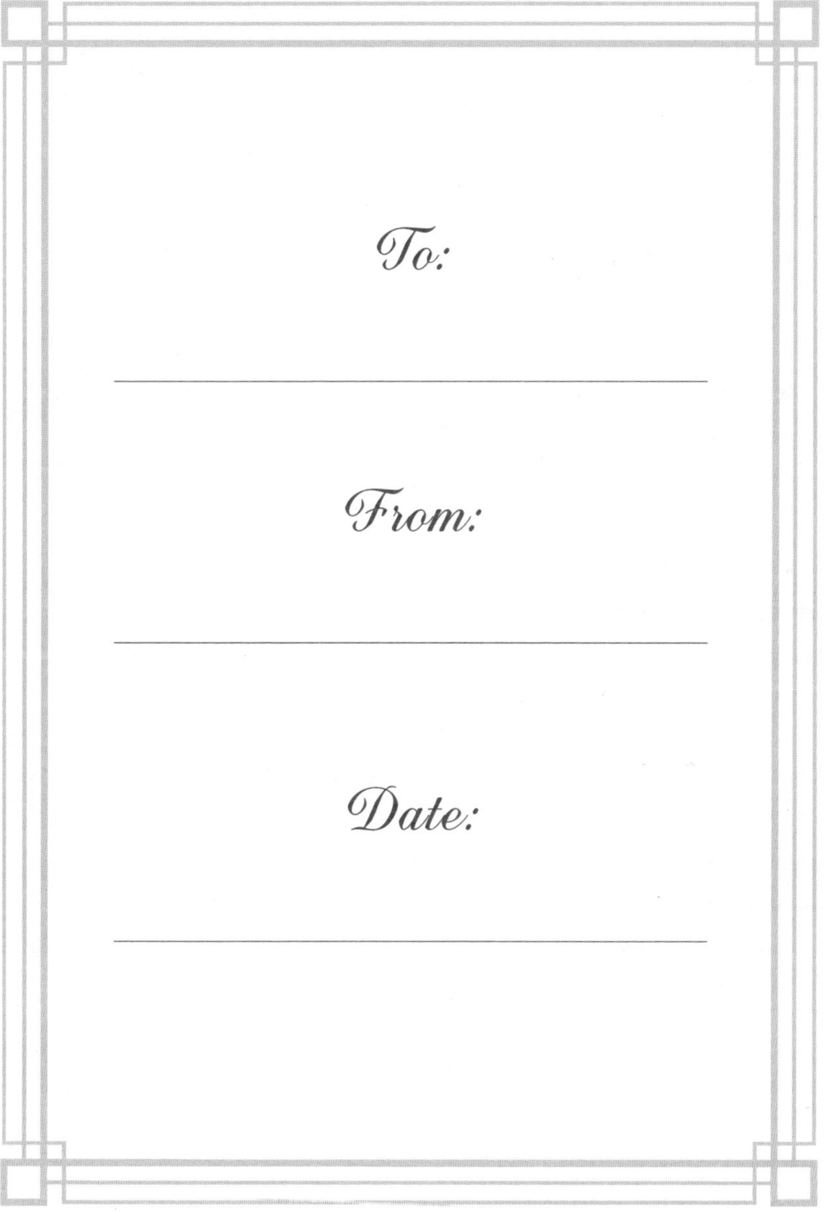

To:

From:

Date:

Visit Christian Art Gifts, Inc., at www.christianartgifts.com.

Drawing Near to God: 365-Day Prayer Devotional

Previously published by Zondervan as notes in *The NIV Prayer Bible*, copyright © 1984.

Published by Christian Art Gifts, Inc., Bloomingdale, IL, USA.

First edition 2024.

Designed by Christian Art Gifts, Inc.

Cover and interior images used under license from Shutterstock.com.

ISBN 978-1-63952-729-8

Printed in China.

29 28 27 26 25 24
10 9 8 7 6 5 4 3 2 1

DRAWING *Near* TO GOD

365-DAY *Prayer Devotional*

BEN PATTERSON

Introduction

"Turn your Bible into prayer." Robert Murray M'Cheyne[1]

This is a book of daily devotions which are designed to help you turn your Bible into prayer. It is a collection of devotional helps, historical and biographical sketches, and book introductions to help you pray from Holy Scripture, Genesis through Revelation, every day of the year.

But why should such a thing exist?

The easiest answer is that whenever you pray through Scripture, you never need wonder whether you are praying according to God's will. Prayer is not a means by which we get God to give us what we want. "Prayer is a means God uses to give us what he wants," writes Bingham Hunter.[2] The Bible tells us what God wants. At first that may seem a little deflating, asking God only for what God already wants to give. By this definition, prayer can sound like a noble and lofty exercise, a soul-purifying meditation on platonic ideals—hardly anything to get the heart beating faster.

But look at what God wants to give! Paul's prayer that the Ephesians might be filled to the measure of all the fullness of God and know a love that surpasses knowledge (Eph. 3:14-21) is better than the best any of us could possibly have imagined and wished on our own. That's only one example of the things the Bible says God wants to give. C. S. Lewis was right:

Indeed, if we consider the unblushing promises of reward and the staggering nature of the rewards promised in the Gospels, it seems that our Lord finds our desires, not too strong, but too weak. We are half-hearted creatures, fooling about with drink and sex and ambition when infinite joy has been offered us, like an ignorant child who wants to go on making mud pies in a slum because he cannot imagine what is meant by the offer of a holiday at the sea. We are far too easily pleased.[3]

To desire what God wants to give, and to turn that desire into prayer is to be expanded in spirit. The purpose of this prayer devotional is to help you understand, desire, and delight in what God wants to give.

The relationship between the Bible and prayer is profound. Picture it this way: Children and other novices to the Bible have long been told that the best way to find the book of Psalms, the longest book in the Bible, is to put their finger in the middle of the Bible—in its heart, so to speak. What is the book of Psalms? It is a book of prayers. And the longest prayer in this longest book is Psalm 119, a prayer about the Scriptures. Prayer is at the heart of the Bible, and the Bible is in the heart of prayer.

But that's just a picture, an illustration of the relationship. Better is a demonstration—the prayer life of our Lord Jesus Christ. At the end of his life, as he hung dying on the cross, he went to Scripture for his prayers. "My God, my God, why have you forsaken me" (Matt. 27:46) is a quotation from Psalm 22:1. "Father, into your hands I commit my spirit" (Luke 27:46) comes from Psalm 31:5. At the point of his greatest anguish and extremity, Jesus turned to the Bible for his prayers. Charles Spurgeon urges us to learn from the fact that when he most needed to pray, Jesus, the grand original thinker, saw no need to be original or extemporaneous.

"How instructive is this great truth that the Incarnate Word lived on the Inspired Word! It was food to him, as it is to us; and, if Christ thus lived upon the Word of God, should not you and I do the same? I think it well worthy of your constant remembrance that, even in death, our blessed Master showed the ruling passion of his spirit, so that his last words were a quotation from Scripture."[4]

As a devout Jew, Jesus' prayer book was the Psalms. A close look at the Psalms shows the Lord's Prayer, the prayer Jesus taught us to pray, to be a summary and distillation of all the prayers that are to be found in the heart of the Bible. It's all there in the Psalms: prayer that God's name be hallowed, his rule be supreme, and his will be done; that our needs be met and our sins forgiven; that we be kept safe from all danger to soul and body.

Paul coined a word to describe the character of Scripture: he said it is "God-breathed" (2 Tim. 3:16). The breath of God permeates the Bible. The breath of God is the Holy Spirit, the same Spirit who spoke light into darkness and turned dust into living beings made in the image of God. This is the Spirit who speaks to us in the Bible, making it "useful for teaching, rebuking, correcting and training in righteousness" (2 Tim. 3:16). We need all these things to be able to pray well, for although the need for prayer is natural, the ability is not. We must be taught and trained in prayer, and if need be, rebuked and corrected. Like the first disciples who asked Jesus to teach them to pray, we may go to Scripture with the same intent and ask the Spirit of Jesus to do the teaching.

Poet George Herbert described prayer as "God's breath in man returning to his birth."[5] The same Breath that gives us breath to pray comes to us through the God-breathed Scriptures. What we inhale in the Word of God, we exhale in prayer.

When the members of his synagogue complained that the words of the liturgy did not express what they felt, Abraham Heschel, the great philosopher of religion, replied that the liturgy wasn't supposed to express what they felt; they were supposed to feel what the liturgy expressed. To be taught by the Bible to pray is to learn to pray and feel what the Bible expresses—to say what it means and mean what it says. *Drawing Near to God* is designed to help the reader listen to the voice of the Spirit in Scripture in such a way that any text can be a text for prayer. Its object is to teach habits of Bible reading that flow into praise and thanks and confession and supplication.

To pray through, in, and from Scripture is not only to pray according to God's will, but also according to what philosopher Peter Kreeft calls "the grammar of existence." Grammar has to do with the proper relationship between words in a sentence, the way things like verbs, nouns, and adjectives are to be positioned relative to each other. Just as a sentence makes no sense when the grammar is bad, our lives make no sense when we fail to appreciate the elemental grammar of our existence: God is God, and we are not. He does not exist for us; we exist for him. Prayer then, as with everything else in life, is ultimately not about us, but about God. Happy are those who know this! For we were made for God and our hearts are restless until they rest in him (Augustine).

Learning to pray Scripture can teach this joyous grammar of existence, because it gets the focus where it belongs—on God, not on ourselves and our perceived needs and feelings. Frankly, our own self-generated prayers can quickly become boring. It's not that God is boring, but we are, and the spiritual ruts and worn-out ways we have come to pray. Biblical prayer raises our desires to heaven, where they are transformed, and our pleasure in prayer is renewed.

The grammar of existence says that God is always there first, ahead of us. We are because he first was and is and will be. "We love because he first loved us" (1 John 4:19). And so we pray, for we also speak because he first spoke. "Our prayer is the answer to God's," wrote P. T. Forsyth. "Herein is prayer, not that we prayed Him, but that he first prayed us, in giving his Son to be a propitiation for us. The heart of the Atonement is prayer—Christ's great self-offering to God in the Eternal Spirit."[6] Prayer is a dialogue, a conversation initiated by God; he speaks, we respond, he responds to our response, and so it goes, forever. To pray is to be lifted up into the eternal fellowship of the community of God—Father, Son, and Holy Spirit.

Since God starts all this by first speaking his word to us, what better place to begin to pray than with his Word in the Bible? We begin with Jesus, God's word incarnate. There would be no conversation at all were it not for his death and resurrection (Heb. 4:14-16)! The conversation continues and is cultivated with his written word.

Joseph Scriven's old hymn about prayer is true: "What a friend we have in Jesus, all our sins and griefs to bear! What a privilege to carry everything to God in prayer!" But we would know nothing about this wonderful Jesus, and his gift of prayer were it not for the Bible! What a friend we have in Jesus, and what a gift we have in the Holy Scripture he has given us. Francis Schaeffer confessed that he would sometimes reach over to the Bible on his nightstand and just pat it as he woke up in the morning. He explained:

"I don't love this book because it has a leather cover and golden edges. I don't love it as a 'holy book.' I love it because it is God's book. Through it, the Creator of the universe has told us who he is, how to come to him through Christ, who we are, and what all reality is. Without the Bible we wouldn't have anything.... I am so thankful for it. If the God who is there had created the earth and then remained silent, we wouldn't know who he is. But the Bible reveals the God who is there; that is why I love it."[7]

That is why we may love it too and learn better how to express our love for the God who gave us his book and ask for the things he wants to give.

Introduction to Genesis

DAY 1: CREATED TO PRAY

Genesis 1:26-28

"God saw all that he had made, and it was very good" (Gen. 1:31).

The book of Genesis tells how the world began in more ways than one.

It says God spoke the creation into existence, out of nothing, *ex nihilo*—that he was not limited in his creative work by any preexistent material but acted in perfect freedom when he made the heavens and the earth. His only limitations, if one can call them that, were his imagination and character. This has enormous significance for prayer. Since God freely created the universe by his word, out of nothing, we can expect God to continue to act in that way. P. T. Forsyth marveled at God's creativity and called him an "infinite opportunist." The universe is not a closed system of cause and effect, it remains responsive to God's word. Nothing is too hard for the Lord. God answers prayer.

Genesis also affirms touchingly, that we were made for God, because we are made like God, in his image. It pleased him, from the beginning, to make humankind able to walk with him in the world and share with him in the care of his creation. Intercessory prayer is on the same order as all the other things we do to share with God in his work. What we do when we pray is no different, fundamentally, than what we do when we plow a field or manage a budget. Both are rooted in Genesis 1:26-28 (see devotion on Day 48).

When sin entered the picture and the image of God was distorted in us, he did not give up on us, but acted to save and to restore his broken and beloved creatures. The first explicit mention of prayer in the Bible comes in this context (Gen. 4:26). When sin broke our fellowship with God, he kept the door open to call on his name and be restored. The communion with God that made the garden of Eden such a delight remains God's great passion for his creatures and will be established one day forever. Prayer will once again be as the air we breathe (Rev. 21:3).

PRAYER: *You made me for yourself, O Lord, and my heart is restless until it rests in you.*[1] *Teach me to pray.*

DAY 2: THE FACE IN FRONT OF THE WORLD

Genesis 1:1-31

"In the beginning God created the heavens and the earth" (Gen. 1:3).

The secret of the world, said G. K. Chesterton, is to know that we only see the back of it. We see everything from behind; trees, clouds, planets, stars, oceans, everything. "Cannot you see that everything is stooping and hiding a face? If only we could get around in front."[1] Behold, the face on the front of the world is God's. That's what this chapter in Genesis is about. Seeing only the backside of the creation, we are tempted to think of it only in terms of space and matter. Seeing the front, the face, as the opening chapter in the Bible does, we must sing. Whatever else Genesis one is, it is a hymn of praise to the God who made all things. You can add your own embellishments to the song by singing of particulars. Does God say the birds and fish and livestock he created are good? You say, as you pray, the crows and dolphins and Hereford cows are good. Make up a tune as you go.

Imagine this chapter as footage from a time-lapse film of the creation. Light bursts forth, waters separate and gather, mountains arise, forests spread, animals appear, millions of millennia dance and flash by. Then the film slows down to real time, and then slow-motion. A man and a woman stand naked and innocent, warm and glistening in the love of God. God's face brightens as he looks at something of himself gazing back at him. "So God created man in his own image, in the image of God he created him; male and female he created them" (Gen. 1:27). Time to sing again. The words of Psalm 8 would be good: "When I consider your heavens, the work of your fingers, the moon and stars which you have set in place, what is man that you are mindful of him…? You made him a little lower than the heavenly beings and crowned him with glory and honor" (Ps. 8:3-5). The next time you are perplexed, disappointed, and discouraged by another person, or yourself, remember you are seeing from behind. In front, there is a face Jesus came to restore to the image of God (2 Cor. 3:18).

PRAYER: *"There's not a plant or flower below, but makes Thy glories known; And clouds arise, and tempests blow, by order from Thy throne; while all that borrows life from Thee is ever in Thy care. And everywhere that man can be; Thou, God, art present there" (from the hymn "I Sing the Mighty Power of God" by Isaac Watts).*

DAY 3: WHEN ALL ELSE FAILS

Genesis 4:26—5:21-24

"At that time, men began to call on the name of the Lord" (Gen. 4:26).

This is the first mention of prayer in the Bible. What is the significance of "at that time"? Look at all that leads up to "that time." In four brief chapters, we read that God created the heavens and earth and pronounced them "good." Then he made a man and a woman, the crown of his creation, in his own image and declared all that he had made "very good." But like a shattered mirror, God's image is broken when the first humans disobey him. You can still see the likeness, but it is terribly distorted. Later Adam and Eve have two sons, Cain and Abel, but Cain kills Abel. The first offspring of God's crowning creation is a murderer! It gets worse before it gets better. Cain has kids and they are a lot like their old man. Soon we hear of a certain Lamech who intends to outdo Cain in malice: "If Cain is avenged seven times, then Lamech seventy-seven times" (Gen. 4:24). Lamech will make Cain's days seem like the good-old-days. Death and violence increase exponentially. "The power of sin is centrifugal.... It tends to push everything out toward the periphery. Bits and pieces go flying off until only the core is left.... In the end nothing at all is left."[1]

"Nevertheless" is a great grace word. So nevertheless, God acts graciously and gives Adam and Eve another child to replace Abel. His name almost is grace; they call him Seth, which probably means "granted." That's the time when people began to call on the name of the Lord. There is a saying, "When all else fails, read the directions." The impulse to pray is a little like that. So far, taking matters into their own hands has got everybody in trouble. We are more apt to see the need to pray when we see how great our needs are; when we run up against the hard edge of our limitations. There's not much we can do in our own name, but "the name of the Lord is a strong tower; the righteous run into it and are safe" (Prov. 18:10).

There is hope. Centuries later, but only a few verses in the Bible, there comes along a man of prayer named Enoch, "who walked with God" (Gen. 5:21-24). Echoes of what was originally intended for all humankind reverberate in those few words (Gen. 3:8). In the fullness of time there will come another child of grace, and communion with God will again be what it was supposed to be (Gal. 4:4-5; Heb. 4:14-18).

PRAYER: *Lord, your name is a strong tower, a refuge for the weary and a pleasure for your children. Forgive my prayerlessness. Remind me often of my need for the delight to pray.*

DAY 4: LIVING BY UNSEEN REALITIES

Genesis 12—13

"I will make you into a great nation" (Gen. 12:2).

The whole question of why God chooses whom he chooses to do his work in the world is a mystery. The Bible's answer is, "so that no one may boast before him" (1 Cor. 1:29). The real story is about God, not his servants. The personal and moral qualities one might look for in a man who was to be the father of millions, and through whom the peoples of earth would be blessed, aren't mentioned in his call, because they are beside the point. All God looked for in Abram was faith. Would he trust God's promise enough to leave what he had known, to travel to something he didn't know, but that God would show him? Note: it was not something God had shown him, but what he would show him. Abram didn't even get a map to where God was taking him; all he got was a promise. His faith was a call to live by unseen realities.

That is the worldview of prayer. When we do something on our own, with what we can see, who gets the glory? We do. When God answers prayer, in ways we can't see, who gets the glory? He does. That way no one can boast. Mere human activity is about us. Prayer is about God. So wherever Abram went, this man of faith pitched tents and built altars (Gen. 12:7; 13:18). Tents are about the seen, what is ours; altars are about the unseen, what is God's. Abram's place of residence was a passing thing, his hope in the God he prayed to was fixed. If God's people are often odd (cf. 1 Cor. 1:26-29), it's only because his methods are too, from the world's perspective. That way no one can boast.

To pray you must hope in God's good promises more than you do in your own good ideas. When you do, you are taken places you never dreamed, for you hear God calling you to:

Leap out from your reedy shallows.
Dive into the moving water.
Eyeless, learn to see truly.
Find in my folly your true sanity.[1]

PRAYER: *God of Abraham, Isaac, Jacob, and our Lord Jesus Christ: teach me to trust your promises, that you may gain great glory, and I might know the joy of communion with you.*

DAY 5: THE FORGE

Genesis 15

"Abram believed the Lord, and he credited to him as righteousness" (Gen. 15:6).

Hear the gospel: "Abraham believed the Lord, and he credited to him as righteousness" (Gen. 15:6). That is really good news. God knows how bad we are at the thing we most need to be good at to meet his holy standards: holiness. It pleases him to accept us as holy when we trust his promises. Think about such a truth and you will be bowled over with the good news. "For it is by grace you have been saved, through faith" (Eph. 2:8).

Now hear the hard part: faith is forged in delay. A forge is a furnace heated to a white-hot temperature. Metal is thrust into the forge until heat makes it malleable, then it is pounded into shape. God's forge for our faith is the gap between the giving of his promise and its fulfillment. Faith is forged in delay, but the temptation in delay is to jump out of the forge. The most common way we do this is by becoming "God's little helpers"—believing we can achieve his ends using our own means.

That's what Abram is flirting with here. In his day, a childless couple could adopt a slave and make him the heir. For Abram, that man is Eliezer of Damascus. True, God had promised Abram and Sarai a child, but that was when Abram was 75 years old. Time has passed, and they're not getting any younger, so maybe what God wants is for them to practice a little common sense, a little conventional wisdom, and do the prudent thing. But God makes it clear once again that he means to give them their own, biological child. Abram believes this and is credited with righteousness. So far, so good. But one chapter later the childless couple will jump out of the forge and try their own methods again, with disastrous results. The Hagar debacle haunts the whole world to this day.

The hardest thing about prayer is the waiting. Jesus told his disciples a parable about prayer so that they would keep on praying and not lose heart. It ended with the question, "When the Son of Man comes, will he find faith on the earth" (Luke 18:8)? Will we still be in the forge, praying and waiting, our faith being tested and strengthened?

PRAYER: *Dear Father, your timing is perfect. You make all things beautiful in your time. Strengthen me to wait and pray with patience and faith.*

DAY 6: FINDING OUT ABOUT PRAYER

Genesis 18:16-33

"Shall I hide from Abraham what I am about to do?" (Gen. 18:17).

In 1952 a doctoral student at Princeton asked a visiting lecturer, "What is there left in the world for original dissertation research?" The visiting lecturer was Albert Einstein. His answer was, "Find out about prayer. Somebody must find out about prayer."[1] The problem is that the question was about science, and prayer won't yield its secrets to scientific methods. God won't be put under a microscope.

But God most definitely wants us to learn about prayer. First, he takes the initiative to get us to pray. Why he does this with Abraham is fascinating. He asks, "Shall I hide from Abraham what I am about to do?" He answers his own question: "Abraham will surely become a great and powerful nation, and all the nations on earth will be blessed through him" (Gen. 18:18). Since Abraham has a key role to play in God's purposes for the world, God decides therefore to bring him into the conversation about Sodom and Gomorrah. Like a king with his royal advisors, God wants Abraham to intercede for the cities!

Blaise Pascal suggested that one of the reasons God gave us prayer was to give us the dignity of causality. Do you appreciate the extraordinary gift God gives in prayer? He works on us by his grace to get us to work on him by our faith. He grants to prayer a power to which he will graciously condescend to submit.

How God gets us to pray is equally fascinating. As with Abraham, he often uses perplexity to draw us into prayer. Abraham's nephew Lot lives in Sodom and may die if God carries out his plan. Abraham is aghast, and remonstrates, "Far be it from you! Will not the Judge of all the earth do right" (Gen. 18:25)? Sadly, many of us would not pray if we weren't driven to our knees. The result is that when the praying is over, we and Abraham discover God is better than we knew him to be before the perplexity. Prayer rejoices in testing because it makes faith pure (James 1:2-4). God himself seems to rejoice in the effects the perplexity has on us. He so wants us to pray that he seems to more than tolerate Abraham's chutzpah in verse 25. He actually seems to enjoy it. In prayer, God calls us to be active partners, not passive spectators.

PRAYER: *Great God! You don't need us, but in your wisdom and love, you call us to this partnership of prayer. Get me out of the grandstands onto the praying field.*

DAY 7: MUSTARD SEED PRAYING

Jan Amos Comenius

"We fix our eyes not on what is seen, but on what is unseen" (2 Cor. 4:18).

Jesus said the kingdom of God starts small but grows, quietly and mysteriously, like a tiny seed planted in the soil (Mark 4:1-20, 26-32). It should not surprise us, therefore, that God's answers to prayer often come in the same way. We pray and we wait and wait and wait. We wonder, did he hear, does he care, has he refused?

In the 1620s, Jan Amos Comenius and a rag-tag bunch of his church members knelt in the snow at the Polish border and prayed a wistful but bold mustard-seed prayer. In the turmoil of Catholic-Protestant rivalry in The Thirty Years War, they had been forced to leave their loved Bohemia. As they knelt shivering, they looked back longingly at their homeland, as Comenius asked God to preserve in Bohemia "a hidden seed to glorify thy name." But Comenius never saw his prayer answered. In 1670 he died an exile, penniless and homeless. He did, however, leave the world 154 books that were seminal in the formation of modern ideas about Christian education.

His prayer was answered 100 years later when a young Count Zinzendorf opened his family estate in Moravia as a refuge for the followers of Comenius. They called their community the Herrnhut or "Lord's Watch" in German. Since they themselves were the fruit of mustard seed praying, they took their name from Isaiah 62:6-7, a great text on mustard seed prayer:

> *I have posted watchmen on your walls, O Jerusalem; they will never be silent day or night. You who call on the Lord, give yourselves no rest, and give him no rest till he establishes Jerusalem and makes her the praise of the earth.*

The Moravian Brethren, as they came to be known, were the pioneers of modern missions. In the first 100 years of their existence, they maintained a continuous twenty-four-hour, seven-day-a-week prayer vigil, and sent 2000 missionaries to the ends of the earth. It was at a Moravian prayer meeting in London that John Wesley felt his heart "strangely warmed." From that encounter came the world-shaking Wesleyan revival, the impact of which we feel to this day.

Comenius prayed for God to preserve in Bohemia "a hidden seed to glorify thy name." From a human perspective, it may have seemed that God did nothing for a century, but for the next two and a half centuries, he went far beyond anything that little bunch of refugees could have ever imagined—beyond Bohemia to the world!

God's ways are not our ways. His timing is not our timing. Where are you in your prayers now? Kneeling with Comenius in the snow? Wondering with Comenius at the end of his life? Read and reflect on the seed parables of Mark 4. Ask the Holy Spirit to strengthen your praying with mustard seed hope.

PRAYER: *Holy Spirit of God! I pray, hoping for things I cannot now see. Strengthen my little mustard seed faith to wait for the day when faith becomes sight. Amen.*

DAY 8: FOR LIFE OR DEATH

Genesis 22:1-19

"God himself will provide the lamb" (Gen. 22:8).

Martin Luther once said, "The only saving faith is that which casts itself on God for life or death."[1] Abraham's faith, in this gut-wrenching story, is "exhibit A" of that truth. It has puzzled and inspired both believers and nonbelievers alike for centuries. In his weakness and grief, Abraham's faith was strong, even though it probably didn't feel that way to him. But believing that God's promise to bless the world through his offspring was true, he "reasoned that God could raise the dead" (Heb. 11:19) if necessary. So, he cast himself on God for life or death.

Abraham's faith has come a long way from the finagling and second-guessing of the Hagar episode. It is different, though not necessarily better, from the faith that wrestled with God over Sodom and Gomorrah. This time he simply says "Yes," to God's command and explains his actions to a confused son who wants to know where the lamb for the offering is: "God himself will provide the lamb for the burnt offering, my son" (Gen. 22:8). He had learned that the only way to keep his life was to lose it in God.

How does one get to that kind of faith? By years of walking, and sometimes stumbling, by faith. The key to a growing faith is the cultivation of a close relationship with God over the long haul. Abraham had grown in intimacy with God by being forced sometimes to trust him in ways he didn't understand. But mostly, it was the day-in, day-out choice to walk by faith in the little things, that taught Abraham to trust God in the big things. That is why the spiritual disciplines, particularly prayer and Scripture reading, are so important. By showing us the face of God when we can see it, they help us to trust when we can't see it.

PRAYER: *Dear Father, help me to see you today, that I might remember what I saw when I can't see you. Teach me to walk by faith, casting myself on you for life or death.*

DAY 9: PRAYER FOR SPOUSES AND MASTERS

Genesis 24:12-15

"Give me success today and show kindness to my master Abraham" (Gen. 24:12).

No one who desires marriage for themselves or for those they love can fail to be moved by the sweetness of this servant's prayer: "O Lord, God of my master Abraham, give me success today and show kindness to my master Abraham" (Gen. 24:12). It is the most natural thing in the world to pray for a spouse because the God we pray to said, "It is not good for the man to be alone. I will make a helper suitable for him" (Gen. 2:18). Proverbs 18:22 encourages confidence in this kind of prayer: "He who finds a wife finds what is good and receives favor from the Lord." God even chose the relationship of husband to wife to be the defining metaphor of his relationship to his church (Eph. 5:22-33). The Lord loves to answer this kind of prayer with a warm, "Yes." But even when his answer is "No" it is for the sake of a different "Yes." His gracious will for most is not his will for all; but it is no less gracious for those who receive a different gift (1 Cor. 7:7).

The servant's prayer is praiseworthy for another reason: it's a prayer to serve his master faithfully. He understands on a deep level that to serve Abraham well is to serve God well through Abraham. The Bible commends this kind of prayer too. Paul urges slaves to obey their "earthy masters with respect and fear, and with sincerity of heart, just as you would obey Christ. Obey them not only to win their favor when their eye is on you, but like slaves of Christ, doing the will of God from your heart. Serve wholeheartedly, as if you were serving the Lord, not men" (Eph. 6:5-7). Serve your earthly master or boss from your heart, and you will find yourself praying for your boss from your heart. Or perhaps you need to pray from your heart that you will serve from your heart!

PRAYER: *Master of all, tune my heart both to sing your praise, and to praise you with my heartfelt service and prayers for my earthly master.*

DAY 10: WRESTLING WITH GOD

Genesis 32

"Your name will be no longer be Jacob, but Israel, because you have struggled with God and with men and have overcome" (Gen. 32:28).

Jacob had been a wrestler from birth. The second of twins, he even came out of his mother's womb grasping his brother Esau's heel—in itself a pretty good wrestling move. His name even meant wrestler, sort of. It was "Jacob" which means, "he grasps the heel" or figuratively, "he deceives" (Gen. 25:26). That had been his career up to this point; he wrestled well, but he wasn't a good wrestler. He was effective, but sneaky, and used his skill to cheat his older brother Esau out of his blessing. Esau's rage required that Jacob spend the next several years of his life in exile. Even there he wrestled with a father-in-law, Laban, who also knew how to put on a few good wrestling moves.

Now, in this chapter, he is going home hoping to reconcile with Esau. The night before he meets Esau he prays, "O God of my father Isaac, O Lord, who said to me, 'Go back to your country and your relatives, and I will make you prosper,' I am unworthy of all the kindness and faithfulness you have shown your servant.... Save me, I pray, from the hand of my brother Esau" (Gen. 32:9-11). Jacob is a different man at a critical point. Now he prays humbly for God's mercy, where before he would have tried to manipulate the situation. But he is not done wrestling. He wrestles with God for the blessing and gets it (Gen. 32:26-29)! God gives him a new name, "Israel," which means "he struggles with God."

God loves this kind of wrestling. Not much good comes from wrestling with people; resentment rises and enemies are usually made. Not much good comes from wrestling with life and work either; sleep comes hard and ulcers form. "In vain you rise early and stay up late, toiling for food to eat" (Ps. 127:2). "Toiling" is another word for fruitless wrestling. Take it to the Lord in prayer. Wrestle with him for the blessing, not people and circumstances. "Resist God, in the sense of rejecting God, and you will not be able to resist any evil. But resist God in the sense of closing with God, cling to him with your strength, not your weakness only... and he will give you strength. Cast yourself into his arms not to be caressed but to wrestle with Him. He loves that holy war. He may be too many for you and lift you from your feet. But it will be to lift you from earth and set you in the heavenly places which are theirs who fight the good fight and lay hold of God as their eternal life."[1]

PRAYER: *My soul clings to you, O God. You alone have the words of life. I will not let go till you bless me.*

DAY 11: AN ELDER'S PRAYER

Genesis 48:15-16

"By faith Jacob, when he was dying, blessed each of Joseph's sons" (Heb. 11:21).

The prospect of one's death acutely focuses the mind. But on what? Astonishingly, for some it only intensifies concerns for personal peace and comfort. But for others it directs their minds toward eternity and the next generation. Jacob is a very old man in this passage. He is near death and the latter is his frame of mind as Joseph brings him his two sons, Ephraim and Manasseh, to be blessed by their grandfather. The faith Jacob is remembered for in the New Testament is not the faith that wrestled with God, but the faith that blessed Joseph's sons. This has much to teach about prayer.

"By faith Jacob, when he was dying, blessed each of Joseph's sons, and worshiped as he leaned on the top of his staff" (Heb. 11:21). To say Jacob did this while he was dying is to say that the blessing was something he himself would not see. That is the faith that so pleases God: "being sure of what we hope for and certain of what we do not see" (Heb. 11:1-2, 6). The verse just before Jacob's mention says the same thing about Isaac's faith, and the verse immediately after about Joseph's faith. Brazilian theologian, Rubem Alves, said hope is hearing the music of the future, and faith is to dance to it. Jacob, though old and infirm, is dancing as he prays his blessing.

How should the elderly pray? They pray with a great abandon to faith and a generous love that will bless the next generation. Bodies may slow down, but our prayers shouldn't. Theologian Karl Barth believed the nearness of death should not shrink our faith but cause the river of responsibility "to flow more torrentially than ever in view of the approaching falls, of the proximity of the coming Judge!"[1] David was comforted that God understood his frailty and mortality: "He knows how we are formed; he remembers that we are dust" (Ps. 103:14). His comfort grows as he considers that even though he will die, God's love will continue to the generations to come: "As for man, his days are like grass, he flourishes like a flower of the field; the wind blows over it and it is gone, and its place remembers it no more. But from everlasting to everlasting the Lord's love is with those who fear him, and his righteousness with their children's children" (Ps. 103:14-17). The passion of every generation should be to know the Lord. But the passion of a passing generation should especially be that the next generation will—and so pray that blessing.

PRAYER: *Eternal Father! Give faith and strength to pray for those who will come after me; and to teach the next generation, even the children yet unborn and those yet to come after them to know the Lord.*

DAY 12: GOD INTENDS IT FOR GOOD

Genesis 50:15-21

"You intended to harm me, but God intended it for good" (Gen. 50:20).

Of course, Joseph's brothers expected him to try to kill them after their father Jacob died. They had it coming to them since years before they had tried callously to murder him. So, they were stunned at what Joseph did when he heard of their fears. First, he wept, then he said to them, "Don't be afraid. Am I in the place of God? You intended to harm me, but God intended it for good to accomplish what is being done, the saving of many lives" (Gen. 50:17-20). The worldwide famine would have destroyed Joseph's brothers and their families had Joseph not been "sent" to Egypt ahead of them.

Over the years, Joseph had gained a perspective on life that is priceless. It is wonderfully captured in the sixteenth century Heidelberg Catechism's description of the providence of God: "Providence is the almighty and ever present power of God by which he upholds, as with his hand, heaven and earth and all creatures, and so rules them that leaf and blade, rain and drought, fruitful and lean years, food and drink, health and sickness, prosperity and poverty—all things, in fact, come to us not by chance but from his fatherly hand."

What Joseph had come to see was that the fundamental issue had not been between him and his brothers, but between him and his God. True, his brothers were scoundrels, but finally it was God who gave them permission to act as they did and God who used their evil to promote good for all of them! Over the years his conflict with his brothers had been transformed into his wrestling with God and with a glorious result: Joseph was freed of his bitterness. The Catechism says this perspective will make us "patient when things go against us, thankful when things go well, and for the future we can have good confidence in our faithful God and Father that nothing will separate us from his love."[1]

This confidence is the fruit of a lifetime of wrestling with God in prayer over the bad things others have done to us. It doesn't relieve them of their responsibility, but it frees us from our slavery to anger and from a victim mentality. Fight them, and the fighting will be endless. Wrestle with God, and you will be free.

PRAYER: *Almighty and loving Father, I thank you that all the things that come to me must first pass through your great heart of wisdom and love. Teach me to think less of the wrongs others have done to me and more of your power to turn those wrongs to my good (Rom. 8:28).*

DAY 13: NIGHT OF FIRE

Blaise Pascal

"You believe in him and are filled with an inexpressible and glorious joy" (1 Pet. 1:8).

Blaise Pascal (1623-1662), was one of the greatest minds in history. His work on probability, experiments with the vacuum and atmospheric pressure, and invention of the first calculating machine established him as a scientist of the first order. The elegance of his prose moved Voltaire to proclaim him the finest writer in France. But what he will most be remembered for are his *Pensees*, a collection of thoughts that, had he lived long enough, were to form the basis of a defense of the Christian faith.

After Pascal's death, a piece of parchment was found sewn into his clothing which he apparently carried with him at all times. It is the record of a decisive and ecstatic encounter he had with God on the night of November 23, 1654. What follows is a portion of what he wrote.

Fire
God of Abraham, God of Isaac, God of Jacob, not of philosophers and scholars.
Certainty, certainty, heartfelt, joy, peace.
God of Jesus Christ.
God of Jesus Christ...
Joy, joy, joy, tears of joy...
"And this is life eternal, that they might know thee,
the only true God, and Jesus Christ whom thou hast sent."
Jesus Christ.
Jesus Christ...
Sweet and total renunciation...
Everlasting joy in return for one day's effort on earth.
I will not forget thy word. Amen.[1]

The god of Pascal's times was an abstract noun, merely part of the intellectual and theoretical landscape, a principle to ponder—not the consuming fire of the Bible, the father of Jesus Christ (Heb. 12:29; John 14:9). The god of "philosophers and scholars" is something you think about; the God of Scripture is someone you meet. And he is much more than interesting and impressive. To meet him face to face is to know "Certainty, certainty, heartfelt, joy, peace... Joy, joy, joy, tears of joy."

What Pascal saw of God is breathtakingly lovely and wonderful. But not everyone has Pascal's experience, and it can be hard to read of it and not ache with envy. Nevertheless, what he glimpsed that night awaits all who hope in Christ. One day, in heaven, when we see God as he is, we too will be as he is, gloriously so (1 John 3:2; Rom. 8:18-21). We pray in this hope, knowing that although we don't see him now, we will be filled with "an inexpressible and glorious joy," for we are receiving the goal of our faith, the salvation of our souls (1 Pet. 1:9).

PRAYER: *Father of Joy! I hope in you, for you have made known to me the path of life, and you fill me with joy in your presence, with eternal joys at your right hand (Ps. 16:11).*

Introduction to Exodus

DAY 14: GOD IS LISTENING!

Exodus 3:7-8, 10

"Moses replied, 'when I have gone out of the city, I will spread out my hands in prayer to the Lord" (Exod. 9:29).

The story of the Exodus gets going when the oppressed people of God begin to pray. God states his intentions to Moses by saying:

> *I have indeed seen the misery of my people in Egypt. I have heard them crying out because of their slave drivers, and I am concerned about their suffering... I have come down to rescue them.... So now, go. I am sending you to Pharaoh to bring my people the Israelites out of Egypt (Exod. 3:7-8, 10).*

It's all there, the building blocks of a theology of prayer. God is a God who hears us, and in his own time, he comes to save.

From what we learn later about the people who prayed, their theology was pretty weak and shallow. No doubt they had very little appreciation of the God they prayed to, or even what it meant to pray, but God was so willing to hear, that he started with them where they were. All who pray should take comfort in that.

There's also some humor in this passage. The people prayed, God heard, and he called Moses to be the answer to their prayers. The problem was Moses wanted nothing to do with this! He was a most unwilling answer to prayer, but he came around. Jesus saw the needs of a helpless and harassed crowd and told his disciples to pray that God would, "send out workers into his harvest field" (Matt. 9:36-38). Think of it: your prayers for the lost and needy may seriously disrupt the life of someone who doesn't even know you. And their prayers may return the favor!

God's desire for communion with his people is what drives him to save and set us free. Everything that follows in Exodus, from the giving of the Law to the building of the Tabernacle, springs from the same divine passion to be present with us. The events of Exodus will one day be fulfilled when God's law is written on our hearts (Jer. 31:31-34), and all the saved of the earth will "serve him day and night in his temple (tabernacle); and he who sits on the throne will spread his tent (tabernacle) over them" (Rev. 7:15). Prayer is a rehearsal for the future.

PRAYER: *Come, Lord, help your people, bought with the price of your own blood, and bring us with all your people to glory everlasting.*

DAY 15: PRAYER AS BIG AS GOD

Exodus 3:1—4:17

"Who am I, that I should go to Pharaoh and bring the Israelites out of Egypt?" (Exod. 3:11).

The question, "Who am I?" has become one of the most tiresome questions of our age. And by the time Moses finishes asking it of God four or five different ways in a conversation spanning two chapters, God is fed up with the question. It starts with surprise and a little humility (Exod. 3:11); moves on to doubt (Exod. 3:13); stalls in the "what ifs" (Exod. 4:1); mumbles in self-deprecation (Exod. 4:10-12); and finally stands up and refuses God's command (Exod. 4:13). Throughout Moses' prayer, the theme is always self-preoccupation.

Prayer is a dialogue with God. Often the dialogue breaks down not because God won't speak, but because we don't want to hear what he says. Two things keep our ears plugged. One is that we tend to believe more in what we believe about ourselves than in what we believe about God. After God's remarkable promises to give Moses miraculous help, Moses still is more concerned about what he can't do than with what God can do. But God's commands and promises are about him, not us, in the same way that our salvation is about his grace, not our works. We're like children holding our father's hand as we cross a busy highway. The question is never how well we hold his hand, but how well he holds ours.

The other attitude that keeps us from hearing God's voice is that most of the time we would rather be tending sheep in Midian than freeing the slaves in Egypt. We're like Moses. We may not like life in Midian all that much, but we prefer the comfort of the boring but predictable, to the insecurity of the fulfilling but unpredictable. A host at a dinner party attended by G. K. Chesterton asked the guests what single book they would not want to be without if stranded on a desert island. Books like the Bible and *The Complete Works of Shakespeare* were put forth. When Chesterton's turn came, he said he would want a copy of *Thomas's Guide to Practical Shipbuilding*!

It's dangerous to pray and really listen to God. Well, not really—actually, the safest place in the world is in the center of God's will. But it may be unsettling, and our fear of that may keep us from hearing God. Thank God he is merciful and relentless. Moses finally did.

PRAYER: *Dear Father, be the center of my life, and the circumference of my hopes. Get my mind off myself and my limitations that I may live and move in your greatness.*

DAY 16: HONEST COMPLAINING OR MERE GRUMBLING?

Exodus 5:22-23

"O Lord, why have you brought trouble upon this people?" (Exod. 5:22).

Things were bad for the people of Israel before God sent his deliverer, Moses. After Moses arrived, things got really bad. Thus, this prayer of Moses in Exodus 5. Have you ever had the courage, or at least the inclination, to pray to God this way?

Moses returned to the Lord and said, "O Lord, why have you brought trouble upon this people? Is this why you sent me? Ever since I went to Pharaoh to speak in your name, he has brought trouble upon this people, and you have not rescued your people at all" (Exod. 5:22-23).

First, the inclination: it's not easy to serve God. In the work of his kingdom, things often get worse before they get better. Abraham enters the Promised Land only to find a famine (Gen. 12:10). Jesus was crucified before he was raised. It is almost axiomatic that the mark of any true work of God is opposition and difficulty. Don't be surprised that there are setbacks and that you struggle. Take it to the Lord.

Second, the courage: sometimes God doesn't really seem to be in control. Are you comfortable telling God exactly how you feel about how things are going? Or do you feel you need to edit your prayers for theological accuracy? It's important that good theology inform the way we pray. But it's also important to know that a healthy relationship with God (and people) requires the freedom to say what you feel—happy or sad, glad or mad. Read the psalms. These are definitely the prayers of people who have a healthy relationship with God.

But keep in mind the difference between honest complaint and mere grumbling. The difference is in the prepositions. Honest complaint speaks to God about the complaint while mere griping talks about God. When you speak to God about your concern, you pray. When you speak only about God to others, you gripe. Honest complaint, like this prayer of Moses, is open-ended and teachable. Behind the prayer is a question mark. Behind mere grumbling is an exclamation point.[1]

PRAYER: *Lord, forgive my grumbling. Forgive also my lack of honest complaint. Take away the fear that love casts out and free me to speak my heart to you.*

DAY 17: THE BATTLE IS THE LORD'S

Exodus 17:8-16

"Moses built an altar and called it the Lord is my banner. He said, 'for hands were lifted up to the throne of the Lord'" (Exod. 17:15-16).

Based on this episode, many "Aaron and Hur" prayer societies were formed to pray for pastors and other Christian leaders in the 19th century. It was believed that as the spiritual life of the pastor went, especially in prayer, so went the success of the spiritual battle in the church. So, people banded together to hold up the pastor in prayer and to intercede for the pastor's intercessory life.

The picture in Exodus is vivid. The typical posture of prayer in the Bible is to stand with arms lifted and hands held out symbolically to receive from the Lord. Added to this, in Moses' case is the staff, the symbol of divine power and conquest. As Joshua leads the troops in battle against the Amalekites in the valley below, Moses stands on the hill above and holds out his staff over the battle. When his arms are raised and the staff is held out, Joshua's army prevails; when Moses tires and the staff is lowered, the Amalekites prevail. So, Aaron and Hur come alongside Moses to provide a rock for him to sit on and to hold up his arms, so he can keep praying.

The image this story gives of spiritual warfare is also vivid. The battle always belongs to the Lord. We succeed only as we are "strong in the Lord and in his mighty power" (Eph. 6:10). The Lord is our Banner (Exod. 17:15). Prayer is one of the chief ways we stay vigilant and fight the battle (Eph. 6:18), and prayer is never a solitary exercise. Even when we pray alone, we pray in the fellowship of the church, the body of Christ. Paul urged the Romans, "by the love of the Spirit, *to join me in my struggle* by praying to God for me" (Rom. 15:30, italics added).

Hold up your pastor in prayer. Leaders need encouragement and protection and hearts to keep on praying.

PRAYER: *Almighty God, our great Warrior and Defender! Teach me to pray boldly in the midst of the battle.*

DAY 18: THE BASIS OF INTERCESSION

Exodus 32:7-14

"O Lord... why should your anger burn against your people, whom you brought out of Egypt?" (Exod. 32:11).

"Now leave me alone so that my anger may burn against them. Then I will make you into a great nation" (Exod. 32:10). Most people would have stumbled over themselves trying to get out of God's way. He was mad, and he had every reason to be. The first commandment he gave was to have no other gods, and the first thing the people did when Moses was away, was to have a pagan orgy around another god. But Moses remained standing before God and interceded for his people. This chapter is the first of three consecutive chapters in Exodus that give a rich picture of the prayer life of one of the Bible's greatest men of prayer. They also provide a model for the prayer life of any follower of Christ.

Moses' intercession was based on three realities. The first was God's self-chosen relationship with his people. When God spoke to Moses and called the people "*your* people whom *you* brought out of Egypt," Moses corrected the Lord and called them, "*your* people whom *you* brought out of Egypt" (Exod. 32:7, 11, italics added). The basis of all prayer is the relationship that God has taken the initiative to form with us. We pray in his name, the name he gave, "Our Father."

Moses also prayed based on God's reputation, pleading with the Lord to consider how he would be thought of by the Egyptians if he executed his fierce anger: "Why should the Egyptians say, 'It was with evil intent that he brought them out, to kill them?" (Exod. 32:12). This isn't manipulation, but a heartfelt prayer that God would get glory in all things. As Jesus taught, we intercede by praying, "Our Father in heaven; may your name be hallowed."

Finally, Moses prayed for the people on the basis of God's promises: "Remember your servants Abraham, Isaac, and Israel to whom you swore by your own self: 'I will make your descendants as numerous as the stars in the sky" (Exod. 32:13). In his usual picturesque way, Martin Luther described what Moses did in this prayer as throwing the sack of God's promises at his feet, and he couldn't step over them! It is beyond exhilarating to pray the promises of God, for they go far beyond the best we could ever think of on our own.

PRAYER: *Dear God, you told us to call you Father. So, I say, Father, may your name be praised and may all peoples on earth praise you. Fulfill your promises to bless your people.*

DAY 19: ON THE PURE LOVE OF GOD

Exodus 33:11-23

"No one can see me and live" (Exod. 33:20).

Sooner or later, conversation with God leads to the desire to see God. Hearing the words of life makes us want to *see* the Speaker. That is where Moses is in this text. Hymn writer Frederick Faber was thinking similar thoughts when he wrote:

How wonderful, how beautiful,
The sight of Thee must be,
Thine endless wisdom, boundless power,
And awful purity![1]

But no one can see God and live. We may see his goodness, but not his face (Exod. 33:19-20).

There is a sense in which God answered Moses' prayer on the Mount of Transfiguration when he saw Jesus shine like the sun (Matt. 17:1-5). We have Jesus' wonderful beatitude that the pure in heart will see God (Matt. 5:8). We also have the hope that puts a lump in the throat of anyone who loves Christ, that "when he appears, we shall be like him, for we shall see him as he is" (1 John 3:2). But for the time being, which is the hardest time to live,[2] we may not see his face. The hope that we may see his face, though for now deferred, does keep us pure (1 John 3:3).

St. Augustine preached a sermon he titled, "On the Pure Love of God." In it he proposed that God made you a Faustian kind of offer. He said you could have everything you want, nothing would be held back from you, there would be no negative consequences for anything you do, and you would live forever. The price? You will never see God's face. Would you make that exchange: everything, but without God? If your answer is "No," you have the pure love of God. Augustine asked, "Did a chill arise in your heart when you heard the words, 'You will never see my face'?" That chill is priceless; it is the pure love of God.[3]

PRAYER: *Glorious God, have you said that no one can see you and live? Then let me die. (from a prayer attributed to St. Augustine)*

DAY 20: WHAT YOU BECOME WHEN YOU PRAY

Exodus 34:29-35

"His face was radiant because he had spoken with the Lord" (Exod. 34:29).

The best thing you can give to others is not your education or your gifts. It is what has happened to you in the time you've spent with God. It is not what you know, but who you've known. Initially Moses didn't realize what had happened to him during those long hours in God's presence on Sinai. Even though he couldn't see God's face and his glory, his own face had begun to reflect some of God's glory. In a way, his prayer of 33:18 was being answered. The people noticed, though. Their observation was not unlike the way the members of the Sanhedrin noticed how bold and articulate Peter and John were: "they took note that these men had been with Jesus (Acts 4:13). There is no substitute for the beauty, power, and goodness that come upon us when we spend time with God.

But there can be a downside to it. It scared the people to see Moses' face, so he toned it down with a veil of some kind. The old Latin Vulgate translation of the Bible mistranslated "radiant" as "having horns." That's why many medieval pictures and statues of Moses have little horns on his head. They make him look a little like the devil. There's a parable here: the closer you come to God and become like God, the more likely some may respond to you as though you were the devil. That's the way it is in this world: "This is the verdict; Light has come into the world, but men loved darkness instead of light because their deeds were evil" (John 3:19). There is no greater privilege or joy than to stand in the presence of God, but it will set you apart.

Jesus said he was the light of the world. He said the same thing about his disciples (John 8:12; Matt. 5:14-16). Prayer is one of the ways we walk in his light and become light.

PRAYER: *I draw near to you, Lord Jesus. Draw near to me as you promised that I may be light in the world as you are light in the world.*

DAY 21: LORD GIVE ME A SENSE OF HUMOR

Thomas More (1478-1535)

"Be joyful always" (1 Thess. 5:16).

Thomas More's long and distinguished career in public service was capped by an appointment to Lord Chancellor of England—one of the highest and most powerful offices in England. That was in 1529. Six years later, in 1535, King Henry VIII, the same man who appointed him to office, had him beheaded. King Henry wanted More to declare him as supreme head of the church in England. More refused, explaining on his way to the scaffold, "I die the king's servant, but God's first."

More had long been ready to die if need be. Beneath all the finery of his position, he often wore a hair shirt. This private penance was to impress upon him the fragility of his life and the emptiness of earthly ambition—each scratch a whispering reminder that though he was in the world, he was not of it. "The worms," he often told his friends, "will one day have it all."

More was also a comic, famous well beyond England for his practical jokes. He even kept in his home a pet monkey and a professional live-in jester. His sense of humor came from the same place as the hair shirt. The pretensions of the world would one day pass away, and his only sure hope was in God alone. Hope kept him encouraged about the future; humor helped him cope with the present. This hope was the lens through which he could see clearly the incongruities and possibilities of this life—the gap between what is and what one day will be.

In a way, More was beheaded because of his sense of humor, or at least because of what it helped him to see. When set against eternity, all the posturing of the most powerful man in England was laughable. More could even laugh at his own death. As he walked up the shaky steps of the scaffold to be beheaded, he said to the executioner, "I pray you, see me safely up, and for my coming down let me shift for myself." When his head was on the block, More asked the executioner to wait while he moved his scraggly beard off the block. He quipped that his beard, after all, had not been found guilty of treason.

PRAY THIS PRAYER OF THOMAS MORE:

"Lord, grant me a holy heart that sees always what is fine and pure and is not frightened at the sight of sin, but creates order wherever it goes. Grant me a heart that knows nothing of boredom, weeping and sighing, let me not be too concerned with the bothersome thing I call 'myself.' Lord, give me a sense of humor, and I will find happiness in life and profit for others."

Introduction to Leviticus

DAY 22: REPLICAS OF GOD

Leviticus 20:16

"You are to be holy to me because I, the Lord, am holy, and I have set you apart from the nations to be my own" (Lev. 20:16).

In a word, the breathtaking command of Leviticus 20:16 sums up not only the purpose of the book of Leviticus, but also the goal of life with God—the premise of prayer. God didn't deliver Israel—and Christ didn't die for our sins—so we could just keep on being who we were before the rescue operation. He saved us from one thing to make us free for something else; to be holy as he is holy, to be with him, and to walk with him. He actually wants to make us like he is. This idea is a scandal to the devils in C. S. Lewis' *The Screwtape Letters*. They cannot imagine that God would really "want to fill the universe with a lot of loathsome little replicas of Himself—creatures whose life, on its miniature scale, will be qualitatively like his own." But that's precisely what God is calling for in that summary command of Leviticus.

How this divine project for the making of holy people is addressed in the book of Leviticus takes some getting used to. Its mass of laws and ceremonies could not seem more remote from modern sensibilities. But their purpose throughout was to take a people with the haziest notions of what it meant to be set apart for God and make that idea concrete in everyday life, in everything they did. The laws didn't actually make anyone holy, but they imbedded deep in the consciousness of a people the dream and desire, the yearning, to be holy. The shadows and signposts that make up Leviticus are fulfilled in the Spirit, the Holy Spirit, who calls us to prayer and makes us cry, "Abba, Father" (Rom. 8:15).

PRAYER:

Thee will I love, my strength, my tower,
Thee will I love, my joy, my crown,
Thee will I love with all my power
In all my works and Thee alone,
Thee will I love 'till sacred fire
Fills my whole soul with pure desire.
(from the hymn by Angelus Silesius, translated by John Wesley)

Father in heaven, fill my whole soul with pure desire—to be holy because you are holy.

DAY 23: AMAZING GRACE AND PRAYER

Leviticus 10:1-3

"They died before the Lord" (Lev. 10:2).

This story always appears in books about difficult passages in the Bible. But it's mostly a passage that mainly moderns struggle to grasp. Earlier generations did not have the same problem we tend to have with it. Why that is the case is the key to understanding the passage and its relevance for prayer.

A cornerstone to justice is that the punishment fit the crime. Parking violations should not result in lethal injection, and genocide should not be punished by picking up rubbish along the highway. The question is, was Nadab and Abihu's use of "unauthorized fire before the Lord" of the parking violation or the genocide variety of sin? True, this kind of thing was expressly forbidden (Exod. 30:9-10), but did its violation warrant death? How you answer that question depends on how seriously you take God and his holiness. If God is not supremely and inexpressibly good and pure, then this little fire violation is no big deal. But if he is, then any violation is cold defiance and treason, profanity of the basest kind. Perhaps you are thinking, but he doesn't do that kind of thing now, to even worse offenses. That's true, but the Scriptures would have us be amazed by that grace—not offended by the justice of what God did to Aaron's sons! The Bible would have us put amazing back into grace.

No person has any right to enter God's presence. In fact, every one of us should tremble at the very thought of sinful people standing before a holy God—the way Isaiah trembled (Isa. 6:5). It is a grace of the highest magnitude that God should allow us access to him through the blood of Jesus (Heb. 10:19). Every time we pray, we should tremble with awe and gratitude that we may. Our confidence should be tempered with deep reverence. Speaking the very phrase, "Our Father," should leave us stunned with wonder.

PRAYER: *Almighty and holy God, you are the Father of Mercies. Sinner that I am, I bless you for the grace that allows me to even call you Father.*

DAY 24: A BLOODY FAITH

Leviticus 17:11-14

"For the life of a creature is in the blood" (Lev. 17:11).

If you were in Jerusalem in the time of Jesus, what you might most have noticed was the presence of smoke in the air, the sounds of bleating sheep and goats, the sight of animals herded to the place of sacrifice, and the smell of burning flesh everywhere—but especially near the Temple. Daily, lambs and goats were brought to the priests and slaughtered. Their blood was smeared on the horns of the altar, the rest poured at its foot. Part of the animal was burned at the altar, the rest outside the city walls. The clergy had the hands of butchers.

The Bible says Jesus came like those lambs, to offer his life as an atoning sacrifice for sin (1 John 4:10). Our faith is inescapably bloody. At its heart it is raw; it is not genteel. Jesus was not a Socrates, drinking hemlock among friends, dying a death of protest. He was not a Buddha, sitting in the lotus position on a mountaintop, dying in deep meditation. He was a lamb slaughtered, a victim bloodied and scourged and impaled on a Roman gibbet.

All of this goes back to passages like this: "The life of the creature is in the blood" (Lev. 17:11). It's easy to miss the point about sacrifice and think that it is about death. This is the source of a great misconception about Christianity. The point of sacrifice is not death, but life released through death—"the life of every creature is its blood" (Lev. 17:14). It is the blood of Christ, the new life released by his death and resurrection, that cleanses and gives us access to God (Heb. 10:22). At the heart of a bloody faith is access to God. We can pray because we now may, thanks to his sacrifice.

PRAYER:

O wondrous love, to bleed and die,
To bear the Cross and shame,
That guilty sinners, such as I,
Might plead Thy gracious Name!
(from the hymn "Approach, My Soul, the Mercy Seat" by John Newton)

Introduction to Numbers

DAY 25: A LONG OBEDIENCE

Numbers 21:7

"So Moses prayed for the people" (Num. 21:7).

In Jewish usage, the book of Numbers goes by the name, "In the Wilderness," taken from the fifth word in the Hebrew text. It is a better name than Numbers, which one suspects has probably kept a lot of people from even beginning to read the book. "In the Wilderness" also captures the story and its meaning for prayer. In his *Confessions*, St. Augustine wrote, "For it is one thing to see the land of peace from a wooded ridge… and another to tread the road that leads to it."[1] God had promised to lead his rescued people to a land of freedom, flowing with milk and honey (Exod. 3:8). That sounded wonderful to a slave people whose workweek was 24/7, without medical and dental coverage and no hope for retirement. They couldn't wait to pack their bags and get going to that great place. But there was just one problem: they had to cross a terrible desert to get there and trust God to give them everything they needed as they traveled. They would have to become pilgrims. It is the struggle to be a pilgrim that forms the plot line of Numbers, or "In the Wilderness."

The spiritual life is a marathon, not a sprint; As Nietzsche said, a "long obedience in the same direction," not a weekend getaway. The gift of freedom and peace is just that—a gift—free, gratis. But it is not cheap. The saved still need to put one foot in front of the other, day-in and day-out. William Carey said his great virtue was that he could "plod." It is more than a virtue; it is an essential resource for the journey. Ninety percent of learning to pray is just showing up faithfully. The journey is full of surprises and challenges, and God has much to teach us along the way. But we won't learn it unless we come to what Andrew Murray called the "school of prayer." The graduates will sing.

PRAY THIS HYMN:

Hitherto Thy love has blest me;
Thou hast brought me to this place;
And I know Thy hand will bring me
Safely home by Thy good grace.

Jesus sought me when a stranger,
Wandering from the fold of God;
He, to rescue me from danger,
Bought me with His precious blood.
(from the hymn "Come, Thou Fount of Every Blessing" by Robert Robinson)

DAY 26: THE LORD BLESS YOU

Numbers 6:22-27

"So they will put my name on the Israelites and I will bless them" (Num. 6:27).

This prayer of blessing is a great prayer to say if you don't have a prayer. But it is just as great even if you do because prayers don't come any better than this one, written or extemporaneous. God prepared this prayer and gave it to Aaron and his sons to say over the Israelites. God's people have been saying it ever since. This prayer of blessing spans the whole biblical story and taps into the richest sources of scriptural truth. Take it a line at a time:

"The Lord bless you": A blessing is not a religious way of saying, "Have a nice day." Blessing is a powerful biblical word; expansive, comprehensive, concrete, touching on all aspects of the good life lived under God: health, abundance, a good marriage, and a happy family (Gen. 9:1; 17:6; 28:3).

"and keep you": God is a warrior and a defender of his people; a shield and fortress (Ps. 121:7-8; 122:1-2). We may pray that God will be who he is.

"the Lord make his face shine upon you... the Lord turn his face towards you": A shining face is a beautiful picture of a friend who delights in you; or of a bridegroom, with love in his eyes, gazing at his bride. God is that way too—read it in Isaiah 62:5. We may pray that he will do what he loves to do.

"and be gracious to you": God is gracious and shows favor to those who don't deserve it (Exod. 34:29-35). In fact, not deserving it is what makes it gracious, the very condition for grace to be grace. We may pray that others will receive the good things they don't deserve.

"and give you peace": Peace is another word like blessing and is often linked with it in the same way the New Testament links "grace and peace." Peace, God's shalom, is comprehensive well-being and equipoise, the kind of blessedness that is experienced as inner peace and tranquility.

"And so they will put my name on the Israelites, and I will bless them": By God's grace, we belong to God! Since we are his, we can be assured that his blessings and delight, his graciousness and peace are ours forever.

Memorize this prayer and you will always be prepared to pray the best for anyone.

DAY 27: A MIRROR OF PRAYER

Numbers 11:10-35

"Why have you brought this trouble on your servant?" (Num. 11:11).

Like its leading characters, the Bible has many models of prayer to emulate. And like its leading characters, it also has many "mirrors" of prayer—prayers prayed by flawed people like us. These prayers are not prescribed but allowed. This prayer is a "mirror" prayer because it reveals flaws. In this passage, Moses is fed up with God's people, and maybe a little fed up with God too. Why else would he say, "Why have you brought this trouble on your servant? What have I done to displease you that you put the burden of all these people on me? Did I conceive all these people? Did I give them birth?" (Num. 11:11-12). Moses is engaged in a little reversal of the appeal he made to God in Exodus 32, where God called his people Moses' people (see Day 18).

Part of the comfort of a prayer like this is the fact that we may pray a prayer like this at all. Venting one's feelings isn't usually the catharsis we think it is. There is no healing inherent in merely spouting off; sometimes it makes things worse, reinforcing negative feelings by the negative feedback of what we hear ourselves say. The healing isn't in the venting, but in the one to whom we vent—God. To know he hears with mercy and without censure is of enormous comfort and encouragement.

But he also answers our "venting prayers." God shows mercy by giving Moses men to share the responsibility that has so weighed him down (Num. 11:16-18). He also punishes them; and while there really isn't a lot of comfort in seeing God punish people who have made life miserable for you—there is a sense of justice being done (Num. 11:31-35).

The best part of God's answer is the reminder that our struggles really aren't about us, but about him. He tells Moses to tell the people, "you have rejected the Lord, who is among you" (Num. 11:20). It's never ultimately about us, it's always about God. Life's burdens are heavy enough without the added burden of narcissism and self-pity. God's response relieves us of that load and yet gives us the dignity of knowing that our struggles bring us into the fellowship of God's sufferings (Col. 1:24; Phil. 3:10).

PRAYER: *Thank you, Lord, that I can be real in my prayers, that I can vent my feelings to you and then watch you work by changing my attitude and helping me through my frustrations with others. I really want to know you, even if it means sharing in your sufferings.*

DAY 28: OUTRAGEOUS GRACE

Six lines from "Prayer of a Soldier about to Die"

"But now that I've met you I'm not scared to die."

The following lines were found on the body of a dead American soldier killed in North Africa in 1944 during the Second World War. His name is not known.

Look, God, I have never spoken to you,
And now I want to say, 'How do you do?'
And see, God, they told me you did not exist,
And I, like a fool, believed all this.
Last night, from a shell-hole, I saw your sky,
I figured that they had told me a lie.
Had I taken time before to see things you had made,
I'd sure have known they weren't calling a spade a spade.

I wonder, God, if you would shake my poor hand?
Somehow I feel you would understand.
Strange I had to come to this hellish place
Before I had time to see your face.
Well, I guess, there isn't much more to say,
But I'm glad, God, that I met you today.
The zero hour will soon be here,
But I'm not afraid to know that you're near.

The signal has come—I shall soon have to go,
I like you lots—this I want you to know.
I'm sure this will be a horrible fight;
Who knows? I may come to your house tonight.
Though I wasn't friendly to you before,
I wonder, God, if you'd wait at your door?
Look, I'm shedding tears—me shedding tears!
Oh! I wish I'd known you these long, long years.
Well, I have to go now, dear God. Good bye,
But now that I've met you I'm not scared to die.[1]

Jesus met a man like this. He too asked for mercy very late in life. Perhaps he would have written some lines like these, but his hands were occupied. They were nailed to a cross, for he was being executed next to Jesus (Luke 23:42). It's never too late to open your heart to Jesus.

PRAYER: *"Remember, O Lord, your great mercy and love, for they are from of old. Remember not the sins of my youth and my rebellious ways; according to your love remember me, for you are good, O Lord" (Ps. 25:6, 7).*

DAY 29: PRAYING FOR THOSE WHO ARE HARD TO PRAY FOR

Numbers 14:13-19

"The Lord is slow to anger" (Num. 14:18).

Some people are easier to pray for than others. At the top of the list are sick children, the terminally ill, close friends, and the persecuted church. Harder are criminals, enemies, and drug addicts. Still, pity and a passion to see the power of God at work can motivate us to pray for these people. At the bottom of the list are the cravenly ungrateful, the gripers and bellyachers—like the people in this text. At first, they complained about the food God gave to keep them alive in the desert. "Not enough variety," they moaned. Now they're complaining about the dangers of entering the Promised Land, a land flowing with milk, honey, and some very large grapes (Num. 13:23, 27).

God finds grumbling ingratitude particularly offensive and decides then and there that this generation of gripers will never enter the good land (Num. 14:11, 22-23). Why is God so offended by this? He is being accused of mismanagement. It's as though his people are dissatisfied customers in a poorly run hotel—his! The roles are reversed into an ugly inversion: they think God exists for their sake, rather they for his. Beneath this attitude of ingratitude is more than spiritual boorishness; it is hatred, of God. "How long will these people treat me with contempt?" asks God (Num. 14:11).

These are the people Moses prays for in this passage. Significantly, he prays for two things: mercy and justice. "Now may the Lord's strength be displayed, just as you have declared: 'The Lord is slow to anger, abounding in love and forgiving sin and rebellion. Yet he does not leave the guilty unpunished'" (Num. 14:17-18). Mercy and justice are not opposites for God is both merciful and just. His mercy tempers his justice but does not eliminate it. "I remember my affliction and my wandering... Yet this I call to mind and therefore I have hope: Because of the Lord's great love we are not consumed" (Lam. 3:19, 21-22).

Christ came and died to make the loveless lovely. So, we must pray for those caught in this particularly gross lovelessness. We must pray that we ourselves do not become ungrateful or complaining and ask God to help us cultivate grateful prayer and praise.

PRAYER: *Open my eyes to your mercies, Lord. Forgive me my ingratitude as I pray for the ungrateful—that their eyes too may be opened.*

Introduction to Deuteronomy

DAY 30: REMEMBER!

Deuteronomy 4:7

"What other nation is so great as to have their gods near them the way the Lord our God is near us whenever we pray to him?" (Deut. 4:7).

The people have good reasons for not feeling very optimistic about what they are about to do: cross the Jordan River and begin wars of conquest for the Promised Land. For one thing, it meant that the last of a cursed generation had to die out so this could happen (Num. 14:20-24). The last prescribed death was done; and the last of a lot of bad news was the somber prelude to the good. But whoever he or she was who died had been loved by someone, and the stage for the glorious conquest had been set with a funeral. More important, none of the people of any generation had a good track record in the forty-year sojourn in the wilderness. Moses' words are impassioned and biting as he reminds them of their repeated failures.

What makes the events and speeches of Deuteronomy so grand is that they describe the renewal of Israel's covenant with God and the promises he had made to them. The people would be called to remember their sin, vividly. But they would also be called to remember God's patience with them, and given the opportunity, to renew their side of the covenant. The word "give" appears 167 times in the book, and 131 of these occurrences refer to God and the multiple ways he had blessed them. Their sin had indeed abounded but so had his grace. That insight is essential to the renewal of faith.

The spiritual disciplines of Scripture meditation and prayer are like daily covenant renewals. Daily, we need to remember God's mercy and goodness, give thanks and pray for his purposes to be accomplished in us, and confess our failures to let him. Gratitude for God's mercy is the foundation of all spiritual renewal, all right living. Like the renewal of the covenant in Deuteronomy, there are three things we need to know live in the joy of God: "first, how great my sin and misery are; second, how I am set free from all my sins and misery; third, how I am to thank God for such deliverance." Prayer is the first act of that thankfulness.[1]

PRAYER: *"How can I repay the Lord for all his goodness to me? I will lift up the cup of salvation and call on the name of the Lord. I will fulfill my vows to the Lord in the presence of all his people" (Ps. 116:12-14).*

DAY 31: WHEN GOD SAYS DON'T ASK

Deuteronomy 3:23-29 (cf. Numbers 20:1-13)

"At that time I pleaded with the Lord" (Deut. 3:23).

God's tone of voice must have meant everything to Moses when he refused Moses' prayer that he be allowed to enter the Promised Land. "'That is enough,' the Lord said, 'Do not speak to me anymore about this matter'" (Deut. 3:26). Was God peeved? Was it, "Stop pestering me about it. You heard me say no, and I meant no."? Or was it more like, "That is the way it must be, dear friend. Please don't ask again."?

Of course, we can't know for sure what God's tone was, but consider this: Moses was a man the Lord spoke with face-to-face as a man would with a friend (Exod. 33:11). And they had had some pretty vigorous conversations, like the time Moses told the Lord to kill him too if he was going to kill the Israelites (Exod. 32:34). God hinted to Jeremiah that, along with Samuel, Moses was one of the two greatest intercessors of all times (Jer. 15:1). In other words, if anyone could get the Lord's attention, these two could. Moses and the Lord had been through a lot together. It must have grieved the Lord to refuse his friend. But his perfect love and wisdom said he must—like he did with his Son in Gethsemane. Nothing gets a father's attention like a child who calls, "Father! You can do anything! Please let this pass from me. But not what I want, but what you want" (Matt. 26:36-46). The Lord must have been saying to Moses, "This is the way it has to be, dear friend."

It's dangerous to second guess God and try to figure out why his superior wisdom and love would not let him grant his friend's last request. We do know this: even though Moses wanted Canaan so badly he could taste it, God was giving him Heaven. And someday, long after he went up on the mountain to die, he would appear on another mountain with Elijah, and he would speak with God's own Son, the Savior of not only Israel, but the world (Matt. 17:1-8). Joshua probably needed him to go too. It was going to be tough to follow Moses in leadership anyway, but if he went along into Canaan, Joshua's job would be impossible.

Enough speculation. What we do know is God is good whether we see him smile or frown—whether he says yes or no.

PRAYER: *My dear Lord and Friend, I will love you when you say yes and when you say no. I will trust when you give my heart's desire and when you don't. Everything you do is good.*

DAY 32: CREED AND PRAYER

Deuteronomy 26

"Say to the priest... 'I declare today to the Lord your god that I have come to the land the Lord swore to our forefathers to give us'" (Deut. 26:3).

Martin Luther's morning and evening prayers typically included the saying of the Apostle's Creed and the Lord's Prayer, followed by a prayer of thanksgiving. For many, the Lord's Prayer and the thanksgiving make perfect sense—but the Creed? It's a nice thing to do, but is so necessary as to do it daily? Luther's sequence was thoroughly and anciently biblical, and it followed the pattern of the liturgy in this text: confess your faith and pray.

When the ancient Israelite brought his thanksgiving offering to the priest, he first confessed his faith and said his creed: "My father was a wandering Aramean, and he went down to Egypt.... But the Egyptians mistreated us and made us suffer.... So the Lord brought us out of Egypt with a mighty hand and an outstretched arm" (Deut. 26:5, 6, 8). Then he placed his offering before the Lord and followed the Lord's command to pray, to "rejoice in all the good things the Lord your God has given to you and your household" (Deut. 26:11).

Biblical prayer is coupled with creed because prayer is a relationship, not a technique. Techniques are about what we can do in ourselves and with ourselves. Prayer is about who we are in God and who he is to us, and that is what creeds are about—like the one in this text and the great creeds of Christian history. In retelling and summarizing the story of our redemption, creeds describe the terms of the engagement we call prayer. They help us talk to the true and living God, not just to ourselves.

Creeds have great power to enrich and deepen prayer. Take the first line of the Apostle's Creed and think of what it can mean for the enjoyment of prayer: "I believe in God, the Father almighty, creator of heaven and earth." That means the God I address as Father is the very one who spoke the universe into existence and continues to rule it by his word. He is more than able to care for me because he is almighty. He is more than willing because he is my Father!

Learn a creed like the Apostles' Creed; it will help you enter the relationship of prayer more thoughtfully and joyfully.

PRAYER: *Father in Heaven! Teach me to apply my mind more fully to our relationship, by deepening my understanding of the propositions and creeds of Christian faith.*

DAY 33: WHATEVER IT TAKES

Deuteronomy 31—32

"And Moses recited the words of this song..." (Deut. 31:30).

Two things make this song so remarkable. One is the audience. It is sung before the whole assembly of Israel, and much of it is sharply critical of how ungrateful Israel has been over the last forty years. God has been inexpressibly good, and the thanks he gets is rebellion and faithlessness from the very people he has been so generous to. The song is a combination of praise and indictment: "He made them ride on the heights of the land and fed them with the fruit of the fields.... They sacrificed to demons" (Deut. 31:13, 17). The theme is repeated many times. One doubts the people were humming along as Moses sang.

Two is the subject, God, and the extraordinary variety of ways he has dealt with the people he came to save. Two of these ways stand out and are very different from each other. On the one hand, God "shielded [Israel] and cared for him; he guarded him as the apple of his eye" (Deut. 31: 10). The word translated "apple" is literally, "little man of his eye." The "little man" is the pupil, the delicate and vulnerable inner part of the eye that we reflexively protect. God has been that way with his people. He has protected and shielded them with the gentle and solicitous care a person gives his own eye.

On the other hand, God has been "like an eagle that stirs up its nest and hovers over its young, that spreads its wings to catch them and carries them on its pinions" (Deut. 31: 11). Mother eagles teach their young to fly by stirring up and essentially destroying the nest her little eaglets have been so comfortable in. This is not a pleasant process, but the young won't want to leave home without it. Then she takes each of them up on her back, throws them off and lets them fall, to force them to use their wings. She does this over and over again until, against their will, they learn to fly. Again, not a pleasant process, but the only way to make a lazy little eaglet—or child of God—fly.

God's dealings with us run the gamut from gentle to rough, tender to tough, teaching to causing terror—whatever it takes. We are unworthy of his love and often ungrateful for it, but he continues to love anyway. And for that, we may sing along with Moses.

PRAYER: *Spirit of the living God, fall afresh on me. Break me, mold me, fill me, use me. Spirit of the living God, fall afresh on me.*

DAY 34: FROM SOCIAL BUTTERFLY TO SAINT

Madame Guyon (1648-1717)

"I have been crucified with Christ and I no longer live, but Christ lives in me. The life I live in the body, I live by faith in the Son of God, who loved me and gave himself for me" (Gal. 2:20).

"Nothing was more easy to me now than to practice prayer. Hours passed away like moments, while I could hardly do anything else but pray. The fervency of my love allowed me no intermission.... So strong, almost insatiable, was my desire for communion with God that I arose at four o'clock to pray."[1]

These are not words one would have expected to hear from the young woman who grew up to become the saintly mystic we know of as Madame Guyon. Born into the pleasure-seeking class in France during the reign of Louis XIV, Mademoiselle de La Mothe (Jeanne Marie Bourvieres) possessed unusual beauty. As her mother lavished upon her dresses and the things of the world, Jeanne read romance novels and spent hours looking at herself in the mirror. When she was fifteen, the La Mothe family moved near Paris where Jeanne continued to climb the social ladder.

Amid the social whirl of Paris, Jeanne was married to M. Jacques Guyon, a wealthy invalid twenty-three years her senior. The marriage was unhappy from the beginning and began a process that caused Jeanne to finally seek her true happiness in God. She was rewarded with a deep sense of God's salvation and presence, and after a mystical experience while walking the river Seine, she wrote, "From this day, this hour, if it be possible, I will be wholly the Lord's. The world shall have no portion in me." In the years that followed, trouble piled upon trouble for Madame Guyon. She went through what St. John of the Cross called the "dark night of the soul," her husband and young son died, a severe case of smallpox left her face disfigured, and she was persecuted and imprisoned in the Bastille by the clergy for what they believed to be her heretical religious views. Through all this, Jeanne Guyon prayed with Job, "The Lord gave and the Lord hath taken away. Blessed be His name."[2] Her contribution to devotional literature was prodigious during those years. The poems, hymns, and books she authored have touched many thousands down to the present day, including Watchman Nee, Francois Fenelon, Hudson Taylor, and John Wesley. The shallow social butterfly had become a woman of great spiritual substance by the time she died in 1717.

She outlined her method of praying Scripture in her book, *Experiencing the Depths of Jesus Christ*, also known as *A Short and Very Easy Method of Prayer*. She recommended to her readers the practice of reading the Bible very slowly, tasting and digesting each verse, a line at a time, moving on only after you have extracted for your soul the essence of the passage. Doing this will bring you to discover that, "The Lord's chief desire is to reveal himself to you and, in order for him to do that, he gives you abundant grace. The Lord gives you the experience of enjoying his presence. He touches you, and his touch is so delightful that, more than ever, you are drawn inwardly to him."[3]

PRAY THIS PRAYER OF MADAME GUYON'S: *"To me remains no place nor time; my country is in every clime; I can be calm and free from care on any shore since God is there."*[4]

Introduction to Joshua

DAY 35: DON'T TAKE IT PERSONALLY

Joshua 1:7-8

"For though we live in the world, we do not wage war as the world does. The weapons we fight with are not the weapons of the world" (2 Cor. 10:3).

A younger pastor asked a wise mentor, an older pastor, what his best advice was for someone beginning in Christian ministry. Without hesitation, the older pastor answered, "Don't take it personally."

"Don't take what personally?" the younger pastor asked.

"Don't take it personally when the work of God seems like fighting a battle," the mentor replied. "It isn't about you, it's about God."

The younger pastor thought about it. Of course, a soldier doesn't get his feelings hurt when the enemy shoots at him. He doesn't look over the top of his foxhole and shout, "Was it something I said?" It's a war and getting shot at goes with the territory.

More than any other book of the Bible, we owe the war imagery of the Christian life to the book of Joshua. God called Joshua to lead the people of Israel in battle for the land that was their inheritance. In the Greek, the name Joshua is rendered *Jesus*. Jesus is a Joshua, but greater than Joshua. The inheritance he secured is greater than anything Joshua accomplished (1 Pet. 1:3-5). And the battle we fight is different from the battles Israel fought, "For though we live in the world, we do not wage war as the world does. The weapons we fight with are not the weapons of the world. On the contrary, they have divine power to demolish strongholds. We demolish arguments and every pretension that sets itself up against the knowledge of God, and we take captive every thought to make it obedient to Christ" (2 Cor. 10:3-5).

But the qualities of faith and character necessary for fighting the good fight remain the same as they were when Joshua and the army of Israel began their assault on Canaan: "Be strong and very courageous.... Do not let this Book of the Law depart from your mouth; meditate on it day and night, so that you will be careful to do everything written in it. Then you will be prosperous and successful" (Josh. 1:7-8). Our greatest weapons are the courage to pray and proclaim the word of God.

PRAYER: *"Father in heaven, you are the Lord of the armies of heaven. Keep me alert to spiritual battle I must fight against the devil, the world, and my own sinfulness!"*

DAY 36: PRAY TO BE ON GOD'S SIDE

Joshua 5:13-15

"As commander of the Lord's army I have come" (Josh. 5:14).

Pray not that God is on our side, but that we are on God's side. That saying attributed to Abraham Lincoln, is the point of this story. Joshua is put in his place when he challenges the warrior standing in the road with a drawn sword, "Are you for us or for our enemies?" He wasn't expecting to hear, "Neither... but as commander of the army of the Lord I have come" (Josh. 5:13-14). Joshua is the one who should be answering the question.

It is good to know your place in the world, but it is critical to know your place before God. The word for this healthy state of mind and heart is humility. God is God, and you are not. God does not exist for your sake, but you exist for his. God comes near to people who know this, but he opposes implacably those who don't (1 Pet. 5:5). He lives in two places: one so high no human can reach it, the other so very low that only the humble can get there: "I live in a high and holy place, but also with him who is contrite and lowly in spirit" (Isa. 57:15). The Latin root for humble is *humus*, as in soil, earth. The earth is where those who pray may kneel.

What Joshua hears is humbling, but it is also heartening. God is not involved in Israel's war—no, the war is God's, and Israel is involved in God's war. What a relief for Joshua, the rookie commander of the army. "Then Joshua fell facedown to the ground in reverence, and asked him, 'What message does my Lord have for his servant?'" Joshua may not be sure of his battle plan, but he can have absolute confidence in God's. What a relief to not have to figure things out yourself, but to submit to God in humble reverence and do his will. That's what prayer is. We are not asking God to do what we want, but to let us be a part of his great plan and to do what he wants. God's plan will blow Joshua's mind and topple the walls of Jericho. Do you have a "Jericho" to face? Be humbled, be heartened, be prayerful.

PRAYER: *Father in Heaven! May your will be done on earth as it is in Heaven. May your will be done by me as faithfully and cheerfully as the angel Joshua met that day.*

DAY 37: ONE FOR ALL, ALL FOR ONE

Joshua 7

"I in them and you in me. May they be brought to complete unity to let the world know that you sent me and have loved them even as you have loved me" (John 17:23).

The individualism of Western culture can make this story hard for us to understand. We think: one man sinned, let the one man be punished for his sin, not the whole community. Thirty-six good men went down that day because of one man's disobedience. We are quite willing to be our brother's keeper, but we don't like the idea of being our brother's victim, especially if we were ignorant of his sin as Israel was of Achan's sin.

God thinks otherwise. The people of God are not a group, but a body. The church is not an organization, but an organism, the body of Christ. You can be a member of a group and have a life outside the group. But you can't be a member of a body and have a life outside the body. An eye or a lung are distinct, wonderfully different within the body, but outside the body they are the same; no more than dull, dead flesh. True individuality happens only in the community of the body of Christ. You are never less an individual than you are in the church, or more an individual than you are in the church. Likewise, the actions and health of every member of a body directly affect the actions and health of every other member. Witness what happens to the rest of the body when the eyes go blind or the lungs go bad. Witness what happened with Achan and Israel.

This has tremendous implications not only for things like morality and church discipline, but for prayer. On the level of individuals, the prayerlessness of one hurts the whole body; just as prayerfulness of one helps the whole body. On the level of the whole body, what would it mean if all the members were praying together in concerted agreement for the things the Head of the body wants for his church? It would be, on a spiritual level, what a body is when all of its members are functioning harmoniously together under the directives of the head. It would be for the work of the kingdom what a great team is to a game, or a great orchestra is to a symphony. It is a beautiful thing when the church acts as one and prays as one (Matt. 18:19-20; John 17:23).

PRAYER: *Jesus, you are the great head of your body, the church. I repent of my individualism and ask that you teach us to pray—together.*

DAY 38: THE FLIM-FLAM MEN

Joshua 9:14

"The men of Israel... did not inquire of the Lord" (Josh. 9:14).

There are a lot of ways to describe what happened to the Israelites when they met the Gibeonites: they were flimflammed, snookered, duped, and deceived. Having heard what the Israelites did to Jericho and Ai, the Gibeonites knew they needed something more than an army to survive the Israelite military machine—they needed a plan. Their plan was to trick Israel into a treaty by making them think the Gibeonites weren't part of the peoples Israel was commanded by God to subdue. So, they made their clothes and food look old and stale, like they had come from a great distance, and they proposed a treaty. The Israelites bought the story. They sampled their provisions, but they did not "inquire of the Lord" (Josh. 9:14). Full of themselves after consecutive victories, they were so confident about what they thought, that they didn't bother to ask the Lord what he thought. The treaty was ratified.

If only they would have prayed about the Gibeonites and their story, this story would have turned out better for God's people. Would've, could've, should've are the language of regrets. Taking the time to pray uses up time in the short run, but it saves time in the long run. When was the last time you thought you were too busy to pray? This morning, perhaps? The Gibeonites were whispering that deception in your ear.

There is another lesson in the story of the Gibeonite deception: simply pursuing God's goals is not enough. We need to use God's means too. Israel had enough faith to hear the Lord say to conquer the land of Canaan. Having heard that much, it was tempting to hurry up and get conquering, and not listen to the rest of what he had to say. God's will covers not only what we are to do, but how and, in the case of the Gibeonites, who we are to do it with. Pray until you hear the Lord speak, and don't stop praying until he stops speaking. In all your ways acknowledge him, and he shall direct your paths (Prov. 3:6).

PRAYER: *God of all wisdom, you know all things and do all things well. Teach me to listen to you so that I might do all things well.*

Introduction to Judges

DAY 39: THE PERENNIAL NEED

Judges 2:10

"Another generation grew up, who knew neither the Lord nor what he had done for Israel" (Judg. 2:10).

"The church is in need of perennial revival because of recurrent spiritual decline," wrote church historian, Earle Cairns.[1] The second generation of Israelites pictured in Judges 2:7 and 10-13, is a case in point. "They *forsook* the Lord, the God of their fathers" (Judg. 2:12, italics added) because they had not known the power and reality of the Lord as their parents had. Jeremiah's favorite word for Israel's spiritual decline is *forsook*: "They have forsaken me, the spring of living water" (Judg. 2:13; cf. 5:7, 19; 9:13). The Ephesian church was in danger of being removed by Christ because, "You have forsaken your first love" (Rev. 2:4). The pattern of spiritual decline, crisis, and revival has repeated itself too many times in biblical and church history to be dismissed as an anomaly. It keeps happening because the enemies of God keep attacking the people of God. If left unchecked, the devil, the world and our own flesh will destroy the church from the inside by false teaching and immorality and from the outside by persecution. We seem to be terminally drawn to forsaking God.

The book of Judges is a kind of cautionary tale about the dangers of not paying attention to our need to be vigilant and prayerful for the purity of the faith. If we do not have God over us to rule us, we will succumb to whatever is around us. This truth is demonstrated in the history of Israel. However, their story is also a story of hope. God's patience is matched only by his creativity in the assortment of people he will use to restore his people. What are we to make of the likes of Ehud, Othniel, Deborah, Gideon, Jephthah, and Samson? They fit as easily in a menagerie or a police line-up, as they do in the hall of fame of faith. But they encourage more than they amaze and amuse, "for God chose the foolish things of the world to shame the wise; God chose the weak things of the world to shame the strong" (1 Cor. 1:27). There's hope for you too!

PRAYER: *Pray for God to revive his people, his church, using the words of Psalm 85:4, 7. "Restore us again, O god our Savior, and put away your displeasure toward us.... Show us your unfailing love, O Lord, and grant us your salvation."*

DAY 40: GOD HAS NO GRANDCHILDREN

Judges 2:10-23

"We will tell the next generation the praiseworthy deeds of the Lord" (Ps. 78:4).

"After that whole generation had been gathered to their fathers, another generation grew up, who knew neither the Lord nor what he had done for Israel" (Judg. 2:10). That statement reads like an epitaph on the graves of those who should have been teaching the next generation about the Lord. And it puts a chill in the heart of every parent who loves their children. What if those who come after us don't know the goodness of God, too? Israel must have been filled with nominal believers.

This is a call to pray for the next generation. What could be more important than to pray that those who follow us will follow the Lord too, only better? What greater tragedy, even indictment, is there than that those who know us best, our families and children, know the Lord least? Psalm 78 is a call to arms—to prayer for the next generation.

"We will not hide them from their children; we will tell the next generation the praiseworthy deeds of the Lord, his power, and the wonders he has done. He decreed statutes for Jacob and established the law in Israel, which he commanded our forefathers to teach their children, so the next generation would know them, even the children yet to be born, and they in turn would tell their children. Then they would put their trust in God and would not forget his deeds but would keep his commands" (Judg. 2:4-7).

The ministry *Moms in Touch* has seen God quietly change school campuses and students' lives as it has summoned moms to "pour out your heart like water in the presence of the Lord. Lift up your hands to him for the lives of your children" (Lam. 2:19). Who is more passionate for the faith of their children than moms? History abounds with the stories of women like Susanna Wesley (the mother of John and Charles) and Monica (the mother of Augustine) who prevailed in prayer for their children. And history was changed because they did.

PRAYER: *Dear Father, from whom your whole family in heaven and earth derives its name, empower me to be faithful in teaching the good news and faithful in prayer for the next generation. Put your Spirit in the hearts of those who come after me, so that they would put their trust in you and no other.*

DAY 41: FIE ON FLEECES!

Judges 6

"I will place a wool fleece on the threshing floor" (Judg. 6:36).

John White's assessment of Gideon's "fleece" prayers may be a little far-fetched, but not too much: "Forget about fleeces. If you've never used them, don't start. If you have, then quit."[1] His reasons for saying this are compelling.

One: Gideon was a semi-pagan, thinking and acting like a semi-pagan, and God was simply being patient and condescending to accommodate his primitive prayer the way he did. It isn't becoming of a Christian to behave like a man of Gideon's ignorance. God uses all kinds of people, some of whom we rightly see as unworthy, like Gideon. He does this to show his sovereign grace. But it is a kind of trafficking in the grace of God to conclude that you can forgo the serious study of Scripture and waiting on God and, instead, give God a few binary choices to show you what to do.

Two: Doing this sort of thing doesn't satisfy our need to know the will of God. It didn't really do it for Gideon, either. The first time he tried the fleece thing and saw it get wet when there was no dew, he still wasn't sure. Maybe there was another hypothesis to explain it, maybe fleeces sometimes do get wet when there is no dew. This kind of crude application of the scientific method always leaves room for more doubt. There is always one more "test" to try, one more way to avoid making a decision. Finally, we all have to learn to walk by faith and not by sight.

Those are White's reasons, but there is one more: the use of "fleeces" circumvents the trying and difficult process of waiting on God and trusting him with less than all of the information we want. God is more concerned about who we are than what we do in a particular situation. Our concerns are often the opposite, and we are drawn to fleeces instead of to spiritual maturity. At least as important as what we wait for in prayer is what happens to our character as we wait.

PRAYER: *Father, you promised that those who hope in you and wait will be strengthened (Isa. 40:31). I am hoping and waiting. Keep me from the temptation to take shortcuts.*

DAY 42: FATHER, MAKE OF ME A CRISIS MAN

Jim Elliot (1927-1956)

In the Fall of 1955, five young men went deep into the rain forest of Ecuador to deliver an invitation. Their names were Nate Saint, Jim Elliot, Roger Youderian, Ed McCully, and Peter Fleming. Their mission was to invite an obscure and warlike people to bring their gifts into the courts of the living God and to sit down with all the other peoples of the earth to feast in his presence (see Ps. 96:7-10; Luke 13:29-30; Rev. 21:22-26). These people called themselves the *Huaorani*, meaning simply, "the people." Everyone who knew of them called them the *Auca*, meaning "savages." Their culture was literally a culture of death: babies were thrown into the river, children buried alive with dying family members, and friends and enemies alike were speared with appalling regularity. But one of the missionaries, Peter Fleming, spoke for them all when he said, "I would gladly give my life for [the Aucas] if only to see those proud, clever, smart people gathering around a table to honor the Son." Many of the Huaorani now gather to honor the Son, but those five missionaries had to first die to make that happen. The Aucas murdered them all on January 8, 1956.

Jim Elliot's wife, Elisabeth Elliot, has preserved many of his prayers and his thoughts on prayer and Christian discipleship. Most of them come out of his student years at Wheaton College.

"That saint who advances on his knees never retreats."

"Father, make of me a crisis man. Bring those I contact to decision. Let me not be a milepost on a single road; make me a fork, that men must turn one way or another on facing Christ in me."

"He is no fool who gives what he cannot keep to gain what he cannot lose."
Consume my life, my God, for it is Thine. I seek not a long life, but a full one, like you, Lord Jesus."

"Father, take my life, yea, my blood if Thou wilt, and consume it with Thine enveloping fire. I would not save it, for it is not mine to save. Have it, Lord, have it all. Pour out my life as an oblation to the world. Blood is only of value as it flows from Thine altar."

"The will of God is always a bigger thing than we bargain for."

"Give me a faith that will take sufficient quiver out of me so that I may sing. Over the Aucas, Father, I want to sing!"[1]

PRAYER: *Select one of the above quotations of Jim Elliot and make it a personal prayer, such as, "Father, make of me a crisis man. Bring those I contact to decision. Let me not be a milepost on a single road; make me a fork, that men must turn one way or another on facing Christ in me."*

DAY 43: WATCH WHAT YOU PRAY FOR AND WHY YOU PRAY FOR IT

Judges 11:30-40

"Jephthah made a vow to the Lord" (Judg. 11:30).

This story of Jephthah's rash and foolish vow leaves one not sure whether to weep, curse, or simply stare into space. He wins a battle for the Lord, but a beloved daughter ends up dead. Still the New Testament lists Jephthah as one of the heroes of faith (Heb. 11:32). What, on earth, does this story have to teach us about prayer?

One lesson is that we must be careful with our vows. The obvious caution is to never make a vow you would hate to have to keep if your prayer were answered. The deeper insight is to know your own heart well enough to know why you are making the vow in the first place. Some vows, like Jephthah's, are really attempts to cut a deal with the Lord; subtle efforts at raising the stakes so he will do what you want. These vows come from anxiety and doubt that the Lord really loves us or fear that we can't trust him to do the right thing unless he gets something from us. That motive is what seems to be behind Jephthah's vow.

The second lesson is to always pray and act according to the best light you can get. Jephthah, like Gideon, was probably semi-pagan in his understanding of the Lord God. His knowledge of the Law of Moses probably did not include the prohibitions against child sacrifice (Deut. 12:29-31; 18:9-10), but he did know something about the importance of keeping one's word. Out of ignorance, he cancelled one law of God with another.

The third lesson is that God rarely overrides our wills and histories to give us information we don't have; but he does honor what we do with what we do have. That is probably the importance of Jephthah's horrific act. He is not praised for what he did (child sacrifice), but for why he did it (keeping his word to God). In a way, we can say the New Testament gives two, but not three cheers for Jephthah's faith.

The fourth lesson is the reason for this Bible: how critically important it is that we know Scripture well-enough to pray from the word of God, according to the will of God! That, in essence, is what Jesus meant about giving us whatever we ask for in his name, according to his character.

PRAYER: *Dear Lord, may I be able to present myself to you, approved as a person of prayer, who does not need to be ashamed and who correctly prays the word of truth (2 Tim. 2:15).*

Introduction to Ruth

DAY 44: PRAYER IN THE WORST OF TIMES

Ruth 2:12

"May you be richly rewarded by the Lord, the God of Israel, under whose wings you have come to take refuge" (Ruth 2:12).

Wedding ceremonies are services of worship on the occasion of a marriage. The event itself is a microcosm of grand and universal realities, and it points to themes far bigger than itself. The tale of Ruth works in the same way and delivers a powerful message of redemption in the context of a love story. Forms of the Hebrew word for redemption appear twenty-three times in this short story, all woven into the fabric of the tale of how two broken and desolate women find hope and a purpose far beyond their greatest hopes. Ruth will become the blushing bride of Boaz, the great-grandmother of David, Israel's greatest king, and an ancestor of the King of kings, the "son of David (Matt. 1:1, 5).

The backdrop of the story is the book of Judges. This is to say it was a time like Hobbe's state of nature in which the life of the Hebrews was usually, "solitary, poor, nasty, brutish and short."[1] Apostasy was egregious, and the wars were bloody. Ethnic hatreds burned with the antipathy between Hebrews and Moabites chief among them. But the story of Ruth, a Moabite woman, was the best of times in these worst of times—like the light that shone in Bethlehem's dark streets centuries later. Bethlehem is where the story of Ruth unfolds, and it teaches a lesson of God's tender willingness to answer prayer in the most intimate and happiest of human relations—and to go far beyond what we ask or even imagine (Eph. 3:21).

PRAYER: *Father in heaven! Give me a faith and a faithfulness like Ruth's, that I may serve you in the darkness.*

DAY 45: PRAYER CHANGES THINGS

Ruth 2:12—3:9

"The Lord bless you, my daughter" (Ruth 3:10).

"Awful things happen to people who pray," writes Virginia Owens. "Their plans are frequently disrupted. They end up in strange places. Abraham 'went out, not knowing where he was to go'—hardly the picture of someone who has struck it rich on a brand-new power source. After Mary's magnificent prayer at the annunciation, she finds herself the pariah of Nazareth society. The well-worn phrase, 'Prayer changes things,' often meant to comfort, is as tricky as any Greek oracle."[1]

What happened to Boaz after he prayed for Ruth wasn't awful, in fact it was thrilling, but it sure disrupted the plans of this middle-aged Bethlehem elder. What followed was an unexpected December wedding, and he and his younger bride becoming the great-grandparents of the great king David. Boaz prayed a blessing for Ruth that God, "under whose wings you have taken refuge" (Ruth 2:12), would be to her like a bird that covers her weak and defenseless young with her wings (cf. Ps. 17:8; 36:7; 63:7). God honored his prayer by letting Boaz be the bird! He was awakened one night with the beautiful woman he blessed lying at his feet, covered by his garment! When he asked who she was, she answered, "I am your servant Ruth.... Spread the corner of your garment over me, since you are a kinsman-redeemer" (Ruth 3:9). These words accomplished two things: they amounted to a Middle Eastern proposal of marriage ("spread the corner of your garment over me"), and they were a play on the word "wings" of the Lord. The word for his garment's "corner" is literally "wings" in the Hebrew. Boaz prayed that God's wings would cover her; Ruth asked that the "wings" of his garment be her cover. God answered Boaz's prayer for Ruth by making him her husband.

The lesson isn't: don't pray for single people unless you plan to marry them. The lesson is: always be ready to be part of God's answer to your prayers. Asking God to help others is not a way of putting the responsibility on his shoulders, but of shouldering the responsibility with him. When we pray for others, we pray not only to him, but also with him who always intercedes for us (Heb. 7:25).

PRAYER: *Father, as I pray for your will for others, make my will one with yours, that I may combine actions with my prayers for them.*

Introduction to 1 and 2 Samuel

DAY 46: A TALE OF THREE MEN

1 Samuel 13:14

"Do not stop crying out to the Lord our God for us" (1 Sam. 7:8).

The books of 1 and 2 Samuel are essentially the story of three men: Samuel, Saul, and David, but especially Samuel and David. Along with Moses, Samuel was the greatest intercessor in the Old Testament. When God wanted Jeremiah to know how determined he was to execute judgment on Judah, he said even Moses and Samuel could not make him change his mind: "Even if Moses and Samuel were to stand before me, my heart would not go out to this people. Send them away from my presence! Let them go" (Jer. 15:1; cf. Ps. 99:6)! Samuel was birthed in prayer, and his training and ministry were rooted in prayer.

This alone makes Samuel a worthy study in the ministry of intercessory prayer. But his role as a prophet, at a critical time in Israel's history, adds even greater significance to his calling as a man of prayer. Samuel is the bridge between the time when Israel was a loose collection of tribes, a theocracy, united by a common faith, and sometimes little more; and when Israel became a monarchy, with a king. It was a perilous move, ambiguous at best, based on questionable motives: "Then we will be like all the other nations, with a king to lead us and to go out before us and fight our battles" (1 Sam. 8:20). But it was a move which God nevertheless sanctioned, even though he knew it was at bottom, a rejection of him (1 Sam. 8:7). There is a profound lesson in this: at a moment of tumultuous change in a nation's history, God's choice of a leader was a man who was both a prophet and an intercessor. The man of the hour was one who would speak about God to the people, and who would speak to God about the people. He embodied P. T. Forsyth's dictum that a leader must be much with the people to know their problems, and much with God to know how to solve them.

After what seemed a misfire with Saul, the magnificent and beloved David became king. But Saul was not so much a misfire as an illustration of the very things Samuel warned the people would happen if they got their king. His story was a tragic and cautionary tale. David, though flawed, was yet a "man after God's own heart" who walked in God's ways with an "undivided heart" (1 Sam. 13:14; Ps. 86:11). Like Samuel, his mentor, David was a man of prayer and the principal author of a book of prayers, the Psalms. Psalms is the longest book in the Bible, and the heart God so loved is often laid bare in these prayers. David was "God's anointed," or messiah, the precursor of the righteous king who would one day come and make everything right, not only for Israel, but for the world. The first messiah, like the ultimate Messiah, was a man of prayer. Again, God's choice of a leader was a man of prayer. David would have been less of a leader had he not been a man of prayer.

PRAYER: *Father in heaven! Teach me to pray like Samuel!*

DAY 47: ANSWERS BIGGER THAN OUR PRAYERS

1 Samuel 1

"I was pouring out my soul to the Lord" (1 Sam. 1:15).

In her culture, the term used to describe Hannah's condition was "barren." The term was more a curse than anything, for childlessness was thought to be punishment for sin of some kind. Hannah was barren; she was hollow at the point in her life where it was most important that she be fruitful and filled. And Peninnah, the second wife, made sure Hannah didn't forget it. Though Hannah was her husband's delight, he had severe limitations in the comfort part of the brain. The "comfort" he offered her was doltish and self-centered: "Hannah, why are you weeping? Why don't you eat? Why are you downhearted? Don't I mean more to you than ten sons" (1 Sam. 1:8)?

Hannah had no place to go but to the Lord. For a moment, even her prayers seemed to be barren, for the high priest Eli almost kicked her out of the temple for being drunk. But the Lord heard Hannah's prayer and gave her a son, and more, a great prophet in Israel. The answer to her prayer was bigger than her prayer. The place where she prayed was bigger too. Like the address Emily gave herself in Thornton Wilder's *Our Town*, Hannah's location was temple, nation of Israel, "planet earth, solar system, Milky Way galaxy, Universe, Mind of God." God heard her prayer from his throne in heaven where he controls history. All Hannah saw was a baby and the relief of her misery. God saw that too, but he also saw his people and their destiny to be a great nation through whom he would bless the whole earth (cf. Gen. 12:1-2). God is a master of efficiency. He could bless Hannah beyond her greatest hopes and bless a people beyond theirs.

Hannah told Eli she was pouring out her soul to the Lord (1 Sam. 1:15), so do we when we pray for the things we care for most deeply. But our souls are small, and they are poured out into the great heart of God who answers better than we can ask or even think (Eph. 3:20-21).

PRAYER: *Father, I trust you to do more with my requests, even my greatest requests, than I can ever hope. Your love, O Lord, reaches to the heavens (Ps. 36:5).*

DAY 48: LISTENING PRAYER

1 Samuel 3

"Then Samuel said, 'Speak, for your servant is listening'" (1 Sam. 3:10).

The fact that the Lord speaks and young Samuel listens is remarkable on two counts. One, "in those days the word of the Lord was rare" (1 Sam. 3:1). Two, the people who should have been listening had stopped a long time ago, and now as Eli snored away and his sons no doubt caroused (1 Sam. 2:12-17), a boy heard from the Lord. God was speaking again. This was good news for everybody but Eli and his boys.

Why now, why Samuel? God has his reasons, which he usually keeps to himself, but some educated guesses or musings can be made. Certainly, God always acts wisely and sovereignly, quite apart from the good things we have done. It would be a mistake to look for qualities in Samuel that moved God to start speaking again. A better approach is to marvel and be thankful that God had decided to speak and had raised up a person who would listen.

It's understanding the act of listening that can help us most. Samuel was on his bed when he heard God. That doesn't mean that we hear God best on a bed, but it is a picture of how we hear God best, which is when we are quiet. John Bunyan's character Eargate couldn't hear because he was stopped up with filth. The filth of modern life usually comes in the form of noise. Though he sometimes uses them, God doesn't like megaphones. "In quietness and trust is your strength" (Isa. 30:15). Samuel's response to God, though coached by Eli, says a lot too. Samuel said, "Speak, for your servant is listening." God is more apt to speak to those who listen than to those who don't. It's not that he is shy, but that he waits to speak until he sees the submission and obedience inherent in the willingness to listen. Obedience opens eyes and ears. "If anyone chooses to do God's will, he will find out whether my teaching comes from God or whether I speak on my own" (John 7:17).

God won't speak until he is ready, and we are ready. The way to get ready is to get quiet, and to resolve to obey what you hear when you hear it.

PRAYER: *Speak, Lord, for I am listening.*

DAY 49: THE DIGNITY OF CAUSALITY

C. S. Lewis (1898-1963)

"Ask and it will be given to you; seek and you will find; knock and the door will be opened to you" (Luke 11:9).

C. S. Lewis described himself at his conversion as "the most dejected convert in all England." Years later, he would look back on that event and muse, "I did not then see what is now the most shining and obvious thing; the Divine humility which will accept a convert even on such terms.... Who can fully adore that Love which will open the high gates to a prodigal who is brought in kicking, struggling, resentful, and darting his eyes in every direction for a chance of escape?"[1]

But that's how it began for the man who became the foremost apologist for Christian orthodoxy in the twentieth century. Lewis brought a capacious and razor-sharp mind to a variety of themes and hardships of the faith that have delighted and instructed readers for decades. Interestingly, he may have written more on the subject of prayer than any other topic. In an essay in *God in the Dock*,[2] Lewis addressed the difficult question, "If God is all wise and all-knowing, He will always do what is best. Why then should our prayers make any difference?"

The answer lies in what can be called God's human project. In his wisdom, God has chosen to work with humans in the unfolding of history, "like a play in which the scene and the general outline of the story is fixed by the author, but certain minor details are left for the actors to improvise." Citing Pascal, Lewis believed God wants to give humans the "dignity of causality" by granting to us the outcome of minor details in the drama. In a sense, prayer is like work, and no more mysterious: both are ways God allows us to affect the world.

So why then, are the things we work for almost guaranteed to have some kind of result, but not the things we pray? Lewis' answer is surprising: "This is not because prayer is the weaker kind of causality," as we may often feel when we pray and wait for an answer, "but because it is a stronger kind." If God were to grant to our prayers the kind of immediate results we expect from our work, the results would be catastrophic. Imagine how disastrous it would be if every prayer we prayed selfishly or foolishly or in anger were automatically granted by God? A single "yes" from God could be far more horrible than any number of his refusals. Otherwise, prayer would be "an activity too dangerous for man and we should have the horrible state of things envisaged by Juvenal: "Enormous prayers which Heaven in anger grants." So, in prayer, "God has retained a discretionary power of granting of refusing it," not because prayer is weak, but because it is so powerful.

When we pray, we should regard God's silences to be at least as meaningful as his voice. His silences are always the silences of his higher designs, his superior sense of timing, and his grand purpose in making our wills one with his.

PRAYER: *Thank you, Lord, for giving me the dignity and privilege of affecting the world through prayer.*

DAY 50: WORK WITH THEM

1 Samuel 8

"It is not you they have rejected, but they have rejected me as their king" (1 Sam. 8:7).

What the people wanted displeased the Lord as much as it displeased Samuel; so the Lord told Samuel not to take it personally: "It is not you they have rejected, but they have rejected me as their king" (1 Sam. 8:7). The Lord reminded him that the people had been doing this kind of thing from the beginning—rejecting him. But when Samuel thought the Lord would send him back to the people with a firm, "No" to their desire, he surprised him with this: "Now listen to them; but warn them solemnly and let them know what a king who will reign over them will do" (1 Sam. 8:9). Samuel did as he was told, and described the kind of oppression any Middle Eastern despot would engage in. The implicit question is: Is that what you want? The people are sure they do and reply, "We want a king over us" (1 Sam. 1:19). When Samuel told the Lord this, he answered, "Listen to them and give them a king" (1 Sam. 8:22). No doubt, this response was much to Samuel's even greater surprise.

What's going on here? The Lord has many ways to answer our prayers. He can answer "yes," or "no," or "wait," or "yes and no," or "yes but..." (see devotion on Rom. 15:30-33). Or, in this case, he can answer with what is, in effect, "Work with them on this." The Lord wants to give them a king, but not the kind they think they want. The people want a strong man who can conduct successful military campaigns against their enemies. The people want the right thing for the wrong reasons. The king God will give will be a king unlike any in the world. He will rule, not as an autonomous despot, but under the law of God (cf. 1 Sam. 10:25), as God's chosen instrument, and ultimately as a type of the King of all kings.

Some of our most misguided and selfish desires can be redeemed. These desires may have come from God originally, but they have become corrupted and distorted by our sinful nature. For instance, the legitimate need for love can mutate into lust, or more subtly, an ill-advised relationship or marriage. God works with us on these things. He knows how we are formed, He knows our weakness, and instead of cutting off our desires, he satisfies our desires with good things (cf. Ps. 103:5, 13-14).

PRAYER: *Father, you have compassion on your children. Satisfy my desires, not with the things I think I need, but with the better things only you can give.*

DAY 51: FAR BE IT FROM ME

1 Samuel 12

"As for me, far be it from me that I should sin against the Lord by failing to pray for you" (1 Sam. 12:23).

The last thing Samuel said he would do for them was the first thing he had done for them. He would keep on praying for the people. Prayer wasn't a last resort, but a first and last resort. Samuel's intercession didn't begin when all his other options ran out, as in, "All we can do now is pray"; other options could come and go, but prayer would remain.

At the high-water mark of his ministry, Samuel could not only be seen praying, but actually leading by prayer (1 Sam. 7:1-11). After the Israelites had been oppressed by the Philistines for twenty years, they finally saw the light, sought the Lord, and repented of their sins. Samuel promised that the Lord would liberate them from the Philistines, and to seal it, he promised to intercede for them. The nation gathered at Mizpah for a service of recommitment. What happened that day is a vivid picture of a people at prayer, led by a man of prayer. As they fasted and prayed, they filled jars with water and poured it out before the Lord, probably as a symbol of their hearts poured out in prayer (cf. 1 Sam. 1:15; Ps. 62:8; Lam. 2:19). Then word came that the Philistine army was bearing down on them to attack them. They said to Samuel, "Do not stop crying out to the Lord our God for us, that he may rescue us from the hand of the Philistines. Then Samuel… cried out to the Lord on Israel's behalf, and the Lord answered him" (1 Sam. 7:8-9) by routing the Philistine army.

Samuel also prayed at the low points of his life. When confronted by the sins of his wicked sons, he turned again to prayer (1 Sam. 8:1-5). When time had run out for Saul, and God had rejected him completely, what did Samuel do? He prayed for Saul: "Samuel was troubled, and he cried out to the Lord all night" (1 Sam. 15:11). Happy or sad, in good times or in bad, Samuel knew he had to give an accounting to God for how he did his work. That's why he prayed so consistently. Do you see your responsibilities in the same light? Far be it from you that you should do otherwise!

PRAYER: *Blessed Master, give me Samuel's spiritual vision, strength, and perseverance that I will not fail to pray for those you have given to my care.*

DAY 52: FROZEN EXPERIENCE

2 Samuel 5:17-25

"As soon as you hear the sound of marching in the tops of the balsam trees.... because that will mean the Lord has gone out in front of you to strike the Philistine army" (2 Sam. 5:24).

When you pray for guidance in any situation, wait on God until you know what he wants, then do what he wants. The next time you face the same situation, repeat what the Lord told you the first time. Right? Wrong. Had David operated on this principle, the second time he met the Philistine army he would have been defeated. The Lord's directive for the first encounter was to attack immediately. For the second encounter, it was to circle around behind them and hold off the attack until he heard "the sound of marching in the tops of the balsam trees.... because that will mean the Lord has gone out in front of you to strike the Philistine army" (2 Sam. 5:24).

Frozen experience will keep you from hearing God's voice. Has God met your needs dramatically in the past, like he met David's needs in the first Philistine confrontation? It was wonderful, but was it so wonderful that you have been tempted to freeze that experience and make it the norm for every other experience to come? Has God been able to speak to you freshly in the present, or have you shackled him to his past dealings with you? What we should learn from the past guidance God gave is that he is faithful, not that he has the same way of dealing with every situation every time. The fact is, no situation is ever exactly like its predecessor. Besides, the situation could be the same, but we are different, and God may have a different way for the different people involved. The permutations could go on and on. Things change, we change, only God doesn't. But he is infinitely able to address every change that comes to us.

What we need to know in every situation is what God promised David: "the Lord has gone out in front of you." That's what guidance is; not a map to read, but a leader to stay close to and follow. Then we not only get to where we need to be, but we enjoy the pleasure of his company.

PRAYER: *Dear Father, if you aren't in front of me, I don't want to go! Still my heart and make me patient to wait for you.*

DAY 53: OPEN MY EYES, LORD

2 Samuel 7:18-29

"Who am I… that you have brought me thus far?" (2 Sam. 7:18).

The price you pay for the wonder and delight David expressed in this prayer, is simply to pay attention to what is around you. The price you pay for spiritual dullness and torpor is dullness and torpor. They are their own reward. Open your eyes to God's goodness to you, and if you cannot say, "Who am I… that you have brought me thus far?" (2 Sam. 7:18), then open them wider. Pray God will make you aware of his mercies. Surely this is what Jesus had in mind when he said we must become like children to enter the kingdom of God.

Annie Dillard writes:

> *An infant who has just learned to hold his head up has a frank and forthright way of gazing about him in bewilderment. He hasn't the faintest clue where he is, and he aims to learn. In a couple of years, what he will have learned instead is how to fake it: he'll have the cocksure air of a squatter who has come to feel he owns the place. Some unwonted, taught pride diverts us from our original intent, which is to explore the neighborhood, view the landscape, to discover where it is we have been so startlingly set down, if we can't learn why.*[1]

"Who am I?" Don't fake it. Be startled. Can you hear the surprise in the question? "It didn't have to be this good, in fact it wasn't and shouldn't have. But it is. I blush at the extravagance of what you have given me, Lord." David will be a king with an eternal dynasty. So will you, only better. If you are in Christ, your sins are forgiven, and he promised, "To him who overcomes and does my will to the end, I will give authority over the nations… [and] I will give the right to sit with me on my throne" (Rev. 2:26; 3:21). Are you surprised at that? Good! Can you say it now? "Who am I?"

PRAYER: *Open the eyes of our heart, Lord. We want to see you, and ourselves, so that we may rejoice with wonder and surprise.*

DAY 55: WHEN OUR EYES ARE OPENED

2 Samuel 12

"I have sinned against the Lord" (2 Sam.12:13).

There's a Russian proverb: "Nothing ages faster than gratitude." David has aged considerably in the time that elapsed between his grateful prayer in chapter 7 and the prayer he prayed in Chapter 12: "I have sinned against the Lord" (2 Sam. 12:13). The man who slept with another man's wife and connived to murder him was hardly grateful (cf. ch. 11).

Blindness to God's mercies will blind you to your sin. "We have two sets of names for vices," said Alexander MacLaren, "one set which rather mitigates and excuses them, and another set which puts them in their real hideousness."[1] We use the mitigating vocabulary for our sin and the hideous vocabulary for other people's sin. Nathan had to enrage David about "another man's sin" to make David see the gravity of his own. True repentance comes only when our eyes are opened, as David's were. Though the route to his sight was indirect, the effect was powerful.

What did David see? He saw his sin as detestable and mean. A rich man with everything had plundered a poor man with little. He saw what he deserved for his sin: death. He even pronounced his own sentence when he said, "As surely as the Lord lives, the man who did this deserves to die" (2 Sam. 12:5)! Greatest of all, he saw the evil of his sin against God against the backdrop of God's goodness toward him: "This is what the Lord, the God of Israel says: 'I anointed you as king over Israel, and I delivered you from the hand of Saul. I gave your master's house to you, and your master's wives into your arms. I gave you the house of Israel and Judah. And if all this had been too little, I would have given you even more. Why did you despise the word of the Lord by doing what is evil in his eyes'" (2 Sam. 12:7-9)? God said he would have done even more for David if he had only asked. David's sin was many things, but worst of all it was cold ingratitude.

"All have sinned and fall short of the glory of God" (Rom. 3:23). What David saw we would profit to see about our sin. There is only one way to reverse the ingratitude that leads to sin, indeed is sin. The remedy is to be grateful for the great mercy that forgives great sin.

PRAYER: *Merciful God, though the thought is terrifying, let me see the greatness of my sin, that I may praise you for the greatness of your forgiveness.*

DAY 56: SEEING THROUGH

2 Samuel 22

"The Lord is my rock" (2 Sam. 22:2).

Whatever David's failures at gratitude were, he will be remembered for his prayers of thanks and praise in the psalms. He is the great lyricist of praise. This prayer sums up much of his life and is virtually the same as Psalm 18. It is a superb example of a perspective that makes thanks and praise possible—call it the capacity to "see through" things.

Look at some of the metaphors David uses for God in this psalm: rock, fortress, deliverer, shield, and stronghold. Then look at the things God gave him and trained him for. God armed him with strength, made his feet like a deer's, trained his hands for battle, strengthened his arms to bend a bow of bronze, and so on. Every one of the things David says about God describe literal, physical things he needed and experienced in fighting battles. He really stood on a rock, hid in a fortress, used a shield, and shot arrows. He was no doubt trained by a real human being to fight with a sword and shield. He certainly spent many hours practicing the skills he would need to fight well. Yet all these things he attributes to God, from God, and through God.

David knew the difference between primary causes and secondary causes. The secondary causes were his tutor in hand-to-hand combat, the fortress he hid in, the strength of his feet on a mountain path. But the primary cause was God: "For from him and through him and to him are all things. To him be the glory forever! Amen" (Rom. 11:36). All these secondary causes were from and through and to God, so to him be the praise forever.

If there is secret to being grateful, it is this: seeing through secondary things to the primary One. Poet George Herbert wrote,

A man that looks on glass,
On it may stay his eye;
Or if he pleaseth, through it pass,
And then the heav'n espy.[1]

The secret of a grateful heart is an eye that will see through the surface to what lies behind it all. Be sure to thank the people in your life who are secondary causes, conduits from the primary Giver. Be thankful for things. But do not forget to see through it all to thank the God who is before and in and after all things.

PRAYER: *I thank you God, for everything and everyone you have given me, and through whom I may see you.*

DAY 57: NO HIGHER CALLING

Susannah Wesley (1670-1742)

"I have learned the secret of being content in any and every situation" (Phil. 4:12).

No one is busier than a mother with ten children; unless the ten were the survivors of the nineteen she gave birth to; unless her husband was a clergyman who was often absent from the home for weeks and months at a time, and was imprisoned for unpaid debts, leaving her to manage both household and parish; unless she also had to suffer the loss of almost everything she owned in fires that twice swept through her home. Susanna Wesley was a very busy woman. Her family teetered on the brink of starvation so many times, that she came to almost dislike the very thought of bread, because she had to work so hard to get it.

Yet for all that demanded her attention, she knew the real battle was spiritual, not against flesh and blood, numerous and needy children with hungry stomachs, and unpaid debts. The way to victory was through obedience and a willingness to suffer; and times of quiet spent in spiritual reading, worship, Scriptural meditation, self-examination, and prayer. Her famous son John Wesley said of her, "For many years my mother was employed in abundance of temporal business. Yet she never suffered anything to break in upon her stated hours of retirement (prayer times), which she sacredly observed from the age of 17 or 18 to 72."[1]

Susanna Wesley was also animated by a keen sense of the high calling of raising children in the knowledge of God. Though gifted intellectually and remembered by many as a woman of unusual beauty, charm, and intelligence, she felt the most strategic use of her life and gifts was to pour herself into her family. She expressed, "I desire nothing in this world so much as to have my children well-instructed in the principles of religion, that they may walk in the narrow way which alone leads to happiness."[2] The world would later feel the impact of her single-minded sense of vocation through the work of her sons John and Charles. But it was not easy for her, and she often longed for quiet and uninterrupted time with God. She prayed:

> *O God, I find it difficult to preserve a devout and serious temper of mind in the midst of much worldly business. Were I permitted to choose a state of life, or positively ask of Thee anything in this world, I would humbly choose and beg that I might be placed in such a station wherein I might have daily bread with moderate care and that I may have more leisure to retire from the world without injuring those dependent on me. Yet I do not know whether such a state of life would really be the best for me; nor am I assured that if I had more leisure I should be more zealously devoted to Thee and serve Thee better than now. Therefore, O Lord, show me that it is undoubtedly best to keep my mind in habitual submission and resignation to Thee....*[3]

PRAYER: *"O Lord, show me that it is undoubtedly best to keep my mind in habitual submission and resignation to Thee."*

DAY 58: DEADLY PRIDE

2 Samuel 24

"David was conscience-stricken after he had counted the fighting men" (2 Sam. 24:10).

Kings and governments take censuses all the time, it's what they do. Israel had taken a census before, without any guilt (cf. Num. 1:2-3; 26:2-4). Sometimes a census is needed as part of preparation for battle or for making wise public policy. The problem with David's census was that there was apparently no real need for a census other than highlighting his pride in what he had accomplished and a desire to brag a little about his power as a king. God took a dim view of this pride and wreaked a terrible judgment on his people. What is wrong with a little pride, a little bragging? What's wrong with it is that it is the root of every other sin. It is, as C. S. Lewis put it, "the complete anti-God state of mind." He explains why:

> *In God you come up against something which is in every respect immeasurably superior to yourself. Unless you know God as that—and, therefore, know yourself as nothing in comparison—you do not know God at all. As long as you are proud you cannot know God. A proud man is always looking down on things and people: and, of course, as long as you are looking down, you cannot see something that is above you.*[1]

Lewis says this raises a terrible question. Is it possible for someone to be very religious and pious but be consumed with pride? It is not. The God this person worships is an imaginary God to whom they pay a penny's worth of false humility to get a dollar's worth of pride toward others. Lewis proposed a test for pride that we should apply to our devotional and prayer life:

> *Whenever we find that our religious life is making us feel that we are good—above all, that we are better than someone else—I think we may be sure that we are being acted on, not by God, but by the devil. The real test of being in the presence of God is that you forget about yourself altogether or see yourself as a small, dirty object. It is better to forget about yourself altogether.*[2]

PRAYER: *Lord, teach me to be so absorbed in thanksgiving and praise that I forget about myself altogether.*

Introduction to 1 and 2 Kings

DAY 59: 500 YEARS OF "GOD-PLUS" VERSUS GOD ALONE

"The Lord warned Israel through all his prophets and seers, but they would not listen" (2 Kings 17:13).

"If men could but learn from history, what lessons it might teach us! But passion and party blind our eyes, and the light which experience gives is a lantern on the stern, which shines only on the waves behind us!" These words by Samuel Taylor Coleridge are the reason the author of the books of 1 and 2 Kings took the trouble to write them. It may be arguable that history repeats itself exactly, but the mistakes of history do so with alarming and deadening regularity. The Books of 1 and 2 Kings aim to identify the mistakes, so they won't be repeated.

Actually, it wasn't so much the mistakes—this mistake and that—but one gigantic mistake, the ultimate folly of worshiping gods other than the true and living God. To make things worse, it wasn't that the people of Israel and Judah ever stopped believing in the Lord. It is just that they wanted the Lord plus all the benefits the other gods might offer. Most of their Canaanite neighbors worshiped gods of fertility and agriculture. Since those were departments vital to everyone's life, it seemed reasonable that the Lord's people should get a little help from some of the "specialists." They wanted to have God and the gods. The appeal of "God-plus" was overwhelming.

The demise of the nations of Israel and Judah at the hands of the Assyrians and Babylonians respectively raised a burning theological question: Did their gods defeat Israel's God when Israel was defeated? The common assumption of the times was that when one nation defeated another nation, the winner's gods beat the loser's gods too. Military defeat brought on a spiritual crisis. The Books of 1 and 2 Kings address this issue by demonstrating how time and again, God's people were defeated not because their God had failed them, but because they had failed their God. That is the light the lantern of 1 and 2 Kings wants to shed on the past and the present.

Jesus said all great prayer begins with three great petitions: that God's name be revered, that his kingdom come, and that his will and no other's be done on earth as it is in Heaven. This is the opposite of "God-plus." To pray the Lord's Prayer is to learn the lessons of Israel's history.

PRAYER: *Father in heaven, thy kingdom come, thy will—and no other—be done on earth as it is in heaven.*

DAY 60: WHATEVER YOU WANT

1 Kings 3:1-15

"God said, 'Ask for whatever you want me to give you" (1 Kings 3:5).

"And God said, 'Ask for whatever you want me to give you'" (1 Kings 3:5). The way you respond to an unlimited offer will say a lot about who you are inside. Multiple-choice offers say more about the person making the offer; after all, he determined the choices. Unlimited offers call forth the heart of the person receiving it. God says, "You can have anything you want, go ahead and ask and it shall be yours," and adds implicitly, "and what you ask will reveal you." Is that why Jesus said, "You may ask me for anything in my name, and I will do it" (John 14:14)? The sky is the limit if you ask in his name. But what you ask will reveal what you know about his name and how congruent your heart is with the heart of God. Your desires say much about you.

Solomon's response could not have been better; he asked for a discerning heart. When he did, he got all the other things he might have asked for thrown in as well. Had he asked only for a good thing, he would have got the good thing and nothing more. Asking for the best got him the best and the good as well. It's like seeking first the kingdom of God and his righteousness. When you do, "all these things will be given to you as well" (Matt. 6:33). Merely good things are the red herrings of life. In mystery novels, red herrings are false clues meant to lead the detective down a wrong path. They get their name from the practice of criminals in the 19th century who dragged smoked herring down a false path to mislead the bloodhounds police used to sniff them out. The enemy of God's best is not the worst, but the less than the best, the good things.

God's complaint is that we want too little, not too much: "We are half-hearted creatures, fooling about with drink and sex and ambition when infinite joy is offered us, like an ignorant child who wants to go on making mud pies in a slum because he cannot imagine what is meant by the offer of a holiday at the sea. We are far too easily pleased."[1] Let your prayers be big—as big as the great and wise God we worship.

PRAYER: *Father in heaven, teach me to so know you and cause me to so love you, that I can ask for anything and receive it.*

DAY 61: JUST LIKE US

1 Kings 17—18

"The Lord heard Elijah's cry" (1 Kings 17:22).

Frankly, most people cannot relate to James' description of Elijah as "a man just like us" (James 5:17). He was fed miraculously by ravens (1 Kings 17:1-6) and by bottomless jars of oil and flour (1 Kings 17:7-16). He raised a boy from the dead (1 Kings 17:17-24), and he totally shut down the prophets of Baal and Asherah in a display of pyrotechnics that kept Israel talking for centuries (1 Kings 18:16-40). Oh, and it didn't rain for three and a half years because Elijah said so and didn't start again until he said so (1 Kings 17:1). If our being able to relate to a man like Elijah is supposed to encourage us to pray, we have a lot of thinking to do about Elijah.

We can identify with his terror at Jezebel's threat and his despondency (1 Kings 19:1-4), but that's about it.

Maybe we're not supposed to identify with Elijah and, therefore, his prayer life. Maybe we're supposed to understand what prayer is and, therefore, identify with Elijah. Maybe Elijah was indeed a man just like us whose experience of prayer shows us that people just like us can see great and wonderful things when we pray. That is the point of James' commentary on these chapters from 1 Kings.

James says prayer is powerful and effective. With both adjectives the sense is of inherent power and effectiveness, of potency and strength just beneath the surface, waiting to be summoned. "Beneath the surface" is usually the way the power and effectiveness of prayer looks. It is not too impressive on the outside—do we really believe those people with their eyes shut and hands folded are moving heaven and earth? It is a stretch of the imagination, but that is exactly what is happening. Read Revelation 8:1-5. And prayer is supernatural in its power and effectiveness: it didn't rain for three and a half years when Elijah prayed. Weather patterns and ocean temperatures, high-pressure systems and low-pressure systems adjusted themselves!

There's one more problem about James' midrash on our texts: what about the prayers of a "righteous man" being answered? Do any of us qualify? By faith in Christ, we are credited as righteous. And in the context of James, Elijah's prayers were his faith in action (James 2:22-23). What holds you back from praying with the confidence of Elijah? He really was just like you, and he saw God's glory because he prayed to see God's glory.

PRAYER: *Almighty God, nothing is too hard for you: weather, food supply, and miraculous signs are easy for you. Take my little faith and grow it!*

DAY 62: WHEN YOU WANT TO GIVE UP

1 Kings 19:1-18

"'I have had enough, Lord,' he said. 'Take my life; I am no better than my ancestors'" (1 Kings 19:4).

"'I have had enough, Lord,' he said. 'Take my life; I am no better than my ancestors'" (1 Kings 19:4). This kind of thing can happen to the best of us, and often does. It's what you feel when it seems your best wasn't enough. Elijah was in the middle of a struggle that pitted the God of Abraham, Isaac, and Jacob against the religion of Baal and Asherah. It was not an interdenominational squabble, like Calvinists and Armenians or Baptists and Methodists. These were two distinct religions with irreconcilable differences. Israel's future as the people of God hung in the balance, and Elijah had expended so much in the struggle, his efforts culminating in a victory on Mount Carmel, or so he thought (1 Kings 18:16-46). But now the evil Jezebel had a contract out on his life, and he wanted to give up. After Carmel, Elijah had been so high; but after Jezebel's murderous pledge, he came down hard (1 Kings 19:1-2). He prayed that God would take his life.

God's answer to his prayer models the ways God cares for his despondent servants. The most priceless is the revelation of his character he gave Elijah. Reminiscent of what he did before with Moses at Mount Horeb, and again at Mount Carmel, God sent a mighty wind, then an earthquake, and then fire. But each time it is said that the Lord was not in any of these. When the Lord does come, it is in a gentle whisper. The message to Elijah is that the way he wanted the Lord to come—in power and judgment—is not the way he will come this time. He will speak softly. More than his wrath, it is his kindness that leads to repentance (Rom. 2:4). Elisha, Elijah's successor, will be remembered more for his acts of mercy than his pronouncements of doom.

Did Elijah's anger at evil get the best of him? It's likely. Twice he told the Lord that he had been very zealous for the Lord and that he was the only one amid a nation of apostates! That was manifestly not the case, as the Lord reminded him (1 Kings 19:10, 14, 18). Excessive anger distorts the facts and makes one feel a victim. The next step is depression, the flipside of anger. Are you weary and despondent? Look into your heart; is it full of anger? Then look to the Lord and his love.

PRAYER: *Dear Father, lest I grow weary and despondent in your service, show me your love for me and for those you have called me to love.*

DAY 63: BREATHE ON THEM, BREATH OF GOD

2 Kings 4

"He went in, shut the door on the two of them and prayed to the Lord" (2 Kings 4:33).

No one knows for sure why Elisha stretched his body over the dead boy's body, mouth to mouth, eyes to eyes, hands to hands (2 Kings 4:34-35). It certainly wasn't ancient Cardio-Pulmonary Resuscitation (CPR). Depending upon one's sensibilities, the action can seem sweet or strange. But it was what the prophet did after he prayed to the Lord for the boy to be raised. Elijah had done the same thing, with the same result (1 Kings 17:21).

Maybe what this story of prayer and healing has for us is not so much a teaching on a particular kind of prayer, but a picture of prayer of a particular kind. Perhaps its intent is to move our compassion more than to add to our prayer repertoire. Sometimes prayer for others is like laying down our lives for them. All intercessory prayer is an act of love, but there are times when one wrestles with God for the life of another, pouring out the heart in tears and loud cries (Lam. 2:19; Heb. 5:7). When Jesus went about healing the sick and those tormented by demons. Matthew said this was the fulfillment of Isaiah 53:4: "He took up our infirmities and carried our diseases" (Matt. 8:17). A close look at Isaiah 53 shows that this bearing of pain was intimately connected with Jesus' ministry of intercession: "For he bore the sin of many and made intercession for the transgressors" (Isa. 53:12). In his prayers for their deliverance, Jesus took on himself their pain. His prayers were more than mere words; they were a further incarnation of God's redeeming love.

George Herbert described prayer as "God's breath in man returning to his birth."[1] Like the story of Elisha, that line isn't about the mechanics of prayer, but the heart of prayer. When God breathed his breath into Adam, he became a living soul. When we pray to the one who gave us breath, our breath, in a sense, goes back to the one who gave it. Does something like that happen in prayer—not mechanically and literally, but spiritually? God breathes his life in us (Rom. 8:15; Come, Holy Spirit!), we breathe back in the prayer of faith, and something of his breath is breathed on others. Intercessory prayer is a miraculous kind of CPR.

PRAYER: *"Breathe on me, Breath of God, Fill me with life anew, That I may love what Thou dost love, And do what Thou wouldst do" (from the hymn "Breathe on Me, Breath of God" by Edwin Hatch).*

DAY 64: THE 7.5-MILLION-DOLLAR MAN

George Mueller (1805-1898)

"But seek first his kingdom and his righteousness, and all these things will be given to you as well" (Matt. 6:33).

The orphans sat in silence as George Mueller rose to pray for their daily bread. The tables were set for breakfast, but there was no food. Just then, there was a knock on the door; it was the local baker. "Mr. Mueller," he explained, "I couldn't sleep last night. Somehow I felt you didn't have bread for breakfast, so I got up at 2:00 AM and baked some fresh bread." Minutes later, another man knocked at the door; this time it was the milkman. His cart had broken down right in front of the orphanage, he needed to empty his cart to repair it, and he wanted to give away all his milk. Breakfast was served.

This kind of thing happened to George Mueller over and over again in a ministry that spanned 57 years. Mueller believed the only one he should ever speak to about his personal needs and the needs of his orphans was God, no one else. He trusted him for every detail of his life. At the end of his life, George Mueller could say that God had provided for over 10,000 orphaned children, answered 50,000 specific prayers, and brought in 7.5 million dollars in contributions (1,453,153 pounds by the days' standards), all in response to simple faith and tenacious prayer. Once he explained his unusual "fund raising techniques" to an incredulous businessman who exclaimed unapprovingly, "Why you live from hand to mouth!" Mueller agreed, saying, "Yes, it's God's hand and my mouth."

He wrote:

> *"When I first began to allow God to deal with me, relying on Him, taking Him at His Word, and set out fifty years ago simply relying on Him for myself, family, taxes, traveling expenses and every other need, I rested on the simple promises I found in the sixth chapter of Matthew, 'I say unto you, take no thought for your life, what ye shall eat, or what ye shall drink; not yet for your body, what ye shall put on… for your heavenly Father knoweth that ye have need of all these things. But seek ye first the kingdom of God and His righteousness; and all these things shall be added unto you' (Matt. 6:25-33). I believed the Word; I rested on it and practiced it. I took God at His Word."*

Despite his amazing experiences, the task of trusting in God for everything was not always easy for Mueller. "I have had my trials and difficulties, and my purse empty… there will always be difficulties, always trials. But God has sustained me out of them, and the work has gone on." He also shrugged off any claims of greatness. "No, this is not, as some have said, because I am a man of great mental power, or endowed with energy and perseverance—these are not the reasons. It is because I have confided in God…. The great point," said Mueller, "is to never give up until the answer comes."[1]

PRAYER: *Nothing is too hard for you, my dear Father. You are completely willing and able to care for me and those I love. I commit us and our needs into your hands.*

DAY 65: CREATURES FROM THE WORLD NEXT DOOR

2 Kings 6

"Elisha prayed, 'O Lord, open his eyes so he may see'" (2 Kings 6:17).

There's a world next door, just around the corner, full of marvelous creatures, closer than you think, and yet a universe away. In fairy tales, it's the place Alice gets to through the looking glass; or the land the Pevensie children enter through an old wardrobe. Elisha's servant saw it when the prophet prayed, "'O Lord, open his eyes so he may see.' Then the Lord opened the servant's eyes, and he looked and saw the hills full of horses and chariots of fire all around Elisha" (2 Kings 6: 17). If there were some kind of spiritual eyeglasses we could put on to see the world next door all around us, we would be as astonished as that servant was. We would know that no matter who or how many our enemies may be, "those who are with us are more than those who are with them" (2 Kings 6:16).

"The angel of the Lord encamps around those who fear him, and he delivers them" (Ps. 34:7). This is not a metaphor; it is literally true. "For he will command his angels concerning you to guard you in all your ways; they will lift you up in their hands, so that you will not strike your foot against a stone" (Ps. 91:11-12). That sounds like fairy tale talk, and it is; except this fairy tale is true. If we could see the times these marvelous creatures have served God by protecting us, we would be amazed? We would also be more confident in prayer. We are never alone. Jesus was so confident of the presence of these beings in the world next door, that when the mob came for him, he told his disciples, "Do you think that I cannot call on my Father, and he will at once put at my disposal more than twelve legions of angels?" (Matt. 26:53).

It is God's business, not ours, to call on the angels to come to our side. Like all his servants, human and otherwise, they are not to be worshiped or prayed to. But they are to encourage us in the spiritual battle we are embroiled in till Christ returns.

PRAYER: *"Praise the Lord, you his angels, you mighty ones who do his bidding, who obey his word" (Ps. 103:20).*

DAY 66: SPREAD IT OUT BEFORE THE LORD

2 Kings 19

"Hezekiah received the letter... and spread it out before the Lord" (2 Kings 19:14).

A dictionary could well define the word "insolence" this way: *See Sennacherib, 2 Kings 19:9-13.* Any sane person would be terrified to say what he said to Hezekiah about God: "Do not let the god you depend on deceive you when he says, 'Jerusalem will not be handed over to the king of the Assyria.' Surely you have heard what the kings of Assyria have done to all the countries, destroying them completely. And will you be delivered? Did the gods of the nations that were destroyed by my forefathers deliver them" (2 Kings 19:10-12)? This is insolence that defies a reply. Hezekiah did the only wise thing that could be done. He took the letter "up to the temple of the Lord and spread it out before the Lord. And Hezekiah prayed to the Lord" (2 Kings 19:14-15).

Sennacherib's letter may have reached the limits of insolence, but today's newspaper headlines can be just as awful in their own way. Things like child abuse, murders, kidnappings, acts of terrorism, rape, robbery, and mayhem defy human reply. They can so stupefy as to leave us mute with outrage and grief. Have you ever felt that way? Spread the newspaper out before the Lord and pray as Hezekiah did! Really. Open the page filled with the outrage, lay it on a table or desk, and read it aloud to the Lord as part of a prayer. Begin as Hezekiah did by remembering God's greatness and sovereignty over the affairs of nations; read a psalm such as Psalm 29, or even verse 15 in this text. Then read the newspaper article aloud to God, beginning with something like, "Almighty God, you know that..." Fill in the details. Then declare God's truth into the situation, as Hezekiah did in verse 18. End by asking him to do what only he can do: to save and to make the kingdoms of this world the kingdom of God. Read Revelation 15:3-4. Then say a hearty "Amen" to what you have prayed. Nothing is too hard for the Lord. 85,000 Assyrian troops died as a result of Hezekiah's prayer; and Sennacherib's own sons assassinated him while he was worshiping his god (2 Kings 19:35-37)!

PRAYER: *"Arise, O Lord, let not man triumph; let the nations be judged in your presence. Strike them with terror, O Lord; let the nations know that they are but men" (Ps. 9:19-20).*

Introduction to 1 and 2 Chronicles

DAY 67: REVIVAL PRAYING

"He answered their prayers, because they trusted in him" (1 Chron. 5:20).

If the books of 1 and 2 Kings are the pathology report, the books of 1 and 2 Chronicles are the prognosis and treatment. Kings explains to exiled Jews how the disaster happened and why. It wasn't because the gods of the Assyrians and Babylonians had defeated the Lord; it was because Israel had abandoned the Lord. God was as involved in their slavery in exile as he was when he delivered them from slavery in Egypt. The first time it was for their salvation, the second time it was discipline for their sanctification. But the people aren't so sure of this. Does he still want them back? Is there still a future and a hope for them? Is their illness terminal? Chronicles say there is a hope. God never stopped loving them and willing that they be a blessing to the world. The treatment is simply: "If my people, who are called by my name, will humble themselves and pray and seek my face and turn from their wicked ways, then will I hear from heaven and will forgive their sin and heal their land" (2 Chron. 7:14). Illustrations of this formula from Israel's history abound in the books.

The message of Chronicles can give great encouragement to prayer, especially prayers of repentance and sorrow for sin. If the promise of 2 Chronicles 7:14 is true, and all of God's promises are, we may be confident that God has a good future for us, no matter how dark and sordid our past. The prophet Hosea gives the message of 1 and 2 Chronicles: "Come, let us return to the Lord. He has torn us to pieces, but he will heal us; he has injured us, but he will bind up our wounds" (1 Chron. 6:1).

PRAYER: *Pray Hosea's prayer with fellow believers, for your church: "Come, let us return to the Lord. He has torn us to pieces, but he will heal us; he has injured us, but he will bind up our wounds" (1 Chron. 6:1).*

DAY 67: DOING GOD'S WILL BY RESISTING GOD'S WILL

1 Chronicles 4:9-10

"His mother had named him Jabez, saying, 'I gave birth to him in pain'" (1 Chron. 4:9).

It was a terrible name to be saddled with from birth. *Jabez* sounded like the Hebrew word for pain, and that's how his mother remembered him. Since she had a painful delivery, she decided he would have a painful identity. Names tell us who we are in a powerfully subliminal way. Before Jabez was able to reflect on his name, and he must have, at some level, believed what his name said about him—discomfort, sadness, grim. We don't know when or how he decided to pray what was essentially a prayer of rebellion: "Oh, that you would bless me and enlarge my territory" (1 Chron. 4:10)! But something deep inside us is very glad he did.

Sometimes to resist the will of God is to do the will of God—if what we resist was meant by God to be temporary and intermediary and, therefore, to be transcended. A child may be born into grinding poverty and ignorance. Though it wasn't God's will that poverty and ignorance exist, it was God's will that the child be born. Should the child acquiesce to poverty and ignorance simply because God willed her birth into those conditions? Not at all. She should resist them in the name of the God who willed she be born into them. For her to resist his lower, temporary will is to embrace his higher, eternal purposes for her blessing. That's the kind of prayer Jabez prayed. His mother gave him a bad name; God wanted better for him, even though he willed that she be his mother.

What difficulty are you facing now? It may be recent, or it may be longstanding. How should you pray about it? For patience, certainly; but surely for endurance too, and for a grateful heart and the trust to accept God's decision. But it may also be his will that you resist his will for you at this moment, to grasp his higher and better will. We may obey God as much when we push our case and plead our cause as we do when we accept our state.

PRAYER: *"Oh Lord, that you would bless me and enlarge my territory! Let your hand be with me and keep me from harm so that I will be free from pain."*

DAY 68: INDISCRIMINATE THANKS

1 Chronicles 23:30

"They were also to stand every morning to thank and praise the Lord. They were also to do the same in the evening" (1 Chron. 23:30).

"They were also to stand every morning to thank and praise the Lord. They were to do the same in the evening" (1 Chron. 23:30). Try to get your mind around the sheer numbers involved in the exercise of thanksgiving in the temple. Thirty-eight thousand Levites are involved. They work in shifts, morning, and evening. Four thousand of the thirty-eight thousand play in the band. The care and abandon given to thanksgiving are extravagant and indiscriminate compared to modern Christian standards, or just about any standards for that matter. Thanksgiving was formalized, to be done twice daily, regardless of how anyone felt that day. No committee was convened to discuss whether they had sufficient reasons to be thankful; God commanded that they just do it, because he believed they always had sufficient reasons whether they felt like it or not. God's mind hasn't changed on this subject.

"Thanksgiving is not a task to be undertaken lightly," writes Virginia Stem Owens. "It is not for dilettantes or aesthetes. One does not dabble in praise for one's own amusement, nor train the intellect and develop perceptual skills to add to one's repertoire. We're not talking about the world as a free course in art appreciation. No. *Thanksgiving is not a result of perception; thanksgiving is the access to perception*" (italics added).[1] We think we need to see something in order to be thankful. But it works the other way: we need to give thanks so we can see. If we wait until we see it, we will never see it. Gratitude is an organ of perception. That's why Paul said to always be joyful, to pray continually and to give thanks in all circumstances (1 Thess. 5:16-18).

But we need help. We must give thanks so that we may be thankful, and we pray for hearts willing to do that. George Herbert prayed a prayer we may all pray.

PRAYER: *Pray George Herbert's prayer.*

Thou that hast given so much to me,
Give one thing more, a grateful heart....
Not thankful when it pleaseth me,
As if Thy blessings had spare days;
But such a heart whose pulse may be
Thy praise.[2]

DAY 69: KEEP DRAWING WATER

1 Chronicles 29:10-20

"David praised the Lord" (1 Chron. 29:10).

This is a prayer to memorize, like Aaron's blessing (Num. 6:24-26). That's because David is to thanks and praise what Andres Segovia is to a guitar, or Arthur Rubinstein to a piano. These people deserve to be imitated. David had spent a lifetime in earnest and vital prayer. In this text we see the grand master at his best, at the end of his life, leading the nation in prayer. We can never thank God too much or in too many different ways. Thanksgiving is an organ of perception; the more we give thanks, the more things we see to give thanks for (see yesterday's devotion).

David's prayer is a real eye-opener or a real "well-opener." Jack Sanford tells of an old well his family used during summer vacations in rural New Hampshire. It was just outside the 150-year-old farmhouse where they stayed. Even in the worst droughts, the old well yielded cold, pure water. Over the years, the family remodeled the farmhouse and made improvements like indoor plumbing and running water. Since the well was no longer needed, it was covered to keep a reserve should the need arise in the future.

One day, years later, Sanford got a hankering for the well's wonderful water. So, he took off the cover, lowered a bucket, and was shocked to discover that the well had gone bone dry. He asked around in the village for an explanation. He learned that wells like that well were fed by hundreds of tiny underground rivulets. When water is drawn from the well, more water flows through the rivulets. When water is not drawn from the well, sediments in the water collect, and the rivulets are stopped up. The more water flows out, the more water flows in.

Our hearts are that way too. The more we give thanks, the more we are able to give thanks. We learn to pray by praying. Sometimes we learn best by learning the prayer of a master, like David.

PRAYER: *Pray aloud this great prayer of 1 Chronicles 29:10-13, until you can pray it by heart and make it your own.*

Praise be to you, Lord,
the God of our father Israel,
from everlasting to everlasting.
Yours, Lord, is the greatness and the power
and the glory and the majesty and the splendor,
for everything in heaven and earth is yours.
Yours, Lord, is the kingdom;
you are exalted as head over all.
Wealth and honor come from you;
you are the ruler of all things.
In your hands are strength and power
to exalt and give strength to all.
Now, our God, we give you thanks,
and praise your glorious name.

DAY 70: "MAN'S EXTREMITY IS GOD'S OPPORTUNITY"

Rees Howells (1879-1950)

"Some trust in chariots and some in horses, but we trust in the name of the Lord our God" (Ps. 20:7).

Rees Howells had seen Will Battery before, a homeless drunk who smelled bad and slept in the boiler room of the local tin mill, an outcast. Still, Howells was drawn to the man and strongly convinced that God wanted to restore him to sanity and salvation. So, he spent all his Sundays with him, taking genuine joy in Will's company and enduring the stares of the townsfolk as Rees and Will walked side by side. For three years Rees prayed for Will, sharing his money and resources until Will finally was converted. "In this way," Rees later commented, "I started at the bottom and loved just one, and if you love one, you can love many; and if many, you can love all."

Such was the work of God in the life of Rees Howells, a simple praying man whose name became synonymous with intercessor—a lightning rod for revival, missionary to South Africa, and founder of the Bible College of Wales.

Believing prayer was the single-most important act he could perform for the future of the world, Howells called college-wide prayer meetings throughout World War II, to cry out to God for the defeat of Hitler and for freedom of the gospel in Europe. Rees was troubled and burdened greatly for the Allied troops, saying "if they suffer more than we suffer for them, it will be our lifelong shame… Lord, don't allow us to pray any differently from what we could if we were on the front line."

In September 1945, the Allied troops attempted to capture a beachhead in Salerno, Italy—a major foothold in the southern approach to Rome. The college was meeting for prayer when Rees suddenly said in a trembling voice, "The Lord has burdened me… with the invasion of Salerno. I believe our men are in great difficulties, and the Lord has told me that unless we can pray them through, they are in danger of losing their hold." The college prayed fervently until exactly 11pm, when everyone spontaneously began praising God, believing that the victory had been won.

A few days later the news came with the headline, "The Miracle of Salerno." It told how enemy artillery was advancing and that, unless a miracle happened, the beachhead would be lost to the Allies. "Suddenly," an eyewitness said, "for no accountable reason the firing ceased, and the Nazi artillery stopped its advance. A deathly stillness settled on the scene. We waited in breathless anticipation, but nothing happened. I looked at my watch—it was eleven o'clock at night. Still, we waited, but still, nothing happened; and nothing happened all that night, but those hours made all the difference to the invasion. By the morning the beachhead was established."

During the war God had called the college to pray for the world, just as Rees had been called to pray for the one soul of Will Battery. In both were embodied what Howells believed to be the main principle of intercession, that "man's extremity is God's opportunity."[1]

PRAYER: *Lord, lead me into the depths of intercession. Make me see the world as you do and join your Son in passionate intercession for the world (see Heb. 7:25).*

DAY 71: PRESCRIPTION FOR REVIVAL

2 Chronicles 7:14

If my people, who are called by my name, will humble themselves and pray and seek my face and turn from their wicked ways, then I will hear from heaven, and I will forgive their sin and will heal their land. (2 Chron. 7:14).

Christians have prayed this ancient prayer-promise, first given to Israel, for centuries as a kind of prescription for revival in the church. What is a revival? There are a lot of ways to think of it but let this be a picture. Have you seen the photo booths at carnivals where people can put their heads in holes over paintings of the bodies of muscle men and princesses and cowboys? The result is usually funny. You see Grandma's face on the body of a muscle man, your bookish Uncle Fred's face over the body of a pirate. The humor is in the incongruity. Sometimes the actual faces of the people who make up the church, the body of Christ, seem incongruous in the extreme, but the result isn't funny. Our faces, which is a way the Bible talks about our inner selves, don't look like they belong on Christ's body. Revival is what happens when spiritual vitality is restored in such a way that the faces and the body match again.

The prayer-promise says there are four things that must happen for God to revive his people:

1. We must humble ourselves; renounce pride and self-sufficiency.
2. We must pray. Genuine prayer comes only from humility. Think of the classic postures of prayer: hands folded, head bowed; hands open and raised toward heaven; face down, prostrate—all are postures of humility and deep dependence on God.
3. We must seek God's face. God's face is his inner self, or his heart. He shows it only to those who want know God as a friend knows a friend, or a lover. To seek God's face is to have your first love restored (Rev. 2:4).
4. We must turn from our wicked ways. The word is *repent*. We cannot seek God's face if we have been seeking something else.

The word *prescription* really isn't a good word to use for this revival prayer-promise. It smacks too much of the mechanical and automatic. But if it helps to underline the certainty, we have that God will keep his promise for he said, "then I will hear from heaven and will forgive their sin and heal their land" (2 Chron. 7:14).

PRAYER: *"Restore us again, O God our Savior…. Will you not revive us again that your people may rejoice in you" (Ps. 85:4, 6)?*

DAY 72: THE BEST POSTURE FOR PRAYER

2 Chronicles 14:2-15

"Lord, there is no one like you to help the powerless against the mighty" (2 Chron. 14:11).

"Then Asa called to the Lord his God and said, 'Lord, there is no one like you to help the powerless against the mighty. Help us, O Lord our God, for we rely on you, and in your name, we have come against this vast army'" (2 Chron. 14:11).

Here is a comical story that has been told as an illustration for prayer: As a telephone repairman worked on the pastor's telephone, he listened as the pastor and two colleagues discussed the best posture for prayer. One said, "I still think the best way to pray is head bowed, hands folded." Another said, "That's fine if it helps you, but I prefer standing with hands open and raised to heaven. It helps me feel my need." The last pastor agreed with the first two, but added, "Both of those have their advantages, but I'm discovering the value of lying face down on the floor. It helps me be humble." Then the telephone repairman spoke up: "I think the best posture for prayer is upside down. I was working on a telephone pole, twenty feet in the air and fell. My harness held me, but I was hanging upside down until I got help."

Asa would have agreed with the telephone repairman—desperate is the best posture for prayer. When he looked at Zerah the Cushite's army, he knew there was no hope, except in God. When people become acutely conscious of their weakness, it does one of two things: it either so unnerves them that they panic, or it drives them to their knees in prayer. Blessed are those who pray when there is no hope. God created the universe out of nothing. He can just as easily save us when we come to nothing. He not only can, but it delights him to do it. His eyes even roam the earth looking for people like Asa (2 Chron. 16:9).

It's too bad this lesson is not one that can be learned once-for-all. Asa got it right once, but he later forgot (2 Chron. 16:1-10). It may take many times to get it right, but each time you learn to trust God a little bit, he will teach you to trust him a little bit more.

PRAYER: *Make Asa's prayer your own the next time you face an impossible situation: "Lord, there is no one like you to help the powerless against the mighty. Help me, O Lord our God, for I rely on you."*

DAY 73: LET THE SINGERS LEAD!

2 Chronicles 20

"We do not know what to do, but our eyes are on you" (2 Chron. 20:12).

Jehoshaphat started in the same prayer posture as Asa (see yesterday's devotion). He was desperate, but perhaps there was a twist in his desperation. The phrase "we do not know what to do" sounds like something he might have said after spending and expending a lot of time and sweat trying to figure out what to do. It sounds like the kind of thing one says after reading and rereading the spreadsheets and budget reports, and everything still points to disaster. In any case, Jehoshaphat is where he needs to be—desperate—and his eyes are on God.

The pattern of his prayer for help is classic and is repeated again and again in the Bible. It bears repeating and underlining: First, he praises God for who God is and what he has promised; that is, he remembers who he is talking to (2 Chron. 20:6-9). Second, he briefly describes the situation (2 Chron. 20:10-11); and third, he asks God to intervene (2 Chron. 20:12). Take note of the relative weight Jehoshaphat gives to these three sections of his prayer. He spends a lot of time praising God (4 verses) and in describing the situation (2 verses) and in asking for help (1 verse). There is a lesson here we need to learn, for so often our prayers reflect a reversed order of priorities. We give a lot of time to weeping and wailing and advising God on what he should do and very little time thanking him for what he can do—and knows to do—better than we do!

The prayer meeting ends with a prophetic word from Jahaziel which so encourages the people that they go into battle with the singers leading! That is an amazing picture of prayer too. Jehoshaphat's prayer is led by praise, and so is his army. They go to meet their enemies singing, "Give thanks to the Lord for his love endures forever" (2 Chron. 20:21). But when they get to their enemies, their enemies are all dead. How pleasing it was to thank God for the victory before they saw the victory. It was pleasing to them and pleasing to God. Let praise and thanksgiving be your banner in prayer of all kinds, and especially your prayers of desperation.

PRAYER: *Jehoshaphat's prayer is another good prayer to make your own: "We do not know what to do, but our eyes are on you."*

Introduction to Ezra and Nehemiah

DAY 74: THE LORD BUILDS

"Unless the Lord builds the house" (Ps. 127:1).

If only relationships were as easy to rebuild as houses or some other non-human, non-personal thing. A twenty-something man was telling his divorced father about the girl he was falling in love with. He said they were going to move into the same apartment and live together for a while to see if their relationship was strong enough for marriage. Both were children of divorce and were wary of marriage. The son explained: "That way, Dad, if it doesn't work out like with you and Mom, we can just split up without the mess."

Pain clouded his father's eyes. He answered, "Rocks split, son; people tear."

The return of the exiles from Babylon to Jerusalem was more like rebuilding a relationship than rebuilding a city. They had felt divorced from and abandoned by God when in exile. It had not been an amicable parting of the ways. But they had come to learn that it was they, not the Lord, who had walked away from the relationship. They had "moved back in" so to speak, but there were a lot of issues to work through—like infidelity to God which was still a sore temptation for them. A pattern of philandering doesn't change overnight. Plus, there were the enemies of God who absolutely did not want a renewed Israel.

God sent two brave and prayerful men to lead this renewal: Ezra and Nehemiah. They were skilled, wise pioneers and administrators. But it was their ministry of intercession that stands out, not alongside their wisdom and courage, but as the source of their strength. Like so many great and godly rebuilders, they knew that unless the Lord did the building, their work was futile.

PRAYER: *Almighty God, send us leaders to lead us into the fullness of your presence in the church. Here am I, send me—if it please you.*

DAY 75: BE A *WE* INSTEAD OF A *ME*

Ezra 9:6-15

"O my God, I am too ashamed and disgraced to lift up my face to you, my God, because our sins are higher than our heads and our guilt has reached to the heavens" (Ezra 9:6).

Two things set this prayer apart from the prayers of many modern Christians in the West. The first, and easier to understand, is the frequency of words like "ours" and "we" and "us" as opposed to words like "I" and "me." Clearly Ezra's chief identity is his Jewishness. He is a "we" before he is an "I." Scholars call that way of thinking, "corporate identity." The individualism of western culture has a hard time getting its mind around this point of view. There is far too much "me and Jesus" in our thinking and praying. There should be a lot more "we and Jesus."

The second thing that sets this prayer apart is the really hard part: it is the fact that Ezra repents of the sins of others as though they were his own. That act takes his "corporate identity" to an even deeper level. But this isn't something peculiar to Ezra, it is the view of Scripture. God's people are members of a body, not an organization. A member of an organization can exist outside the organization; a member of a body is dead outside the body. And the body stretches out not only in space, but in time. Read Hebrews 11:40. It says that a great cloud of witnesses who came before us (and are now dead) are not just waiting for us to finish the race as they have. No, it says they are waiting for us to finish the race *so they can, too*! "God had planned something better for us so that only *together with us would they be made perfect*" (Heb. 11:40; cf. 12:1-2, italics added).

We are linked to one another in ways we must understand if we are to give to intercessory prayer the urgency it deserves. What I do for another, or fail to do for another, has profound implications for that person's wellbeing. Ezra is stricken over the effect others' sins have had on the whole people; so much so that he repents as one of them. In the final analysis, this kind of praying is not about "corporate identity," it is about love. Ask God to expand your sense of your self, so you can pray for others as you would for yourself. In this way, you love your neighbor as yourself.

PRAYER: *Father, teach me when I pray, to think "we" and "ours" more than I think "me" and "mine."*

DAY 76: NO ONE IS AN ISLAND

Nehemiah 1:4-11

"They are your servants and your people, whom you redeemed by your great strength" (Neh. 1:10).

This is the second of three prayers of Ezra and Nehemiah that we will look at in these devotions. All three prayers are exemplars of the mind of an intercessor—that deep sense of solidarity with a people that will treat their sins as their own and plead for God's mercy for "us," not "them." John Donne's famous meditation captures the perspective of these great men of prayer:

> *No man is an Island, entire of itself; every man is a piece of the Continent, a part of the main; if a clod be washed away by the sea, Europe is the less, as well as if a promontory were, as well as if a manor of thy friends or of thine own were; any man's death diminishes me, because I am involved in Mankind; And therefore never send to know for whom the bell tolls; It tolls for thee.*[1]

Only love can cause us to see others this way. Paul told husbands to love their wives as they love their own bodies, for that is how Christ loves the church—as his own body (Eph. 5:25-33). Ezra and Nehemiah love the people of God the way Christ loves the church.

In this prayer, Nehemiah drew on a text from Moses' intercession, by allusion, and put himself in the same place Moses was when he pled with God for the life of the nation. Ezra prayed, "They are your servants and your people, whom you redeemed" (Neh. 1:10). The first time that kind of prayer was prayed, Israel was close to extinction (cf. Deut. 9:25-29). At that time, Moses did a daring and provocative thing: he "stood in the breach before [God] to keep his wrath from destroying" the nation (Ps. 106:23). Now Nehemiah does the same thing.

What would happen to your personal prayer life, and the prayers of your church, if these were the perspectives you brought to prayer: a deep sense of solidarity with the people you pray for and courage to stand in the breach between them and destruction? It would be harder to get drowsy and to be trivial when you pray.

PRAYER: *Holy God, my heart is narrow! Expand it with your holy presence that I might make room for others in my prayers.*

DAY 77: THE SACRAMENT OF GEOMETRY

Simone Weil (1909-1943)

"Whatever you do, work at it with all your heart, as working for the Lord. It is the Lord Christ you are serving" (Col. 3:23-24).

In 1938, while at the Benedictine abbey of Solesmes, Simone Weil had a mystical encounter with God. As she read a poem by George Herbert, "Christ came down and seized me," she later wrote to a friend. Although Weil never was formally baptized or joined a denomination, she continued to have an intense interest in Christianity during the few remaining years of her life. She died in 1943 of starvation and pulmonary tuberculosis after refusing to eat in order to show solidarity with the French under Nazi occupation.

Weil's early years were impassioned and restless. Born in Paris in 1909, she obtained her undergraduate degree with honors at age fifteen and spent her young adulthood teaching philosophy and involving herself in causes of social reform. As a writer, she contributed to several communist and socialist publications. As an activist, she became an advocate for the unemployed and the lower-class worker, even taking a job in an automobile factory to better understand the worker's plight. But it was in her thinking and writing as a fervent (though somewhat unorthodox) Christian that she made her most enduring contributions.

Her essay, "Reflections on the Right Use of School Studies with a View to the Love of God," has inspired many Christian students to see their studies as more than mere academic pursuits, but as means to a higher end. This higher end is the love of God, and it is achieved through a rigorous discipline which Weil calls "the faculty of attention." The concept is simple: All academic pursuits train the mind to focus its full attention on the problem or the task at hand. Weil believed this focus of attention is the very substance of prayer, in which God is the subject. In this way, learning has value in and of itself as a lower means to the higher end of loving God in prayer.

"The solution of a geometry problem does not in itself constitute a precious gift," wrote Weil, "but the same law applies to it because it is the image of something precious. Being a little fragment of particular truth, it is a pure image of the unique, eternal, and living Truth, the very Truth that once in a human voice declared: 'I am the Truth.' Every school exercise, thought of in this way, is like a sacrament."

But Weil warned against approaching prayer and learning with the stoic drudgery of a homework assignment. "Contrary to the usual belief… the type of willpower that makes us set our teeth and endure suffering… has practically no place in study. The intelligence can only be led by desire. For there to be desire, there must be pleasure and joy in the work. The intelligence only grows and bears fruit in joy. The joy of learning [and praying!] is as indispensable as breathing is to running."[1]

PRAYER: *"Teach me, my God and King / In all things thee to see / And what I do in anything / To do it as for thee" (George Herbert).*

DAY 78: LOVE TO TELL THE STORY

Nehemiah 9:1-37

"Stand up and praise the Lord your God,
who is from everlasting to everlasting" (Neh. 9:5).

It has been said that history is *His Story*, God's story. If life is a story, and God is the author, then everything depends on understanding where you are on the plot line. The happiness or sadness of any moment is meaningful only in the context of the whole narrative. Given the enormous and daunting difficulty of rebuilding a shattered nation, it's a good thing that Nehemiah knows the story well.

In his prayer for Israel, Nehemiah touchingly retells the story to God, making his case from the story God has been writing for God to continue to rescue his people despite their sin. He starts with creation, moves to Abraham, and then recalls the rescue from captivity in Egypt, the giving of the law on Sinai, the rebelliousness of his people in the wilderness, the conquest of Canaan, and the national apostasy that has gotten them where they are now.

At every turn in the story, Nehemiah returns to the theme of God's amazing grace. Regarding creation, he prays, "You give life to everything" (Neh. 9:6). Remembering Abraham he says, "you have kept your promise because you were righteous" (Neh. 9:8). In Israel's deliverance from slavery, he marvels, "you sent miraculous signs and wonders" (Neh. 9:10). In the subsequent ingratitude and rebelliousness of the people in the wilderness, Nehemiah recalls how God had been, "a forgiving God, gracious and compassionate, slow to anger and abounding in love" (Neh. 9:17). Regarding the apostasy of the kings of Israel and Judah, Nehemiah prays: "But in your great mercy you did not put an end to them or abandon them, for you are a gracious and merciful God" (Neh. 9:31).

All this retelling of the story brings Nehemiah to the present and to his prayer for God to keep writing the story the way he always has: "Now, therefore, O our God, the great, mighty and awesome God, who keeps his covenant of love, do not let all this hardship seem trifling in your eyes" (Neh. 9:32). In other words, it's been bad for us before, and it's just as bad now. Please save us.

This kind of praying does three things for us: it keeps us clear on what we may expect from God, it encourages us by strengthening our faith, and it gives us joy to remember how God has been good to us—it is fun. With the Lord, it pleases him when his people start thinking the way he always has.

PRAYER: *"I love to tell the story / 'tis pleasant to repeat What seems each time I tell it, more wonderfully sweet" (Katherine Hankey, from the hymn "I Love to Tell the Story").*

Introduction to Esther

DAY 79: A CHOREOGRAPHY OF COINCIDENCES

"Gather together all the Jews who are
in Susa, and fast for me" (Esther 4:16).

What are we to make of a book in the Bible that doesn't even mention God? Sometimes actions speak louder than words. God's words are acts and his acts are words spoken to those with ears to hear. What God says, he does; and what he does is always consistent with what he has said.

Though the story opens with the threat of genocide, the Jews seem to be the luckiest people on earth when the story concludes. How lucky for them that Esther was such a gorgeous woman. How fortunate that she beat the other women out in the Bride-for-Xerxes competition. How lucky for them that Mordecai just happened to overhear an assassination plot. Coincidences collect, one upon another, and Lo! the evil Haman ends up falling in the pit he dug for others.[1]

But maybe the Jews are just a little too lucky, like the suspicious character who keeps beating the house in roulette. Maybe there is some manipulation of the game going on somewhere. To use a line by songwriter David Wilcox, there is a choreography in these coincidences. That is the point of a story in which the main character, God, isn't mentioned. That is the way he seems to carry out so much of his governance of the world—incognito, choreographing coincidences, working quietly behind the scenes. Or maybe it's the other way around as Chesterton suggested. Maybe we are the ones behind the scenes. Maybe we are looking at the world from behind, and if we could get in front we would meet, face-to-face the smiling Providence who seems so quiet.[2] Esther thinks so and would encourage us to not lose heart when our prayers seem to fall into a silent abyss.

PRAYER: *Praise our sovereign God using the words of the Apostle Paul.*

Oh, the depth of the riches of the wisdom and knowledge of God!
How unsearchable his judgments,
and his paths beyond tracing out!
"Who has known the mind of the Lord?
Or who has been his counselor?"
"Who has ever given to God,
that God should repay them?"
For from him and through him and for him are all things.
To him be the glory forever! Amen (Rom. 11:33-36).

DAY 80: FOR SUCH A TIME AS THIS

Esther 4

"And who knows but that you have come to royal position for such a time as this" (Esther 4:14).

The stakes could not have been higher: the very existence of an entire people hung in the balance. If Haman, the ancient Hitler, had his way there would be genocide, and the Jews would cease to exist in Persia. Everything now seemed to focus in on the lovely Esther. She was the only hope of her people, if there was any hope. What she did with the opportunity before her, how she seized the day, would affect generations to come. Her uncle Mordecai urged her to act: "Who knows but that you have come to royal position for such a time as this" (Esther 4:14).

The maxim "know yourself" was inscribed on the Greek temple of Apollo at Delphi. In the ancient world, knowing one's own limits was thought to be the heart of wisdom. However, the Bible says wisdom is to, "know your time." In the Greek, time is spoken of in two ways, *chronos* and *kairos*. *Chronos* is time as an abstract measurement, like what you see on a clock. *Kairos* is time as a season or a moment; it is about meaning, not measurement. *Kairos* is what the Bible is interested in. Jesus was sometimes irritated when people didn't know their *kairos* (Matt. 16:2-3). Other times he was heartbroken, as when he wept over Jerusalem, "because you did not recognize the time (*kairos*) of God's coming to you" (Luke 19:44).

One of the ways the Bible speaks of prayer is in the language of watchfulness and alertness (Isa. 62:6-7; Eph. 6:18; 1 Pet. 5:8). To pray is, by definition, to be alert to the moment and to know what time it is because prayer is birthed in an awareness of God's *kairos*: "I tell you, now is the time (*kairos*) of God's favor, now is the day of salvation" (2 Cor. 6:2). For this very reason, Jesus was grieved and frustrated because his disciples would not watch and wait with him in Gethsemane. By "watch" he meant stay awake and pray, for to pray was to be awake. He said, "The spirit is willing, but the body is weak" (Matt. 26:41). Prayer would keep them from falling into temptation, but the disciples couldn't stay awake because they didn't know what time it was.

Getting up in the morning to pray or setting aside time in the evening to pray is about much more than the clock and your schedule. It is understanding that whenever you come to pray, you do so "for such a time as this." Who knows what your prayers may mean for the world?

PRAYER: *Holy Spirit! Remind me what time it is. Awaken me each day to the time of my life. Teach me that it is always time to pray.*

Introduction to Job

DAY 81: THINGS TOO WONDERFUL FOR ME

"You asked, 'Who is this that obscures my plans without knowledge?' Surely I spoke of things I did not understand, things too wonderful for me to know" (Job 42:3).

If God is God, he can't be good. If God is good, he can't be God. That is the way Archibald MacLeish sums up the conundrum of Job in a modern retelling of the story in his play, *J.B.* It's also a pithy way of stating what, for Christians and Jews, is the problem of evil. How could a God who is infinitely powerful, wise, and good allow a world in which the innocent suffer? On the one hand, if God is infinitely powerful and wise, can he also be good? On the other hand, if God is good, can he also be what a God is supposed to be; infinitely powerful and wise? Surely his power and wisdom must in some way be limited.

The book of Job raises the problem of evil but does not answer it—at least in the way we pose the problem. It does something better. It gives us a vision of God's grandeur and mystery that is more satisfying than any other answer could ever be. Besides, answers are overrated. For the philosopher in all of us, one answer always leads to many more questions which, when answered, pose yet more questions, *ad infinitum*. The book of Job also encourages us to pray, and if need be, to wrestle with God through our suffering. When we read Job through the lens of Jesus' life, death, and resurrection (since Jesus was the ultimate innocent sufferer), we are assured that we need no longer wonder whether God cares. We pray to a sympathetic High Priest who suffered as we have (Heb. 4:15-16).

PRAYER: *O holy One, you are God, and I am not. I bow trembling before your infinite majesty and wisdom and trusting in your ineffable love. Teach me your ways, guide me into your glory.*

DAY 82: A HUMBLE AND GRATEFUL GUIDE

Job 1:21

"The Lord gave, and the Lord has taken away;
may the name of the Lord be praised" (Job 1:21).

God was proud of his servant Job, and Job's prayer above shows why. First, there was the remarkable humility of his prayer. Job knew all along that everything he had came from God. Naked he arrived in this world; naked he would depart. Everything he considered his own he had by gift, not by right. Second, there was Job's amazing expression of gratitude when he learned he had lost the people and things most precious to him. His attitude wasn't: *the Lord took what was mine*, but *the Lord gave and then took what was already his*. Job's prayer was, "Thank you that I ever had them at all." Humility and gratitude are the irreducible minimums of prayer. The grateful are humble, or they wouldn't be grateful. God dwells only with the humble (Isa. 57:15; 1 Pet. 5:5). Until we know we have no ground to stand on before God, we have no ground to stand on before God.

Job's humility and gratitude will be severely tested. He will be pushed out to the very edge of humanity and return holier and happier. Kierkegaard pictured him as standing at an outpost, from which he could lead the rest of us through the dark wilds of suffering. Job is a guide who gives us hope and reassures us that what we thought isn't possible is possible. When Job's story ends, "the terror is endured, the horror experienced, the battle of despair waged, to the honor of God, to his own salvation, to the profit and happiness of others. In joyful days, in fortunate times, Job walks by the side of the race and guarantees it its happiness, combats the apprehensive dream that some horror may suddenly befall a man and have power to destroy his souls as its certain prey."[1]

Job is a great prayer partner. His prayers aren't tidy because his life isn't tidy. Because of this, he teaches prayer, but mainly he encourages us to pray just as we are. He is one of the original, "Just as I am" pray-ers.

PRAYER:
Just as I am, tho' tossed about
With many a conflict, many a doubt,
Fightings within, and fears without,
O Lamb of God, I come!
(from the hymn "Just As I Am" by Charlotte Elliott)

DAY 83: THE MINISTRY OF SILENCE AND PRAYER

Job 2:11-13

"Then they sat on the ground with him for seven days" (Job 2:13).

When Job's friends arrived on the scene and saw Job's suffering, they sat on the ground and were silent for seven days. The moment they opened their mouths, his suffering got a lot worse. Job hadn't yet asked why he was suffering, but in case he did, they wanted him to know why. The reason was, to their way of thinking, simple. Good things happen to good people, and bad things happen to bad people. The universe is morally ordered by a God who punishes evil and rewards good. Bad things had happened to Job, exceedingly bad things. Therefore, Job must have done some exceedingly bad things. Job's friends had a lot of Bible to back them up (cf. Ps. 37:25; Prov. 12:21). But they were wrong. Job knew they were, and God said they were (Job 42:7).

Their error can be put this way: they were superficially right, but fundamentally wrong. God does punish evil and reward good, the Bible says so. But there are exceptions and mysteries in this world. Job's friends were using their Bible like an owner's manual. They looked at Job's symptoms, checked their listing in the index, read the appropriate pages, and drew their conclusions. The problem is that the Bible isn't an owner's manual because God isn't a mechanism. Job isn't either. Both are persons. The moment we forget that axiomatic truth, we make ourselves the god of God. We elevate our theology, what we think about God, to the level of God. Their reading of the Bible was bigger in their minds than the God of the Bible. They were superficially right, but fundamentally wrong.

How much better it would have been if Job's friends were slow to speak and quick to listen? How much better it would have been, if when they spoke, it was to ask questions and to listen to Job and then to pray with Job—especially pray. A ministry of silence and prayer would have been healing to Job and honoring to God. The Spirit who moves us to pray is the *paraclete*, the spirit of encouragement who comes from the God of all comfort (Rom. 8:15-16; John 14:16; 2 Cor. 1:3-4). Consider how quiet the Spirit's ministry is and do likewise.

PRAYER: *Holy Spirit of God, our great comforter and friend! Teach me to listen and pray with those who suffer.*

DAY 84: LITTLE LEFT TO LOSE

Polycarp (69 AD-155 AD)

"They overcame him by the blood of the Lamb and by the word of their testimony; they did not love their lives so much as to shrink from death" (Rev. 12:11).

Polycarp, the bishop of Smyrna, was a very old man when he was ordered to stand before the proconsul. At age 86, with his body weak and his life nearly over, it seemed that his options were few, like the choice the proconsul gave him: either renounce Christ or die. But there is freedom in having little to lose. When the proconsul demanded he renounce his faith in Christ, Polycarp answered, "I have served him for eighty years, and he has never done me wrong: how can I blaspheme my king who saved me?"

"I have wild beasts," said the proconsul.

"Call them," replied Polycarp.

"If you make light of the beasts," retorted the governor, "I'll have you destroyed by fire."

Polycarp answered, "The fire you threaten burns for a time and is soon extinguished: there is a fire you know nothing about—the fire of the judgment to come and of eternal punishment, the fire reserved for the ungodly. But why do you hesitate? Do what you want."

The crowd quickly gathered wood and built a pyre. After Polycarp said a prayer, the men in charge lit the fire and a great flame shot up. In moments, one of the last men to have personally known one of the apostles was gone. Polycarp's predecessor in Smyrna had been the Apostle John. The year was 155 A.D.

Theologian Karl Barth said the approach of the end of life should be like the approach of a waterfall, where "the river of responsibility should flow more torrentially than ever in view of the… proximity of the coming Judge!" Just as a river speeds up its pace as it nears the precipice of the falls, so old age should be a time to follow Christ with more abandon than ever before. Why hold back and play it safe when the time is so short? Polycarp didn't. He knew the choice was not whether to die, but when—and that knowledge made him a free and courageous man. There really is a freedom in having little left to lose.

PRAYER: *Consider and say aloud Polycarp's prayer on the day of his death:*

"O Father of thy beloved and blessed Son, Jesus Christ, through whom we have come to know thee, the God of angels and powers and all creation, and of the whole family of the righteous who live in thy presence; I bless thee for counting me worthy of this day and hour, that in the number of the martyrs I may partake of Christ's cup, to the resurrection of eternal life of both soul and body in the imperishability that is the gift of the Holy Spirit."[1]

DAY 85: GOD'S QUESTIONS

Job 38

"Then the Lord answered Job out of the storm" (Job 38:1).

God answers Job's questions with a question of his own: "Who is this that darkens my counsel with words without wisdom?" (Job 38:2). God's "counsel" is his design, his purpose and plan in the world. Job has been questioning increasingly God's fairness in his management of the world. God's question is mostly rhetorical—"Who is this?" as in "Who do you think you are?" Then God follows up with a barrage of questions spanning chapters 38-41, all of which add up to a huge, "Who do you think you are?"

The point is not lost on Job. When God is finished with his questions, Job is finished with his. "I know that you can do all things; no plan of yours can be thwarted. You asked, 'Who is this that obscures my counsel without knowledge?' Surely, I spoke of things I did not understand, things too wonderful for me to know" (Job 42:2-3). Note that God did not even attempt to answer any of Job's questions. He barely acknowledged them. All he did was confront Job with two things: Job's smallness and God's greatness. And that answer was sufficient for Job. God had said, this is as far as your intellect can go. The universe I made and manage is wilder and bigger and more terrifying than you can ever understand.

The effect of great pain is claustrophobic. Your pain can become the whole world to you. Suffering makes egotists of us all. God's treatment of Job, though harsh, relieved him of the burden Job and his friends created. It is difficult enough to suffer in a world we don't understand; it is too heavy a burden to believe that our circumstance, not God, is what was and is and ever will be, world without end. Job's great humility was chastened and deepened.

The greatest of innocent sufferers was Jesus. When he prayed in Gethsemane, he was very clear about the lesson of Job. His world was big and his humility deep. So, he prayed, "Abba, Father, everything is possible for you. Take this cup from me. Yet not what I will, but what you will" (Mark 14:36). We can learn to pray the same way too, from the heart.

PRAYER: *"Abba, Father, everything is possible for you. Take this cup from me. Yet not what I will, but what you will."*

DAY 86: THE ANSWERER IS BETTER THAN ANSWERS

Job 42

"Now my eyes have seen you" (Job 42:5).

When God confronts Job with questions of his own, Job is crushed. He says, "Therefore I despise myself and repent in dust and ashes." Our English word, "despise," isn't strong enough. The Hebrew is literally "to melt" or "to flow." For what does Job despise himself? It certainly wasn't any sin his friends were sure he had committed. It was the monstrous, spiritual crime of putting God on the judgment stand. Now Job is embarrassed and revolted at himself. He is terrified by what he has done.

But Job is also satisfied. God answered none of his questions with an answer, only more questions. But Job is satisfied because he has seen something of the Answerer: "My ears had heard of you but now my eyes have seen you" (Job 42:5). That is enough. Job is like the resistance fighter in British philosopher, Basil Mitchell's, parable. His country is captive to an evil army of occupation. One night he meets a stranger who makes a deep impression on him. The stranger tells him that he is a leader of the resistance and urges him to trust him no matter what he sees later. When the night is past, and they part company, the resistance fighter is completely confident that this stranger is who he said he was. They never meet again in conditions of intimacy, although the resistance fighter meets the stranger often. Sometimes he sees him helping his friends in the resistance, and they say, "Look, he is on our side, he is helping us." Other times he sees him dressed in the uniform of the army of occupation, handing over patriots to the firing squad. Then his friends will curse the stranger. But the fighter will insist, "He is still on our side; the stranger knows best."

Nothing could be more important to spiritual health in a seemingly chaotic world than to know the Lord, to seek his face in his word and in prayer. Do you know him, or have you just heard about him? Until you know him personally, all you may know about him cannot sustain you in a crisis.

PRAYER: *"My heart says of you, 'Seek his face!' Your face, Lord, I will seek" (Ps. 27:8).*

Introduction to the Psalms

DAY 87: THE APPLE OF GOD'S EYE

"Keep me as the apple of your eye" (Ps. 17:8).

The psalms are easy to find in the Bible. Just put your finger somewhere near the middle of your Bible, open it at that point, and you will find the book of Psalms. The psalms are not quite the heart of Scripture—Jesus is—but they are all about what it means to be in relationship with him. The psalms are also the longest book in the Bible, by far. The psalms are a book of prayers. That should tell us how important prayer is to a vital relationship with God.

The phrase, "divine-human encounter" is a favorite among Bible scholars. It is another way of describing what the psalms help us do: encounter God and have a relationship with him. The psalms help us to meet with God as a friend would meet with a friend, or a subject with a king, a child with a father or mother, a husband and a wife, or a sheep and a shepherd. God is amazingly concrete and personal in the psalms. While the psalms are a rich source for theological reflection, they are not to be reduced to academic speculation about God. In the psalms, God is not Alfred North Whitehead's "principle of concretion," Henry Nelson Wieman's "integrating factor in experience," or Paul Tillich's "ground of all being." These gods are for contemplation and discussion only, not for prayer. The Book of Psalms sets the stage for us to encounter God in the most intimate way, the way Jesus taught. We learn to speak to God as "Abba"—Father, dear Father (Ps. 68:5-6).

The psalms are unique for another reason. They are remarkable because of who we pray with as we pray them. When we pray the psalms, we pray with God's people who have come before us, from ancient Israel to the church. We enter a mystical fellowship stretching back in time, known as the "communion of saints." We are never less alone than when we pray the psalms. And more wondrous, we also pray *with* our Lord Jesus who prayed them—and *to* him for the psalms anticipated him (Luke 24:44). The same prayers and laments Jesus prayed, we may pray with and to him, the second person of the Trinity. He is the fulfillment of Israel's hope, who lives to intercede for us (Heb. 7:25).

PRAYER: *"Keep me as the apple of your eye; hide me in the shadow of your wings" (Ps. 17:8).*

DAY 88: THE BLESSED LIFE

Psalm 1

"He is like a tree planted by streams of water, which yields its fruit in season and whose leaf does not wither" (Ps. 1:3).

"Life isn't a supermarket for truth" is one way to paraphrase this psalm. Contrary to modern popular religious tastes, there aren't many varieties of truth, like the varieties of food in a supermarket. We like to customize faith, like we might mix and match items in a big store. There are many ways to be nourished spiritually, right?

Wrong. There are but two choices: one way leads to blessedness and life; the other way leads to death. One way plants you, the other uproots you. Both ways begin with how you think and then progress in opposite directions. The blessed way delights in and meditates on God's law. It brings health and fruitfulness. The way of death descends from thinking about sin to doing it and then promoting it ("counsel of the wicked... way of sinners... seat of mockers"). Those who follow the way of death end up rootless and blown about like dust in a windstorm.

There is only one way to life, but the ways life shows itself are nearly endless, like the varieties of fruit in the world: raspberries, avocados, kiwis, apples, bananas, and papayas—the list would fill pages. Trees aren't water pipelines; they are living organisms, fruit bearers, like people. There is a dull sameness to sin and death—all corpses look more or less alike—but there is a rich variety to the ways life expresses itself in the people who are planted in it. God is the author of life, and he revels in originals. Look around at his creation; he is not a cookie-cutter God.

We are planted in life by delighting and meditating on God's truth in Scripture. Scriptural meditation is like a dialogue or conversation. You listen carefully to what God says and then talk to him about what you hear through praise, confession, petition, questioning, weeping, laughing, and longing. Then you listen some more and say some more. Bible reading and prayer go together the way listening and speaking go together in good conversation. Both lead to delight in the partner in the dialogue.

PRAYER: *Father in heaven! Deepen my conversation with you through prayer and the truth of your Word.*

DAY 89: WHAT DOES IT MEAN TO BE A HUMAN BEING?

Psalm 8

"What is man that you are mindful of him" (Ps. 8:4).

How do you begin your work each day? Are you enthusiastic like the seven dwarves in the Disney classic *Snow White*? "Hi ho, hi ho, it's off to work we go!" Or are you merely resigned, like the bumper-sticker, "I owe, I owe, it's off to work I go"? Try this: go to work with this psalm on your lips, and with it, a profound sense of wonder and gratitude for the place and the work God has given you in his creation.

Begin the way the psalmist begins. Consider first the majesty of God and the magnificence of God's creation. "O Lord, our Lord, how majestic is your name in all the earth! You have set your glory above the heavens.... When I consider your heavens... what is man that you are mindful of him" (Ps. 8:1, 3a, 4a)? That question can be asked mockingly of the arrogant (Ps. 144:3, 4), or desperately as a plea for mercy (Job 7:17), or in astonishment as it is asked here. What can we be in a universe so large that its center is everywhere, its circumference nowhere (Pascal)? What can we be to a God so great that this massive universe is but the work of his fingers, his "needlepoint," so to speak?

What we are to this God is, "a little lower than the heavenly beings and crowned... with glory and honor" (Ps. 8:5). We are made in his image (cf. Gen. 1:26-31) and appointed as "ruler over the works of [his] hands" (Ps. 8:6). That's where your work comes in. No matter how small and insignificant it may seem to you, if your work is worth doing at all, it is a piece of God's world to be cared for in his majestic name. That amounts to nothing less than glory and honor.

So, frame your day's work in worship. Begin with praise—the way a child praises God (Ps. 8:2), surrendering yourself simply and unquestioningly to his greatness. Affirm with humble thankfulness your place in this great God's world (Ps. 8:5-6). Then work as though you believed it was true, learning from Christ who shows us how to work with gentleness and humility (Matt. 11:25-30).

PRAYER: *Thank you for the work you have given me to do and the dignity of working. Sustain me in my work with a vision of the honor and glory you give your servants in the world.*

DAY 90: THE PLEASURE OF GOD'S COMPANY

Psalm 16

"You will fill me with joy in your presence, with eternal pleasures at your right hand" (Ps. 16:11).

Jonathan Edwards thought of God the way David thought of God in this psalm. It was for "sweet delight in God" that he gave himself to God. He wrote:

> *The first instance I remember of that sort of inward, sweet delight in God and in divine things, that I have lived much in since, was on reading these words, 1 Timothy 1:17: 'Now unto the King eternal, immortal, invisible, the only wise God, be honor and glory for ever and ever. Amen.' As I read the words, there came into my soul, and was as it were, diffused through it, a sense of the glory of the Divine Being; a new sense, quite different from anything I ever experienced before. Never any words of Scripture seemed to me as these did. I thought with myself, how excellent a Being that was, and how happy I should be, if I might enjoy that God, and be rapt up to Him in Heaven, and be, as it were, swallowed up in Him forever.*[1]

Edward's words are a variation on the theme of verse eleven: "You have made known to me the path of life; you will fill me with joy in your presence, with eternal pleasures at your right hand."

A modern myth has it that the way to happiness and freedom is broad and filled with many choices. The more we can do when we want to do it, the freer and happier we think we will be. The Bible takes the opposite point of view. The way to joy is narrow and singular (cf. Matt. 7:13-14; see also devotion on Psalm 1, Day 88). It is like getting married. Faithfulness to one partner for life radically narrows one kind of choice, but it opens a universe of other glorious possibilities. Those who want to keep their options open are the ones who are trapped. This psalm is the prayer of a single-minded man who knows that apart from God he has no good thing. God has assigned him his portion and his cup, and he has set the Lord always before him. The pleasure of God's company is the only path of freedom and life.

PRAYER: *Gracious God! You have made known to me the path of life; you will fill me with joy in your presence, with eternal pleasures at your right hand. Praise your holy name.*

DAY 91: JUST AS I AM

Charlotte Elliott (1789-1871)

"When he saw the crowds, he had compassion on them, because they were harassed and helpless, like sheep without a shepherd" (Matt. 9:36).

It was a bad time for Dr. Malan to ask Charlotte the question. In pain and depressed, she didn't want to be asked if she felt the peace of God in spite of her circumstances. A debilitating sickness had afflicted her in her thirties and had left her in pain and frequently bedridden until the end of her life.

But Dr. Malan's question pricked her conscience. Though she had been raised in a Christian home, she knew little of Christ's peace. She sought Malan out. "I am miserable," she admitted to him. "I want to be saved; I want to come to Jesus, but I don't know how." Malan's reply was destined to affect millions. He said, "Come to him just as you are."

Charlotte's health didn't improve, but from that moment she lived in the peace of Christ, "a man of sorrows, and familiar with suffering" (Isa. 53:3). Confined to her home, Charlotte wrote hymns to be sung in church, penning nearly 150 before her death on September 22, 1871.

One day Charlotte was feeling especially sick. Again, she wondered despairingly how she could serve God as an invalid? Feeling dejected and useless, she began to write. The words flowed out of her, echoing the words of Dr. Malan years before:

Just as I am, without one plea
But that Thy blood was shed for me,
And that Thou bidd'st me come to Thee,
O Lamb of God, I come! I come!

Charlotte sent the hymn anonymously to a Christian publication and forgot about it. Years later, one of her doctors handed her a poem inside a tract, hoping it would console her. Charlotte was amazed to find herself reading her own poem! "Just as I Am" had become so popular that it had circulated across England and found its way back to her bedside.

After her death, more than 1000 letters were found among Charlotte's belongings thanking her for writing the hymn. Years later, in 1934, a skeptical young man attended a revival meeting in South Carolina. As the choir sang "Just as I Am," he made his way to the front and gave his life to Christ. The young man's name was Billy Graham. Only heaven knows how many millions of lost and dejected souls have been encouraged as Charlotte's hymn has been sung at Billy Graham evangelistic meetings around the world.

PRAYER:

Just as I am—Thou wilt receive,
Wilt welcome, pardon, cleanse, relieve,
Because Thy promise I believe—
O Lamb of God, I come, I come!

DAY 92: THE GLORY AND POWER OF GOD'S WORD

Psalm 19

"The heavens declare the glory of God....
The law of the Lord is perfect" (Ps. 19:1-7).

There is no greater celebration of the Scriptures in the Bible than this psalm. One is longer (Ps. 119), and one is more succinct (2 Tim. 3:16-17), but none are greater. What does David think of when he looks at the sun and the other stars? He thinks of the Bible (Ps. 19:1-6)! Poet Gerard Manley Hopkins wrote, "The world is charged with the grandeur of God. It will flame out like shining from shook foil."[1] David might add, "It will flame out like light from the Scriptures, too." The medieval church thought Galileo a heretic when he asserted that God had two books, the creation and the Bible. But David was a "heretic" thousands of years before when he praised the God who speaks both in the skies (Ps. 19:1-6) and the Scriptures (Ps. 19:7-14).

Is the Bible hard for you? Dry? Uninteresting? Don't worry, you're in good company. Martin Luther said, "Sometimes there has been more in a line of Scripture than I could bear to stand under. Other times, the Bible has been to me as dry as a stick." You shouldn't worry, but you shouldn't be blasé either. Remember, the Bible is a critical part of the dialogue with God we call prayer, the chief part of his side of the conversation.

There are some things you can do to help this. Practice the lesser-known spiritual discipline of imaginative association. Connect in your imagination the wonder and beauty you see in a night sky with the contents of this book. Look at the Milky Way and think, "The Bible is like that." Also ask yourself, do I really expect or want to meet God when I read the Bible? "It's not what I don't understand in the Bible that worries me," wrote Mark Twain. "It's what I do understand." Maybe your apathy toward the Bible is a smokescreen to hide your fear of exposure (note Ps. 19:2-13). Finally, ask yourself, "How would I act if I believed there is treasure hidden in the Bible?" If you had in your hands a map showing where you could find great material treasure, wouldn't you apply yourself diligently to crack any code or language and overcome any mountain, weather, or foe to find the treasure? What is to be found in Scripture is "more precious than gold, than much pure gold" (Ps. 19:10).

PRAYER: *Father in heaven! Open my eyes to see wonderful things in your word; and open my mouth to sing your praise.*

DAY 93: THE GOOD SHEPHERD

Psalm 23

"The Lord is my shepherd" (Ps. 23:1).

The idea of God being a shepherd to his people is not unique to this psalm. The picture appears many other places (Ps. 28:9; 79:13; 80:1; 95:7; 100:3). It was also used widely in the ancient Near East, and the Bible, as a metaphor for a king. It worked well. Most people knew what shepherds did to protect and care for their flock.

What makes this psalm so special is how personal it is. For God to be a shepherd to his flock or his people, the nation of Israel, is one thing; but for God to be David's personal shepherd is something else quite wonderful. Read it aloud and take in the staggering message that God makes *you* lie down in green pastures, leads *you* beside quiet waters and restores *your* soul. If God is not really this intentional in his care for each of us personally, then praying this psalm is to engage in an act of almost criminal narcissism. But Jesus assured us that God does care for us in this way (John 10:11-14). He has even numbered the hairs on our head (Matt. 10:29-31). Let that truth sink in as you pray this psalm. There is great joy in the comfort it brings.

There is also a great awe that can come with it. An astronomer, who was also a Christian, had lectured at a university on the immensity of the universe. During the question-and-answer session that followed, a student who was not a believer asked the astronomer a provocative question: "How can a God big enough to manage the cosmos you just described, possibly be involved in the personal lives of his followers—as you believe he is?" The scientist answered quietly, "The God I believe in is bigger than you think." God's love and wisdom are immeasurable, both in the extent he goes into space, and the depth he enters into our hearts. A truly big God can do both.

Be awed and be joyful. Savor also this truth: the Shepherd wants your friendship. His goodness and mercy will pursue you all your life, so you may dwell in his house forever (Ps. 23:6).

PRAYER:
All the way my Savior leads me;
Oh, the fullness of his love!
Perfect rest to me is promised
In my Father's house above:
When my spirit, clothed immortal,
Wings its flight to realms of day,
This my song thru endless ages:
Jesus led me all the way.
(Fanny Crosby, from the hymn "All the Way My Savior Leads Me")

DAY 94: SAFETY IN GOD'S PRESENCE

Psalm 27

"My heart says of you, 'Seek his face!' Your face, Lord, I will seek" (Ps. 27:8).

What do you need most when your enemies surround you? A safe place to escape to, a fortress, a hiding place, of course. This is what David yearns for throughout the rest of his life: "One thing I ask of the Lord, this is what I seek: that I may dwell in the house of the Lord all the days of my life, to gaze upon the beauty of the Lord and to seek him in his temple" (Ps. 27:4).

But it would be a serious misreading of this prayer to conclude that he wanted to exchange public life for the life of a priest or monk. David knew that no one was allowed to live in the temple. What he wanted was to enjoy daily and forever what the temple stood for—the presence of God. God's house is the whole world (cf. Ps. 36:8). What David wanted was the pleasure and protection of unbroken communion with God in his house. That was what entering a human house stood for in the ancient Near East: it was a place of fellowship and safety. So strong was the custom of home being a place of refuge that if even your mortal enemy was able to enter your house, you were bound to protect him!

It's not where you are but who you're with that makes all the difference. Threat, fear, and worry cannot touch you in God's presence. Not even disaster and death can separate you from his love (Rom. 8:31-39). The endless distractions and demands of life are unified and ordered in God's presence. The one thing needed (cf. Luke 10:41-42) is to "gaze upon the beauty of the Lord and to seek him in his temple." What David prays for is the breakdown of the wall between the sacred and the secular. So must we. There are no compartments, no inside and outside, to God. He sees our thoughts and motives as clearly as he sees our actions. "The earth is the Lord's, and everything in it" (Ps. 24:1). If this be true, then everything we do is done in his temple and falls under the heading "sacred."

PRAYER: *Lord, one thing I ask of you, this is what I seek: where I work and where I study; where I think and where I eat; in my car and in my home, that I may gaze upon your beauty and seek you.*

DAY 95: THE INEXHAUSTIBLE GOD

Psalm 36

"Your love, O Lord, reaches to the heavens" (Ps. 36:5).

Go outside, look up to the heavens, and stretch your imagination: In August of 1989, the unmanned spacecraft, Voyager 2, flew over the polar ice cap of the planet Neptune, 2.8 billion miles out on the edge of our solar system. It transmitted astonishing photographs of a strange and stormy world; a planet covered by a thick haze of helium and hydrogen, with 1,500 mile-per-hour winds pushing great frozen clouds of methane across its surface. In Neptune's southern hemisphere, the spacecraft recorded a tremendous storm system—a continuing counter-cyclone that was as big across as the Earth. Traveling at speeds over 60,000 miles per hour, it took Voyager 2 twelve years just to get to the outer rim of our solar system. Long after it has ceased to send signals back to Earth, it will still be traveling through empty space. In the year 40,176, it will likely pass within 1.7 light years of the star Ross 248, and in the year 296,036, will perhaps come within 4.3 light years of the star Sirius!

Now read verse 5: "Your love, O Lord, reaches to the heavens, your faithfulness to the skies." God's love is there. It reaches that far and farther. It is unsearchable. You could perform other such exercises of the imagination to get your mind around this text. His righteousness is as unshakable as the Himalayas, and his justice is as profound as the deepest ocean (Ps. 36:6). But you get the idea.

God's love and justice are that big, and this small and intimate: "O Lord, you preserve both man and beast. How priceless is your unfailing love! Both high and low among men find refuge in the shadow of your wings. They feast on the abundance of your house; you give them drink from your river of delights. For with you is the fountain of life; in your light we see light" (Ps. 36:6-9). Like a gracious host, the inexhaustible God stands at the door and welcomes us into the bounty of his house. He bids us drink from his delightful river and gives us his light, his truth and life, and wisdom to appreciate and enjoy his world—and the world to come (cf. Rev. 22:1). Be thankful and rejoice!

Based on all this, many ancient Jews prayed each morning: "Continue your love to those who know you, your righteousness to the upright in heart" (Ps. 36:10). Indeed. It's a good tradition to keep up.

PRAYER: *"And, we pray give us such an awareness of your mercies, that our hearts may be sincerely thankful, and that we may show forth your praise not only with our lips, but in our lives" (from The Book of Common Prayer).*

DAY 96: SAVED TO SERVE

Psalm 40

"I desire to do your will, O my God" (Ps. 40:8).

In his great hymn, "When I Survey the Wondrous Cross," Isaac Watts wrote an excellent paraphrase of the first eight verses of this psalm: "Love so amazing, so divine, Demands my soul, my life, my all." The flow of the hymn matches the flow of the psalm. A great love has saved a great sinner; the only appropriate response is a great offering—one's very self in love and gratitude. Watts' hymn and David's psalm should be read as the spiritual autobiography of every Christian.

David was in a terrible mess before God acted on his behalf. He was stuck in a "slimy pit," but God lifted him "out of the mud and mire and set [his] feet on a rock" (Ps. 40:2). He must declare God's goodness, but how? The fitting declaration is his whole life offered as a sacrifice. David's description of this sacrifice is striking. The ritual sacrifices of Jewish religion are not what God wants; he knows that full well, having seen the emptiness of his predecessor Saul's superficial observance (1 Sam. 15:22-23). So, David will be the sacrifice—a living sacrifice! "Sacrifice and offering you did not desire, but my ears you have pierced" (Ps. 40:6). The Hebrew word for "pierced" is literally, "dug." Translators wrangle over whether the "digging" spoken of here refers to the practice of piercing a slave's ear when he lovingly offers himself to his master for life (Exod. 21:6); or whether it means simply "opened" as in ears opened to hear and obey God's word (Isa. 50:4-5). The latter makes more sense, but both options paint a picture of the total response fitting a total salvation; and anticipate the perfect sacrifice made by Christ for our salvation (Heb. 10:5-10).

Having made his life a living sacrifice, the Bible takes on new meaning for David. Now he can say, "Here I am, I have come—it is written about me in the scroll. I desire to do your will, O my God; your law is within my heart" (Ps. 40:7-8). The scroll is the word of God, and he sees it no longer as a collection of abstract rules, but as his Savior's loving will, written to him and about him. In fact, God's will is even written on his heart!

David's story is your story if you name Christ as your Savior. Pray that your response will be as appropriate as David's was (Rom. 12:1-2).

PRAYER: *Here I am, Lord, I am yours. I desire to do your will; your law is within my heart.*

DAY 97: PRAYER AND DEPRESSION

Psalms 42—43

"Why are you downcast, O my soul? Why so disturbed within me? Put your hope in God, for I will yet praise him, my savior and my God" (Ps. 42:5-6).

Not all depressions are the same. Some are circumstantial, the result of loss or disappointment or fatigue; some are clinical and more complex. But whatever their nature or source, their symptoms are very similar: the numbing dread that the darkness and grief are impenetrable and immovable, and the lie that what is passing is eternal. These two psalms give some very helpful clues as to how to deal with depression.

The first is to talk to God about your depression. Pray the depression. That is what these psalms are: addresses to God about how the psalmist feels. You can be brutally honest; the psalmist certainly is. He prays, "I say to God, my Rock, 'Why have you forgotten me? Why must I go about mourning, oppressed by the enemy?' My bones suffer mortal agony as my foes taunt me, saying to me all day long, 'Where is your God'" (Ps. 42:9-10)? It's always better to talk to God about how you feel about God than to others about how you feel about God. The most destructive aspect of any depression is the sense of abandonment by God. So talk to him about that! Prayer can turn the chasm into a bridge.

Talk to yourself about your depression. Three times, the psalmist says, "Why are you downcast, O my soul? Why so disturbed within me? Put your hope in God, for I will yet praise him, my Savior and my God" (Ps. 42:5, 11; 43:5). Feelings can be like unruly children, and like unruly children, they must not be allowed to have the last word. Let them sound off, but also let them know about what is true. It may seem a little schizoid to talk to yourself this way, but the power of depression is schizoid; it splits you off from what is true. It takes a piece of the picture and makes it the whole picture. Talk back to yourself and affirm the truth that, "I will yet praise him, my Savior and my God." Let your faith speak to your faith.

Remind yourself that your deepest need is God—whether you are depressed or not. Unpleasant as it is, depression can be a reminder that we are not whole without God, no matter how well we may feel. You may even be so bold as to thank him for that! "As the deer pants for streams of water, so my soul pants for you, O God. My soul thirsts for God, for the living God. When can I go to meet with God" (Ps. 42:1-2)?

PRAYER: *By day, O Lord, you direct your love, at night your song is with me—a prayer to the God of my life. Why are you downcast, O my soul? Put your hope in God, for I will yet praise him, my Savior and my God.*

DAY 98: IF YOUR RIGHT HAND OFFENDS YOU

Thomas Cranmer (1489-1556)

"Whoever acknowledges me before men, I will also acknowledge him before my Father in heaven. But whoever disowns me before men, I will disown him before my father in heaven" (Matt. 10:32-33).

It is not too much of an exaggeration to say Thomas Cranmer, the compiler of *The Book of Common Prayer*, the Anglican prayer book, was the man who taught England to pray. In many ways Cranmer's life was a microcosm of his age. Sixteenth-century England was a time of revolution, passion, and intrigue. This time period saw King Henry VIII wade his way through six wives and the kingdom totter uncertainly between Protestantism and Catholicism.

Cranmer had been a brilliant student at Cambridge. His excellent scholarship earned him the status of fellow of Jesus College where he eventually became a lecturer and authority on original biblical texts. Eventually Cranmer became Archbishop of Canterbury.

In the years that followed, Cranmer used his influence to shepherd the Reformation of the Church of England. His greatest work was *The Book of Common Prayer*, which expressed the Protestant faith in the vernacular of the people instead of Latin. Also, with the support of Anne Boleyn, Cranmer helped translate the Bible into English. Soon every church had an English Bible chained to a pillar.

When the ardent Catholic, "Bloody Mary" became queen, however, Cranmer was stripped of his position and imprisoned. He was then forced to watch his friends Ridley and Latimer burned, and he was tortured and brainwashed until he signed a recantation of his Protestant beliefs. Wanting to make a public spectacle of Cranmer, Mary scheduled a public ceremony in which Cranmer would read his recantation.

On March 21, 1556, a crowd gathered in the Church of Great Saint Mary in Oxford. Cranmer mounted the stage and prayed a prayer that rocked the crowd: "O Lord, whose property is always to have mercy… Now I come to the Great Thing that troubleth my conscience more than any other thing that I ever said or did in my life; and that is the setting abroad of writings contrary to the truth…writ for fear of death and to save my life… and forasmuch as my hand offended in writing contrary to my heart, therefore my hand shall first be punished… it shall first be burned."

Livid, his enemies hurried him to the place of execution, where he was chained to the stake. As the flames rose around him, he thrust his right hand into the fire, the same hand that had signed the recantation, crying, "This hand hath offended." He was soon dead, but the prayers he wrote have been prayed for centuries.

PRAYER: *"O Lord, who hast taught us that all our doings without love are worth nothing; send thy Holy Ghost and pour into our hearts that most excellent gift of love, the very bond of peace and all virtues, without which whosoever liveth is counted dead before thee; grant us this for thy Son Jesus Christ's sake" (Thomas Cranmer).*

DAY 99: BRING IT ON!

Psalm 46

"God is our refuge and strength, an ever-present help in trouble" (Ps. 46:1).

Let the worst come, the psalmist says. Bring it on, we can handle whatever comes because "God is our refuge and strength, an ever-present help in time of trouble" (Ps. 46:1). Then the psalmist conjures up the worst, what we might today describe in terms of nuclear holocaust: "though the earth give way and the mountains fall into the heart of the sea, though its waters roar and foam and the mountains quake with their surging" (Ps. 46:2-3). There are other bad things that can happen and do happen. Enemies may attack us and nations continually fight amongst themselves (Ps. 46:5-6), but God is God, and they are not, so we will not fear.

One of the most famous verses in the Bible is Psalm 46:10: "Be still, and know that I am God." It is often read in a tone of calm assurance and comfort or as a call to be still and peaceful in one's soul. While that is always good advice, it is probably not the tone of the verse. The Hebrew is more like "Hush!" or "Enough!" Since it is spoken to warring and violent peoples, we should read it as a stern rebuke. God gets in the face of arrogant and angry nations and says, "Stop! Right now!" The closest New Testament parallel are the words Jesus shouted to the storm, "Quiet! Be still" (Mark 4:39)! That's how God speaks to our enemies.

He usually speaks to us quite differently. The psalmist describes it this way: "There is a river whose streams make glad the city of God, the holy place where the Most High dwells" (Ps. 46:4). Jerusalem is the city of God spoken of here, but Jerusalem had no river like her powerful enemies. Egypt had the Nile, Babylon had the Tigris and Euphrates, but Jerusalem had only a little creek, at most. The river who made her glad was the presence of God. God's people can drink to their deepest satisfaction from this "river of delights" (Ps. 36:8)! God's word to the nations is "Hush!" His word to us is, "The Lord Almighty is with us" (Ps. 46:7). Believe this and let God rebuke your enemies and calm your fears.

PRAYER: *You are my refuge and strength, O Lord, a very present help in trouble. I will not be afraid of anything.*

DAY 100: THE BIBLE IS AN ADULT BOOK

Psalm 51

"Against you, you only, have I sinned" (Ps. 51:4).

Churches ought to put a neon sign outside the entrance to their buildings, shaped like an arrow, pointing inside, and reading "Adult Books." When curious, so-called "adults" walked in the door, they would find inside a stack of Bibles. In the truest sense of the word, the Bible is an adult book. To teach it to children we must often delete some portions and dilute others. Portions of the Bible, if made into a film, might get an R rating. The story of sin that lies behind this great psalm of David's is one such portion. It is a story of adultery and murder as lurid as anything Hollywood has ever filmed. You can read the story in 2 Samuel 11 and 12.

Uriah, if he were able, might have argued with David's confession that it was against God and God alone that he had sinned (Ps. 51:4). David had, after all, murdered Uriah to cover up his adultery with Uriah's wife, Bathsheba. But this psalm of confession is a radical prayer. The word radical comes from the Latin *radix* which means root. David has thought long and hard about the roots of this sin against Uriah and sees that it began with his disregard of God. In this, he predates Paul's searching analysis in Romans 1:21: "For though they knew God, they neither glorified him as God nor gave thanks to him, but their thinking became futile, and their foolish hearts were darkened." From this fundamental futility and darkness comes every other transgression and iniquity against others. Uriah would never have been murdered if David had attended to his relationship to God.

David's radical approach extends deep into his own heart as he acknowledges that God isn't interested in outward, superficial obedience but inward purity: "Surely you desire truth in the inner parts; you teach me wisdom in the inmost place" (Ps. 51:6). So, he prays for a radical cure for a radical sin: "Create in me a pure heart, O God, and renew a steadfast spirit within me. Do not cast me from your presence or take your Holy Spirit from me. Restore to me the joy of your salvation and grant me a willing spirit, to sustain me" (Ps. 51:10-11).

Confess your sins as David did. Your sin may not be as grievous as his was, but it is no less radical in its origin, and requires no less radical a cure.

PRAYER: *Lord, I have sinned against you, and only you. Forgive me, for Christ's sake, and restore to me the joy of your salvation.*

DAY 101: HUNGER FOR GOD

Psalm 63

"My soul thirsts for you, my body longs for you" (Ps. 63:1).

David was physically hungry and thirsty when he wrote this psalm in the wilderness of Judea, but he saw in the longings of his body a deeper meaning. His hunger and thirst were signposts to his need for God. This realization brought dignity to his cravings. He was more than his belly; he was made for God. Hungry and thirsty in the same wilderness, Jesus did the same thing with his bodily yearnings when he rebuked Satan: "It is written, 'Man does not live on bread alone, but on every word that comes from the mouth of God'" (Matt. 4:4; Deut. 8:3).

Here is a great way to pray: turn your longings and hungers toward God. Do not pray only that they be removed. Pray that they become reminders and parables of your need of God. Pain and suffering or frustration and anxiety can become sacramental experiences if you let them lead you to their deeper meaning in God.

The poet George Herbert painted a vivid picture of the meaning of the empty places in our lives. He pictured God, having made a kind of empty husk of a human, pouring from a glass of good things into him, filling him with strength, beauty, wisdom, honor, and pleasure. But he stops pouring with one thing left—rest—or satisfaction. He decides it would hurt the human to have this last gift.

For if I should (said he)
Bestow this jewel on my creature,
He would adore his gifts instead of me,
And rest in Nature, not the God of Nature.
So both should losers be.

Yet let him keep the rest,
But keep them with repining restlessness:
Let him be rich and weary, that at least,
If goodness lead him not, yet weariness
May toss him to my breast.[1]

Thank God for your emptiness, and let it lead you to him. God fills up only empty hearts.

PRAYER: *Thank you, Father, for the emptiness I sometimes feel. Let it point me to your Son, the Bread of Life.*

DAY 102: WHOM HAVE I IN HEAVEN BUT YOU?

Psalm 73

"God is the strength of my heart and my portion forever" (Ps. 73:26).

"Of the Seven Deadly Sins, anger is possibly the most fun," writes Frederick Buechner. "To lick your wounds, to smack your lips over grievances long past, to roll over your tongue the prospect of bitter confrontations still to come, to savor to the last toothsome morsel both the pain you are given and the pain you are giving back—in many ways it is a feast fit for a king. The chief drawback is that what you are wolfing down is yourself. The skeleton at the feast is you."[1]

Asaph, the writer of this psalm, looks back on how things were for him at one time and admits that he was being consumed by bitterness and anger. He was full of envy for what seemed to be the unchecked arrogance and rapaciousness of the wicked. Not only were they getting away with murder and theft, but they were also even prospering. God seemed worse than an absentee landlord; he appeared unfazed and uninterested. Asaph almost shot his mouth off about God and the uselessness of living a good life. He's glad he didn't (Ps. 73:15). In retrospect, he says to God, "When my heart was grieved and my spirit embittered, I was senseless and ignorant; I was a brute beast before you" (Ps. 73:21-22).

What changed things for him was entering the sanctuary one day and gaining a refreshed vision of God's love and justice. In worship Asaph remembered that a holy God will not let sin go unpunished (Ps. 73:16-20). Even better, in worship he remembered the sweetness of God's love. He prays some of the sweetest words of friendship with God in all of Scripture:

> *Yet I am always with you; you hold me by my right hand. You guide me with your counsel, and afterward you will take me into glory. Whom have I heaven but you? And earth has nothing I desire besides you. My flesh and my heart may fail, but God is the strength of my heart and my portion forever (Ps. 73:23-26).*

Let the wicked enjoy their temporary successes! He now knew that "the man that had everything minus God is a pauper; and the other who has God minus everything is 'rich to all the intents of bliss.'"[2] The cure for anger, envy, and bitterness is gratitude for the goodness of God's friendship.

PRAYER: *Whom have I in heaven, but you? And earth has nothing I desire besides you. Lord God, you are the strength of my heart and my portion forever!*

DAY 103: REVIVE US AGAIN

Psalm 85

"Will you not revive us again, that your people may rejoice in you?" (Ps. 85:6).

It happens in marriages and between friends, in families and in churches. Love grows cold and passion fades and what once was personal and intimate becomes rote and formal. But if even the memory of what once was remains, it can be enough to spur renewal, or revival. This is especially the case with God's people. The risen Christ urged the Ephesian church to remember and be revived. He wrote, "You have forsaken your first love. Remember the height from which you have fallen! Repent and do the things you did at first" (Rev. 2:4-5). In the same way, this psalm of the Sons of Korah remembers what once was (Ps. 85:1-3) and prays for the revival of God's people: "Will you not revive us again, that your people may rejoice in you" (Ps. 85:6)?

What is revival? The prayer itself provides the definition and the goal of revival which is "that your people might rejoice in you." As in a marriage, to be revived in faith is to be renewed in love and joy. Having powerful faith to move mountains and courage to willingly be consumed by fire but lacking love is to have a dead faith (1 Cor. 13:1-3). Far from being honored by mere, empty obedience, God is insulted. No, as John Piper says, God is glorified in us only as we are satisfied in him.

The psalm provides a lovely picture of revival, very much in keeping with its definition: "Love and faithfulness meet together; righteousness and peace kiss each other" (Ps. 86:10). Could anyone wish for anything more? The quality of life takes on a kind of marital bliss, and heaven and earth meet as, "Faithfulness springs forth from the earth, and righteousness looks down from heaven" (Ps. 85:11). A clearer picture comes from the first chapter of John's gospel: "The Word became flesh and made his dwelling among us. We have seen his glory, the glory of the One and Only, who came from the Father, full of grace and truth" (John 1:14). Revival is the presence of Christ, dwelling among us in love, in our hearts (Eph. 3:17).

The history of the of God's people seems to be a history of recurrent spiritual decline (cf. Judg. 2:7, 10-13). That's the bad news. The good news is that God is always ready to hear his people pray, "Will you not revive us again, that your people may rejoice in you?"

PRAYER: *Dear Father, our love has grown cold, our faith is weak; revive us again that we might rejoice in you!*

DAY 104: INNER HEALTH MADE AUDIBLE

Psalm 95

"Come, let us sing for joy to the Lord; let us shout aloud to the Rock of our salvation" (Ps. 95:1).

Some people have a low opinion of a God. They see him as a selfish deity who demands that his people do such things for him as: sing for joy, shout aloud, give thanks, extol him with music and song, bow down and kneel before him. They think this "god" is just an expression of human narcissism, an imaginary deity who needs his ego stroked just like us. Or worse, they wonder if God is really this way—a cosmic egotist who sits up in heaven thundering and demanding compliments.

The truth is God doesn't need our praise, but we need to give it. We need to praise the God who is worthy to be praised because the praise of God is what makes us human. We will not be fully human until God is fully God to us—in our mind, heart, soul, strength, and imagination. The Apostle Paul declared that we become what we worship, for "we, who with unveiled faces all reflect the Lord's glory, are being transformed into his likeness with ever-increasing glory" (2 Cor. 3:18). The church father Irenaeus was echoing Paul when he wrote, "The glory of God is man fully alive, and the life of man is the vision of God."

The evidence is all around us, even in ordinary life. C. S. Lewis declared praise to be a principle that holds true for all humanity, both for believers and non-believers.

> *The world rings with praise—lovers praising their beloved, readers their favorite poet, walkers praising the countryside, players praising their favorite game. We hear praise of weather, wines, dishes, actors, motors, colleges, countries, historical personages, children, flowers, mountains, rare stamps, rare beetles, and on and on. I had not noticed how the humblest, and at the same time most balanced and capacious minds, praised most, while the cranks, misfits and malcontents praised least.... Praise almost seems to be inner health made audible.*[1]

Praise is good for you! It's healthy. It makes you better than you were before you praised God. It's "inner health made audible" in the truest and eternal sense of the word. For "the worth and excellency of a soul is to be measured by the object of its love."[2]

PRAYER: *"Lord God! I praise you, for you are the great King above all Gods! You are my maker, and I am the sheep under you care!"*

DAY 105: THE SON OF THESE TEARS

Monica, Part 1

"Then Jesus told his disciples a parable to show them that they should pray and not give up" (Luke 18:1).

Monica's situation is a classic scenario: a godly, faithful mother loving an ungodly, faithless child. What's the mother to do? Pray. The time is the fourth century AD; the mother is Monica; the son is the brilliant, egotistical, heretical, and licentious Augustine. Mother and son have wills of steel. Her will is an irresistible force, his an immovable object.

Monica visited the local priest to make a modest request. She asked if he would he do her a favor and have a talk with her son convincing him to refute his errors, drive out the evil in him and replace it with the good. Put simply, would the priest do everything she, Augustine's mother, had not been able to do? The priest was not the first nor the last to hear such an unreasonable request from a distraught parent. He answered wisely, and he graciously refused her request. Augustine later wrote: "He told her that I was still unripe for instruction because, as she had told him, I was brimming over with the novelty of the heresy and had already upset a great many simple people with my casuistry."

In other words, Monica's son was having too much fun being a fool, and making others foolish, to be persuaded to do otherwise. There was but one thing to do: pray. "Leave him alone," he said. "Just pray to God for him. From his own reading he will discover his mistakes and the depth of his profanity."

The priest then gave a personal testimony of how he had once been right where Augustine was but had been brought to the truth even though his mother was herself a heretic. His point seemed to be that nothing is too hard for God. Human extremity is God's opportunity—you can't fix him, I can't fix him, only God can fix him, so trust in God.

Monica didn't like that answer, so she pressed her case and pestered the priest some more, this time with tears. The priest had enough. He answered, "Leave me and go in peace. It cannot be that the son of these tears should be lost."

Augustine wrote: "In later years, as we talked together, she used to say that she accepted these words as a message from heaven."[1] Message from heaven they were because Monica prayed, and the son of her tears became Saint Augustine, one of the most powerful voices the Christian church has ever had. He became the author of the monumental *City of God* and the matchless *Confessions*. Jesus said we should always pray and not give up (Luke 18:1). Thank God that Monica did not give up. The faith of millions has been enriched through the faithful prayers of this tenacious woman.

PRAY THIS PRAYER THAT HER CONVERTED SON PRAYED:

Eternal God,
the light of the minds that know thee,
the life of the souls that love thee,
the strength of the wills that serve thee;
help us so to know thee that we may truly love thee,
so to love thee that we may fully serve thee,
whom to serve is perfect freedom.[2]

DAY 106: PRAISE THE LORD, O MY SOUL

Psalm 103

"Praise the Lord, my soul" (Ps. 103:22).

Frederick Lehman's hymn to the love of God expresses gratefully the impossibility of ever adequately describing the love of God:

Could we with ink the ocean fill,
And were the skies of parchment made;
Were every stalk on earth a quill,
And every man a scribe by trade;
To write the love of God above
Would drain the ocean dry,
Nor could the scroll contain the whole,
Though stretched from sky to sky.

O love of God, how rich and pure!
How measureless and strong!
It shall forevermore endure,
The saints' and angels' song.

Yet unfathomable as his love is, we must keep trying to sing of it. Psalm 103 offers one of the best ways to try. Using its words and structure as a guide, pray through four stages.

Praise him for what he has done for you personally (Ps. 103:1-5). What has God been to you? He forgives, heals, redeems, crowns, and satisfies—list the ways you have known him to do this. Praise him that he loves you from youth to old age, even renewing your youth like the eagle's (cf. Isa. 40:30-31; Ps. 92:14).

Praise him for his patient love for his people (Ps. 103:6-14). Maybe you've never thought to do this before, but it will greatly deepen your appreciation of the love of God. Use what you know of biblical history, or church history, and do what David does. Think of God's patience with a people who have never distinguished themselves by their faithfulness and of a God who nevertheless has. Their story is our story too. "Nevertheless" is a great grace word!

Praise God for his faithfulness in death (Ps. 103:15-18). Remember that life is short, and your only firm hope is in the eternal Father who made you and sympathizes with your frailty. The idea here is not to be somber but sober enough to understand in a fresh way your hope in God's love.

Praise God with the whole created order (Ps. 103:19-22). Actually pray in such a way that the exhortations of verses 20-21 become your exhortations. Tell the angels to praise God. Tell creatures and plants and mountains and bodies of water to praise God! David did. So did St. Francis. Address them by name: "Azaleas and whales, Gobi Desert and Lake Michigan—praise the Lord!"

PRAYER: *Praise the Lord, O my soul! All that is within me, praise his holy name!*

DAY 107: THE BIBLE AND PRAYER

Psalm 119 (selected)

"Blessed are they who walk according to the law of the Lord" (Ps. 119:1).

The longest book in the Bible, the psalms, is a book of prayer. The longest psalm in this book of prayer is a psalm celebrating the law, the word of God. There is a strong, though implicit, message in this pattern. In the heart of the Bible is a book about the life of prayer, and Scripture is critical to the life of prayer. Scripture is so important to prayer for two reasons. One, Scripture emphasizes God's side of the prayer conversation. It is not the only way God speaks, but it is the norm by which we know he is speaking. God speaks through his Spirit into our hearts, for example. But if what we think we hear the Spirit saying in our heart conflicts with Scripture, we can be sure it is not the Spirit speaking. Two, Scripture teaches us how to hold up our end of the prayer conversation. The psalms, for instance, may not always express what we feel, nor should they (cf. Ps. 137:8-9). But, more often than not, they are models of prayer—and we will do well if we learn to feel what they express.

What follows are some highlights from this psalm of the word of God. Use them as material for praise, confession, and petition.

Don't worship the book, but the God of the book. By reading the book, "I seek [God] with all my heart" (Ps. 119:9-10).

Pray that the Holy Spirit will give you understanding when you read. "Open my eyes that I may see wonderful things in your law" (Ps. 119:18).

God's word shows the way of freedom. "I run in the path of your commands, for you have set my heart free.... I will walk about in freedom, for I have sought out your precepts" (Ps. 119:32, 45).

The word of God is absolutely faithful. "Your promises have been thoroughly tested, and your servant loves them" (Ps. 119:140).

The word of God will keep you from sin. "I have hidden your word in my heart that I might not sin against you" (Ps. 119:11). There is an old saying, "This book will keep you from sin, and sin will keep you from this book."

The word of God can make you wiser than your teachers. "I have more understanding than the elders, for I obey your precepts" (Ps. 119:100).

The word of God gives guidance in life. "Your word is a lamp to my feet and a light to my path" (Ps. 119:105).

PRAYER: *Set my heart free, that I may run in the path of your commands!*

DAY 108: ROAD SONGS

Psalms 120—134

"They go from strength to strength till each appears before God in Zion" (Ps. 84:7).

Psalms 120 to 134 have long been known as the "Psalms of Ascent." They were sung by Jewish pilgrims on their way to Jerusalem to celebrate any of the three great festivals devout Jews celebrated each year: Passover, Pentecost, and Tabernacles. Jerusalem was the highest city in Palestine, so the journey was literally an "ascending" trip.

For centuries, the church has also prayed these "road songs" as metaphors for the Christian journey of discipleship, the pilgrimage toward our upward calling in Christ (Phil. 3:14). The roots of this notion go deep in the soil of the Bible. Abraham, the father of all who believe (Gal. 3:7), the archetypical man of faith, was a traveler and a pilgrim. He was "*called* to go to a place he would later receive as his inheritance. By faith he made his home in the promised land as a stranger in a foreign country, for he was looking forward to the city whose foundations, whose architect and builder, is God" (Heb. 11:8-10, italics added). Abraham's sons, Isaac, and Jacob, also waited by faith, as did their children and their children's children for more than 400 years in Egypt, until they were again called out to continue to go to the land God had promised Abraham. The Hebrew word for the congregation of Israel means just that: it is *qahal*, "the called-out ones."

In the Old Testament, the people of God were pilgrims—those called out to go to the land God would show them. According to the New Testament, Christians are also called to live as pilgrims, "as aliens and strangers in the world" (1 Pet. 2:11). Not surprisingly, the church is also the *ekklesia*; from the Greek *ek*, "out," and *klesis*, "to call."

Pilgrims need a map to show them where they are, where they need to go, and how to get there. The psalms of ascent are like a map, dealing with the essentials of discipleship—the perspectives, skills, and disciplines necessary for the journey. The themes are easy to detect, and you may make them your own as you learn to pray them as road songs for your journey.[1]

PRAYER:

Guide me, O Thou great Jehovah,
Pilgrim through this barren land;
I am weak, but Thou art mighty;
Hold me with Thy powerful hand.
Bread of heaven, Bread of heaven,
Feed me till I want no more.
(from the hymn "Guide me, O Thou great Jehovah" by William Williams)

DAY 109: PATIENT, PERSISTENT PRAYER

William Carey (1761-1834)

"So our eyes look to the LORD our God, till he shows us his mercy" (Ps. 123:2).

What do fast food, high-speed Internet, and cell phones all have in common? Two words: instant gratification. Instant gratification is everywhere in our culture, and it threatens to give us an unrealistic view of prayer and of God's greater work, if we're not careful. Fortunately, we have the lives of people like William Carey to teach us the opposite.

Born in 1761 in England, Carey grew up a poor Anglican and wanted nothing more than to be a professional gardener. Unfortunately, a skin disease kept him from working in the sun, so he took up an apprenticeship under a local shoemaker. In between shifts, he kept a strict regimen of study, teaching himself the classics, the sciences, and Greek and Hebrew translations of the Scriptures. Soon he became a Calvinist Baptist preacher with a growing passion for sharing the gospel overseas. Carey's enthusiasm for missions was met with indifference and suspicion by his fellow pastors. Undaunted, he continued preparations and fundraising, and finally in 1792, he sailed with two other men for India.

But if Carey experienced trouble and opposition before he reached the mission field, nothing could compare to the trouble he experienced once his work began. Carey immediately set about building India's first printing press. He worked long hours for twenty years, translating scripture into as many languages and dialects as he had energy for. Suddenly in 1812, a fire burned the printing building to the ground, destroying Carey's entire library, dictionaries, deeds, ten translations of the Bible, his completed Sanskrit dictionary, and the typesets for printing over ten different languages.

Shocked beyond words, Carey wept over the destruction. But the fire didn't quench his spirit. "The Lord has laid me low," he said, "that I may look more simply to him." Soon he had set up a new shop and began again the painstaking work of scholarly translation. "The loss is heavy," he said, "but as traveling a road the second time is usually done with greater ease than the first time…we are not discouraged; indeed, the work is already begun again in every language. We are cast down but not in despair."

When the world heard about the catastrophic fire, money began pouring in. Soon the operation was once again underway, and Carey and his staff redoubled their efforts. By the time of his death, Carey's organization had translated and published the entire Bible into six different languages and published selected passages and books into forty-four!

PRAYER: *Father, forgive me for how easily I am discouraged. Strengthen me by your Spirit to be patient with you and your eternal purposes and to not lose heart in prayer and service.*

DAY 110: HOW GOOD AND PLEASANT

Psalm 133

"How good and pleasant it is when brothers live together in unity" (Ps. 133:1).

Some things are good but not pleasant; and some things are pleasant but not good. You can probably think immediately of things that fit the "good but not pleasant" category: any sort of medical or dental procedure, for instance. Maybe you can think of many more things that qualify as "pleasant but not good" (as in good for you). Most of these probably have to do with food.

Only a very few things qualify as both good and pleasant. This psalm says unity among God's people is one of these rare blessings. It is fun, and it is good for you! It is as though the priestly oil that anoints and consecrates Aaron, is poured down on God's people, consecrating them in the same way. It is like the dew from Mount Hermon that refreshes and nourishes Zion. It is a very, very good thing when God's people get along with each other. God is glorified, and people flourish and are joyful. "For there the Lord bestows his blessing, even life forevermore" (Ps. 133:13).

Jesus must have had this in mind when he prayed that his church would be one, as he and his Father are one. Jesus asked God to make his followers "one as we are one: I in them and you in me. May they be brought to complete unity to let the world know that you sent me and have loved them even as you have loved me" (John 17:22-23). Jesus believed that unity in the church would be such a powerful demonstration of the presence of God in the church, "precious oil poured on the head," that it would make believers of nonbelievers. This is because God is a good and pleasant fellowship of Father, Son, and Holy Spirit. God is one as three and three as one. God is a loving community. For the Christian community to be *one* is for them to be a little bit of heaven on earth. Pray Psalm 133 for your church. When you do, you pray with Jesus himself, and it's good for you.

PRAYER: *Father, Son, and Holy Spirit, may we in the church be one as you are one; that the world may know that Jesus is the Son of God and that we are beloved of the Father.*

DAY 111: YOU KNOW ME!

Psalm 139

"O Lord, you have searched me and you know me" (Ps. 139:1).

At the Museum of Modern Art in New York City, there is a sculpture of a hand by the French sculptor Auguste Rodin. Two clay figures of a man and a woman appear to be emerging out of its palm. It is one of Rodin's favorites. He called it "The Hand of God." Picture that hand and know this: Before you cared about God (and whether or not you ever do), God has held you in his hand. That is the message of this psalm.

It's significant that the Scripture says God has held you by his hand, not his intellect. Surely his intellect, if one can call it that, comprehends us completely. But there is small comfort in the idea of a giant mind knowing all there is to know about us. It's even scary—like a surveillance camera capturing everything we do and think and say. God's knowledge of us is not the knowledge of a jailor, but a lover. "O Lord, you have searched me, and you know me. You have laid your hand upon me. Such knowledge is too wonderful for me" (Ps. 139:1, 5, 6).

His hand has held you not only by his knowledge of you, but also by his presence with you (Ps. 139:7). There is no place you can go and not find God there with you, and ahead of you. A child was asked how she knew there was only one God. She answered, "Because he's so big there isn't room for anyone else." There is room for you, however. He is everywhere present, not just as a fact of his deity, but because of his love. Further, his hand has done more than hold you; he has shaped you by creating you, even knitting you together in your mother's womb. You are a marvel (Ps. 139:13-16).

The wonderful upshot of all this is that when you pray, he knows what you need before you ask (Matt. 6:8). If you bring some great and troubling situation to him, you need not worry that he will say, "Really? Oh that's terrible. I had no idea. Let me think about what to do." God is master of the situation before you pray about it. In fact, you are praying about it because he has moved you to pray, so be at peace. "How precious to me are your thoughts, O God" (Ps. 139:17)!

PRAYER: *Lord and Giver of life, thank you for making me fearfully and wonderfully! Search me and know me; show me if there is anything in me that offends you.*

DAY 112: SAYING NO TO SAY YES

Monica, Part 2

"For our light and momentary troubles are achieving for us an eternal glory that far outweighs them all" (2 Cor. 4:17).

Despite her tearful prayers, Monica's son Augustine had not yet become a Christian. She had been assured by a wise priest to pray with hope, believing "it cannot be that the son of these tears should be lost." But if anything, since that time, things seemed to be getting worse. Now Augustine wanted to leave Monica and his home in Carthage to sail to Rome in order to pursue his profession as a teacher of rhetoric. Carthage in the fourth century AD was a conservative, North African town in what was the "Bible Belt" of the Roman Empire. Rome was cosmopolitan and immoral, filled with the temptations of flesh and mind. Monica knew how susceptible Augustine was to both. A trip to Rome would seal his doom, she was sure of it! "She wept bitterly to see me go," Augustine wrote, "and followed me to the water's edge, clinging to me with all her strength in the hope that I would either come home or take her with me." What a scene it must have been to see this brilliant young adult and his mother struggling and arguing at the docks! Again, it was the irresistible force versus the immovable object.

Augustine decided the only way out was to lie. He told his mother he wouldn't be leaving after all, at least for a while. He said he needed to wait for the wind to rise and wanted to visit a friend before departure. But that night, he secretly sailed away. The next day Monica was "wild with grief, pouring her sighs and sorrows" out to God, sure he had not listened to her prayers.

But it was in Rome, the last place his mother wanted him to go, that Augustine found what she most wanted him to have. For it was there he met his intellectual equal, Ambrose, a Christian bishop, and was converted. Through the painful breach between mother and son, God in his sovereign love did something wonderful for both. Augustine thanked God for, "letting my own desires carry me away on a journey that was to put an end to those desires." What looked like running away from God had really been running to God. In much the same way, Monica, against her will, actually got what she most wanted in a way she least expected. In his *Confessions*, Augustine wrote that in refusing Monica's prayer, God, "in the depth of [his] wisdom, granted the wish that was closest to her heart."[1]

God is the master of all things, even the wills that resist his. He always reserves the right to be God and answer our prayers not our way, but his way. This is a bitter lesson for some, but ultimately one of the sweetest lessons of all. When God says "No," he says it to say a greater "Yes!"

PRAYER: *Father in heaven! I will trust you even when I can't see the good you are working in my life and in the world. Fix my eyes not on what is seen, but what is unseen (2 Cor. 4:18).*

Introduction to Proverbs

DAY 113: THE BEGINNING OF WISDOM

"For attaining wisdom and discipline; for understanding words of discipline" (Prov. 1:2).

What is wisdom? Knowing what it is not will help to understand what it is. Wisdom is not genius or intelligence. Mere intelligence without wisdom is like a fast runner on the wrong road. The advantage of speed is really a disadvantage, for all it does is help the runner get further away from his destination. To be smart but not wise is to be able to invent even more ways to be stupid. The history of modern philosophy is filled with examples of this. The race does not always belong to the swift, in more ways than one.

Wisdom is knowing the right path to run. It is the moral insight that shows you how to be good so you can live well. "I run down the path of your commands, because you have set my heart free" (Ps. 119:32).

Our Lord Jesus made the same point with a different metaphor when he said, "Therefore, everyone who hears these words of mine and puts them into practice is like a wise man who built his house on the rock. The rain came down, the streams rose, and the winds blew against that house, yet it did not fall, because it had its foundation on the rock." The foolish man, he went on to say, built on sand, and when the rains came, the house collapsed (Matt. 7:24-27). In other words, if his life was a house, he could have built something worthy of the cover of *Architectural Digest*, but it would be worthless after the first storm. What a tragedy to have a high IQ, a great education, and a fool's outlook.

Proverbs is filled with things even a child can understand; and things those who won't be a child won't understand. It's therefore a great book to read on your knees, humbly and prayerfully. "At that time Jesus, full of the Holy Spirit, said, 'I praise you, Father, Lord of heaven and earth, because you have hidden these things from the wise and learned, and revealed them to little children. Yes, Father, for this was your good pleasure'" (Luke 10:21).

PRAYER: *"Show me your ways, O Lord, teach me your paths; guide me in your truth and teach me, for you are God my Savior, and my hope is in you all day long" (Ps. 25:5).*

DAY 114: THE LIGHTHOUSE

Proverbs 1:7; 9:10; 14:26-27

"The fear of the Lord is the beginning of knowledge" (Prov. 1:7).

You may have heard this legend. A large battleship was coursing through the North Atlantic Ocean in a heavy fog, when the captain saw a light out ahead. Since his ship appeared to be on a collision course with whatever the light was, he radioed immediately, "Alter your course, ten degrees south." The message came back, "Alter your course ten degrees south." Irritated, the captain, radioed, "This is captain Dillard, I repeat: alter your course, ten degrees south." The message came back, "This is ensign Collins, I repeat: alter your course ten degrees south." The situation was approaching a crisis. The captain bellowed, "This is a battleship, you idiot! Alter your course ten degrees south!" The message came back, "This is a lighthouse, sir. Alter your course ten degrees south."

The topic sentence of the book of Proverbs is like a lighthouse: "The fear of the Lord is the beginning of knowledge, but fools despise wisdom and discipline" (Prov. 1:7). If you are not clear on this fundamental truth, you may be clear about a lot of other things—your name, the kind of ship you're on—but you are headed for disaster. Money, intelligence, and good looks will just be part of the wreckage.

The greatest commandment, according to Jesus, is that we love God with our whole being (Matt. 22:37). If loving God is the greatest thing we can do, and fearing him is the beginning of everything else, how do the two fit together? Can we both love God and fear him? Doesn't one cancel out the other? Some translations render the word "fear" as "reverence." While accurate, they miss the strength of the word which is literally "fear" in the Greek text. What Jesus is getting at is that our respect for God should be like fear in its intensity. The sight of something you fear marvelously focuses your mind. It blocks out everything else. In this sense, then, you can truly love only who you fear. There can be no deep love without a corresponding deep reverence that is like terror. Fear and love are linked in exciting ways in the Bible: "But with you there is forgiveness; therefore, you are feared" (Ps. 130:4).

When you pray, whether you use the words or not, let your "Father," always be "Father in heaven." For God is both closer than a friend and higher than the greatest king; a lighthouse guiding you home, or a rock upon which you are broken (Rom. 9:33).

PRAYER:

O, how I fear Thee, living God,
With deepest, tend'rest fears,
And worship Thee with trembling hope
And penitential tears!

Yet I may love Thee too, O Lord,
Almighty as Thou art,
For Thou hast stooped to ask of me
The love of my poor heart!
(from the hymn "My God, How Wonderful Thou Art" by Frederick William Faber)

DAY 115: STRAIGHT PATHS AND MATURE PEOPLE

Proverbs 3:5-6; 16:3

"In all your ways acknowledge him, and he will make your paths straight" (Prov. 3:6).

This proverb isn't a promise for an easy, obstacle-free life. It says God will make your paths straight. There are still rugged mountains to climb, deserts to cross, rivers to ford, and jungles to bushwhack. That's where wisdom comes in. There is a bonus in this; for in the straightening of our paths, we too are made straight. "Consider it pure joy, my brothers, whenever you face trials of many kinds, because the testing of your faith develops perseverance. Perseverance must finish its work so that you may be mature and complete, not lacking anything." The struggles can be good for us if we have the wisdom to handle them. So, "If any of you lacks wisdom, he should ask God" (James 1:2-5). There you have it: as paths are made straight, people are made mature.

"In all your ways acknowledge him." What does it mean to acknowledge the Lord in all our ways? It means to live by his word in every circumstance, in every place we find ourselves. There is a story about a father and a son who were traveling to a city in a far country. The journey would take several days. As they walked over mountain passes and through forests, the boy wanted to explore things. They would enter a meadow, and the boy would want to run to the other side. If they passed a rock outcropping, the boy would beg his dad to let him climb it. The boy got bolder and bolder as they journeyed. One day he wanted to go a greater distance off the road than he had yet ventured. The father agreed that he could, but as the boy started off, he felt a tinge of fear. He asked, "How can I know if I've wandered too far away, father?"

The father smiled and answered, "I'll call your name every few minutes and you answer. You call my name every few minutes, and I'll answer. If you get to a place where you can't hear my voice very well, you've wandered too far"

That's what it looks like to acknowledge the Lord in all our ways. It is a picture of prayer and the word of God—his voice calling to us, and our voice calling to him.

PRAYER: *O dear Father! Speak, for I am listening. Hear me when I pray.*

DAY 116: WISDOM IS SUPREME

Proverbs 4:7-9

"Though it cost you all you have, get understanding" (Prov. 4:7).

"Whatever else you get" is an alternate way to translate, "Though it cost you all you have" (Prov. 4:7). The image is of a marketplace with so many things to buy; some good, some cheap, only a few excellent. "Whatever else you get in this marketplace of goods and wares, make sure you get wisdom, because wisdom is supreme." The truth is, there are a lot of things you could buy, but it's hard to know what is worthwhile. Archbishop William Temple said the world is like a jewelry store in which vandals have switched the price tags around. Some items with high price tags are worthless while truly precious items have been shoved to the back of the shelf and priced cheaply. Wisdom is one of these precious items. Sometimes we forget where to look for it. "Where is the Life we have lost in living?" wrote T. S. Eliot.[1] "Where is the wisdom we have lost in knowledge? Where is the knowledge we have lost in information?"

To pray for wisdom is to ask for eyes to pick out what is wise amid the marketplace of wisdom substitutes. "And this is my prayer: that your love may abound more and more in knowledge and depth of insight, so that you may be able to discern what is best" (Phil. 1:9-10). To pray for wisdom is also to ask for God to change your heart to want wisdom more than any other thing. "Though it cost you all you have, get wisdom." Wisdom, like the God of wisdom, and the kingdom of God, is given only to those who treasure her and seek her with all their heart. Anything less will yield something less. Anyone who comes looking for God "must believe that he exists and rewards those who earnestly seek him" (Heb. 11:6). Those who seek the kingdom must be willing to part with everything they have for the joy of securing it (Matt. 13:44-46).

PRAYER: *Open my eyes that I might see what is wise. Open my heart, that I might want what is wise.*

DAY 117: THE PROVERBS 31 WOMAN

Proverbs 12:4; 31:10-31

"A woman who fears the Lord is to be praised" (Prov. 31:30).

There actually was an ad in the "Personals" section of a newspaper for the kind of woman praised in these proverbs. It was headlined: "Are You My Proverbs 31 Woman?" The description the man who ran the ad gave of himself made one doubt that a woman of the wisdom and discretion described in these proverbs would be interested. But the ad was a kind of prayer, and one couldn't fault him for his prayer. It is a worthy prayer for a man to pray for God to give him a wife like this. And it is a worthy prayer for a woman to pray that she would be like this.

The question begged here is why isn't there a "Proverbs 31 Man" described somewhere in the proverbs? Any answer to that question would be purely speculative. One thing is certain, however: the Bible is full of commands for qualities of character that apply equally to both sexes. Each of the qualities praised in the "Proverbs 31 Woman" can be found elsewhere in Scripture in contexts that apply to both men and women. Further, Paul's instructions for husbands call men to a level of love and sacrifice unmatched in religious literature of any kind (Eph. 5:25-33).

The best thing to do with the beautiful, full-length portrait of a great woman in Proverbs 31 is to thank God for women like that. If you are a woman, it is also a call to thank God that you can have the kind of wise influence the Bible says you can have. We should thank God that the Word of God highly treasures women. We can pray for wives and mothers and sisters and friends to grow in the grace and knowledge of God. We can pray for men whose wives fall far short of this ideal. William Carey and John Wesley had terrible marriages, but powerful ministries. Surely someone saw their "thorn in the flesh" and prayed that God's grace would be sufficient for them in their weakness.

PRAYER: *Father in Heaven! We turn our eyes away from the false images of womanhood promoted by the commercial interests of our culture. Stir us all up to desire and prize the kind of woman you prize.*

DAY 118: LIPS AND LIVES

Proverbs 15:8, 29; 28:9

"The Lord detests the prayer of the wicked" (Prov. 15:8).

"But the prayer of the upright pleases him" (Prov. 15:8b). This is the kind of prayer and pray-er God delights in: the one whose life and prayers match up. What we ask for and who we are should line up with each other. When David came to understand this, it lit up his life. He gushed, "Sacrifice and offering you do not desire... burnt offerings and sin offerings you did not require. Then I said, 'Here I am, I have come.... I desire to do your will, O my God; your law is within my heart'" (Ps. 40: 6, 7, 8). God takes this kind of prayer into his confidence and grants him the joy of no longer being only a servant, but an intimate friend (Gen. 18:17-19; Job 29:4; Ps. 25:14; John 15:15). What could be better than that?

But what could be worse than this: "The Lord detests the prayer of the wicked" (Prov. 15:8a). This is the person whose prayers and life conflict. Prayer and deed are two distinct and separate categories. God hates this kind of praying for the obvious reason: it betrays and mocks God to ask him to do what you won't do or to praise him with lips, but not a righteous life. It's doubly galling to God because he always sees us comprehensively. He knows exactly what we've done as we pray. It's not that he's let down later, after he has heard us pray; but he is disappointed as he hears us pray.

"The Great Thanksgiving" in *The Book of Common Prayer* frames the matter neatly when it prays, "give us such an awareness of your mercies, that our hearts may be sincerely thankful, and that we may show forth your praise not only with our lips, but in our lives, by giving up ourselves to your service, and by walking before you in holiness and righteousness all our days." Lips and lives: that's the kind prayer that pleases God.

PRAYER: *Dear Lord, "give us such an awareness of your mercies that our hearts may be sincerely thankful and that we may show forth your praise not only with our lips, but in our lives, by giving up ourselves to your service, and by walking before you in holiness and righteousness all our days."*

DAY 119: TWO TOWERS

Proverbs 18:10-11

"The name of the Lord is a strong tower" (Prov. 18:10).

There are two towers spoken of in Proverbs 18:10-11. One tower is unseen and impregnable, the other seen but wholly imaginary. The imaginary tower is "the wealth of the rich" kept in "their fortified city; they imagine it an unscalable wall" (Prov. 18:11). The imaginary tower represents all human efforts for salvation and security. In their heart of hearts, those who trust in this tower must know that if it isn't scaled by an army, what they've kept in it will be swallowed up in death. So, it takes a great deal of imagination and diversion to prop up this tower. Pascal tried to shock the people of his day into seeing this. He wrote, "Imagine a number of men in chains, all under the sentence of death, some of whom are butchered in the sight of others; those remaining see their own condition in that of their fellows and, looking at each other with grief and despair, await their turn. This is an image of the human condition." Knowing that all mortals will die and lose everything, how can anyone possibly keep trying to hide in that tower? Pascal's answer was, "Being unable to cure death, wretchedness and ignorance, men have decided, in order to be happy, not to think about such things."[1]

The impregnable tower, though unseen, is none other than the name of the Lord. God's name is his character, expressed in his word and in his mighty deeds to save. Because he is unchanging, his word is unchanging. Heaven and earth will pass away, but his word is the strongest of towers and will not (Matt. 24:35). His pleasure is in those who trust him in everything. Nothing else impresses God; not strength, beauty, or intelligence. Why should they? He is God! (cf. Ps. 144:10-11) Nothing can separate us from his love in this strong tower (Rom. 8:37-39). But note, you have to run to this tower. You must seek the Lord and trust the Lord with your whole heart. Imagination requires no effort, faith does.

PRAYER:

A mighty fortress is our God,
A bulwark never failing;
Our Helper He amid the flood
Of mortal ills prevailing.
(from the hymn "A Mighty Fortress" *by Martin Luther)*

DAY 120: SINK OR SWIM

The Churches of Ipswich

"Again, I tell you that if two of you on earth agree about anything you ask for, it will be done for you by my Father in heaven" (Matt. 18:19).

One of the saddest chapters in the history of American Christianity is what happened to the churches of New England in the hundred years that spanned the late eighteenth and early nineteenth centuries. During that time, church after church and seminary after seminary moved from the historic Christian faith to apostasy, as one by one they embraced the heresies of Unitarianism and Universalism. It was as if a flood of spiritual darkness engulfed the Northeast. But there were some heroic exceptions to this decline, notably four churches in the town of Ipswich, along Cape Anne, Massachusetts.

In 1760, John Cleaveland became pastor of the Second Church of Ipswich. When he arrived, he sensed immediately the spiritual malaise in his congregation and called his people to engage in a "Concert of Prayer"—a cross-denominational prayer strategy based on the writings of Jonathan Edwards and a group of pastors from Northern Scotland. The plan was to pray for two things: the revival of religion in the church and the spread of the kingdom of God in the world. They were to pray every two weeks, either in small groups or privately, and then to meet quarterly in an all-church prayer meeting. The church did all this faithfully for twenty years. Though the work started small, within three years Cleaveland's church began to experience a revival of love for God and a wave of conversions. Little by little, the revival spread throughout the region.

In 1780 Cleaveland invited three other Congregational churches in Ipswich to join in the "Concert of Prayer." The churches agreed. Quarterly prayer meetings were rotated among the four churches, and in the following years, each of the churches enjoyed periodic revivals. This "Concert of Prayer" continued uninterrupted for one hundred years, celebrating its centennial celebration on December 31, 1859. Remarkably, for the hundred years they were involved in the "Concert of Prayer," the four churches remained true to the historic Christian faith. While most of New England's protestant churches were drowning in a sea of spiritual darkness, the churches in Ipswich had learned to swim.

The century of prayer ended with the outbreak of the Civil War. Within twenty years all four churches sank into the very apostasy they had avoided for so long. Sadly, the churches in Ipswich had forgotten how to swim. For a church to choose to pray or not to pray is not merely to decide whether to engage in a nice spiritual discipline. It is to choose between life and death.[1]

PRAYER: *Great God! Eternity hangs in the balance. Teach us to pray as though we realize this for our church, our city, our nation, and the world.*

DAY 121: BRING IT INTO THE LIGHT

Proverbs 28:13

"He who conceals his sins does not prosper" (Prov. 28:13).

G. K. Chesterton said the only Christian doctrine that is empirically verifiable is the doctrine of original sin. We see its devastation all around us. It is possible that this proverb also meets the empirical test: "He who conceals his sins does not prosper." According to David, lack of prosperity is something of an understatement: "When I kept silent, my bones wasted away through my groaning all day long" (Ps. 32:3). Guilt works like a corrosive agent on the heart. The greater power of sin is not in the act, but in the concealment of the act. Studies of addictions show that it is in secrecy that they gain control of a person's life. Sin is birthed in darkness and flourishes in darkness. Bring it into the light and it withers.

"But whoever confesses and renounces them finds mercy." The first step is confession. To confess your sin is not to tell God what he doesn't already know; it is to agree with what he already knows. When that happens, a miracle takes place—what came between you and God now connects you. The second step is renunciation. Simply confessing your sin does not bring it into the light—it must be renounced as it is confessed. There is a kind of fellowship in sin that revels in self-disclosure. Have you ever overheard people roll their eyes and laugh as they regale each other with tales of drunkenness and sexual indulgence? Some quip, "I don't want to go to heaven because I'll have no friends up there." The lightweight virtues of sincerity and frankness often outweigh the heavier virtues of chastity, temperance, and integrity. "At least he's honest," we will say. But what we need is mercy, not reassurance and social acceptance. We are dying for lack of forgiveness, not low self-esteem.

David knew how bad it felt to keep his sin hidden. He also knew how great it felt to confess and renounce it: "Blessed is he whose transgressions are forgiven whose sins are covered. Blessed is the man whose sin the Lord does not count against him, and in whose spirit is no deceit" (Ps. 32:1-3).

PRAYER: *Merciful God! I confess and renounce my sin. Take away the darkness and depression inside; restore to me the joy of your salvation.*

DAY 122: JUST TWO THINGS

Proverbs 30:7-9

"Two things I ask of you, O Lord; do not refuse me before I die" (Prov. 30:7).

This prayer is either a gross oversimplification or a masterful distillation. "Two things I ask of you, O Lord; do not refuse me before I die" (Prov. 30:7). Only two things, is that all? But those two things cover a lot of territory, spiritually. For one thing, they address both our minds and bodies. The first is, "Keep falsehood and lies far from me" (Prov. 30:8a). That speaks to the mind, the ideas, and attitudes that enter us through our eyes and ears. The second is, "Give me neither poverty or riches, but give me only my daily bread" (Prov. 30:8b). That speaks to our bodies, our physicality. Between these two statements, pretty much all that we are physically, emotionally, mentally, and spiritually is covered.

Sin is a lie—the lie. The enemy of our souls is "a liar and the father of lies" (John 8:44). One of the most persistent temptations we face is to live on the level of our physical appetites. Appetites aren't inherently bad because God made our bodies good. But the lie of sin will convince us that we are no more than our bodies. When Jesus told Satan, the Liar, that "man does not live on bread alone, but on every word that comes from the mouth of God" (Matt. 4:4), he gave two gifts to our humanity: On the one hand, he affirmed our physicality—that God made us to need bread. On the other hand, he affirmed our spirituality—that God made us more than our stomachs.

There's yet more to this prayer. The proverb explains the reason for these two requests: "Otherwise I may have too much (bread) and disown you and say, 'Who is the Lord?' Or I may become poor and steal, and so dishonor the name of my God" (Prov. 30:9). The prayer is a prayer not to be led into temptation. It is the prayer of one who knows his weakness and asks God to protect him from his weakness. It is a humble prayer. The Bible never encourages us to pray to be tested so we can show how strong we are. Rather, Jesus said to pray that we not be tested. True, we should expect to be tested, and when tested we should pray for strength and endurance—but never that we be tested.

All that in a simple prayer for two things. Actually, the prayer may not be so simple after all since Jesus said only one thing is needed (Luke 10:41-42). But it's a good place to start.

PRAYER: *"Two things I ask of you, O Lord; do not refuse me before I die: Keep falsehood and lies far from me: Give me neither poverty or riches, but give me only my daily bread."*

Introduction to Ecclesiastes

DAY 123: "MEANINGLESS, MEANINGLESS... UTTERLY MEANINGLESS!"

"All of them are... a chasing after the wind" (Eccles. 1:14).

Simone de Beauvoir had attained everything she had ever aspired to as a writer, existentialist philosopher, and proto-feminist. She was interviewed by *Time Magazine* when she was 57 years old. Despite her accomplishments, de Beauvoir had little sense of fulfillment as she looked back over her life, and she was obsessed with her mortality. "The most important, the most irreparable thing that has happened to me is that I have grown old. How is it that time, which has no form or substance, can crush me with so huge a weight that I can no longer breathe?" At 57, she found herself, "hostile to the society to which I belonged, banished by my age from the future, stripped fiber by fiber from my past.... The promises have all been kept. And yet, turning an incredulous gaze toward that young and credulous girl (I once was), I realize with stupor how much I was gypped."[1]

Her disillusionment is at the heart of the issues explored by this remarkable book, the most modern sounding of all the books in the Bible. Professor Peter Kreeft says that whenever he is called upon to teach the Bible in a college classroom, he begins with Ecclesiastes, not with Genesis, for Ecclesiastes raises all the critical questions the rest of the Bible answers. One-by-one, the writer looks at the ways humankind has attempted to find meaning apart from the God of the Bible; and one-by-one he finds them inadequate. The pursuit of wisdom leads only to frustration and pain. The pursuit of pleasure leads only to disappointment. But whether one pursues wisdom or pleasure, in the end both are eroded by time and swallowed up in death.

After the ascription, the first word of the book of Ecclesiastes is "meaningless!" The last words are, "Now all has been heard; here is the conclusion of the matter: Fear God and keep his commandments, for this is the whole duty of man. For God will bring every deed into judgment, including every hidden thing, whether it is good or evil" (Eccles. 12:13-14). The journey from that beginning to that ending is provocative, puzzling, and sobering. But it is a journey worth taking to discover afresh that fulfillment is only found in God. Apart from the God who hears and answers prayer, the alternative is suicide or a rather gloomy pursuit of temporal satisfactions. To pray the themes of Ecclesiastes is to feel an acute sense of gratitude and relief that, because of Christ, life is not, "meaningless!"

PRAYER: *In you, Lord Christ, are hidden all the treasures of wisdom. Because of your victory over sin and death, nothing I do in your name is a chasing after the wind.*

DAY 124: THE BLESSINGS OF THIS LIFE

Ecclesiastes 2:24-26

"A man can do nothing better than to eat and drink and find satisfaction in his work" (Eccles. 2:24).

The writer of Ecclesiastes misses no folly or foible of the human condition. But even amid all the meaninglessness, he sees that there are certain things God has given humans that are very good and satisfying. Two are mentioned here: good work and good food (Eccles. 3:22; 5:18-20; 8:15; 9:7-10); and a third thing is mentioned elsewhere: a good marriage (Eccles. 9:9). The whole world may seem cockeyed, but with these earthly pleasures, life can still be good. But there are two provisos: that God blesses these gifts and enables us to enjoy them (Eccles. 5:19), and that we know they are gifts from God, not our own doing.

There is an important theology of pleasure implicit in these verses. Two things stand out. One, God's good gifts in creation are good. Food, work, and marriage are inherently worthwhile. The world is the Lord's manor, his estate, and in his Word he magnanimously encourages us to enjoy being his guests. "Both high and low among men find refuge in the shadow of your wings. They feast on the abundance of your house; you give them drink from your river of delights. For with you is the fountain of life; in your light we see light" (Ps. 36:7-9). Two, apart from God, our earthly joys are too confined or too narrow. Earthly pleasures are good in themselves because God made them, but because the pleasures are not God, they can't satisfy the way only God can. Many earthly joys will diminish as we age and as our senses dwindle (cf. Eccles. 12:1-8). For the gifts to be all they can be, we need the Giver with the gift.

It is common for evangelical Christians to pray before meals. Some call the prayer "giving thanks," others call it "saying grace." Both ways are good. Of course, we should be thankful, and our gratitude is enhanced to the degree that we see grace. It would also be appropriate to call these prayers "pleasure prayers." The only way to improve on the pleasure of mashed potatoes and gravy or a joyous evening of family laughter is to say, "Thank you."

PRAYER: *Thank you, gracious and generous Father for all the blessings of this life. We feast on the abundance of your house, and you give us drink from your river of delights. "For with you is the fountain of life; in your light we see light" (Ps. 36:8, 9).*

DAY 125: TOO MUCH BUT NOT ENOUGH

Ecclesiastes 3:1-22

"He has also set eternity in the hearts of men; yet they cannot fathom what God has done from the beginning to end" (Eccles. 3:11).

The world is too much for us. We are dwarfed by its glorious and inexorable movements and seasons. For instance: "There is a time for everything, and a season for every activity under heaven: a time to be born and a time to die" (Eccles. 3:1-2). There you have it—our birth and our death, the two most important events of our life, are things we have absolutely no control over. There are many other things we do not control as the following verses show (Eccles. 3:1-8). Eternity rules time and all who move through it. Times and seasons come and go, and only God knows when, why, or how This unsettling knowledge can make us wise, as in the fear of God (Prov. 1:7), which is what the writer of Ecclesiastes says it's supposed to do: "And I know that everything God does will endure forever; nothing can be added to it and nothing taken away from it. God does it so that men will revere him" (Eccles. 3:14).

Yet, dwarfed as we are by the world, the world is not enough for us. We were made for more than the world can give. Moving through times we cannot control, we long for more. God made us that way: "He has made everything beautiful in its time. He has also set eternity in the hearts of men; yet they cannot fathom what God has done from beginning to end" (Eccles. 3:11). The world may dwarf us, and the weight of time eventually crush us, but we are greater than both. "Man is but a reed, the most feeble thing in nature; but he is a thinking reed," wrote Pascal. "If the universe were to crush him, man would still be more noble than that which killed him, because he knows that he dies and the advantage which the universe has over him; the universe knows nothing of this."[1] Pascal believed our greatness is that of a deposed king; we were made for more, we lost it, and we want to get it back.

Thoughts like these both humble and ennoble us. We are wretched when seen only against the backdrop of the universe. But God made us for himself, and we are restless until we find rest in him (from Augustine's *Confessions*). Only deposed royalty who have been humbled find their way back.

PRAYER: *You made me for yourself, Lord. My heart is restless for you; I hunger and thirst for you as in a desert. Satisfy me with your love.*

DAY 126: THE SACRIFICE OF FOOLS

Ecclesiastes 5:1-7

"Therefore stand in awe of God" (Eccles. 5:7).

This passage is to prayer and worship what Proverbs 1:7 is to wisdom: "The fear of the Lord is the beginning of knowledge." Awe of God in prayer and worship is a subset of wisdom. "Guard your steps when you go to the house of God" (Eccles. 5:1). That means, pay attention to what you are there for and Who you are there to honor. The promise of the New Testament still holds. You may enter the holy place with confidence (Heb. 4:16) but not carelessness. We come into God's presence by the grace of his Son, but grace never gives us license to be irreverent. The most essential and appropriate response to grace is gratitude, and gratitude is never casual. The greater the grace, the greater the gratitude and reverence.

The worst kind of irreverence is mindless worship according to this passage. It is the sacrifice of fools who don't think about what they are doing, who speak before they think, and who make empty promises to God. Their words and prayers are like the mumblings and ramblings of someone in a troubled sleep. The only thing worse than a silent fool is a talkative fool.

How do your prayers and the worship you offer God stand in the light of this text? On the continuum between garrulousness and awe, where does the worship of your church fall? Remember God is the center of worship, not you and your feelings and friends. Feelings and friends matter and are properly brought before the light of God for their sanctification. But when they, not God, become the center, you know how serious an offense that is. The Bible's word is idolatry. "God is in heaven, and you are on earth, so let your words be few' (Eccles. 5:2). It doesn't say let your words be eloquent or theologically profound. Sometimes the greatest eloquence is in simple, listening silence.

PRAYER: *Holy God, teach me the discipline and grace of silence. I shut my mouth and open my ears. Speak, so I may speak well of you.*

DAY 127: TAKE THE TIME

Andrew Murray (1828-1917)

"He is always wrestling in prayer for you, that you may stand firm in all the will of God, mature and fully assured" (Col. 4:12).

As a young man, Andrew Murray spent a lot of time on horseback, riding for weeks of uninterrupted ministry in the sunbaked South African territory of Bloemfontein, an area covering 50,000 square miles. Boers (Dutch-speaking South African farmers) traveled great distances to hear the famous Murray preach. Barely into his twenties and with a frail frame, Murray earned the nickname "the boy preacher." One Dutch farmer, upon seeing Murray for the first time, was overheard as saying "Why, they have lent us a girl to preach to us."

Andrew Murray had grown up in South Africa, the child of a Dutch Reformed preacher. When he was ten years old, he left home and traveled to Scotland for schooling. His interest in theology and revival brought him to seek further education in Holland and Germany before he finally returned to South Africa to begin his career as a preacher.

People flocked to hear him speak. He saw conversions at nearly every evangelistic service. Because of all this, he felt a growing conflict with "pride and self-complacency… in my heart." Soon Murray found himself too sick to travel or to preach. Hours spent traveling were replaced by hours of quiet waiting on God. Murray's daughter later wrote of this period in his life: "It was after this 'time of silence' when God came so near to [Murray] and he saw more clearly the meaning of a life of full surrender and simple faith. He began to show in all relationships that constant tenderness and unruffled lovingkindness and unselfish thought for others which increasingly characterized his life from that point. At the same time, he lost nothing of his strength and determination."

The years that followed were richly productive. Revival came to Murray's church, which led to an invitation to speak at the Keswick and Northfield Conventions. His involvement with these movements led eventually to a prayer movement for worldwide revival. The Welsh revivals of the early 1900's traced their roots back to the Keswick Convention and to missionaries such as James Hudson Taylor, A.T. Pierson, and Samuel Zwemer. These men considered the Keswick convention to be "hunting grounds" for the new generation of missionary recruits. In his lifetime Murray wrote over 250 books and articles on theology, mission work, and prayer. Many of his books are still in print.

But Murray never forgot the lessons of quiet waiting in his youth. His life was sustained by a perpetual hunger for God's presence. His cry was a constant call back to that still place where the soul meets the Word of God: "Take time to read His Word as in His presence, that from it you may know what He asks of you and what He promises you. Let the Word create around you, create within you a holy atmosphere, a holy heavenly light, in which your soul will be refreshed and strengthened for the work of daily life."

PRAY THIS PRAYER OF ANDREW MURRAY: *"May not a single moment of my life be spent outside the light, love, and joy of God's presence and may not a moment without the entire surrender of myself as a vessel for Him to fill full of His Spirit and His love."*[1]

DAY 128: A GOOD YOUTH AND A GOOD DEATH

Ecclesiastes 11:7—12:8

"Be happy, young man, while you are young, and let your heart give you joy in the days of your youth" (Eccles. 11:9).

In many collections of famous photographs there is a picture of two woman peering at each other from opposites sides of a giant redwood tree. One is youthful, a lovely nude, full of life and promise. The other is very old and somewhat shrunken, dressed in a sweater, sensible skirt, and oxfords. Both are smiling faintly at what they see. They seem amused. Youth looks at old age, and old age looks back—like in this fascinating meditation.

It's good to be young, and youth is wasted on the young if they don't know that. "Be happy, young man, while you are young, and let your heart give you joy in the days of your youth" (Eccles. 11:9). The young also waste their youth if they are not reflective and sober about their youth. Be joyful, yes, but also be aware that your youth is a temporary gift from God that you will have to give an account for someday. "Know that for all these things God will bring you to judgment.... Remember your creator in the days of your youth before the days of trouble come and the years approach when you will say, 'I take no pleasure in them'" (Eccles. 11:9, 12:1). Don't let the passions of youth make you nearsighted; keep the long view before you.

To state the obvious, as long as we can remember we've all been alive. It's hard to imagine being dead, not to mention unpleasant. Even the very old can look at their aging selves with incredulity. Generations before us weren't this squeamish about the subject, and they used to pray regularly that God would grant them a good death. Peter Kreeft has written movingly on how all prayer is a preparation for a good death. "Prayer is a rehearsal for death; prayer is a little death. For to pray is to enter God's presence, and to enter God's presence we must die.... This is a blessed death; we die to our own presence, our own I AM. We stop being our own god and let God be God.... Prayer is the preparation for the last turning to God... because in it we are not only taken out of ourselves but also into the presence of God. Prayer is heaven on earth."[1] You remember your Creator not only in the days of your youth but also in your old age when you pray.

PRAYER: *Our Lord and Creator, "teach us to number our days aright, that we may gain a heart of wisdom" (Ps. 90:12).*

DAY 129: PART OF THE PERMANENT

Ecclesiastes 12:9-14

"Now all has been heard; here is the conclusion of the matter: Fear God and keep his commandments, for this is the whole duty of man" (Eccles. 12:13).

J. B. Phillips' paraphrase of 1 John 2:15-17 is also a good New Testament paraphrase of the ending of Ecclesiastes:

> *Never give your hearts to this world or to any of the things in it. A man cannot love the Father and love the world at the same time. For the whole world-system, based as it is on men's primitive desires, their greedy ambitions and the glamour of all they think splendid, is not derived from the Father at all, but from the world itself. The word and all its passionate desires will one day disappear. But the man who is following God's will is part of the permanent and cannot die.*[1]

Only God lasts. We won't, and the things that so attract us won't. The rational choice then, the realistic decision, is to do God's will. So much in life is really beyond our control and a striving after the wind, "sound and fury, signifying nothing." Here is one thing we can build on and bank on, the one real choice we can make to do something of eternal consequence—the will of God. Nothing else we do can make us "part of the permanent."

The resurrection of Jesus Christ from the dead proves it. It is the final answer to the cry, "Meaningless! Meaningless!…Utterly meaningless! Everything is meaningless" (Eccles. 1:2).

When the perishable has been clothed with the imperishable, and the mortal with immortality, then the saying that is written will come true: 'Death has been swallowed up in victory. Where, O death, is your victory? Where, O death, is your sting?'… Therefore, my dear brothers, stand firm. Let nothing move you. Always give yourself fully to the work of the Lord because you know that your labor in the Lord is not in vain. (1 Cor. 15:54-55, 58)

PRAYER: *"Grant, O Lord, that we may live in thy fear, die in thy favor, rest in thy peace, rise in thy power, reign in thy glory; for thine own beloved Son's sake, Jesus Christ our Lord." (William Laud).*[2]

Introduction to the Song of Songs

DAY 130: LOVE IS STRONGER THAN DEATH

"For love is as strong as death" (Song of Songs 11:7).

"As a bridegroom rejoices over his bride, so will your God rejoice over you" (Isa. 62:5). If you have never thought of God looking at you as his beloved, you should because he does. "The Bible is about marriage," wrote David Hubbard.[1] In the very beginning there is a wedding, the union of the first man and first woman, naked but not ashamed (Gen. 2:23-25). At the end, when history is consummated, there is a huge wedding feast (Rev. 19:7-9). In between the beginning and the end, God's relationship with his people is underlined with marriage metaphors. Hosea must faithfully love and stay married to the strumpet Gomer as a picture of what God must endure with Israel. Jesus is the Bridegroom whom his friends should enjoy as long as he is with them (Matt. 9:14-15; 25:1-13; John 3:29). Human marriage is the chief New Testament metaphor for God's marriage to his church (Eph. 5:21-33).

In the middle of the Bible, nestled between the Law and the Prophets, is a little book that does nothing else but celebrate the pleasure, joy, communion, and ecstasy of sexual love in marriage. Other parts of the Bible have much to say about the seriousness of the marriage covenant. Only Song of Songs says it is fun—in great, playful detail. Some of its images and metaphors are not suitable for children. It contains no hymns, liturgy, oracles, or visions—just love songs.

Song of Songs is lighthearted, but not light-headed. It will make you yearn and blush and smile, but it will also make you think and rethink the love of God that created marriage. To pray its themes is to be awakened to new dimensions of what it means to be part of the church, the bride of Christ. Some of these ideas you may not be ready for. All point to the center of the faith we confess, that the love which went to a cross "is as strong as death, its jealousy unyielding as the grave. It burns like a mighty fire, like a mighty flame (Song of Songs 8:6).

PRAYER: *The earth is filled with your love, O Lord; teach me your decrees (Ps. 119:64).*

DAY 131: PASSION AND RESTRAINT

Song of Songs 2:7

"Do not arouse or awaken love until it so desires" (Song of Songs 2:7; 3:5; 8:4).

The three times this plea for restraint appears in Song of Songs, it is preceded by language of intense sexual excitement and longing. Space doesn't allow for exposition of the many images used, but two will illustrate. The man says his beloved is "like a mare harnessed to one of the chariots of Pharaoh" (Song of Songs 1:9). A mare is a female horse, and Pharaoh's army didn't use them; his horses were all male horses. Anyone familiar with animal husbandry knows the effect the presence of a female horse has on male horses. It can be nothing short of pandemonium. The man's compliment may not appeal to modern tastes, but his expression of appreciation for her sexual attractiveness is vivid and definite. She not only looks good to him, but to others also! For her, he is like "a sachet of myrrh resting between my breasts" (Song of Songs 1:13). Her image is a little more genteel than his, but no less vivid. That is what he is to her and what she wants him to be, literally. To repeat, these are but two of many images of sexual excitement and longing, and not even the most graphic.

Unmarried couples who feel this way about each other have a hard time keeping their hands off each other which is exactly what the Song urges them to do, until marriage. The experience of love-making is too powerful, too consuming, to stir up until the lovers are ready; and no couple is ready until they are ready to make the lifelong covenant of fidelity and love we call marriage. The call for restraint is for the sake of sexual joy. In Song of Songs 2:7, the couple is charged by a solemn oath, "by the gazelles and by the does," to hold back. These creatures are symbols of passion (see Song of Songs 4:5; 7:3). The point is this: for the sake of all you desire sexually, be restrained sexually. Sexual restraint is pro-sex, not anti-sex.

Our prayers for the unmarried must be fed by this perspective. So should our encouragements for them to be pure. Also, a good way to pray for sexual purity is to pray with thanksgiving for the gift of sex and with praise to the God who gave it.

PRAYER: *Dear Father, our sexuality was your good idea; may we always be thankful and respectful of what you gave. And may we show our thanks by living lives of purity and holiness so that love may be aroused and awakened when it desires!*

DAY 132: THE POWER OF LOVE

Song of Songs 8:6-7

"Place me like a seal over your heart" (Song of Songs 8:6).

Lovers sometimes ask each other, "How much do you love me?" The greatest answer is, "I love you enough to marry you." These two verses speak of marital love as the most powerful and indomitable of all human affections. It asks to be placed "like a seal over your heart." A seal was the personal stamp, the image pressed by a signet ring into the wax, that sealed and guaranteed the contents of the scroll to be the owner's. "Let me be pressed into your heart that way," is what marital love asks.

To love someone enough to marry is to commit to a kind of love that "is as strong as death." Death is total—one can't be a little bit, or mostly, dead. Either you are dead or you're not. Death is final—the dead have no further plans for themselves, no more options. Death is irreversible—there is no turning back. Only death, physical or spiritual, can separate a husband and a wife. Death is permanent and so is love. "Love never fails.... And now these three remain: faith, hope and love. But the greatest of these is love" (1 Cor. 13:8, 13).

Someone asked Jesus, "How much do you love me?" He replied, "This much," and then he stretched out his arms and died. Other kinds of human love are compared to the love of Christ, friendship being one of them (John 15:14). But marital love has special status as the most characteristic of God's love for his church. The Bible is indeed a book about marriage.

The text doesn't mention how mundane the arena in which this powerful love is lived out. It's easy to see love in daydreams about a future spent together. It's harder to recognize amid diapers, packed schedules, sickness, disappointment, and misunderstanding. That is where prayer becomes so important, because prayer is mundane too. Like marital love, so much of prayer is just being there, showing up day by day. It too is a daily kind of dying to the kingdom of self.

PRAYER: *My dear Savior, you have set me like a seal over your heart. Your love for us is even stronger than death. All praise and honor be to your holy name! Strengthen us to love each other this way.*

DAY 133: GOD GUIDES

Mary Geegh (1898-1999)

"Speak, Lord, for your servant is listening" (1 Sam. 3:10).

The whole practice of prayerful listening was a brand-new idea to the missionary to India.

Mary Geegh had just determined to listen to God for guidance in everything. She would ask the Lord to lead her in the specific situations she brought to him and wait quietly for him to speak. She would then write down what she heard in a notebook and do it, whatever it was. But one particular response was a stretch. In her morning prayers, Mary had asked God what she should do to dissolve the critical feeling she had toward another woman in the village. The thought came, "Take her a fresh egg." That didn't sound like divine guidance to her; it seemed like foolishness. Why not take her a dozen eggs? Why just one? Wouldn't she be insulted? So, Mary wrote it down in the notebook but wrote it off in her mind.

She went to teach her classes at the mission school and came home for lunch. When she walked into her house, she saw in her living room a chicken perched on the armchair. The hen flew down, and Mary saw on the armchair a freshly laid egg! She remembered what she had heard that morning and written in her notebook. But she still argued with God. Mary said, "She'll laugh at me." God said, "Results are not your business. Your business is obedience." So, Mary took the egg to the woman's house and gave it to her little boy to take to her.

That evening the woman came to her house and asked, "How did you happen to bring that egg? It was so fresh and good." She explained that her family had not had enough to eat that morning, and she hadn't eaten anything that day. The appearance of that one egg later in the day was for her a clear sign of God's love. She ate it and was deeply satisfied. From that day on the tension was gone between the two women.

Mary first learned this method of guidance from another missionary, Dr. L. R. Scudder. After seeing the remarkable way Dr. Scudder was led by the Holy Spirit in his ministry, she asked him, "How do I begin to have the power of the Holy Spirit, to help people?" He replied, "The first step is to 'wait'…'be still'…'listen.' Then be *definite* about your sins—daily; with notebook and pencil, write down the things the Holy Spirit speaks to your mind; determine to obey. Then share with others who come to you for help how the power of Christ changes you."

Mary Geegh practiced quiet listening and obedience for the rest of her life until she died at the age of 101 years. Many of her experiences of guidance are recorded in a little book she titled simply, *God Guides*. Some of the stories are astonishing, and all are vivid demonstrations of how God delights to sweetly lead a humble servant who will listen and obey.[1]

PRAYER: *"Speak, Lord, for your servant is listening" (1 Sam. 3:10).*

Introduction to Isaiah

DAY 134: "HERE IS YOUR GOD!"

"To whom, then, will you compare God" (Isa. 40:18).

Lord Kenneth Clark, the narrator of *Civilization*, once told a reporter, "I still go the Chartres Cathedral each year and to the Parthenon every three years. Very good. Keeps your standards high." What is true of Chartres and the Parthenon is true in spades of God. To gaze steadily and lovingly at the God of Scripture is to raise one's standards of what is true and good and lovely. Our standards will never be higher than our view of God. Nor will our lives.

Isaiah has been called the theologian of the Old Testament because of his exalted descriptions of God. His call came out of a stunning and profoundly unsettling vision of God's holiness (Isa. 6). Isaiah 40 is one of the greatest proclamations of the grandeur of God in prophetic literature. But with all his apprehension of God's greatness, Isaiah is a pastor-theologian who is able to see the practical implications of serving such a God. Many have found hope and encouragement by praying passages from Isaiah. To renew his sense of call, a dispirited pastor once hiked through the Grand Canyon memorizing and praying Isaiah 40. He was never the same after that time.

Isaiah's consciousness, like all the prophets, placed him in a universe dominated by the presence of God. In this sense, they were the most blessedly unbalanced of people. They were like magnifying glasses, held at just the right angle to focus the light of the sun most intensely on one spot. They were spiritual arsonists, starting fires when they spoke. Their prophecies ignited the people and culture of their day and do so even now. Read and pray the prophets at your own risk; it doesn't take much exposure to catch fire.

PRAYER: *"Then sings my soul, my Savior God to Thee, 'How great Thou art!'" (from the hymn "How Great Thou Art" translated by Stuart K. Hine)*

DAY 135: HOLY TERROR

Isaiah 6:1-7

"I saw the Lord" (Isa. 6:1).

Why should Isaiah's awe-filled experience of God's holiness matter to you? First, God's holiness is his most essential quality, more essential than even his love and justice. Holy is the word that modifies everything else. His love is a holy love; his justice is holy justice. We cannot understand God's love until we understand his holiness. God's holiness is his distinct and unapproachable otherness, morally and spiritually.

Second, Jesus said the first thing we should pray for is that we and others would know and honor God's holiness. "Hallowed" is an old word for holy. "May your name be hallowed," means, "may your name be held as holy, regarded and spoken and worshiped as holy."

Third, holiness is not only God's essential quality, but it is also our calling. "Just as he who called you is holy, so be holy in all you do; for it is written, 'Be holy, because I am holy'" (1 Pet. 1:15-16). Our calling to be holy should create a tension in us that is both terrifying and thrilling. The terrifying part is that we are not holy, as Isaiah so shatteringly realized. But we are called to be what we are not—yet! That is the thrilling part, for just as the seraphs flew to Isaiah with a live coal from the altar and touched it to his lips, so God wills to make us holy. The saying that God loves us just as we are, but too much to let us stay the way we are is exactly true.

> *To ask that God's love should be content with us as we are is to ask that God should cease to be God: because he is what he is, his love must, in the nature of things, be impeded and repelled by certain strains in our present character, and because he already loves us he must labor to make us lovable.... Love may forgive all infirmities and love still in spite of them: but Love cannot cease to will their removal. Love is more sensitive than hatred itself to every blemish of the beloved.... Of all powers he forgives most, but he condones least: he is pleased with little, but demands all.*[1]

PRAYER: *Holy Father! You have called me to be holy because I belong to you. May it be so; you have my trembling permission to make me so.*

DAY 136: TESTING GOD'S GOODNESS

Isaiah 7:10-14

"I will not put God to the test" (Isa. 7:12).

There are two ways to put God to the test, both are bad because it's always bad to put God to the test. The first way is to say to God, "I won't trust you until you show you can be trusted." This is what happened in the desert when God tested his people to see if they would trust him for water, but the people in turn tested God. The people had grumbled a lot in the wilderness, but they found God to be faithful, and presumably, they had grown in faith. Now, at Massah, he expands the frontiers of their faith by forcing them to trust him for water, too. Not a big test, one would think, but still a test: Was God only a god of food? Was he also a god of water? The people flunked their test by putting God to the test (Exod. 17:2). They grumbled and complained so much that their sin was memorialized in two psalms (Ps. 81:7-8; 95:9). They wouldn't trust God for water until he gave it. Their sin was unbelief.

The second way to put the Lord to the test is to do what Ahaz did in this text. God wanted to give Ahaz a sign of his love; so much so that Ahaz could ask for anything, and God would stop at nothing to give it, "whether in the deepest depths or in the highest heights" (Isa. 7:10). But Ahaz refused the offer, piously it seemed: "I will not ask; I will not put the Lord to the test" (Isa. 7:12). But this was in fact, testing God. Isaiah was disgusted: "Will you try the patience of my God also" (Isa. 7:13)? If Ahaz were to take God up on his offer, it would mean he would have to change his evil ways. The man was a scoundrel (cf. 2 Kings 16), and for him to trust God in this would be a kind of submission which would lead to submitting to God in other things. Ahaz's sin, like Israel's, was also unbelief.

The question of testing God is always in the forefront of prayer. We can test him by refusing to believe his promises. We can test him by having a mouth that says one thing and a heart that wants another. Ask yourself: What would I do or how would I be different if I fully experienced God's goodness to me? Could I keep living the way I have been?

PRAYER: *Gracious God! May I not insult you by refusing your love. Take away my love of sinning, that I may have room for you.*

DAY 137: DRINK, THANK, PRAY, AND PROCLAIM

Isaiah 12

"In that day you will say..." (Isa. 12:1).

There are four things we need to do with this song, all of which are sung about in the song. The first is simply to drink from the well of salvation (Isa. 12:3). It's a promise by none other than Jesus himself, that whoever believes in him will drink living water, and the water will become a spring of water welling up inside (John 4:10, 13-14). That is his extraordinary offer. Are you thirsty for something deeper and more satisfying than you have ever drunk? Drink of Jesus. The leader of no other world religion makes this offer; Jesus alone says he is the offer, not a law or a way or a code of morals. He desires to be a part of you, like water in your body—every cell nourished and refreshed.

The second thing we need to do is give thanks for the water. The language and means you use should be exuberant: "Give thanks... sing to the Lord... shout aloud and sing for joy" (Isa. 12:4, 5, 6). Karl Barth said grace elicits gratitude like the sound of an echo; that gratitude follows grace like thunder follows lightning. The bigger the lightning, the louder the thunder; the greater the grace, the greater the thanks.[1]

Third, we should "call on his name" (Isa. 12:4). That is biblical language for prayer and worship, but especially prayer though the two are easily separated. God so loved the world that he gave his only son that we might have eternal life. Eternal life is more that interminable life which would be horrible to contemplate. Eternal life is the life of God, which does last forever, but is so much more. It is the quality of life with God and in God. It is communion in the holy and loving fellowship of the Trinity. That is prayer in all its glory!

Fourth, we should proclaim God's goodness among the nations: "Make known among the nations what he has done... let this be known to all the world" (Isa. 12:4, 5). All our worship of the God who saves and satisfies us should point to missions. As John Piper puts it, "Worship is the fuel and goal of missions." The goal of missions, "is the gladness of the peoples in the greatness of God." But worship also fuels missions. "Passion for God in worship precedes the offer of God in preaching. You can't commend what you don't cherish."[2]

PRAYER: *Using this passage as a guide, write your own paraphrase as a prayer along these four themes: drink, thank, pray, and proclaim.*

DAY 138: ON THIS MOUNTAIN

Isaiah 25:6-9

"The Lord Almighty will prepare a feast of rich food for all people" (Isa. 25:6).

There is so much to hope for in these lines, and so much to pray for. If prayer is the means God has provided to give us what he wants, this vision of God's good future makes prayer the most joyous of activities. We may pray for the day when God will serve us at a great feast. This is what God wants to do: "On this mountain the Lord Almighty will prepare a feast of rich food" (Isa. 25:6). It is God's pleasure to serve us! The Son of Man did not come to be served, but to serve (Mark 10:45) because his Father has served from the beginning and will serve in the end. Amazing. If we won't let him serve us, we can have no part of him (John 13:8).

We may pray that the whole world will enjoy God's blessings. The feast is "for all peoples" on this mountain. This is underlined by the use of "peoples" (ethnicities), "nations" (political groupings), and "faces" (individuals). What began with a childless couple in the ancient Middle East will culminate in a blessing for the whole world. God's house was to be a house of prayer for all nations, Jesus said so (Mark 11:17). And no matter how his people failed to grasp that in the past, in the future it will be so (cf. Rev. 22:21-26).

We may pray for the end of death. God wills to "destroy the shroud that enfolds all peoples, the sheet that covers all nations; he will swallow up death forever" (Isa. 25:7-8). Death is now the Great Swallower (cf. Ps. 49:14), but proud death will be swallowed up! Paul partially quotes this verse in his resurrection manifesto in 1 Corinthians 15:55. It no doubt inspired poet John Donne to write some of his most famous lines,

Death be not proud, though some have called thee
Mighty and dreadful, for thou art not so....
One short sleep past, we wake eternally,
And death shall be no more; death thou shalt die.[1]

PRAYER: *Come, Lord, and call your people from east and west and north and south! Set the table and we will feast with you and with each other forever.*

DAY 139: BECAUSE HE TRUSTS IN YOU

Isaiah 26:3-4

"Trust in the Lord forever" (Isa. 26:4).

A great gospel counterpart and illustration of these two verses is the story of the time Jesus and his disciples were in a boat crossing the lake and were caught in a furious storm (Mark 4:35-41). The boat was being swamped, and the disciples were frantic. "But Jesus was in the stern, sleeping on a cushion." There you have it: perfect peace. And for the disciple's, perfectly irritating peace: "Teacher, don't you care if we drown?" You probably remember the rest of the story. Jesus was steadfastly asleep because he trusted his Father's power.

How could anyone be so calm when everything else was unraveling? Isaiah's explanation is: "You will keep in perfect peace him whose mind is steadfast *because he trusts in you*" (Isa. 26:3, italics added). Trust is at once the easiest and hardest thing to do. It's not complicated, because even (or especially) children get it. Trust is simply relinquishing your hold on things and letting God hold them. God is holding them anyway, so trying to hold them yourself is impossible. That's why not trusting God is so exhausting; it is our effort to control what can't be controlled. C. S. Lewis said coming to faith was like diving into a pool of water. It wasn't so much something he did, as something he stopped doing, holding on and holding back.

A little boy was trapped on the second floor of a house on fire. He stood at the window, surrounded by smoke and flames, crying for help. He heard his Daddy's voice below yelling for him to jump into his arms. "But I can't see you Daddy," he cried. His Daddy shouted back, "That's OK. I can see you so jump." We walk by faith, not by sight, do we not? Beneath us are the everlasting arms (Deut. 33:27). We need not fear what we see, because the One we cannot see has everything under control. "Trust in the Lord forever, for the Lord, the Lord, is the Rock eternal" (Isa. 26:4).

PRAYER: *Almighty God! You are the Rock eternal. You are the only one worthy of all my confidence. I believe, help me when I don't.*

DAY 140: THE LORD LONGS TO BE GRACIOUS TO YOU

Isaiah 30:15-18

"In repentance and rest is your salvation" (Isa. 30:15).

So often, the things God tells us to do seem counter-intuitive to our worldly minds. Here is one example. Judah is in a highly charged, military crisis that seems clearly to call for alliances, armaments, and fast horses. God describes with dead-on accuracy where that mentality will take them: the faster they run, the faster their enemies will run (Isa. 30:16). We know that's true, don't we? Have you ever experienced demands on your time that only seemed to increase the harder you worked? Have you lived out your own version of the Greek myth of Sisyphus? He was the man cursed by the gods to spend an eternity toiling and straining to push a giant boulder to the top of a hill, only to have it roll back to the bottom when he got to the top—over and over and over again, forever.

The Lord says there is a better way: "In repentance and rest is your salvation, in quietness and trust is your strength" (Isa. 30:15). The Hebrew word for strength is literally "warrior strength." The best way to be strong like a warrior is to stop trying to be strong the way a warrior gets strong. Let the Lord be your strength, for "the Lord longs to be gracious to you; he rises to show you compassion" (Isa. 30:18). God is not only more than able to help you, but he is also more than willing to help you. Even as you move in his direction, you will see him rising to meet you; like the waiting father in Jesus' story (Luke 15:20).

We live in an activist culture. We believe that no one should just stand there but should do something, anything. The worst thing to do is nothing. But very often, God's approach is the opposite. God says, "Call to me and I will answer you and tell you great and unsearchable things you do not know" (Jer. 33:3).

PRAYER: *In repentance and rest is my salvation, in quietness and trust is my strength. Thank you, Lord.*

DAY 141: A CANDLE BURNING BRIGHTLY

Robert Murray M'Cheyne (1813-1843)

"For to me to live is Christ and to die is gain" (Phil. 1:21).

All his life Robert Murray M'Cheyne seemed to move at an accelerated pace. At age four he taught himself to read and write the Greek alphabet. He began high school at age 8. At 14 he was admitted to Edinburgh University.

In college he was "of a lively turn," spending all of his free time dancing, card playing and enjoying music. It took the death of his beloved older brother to shake up Robert and get him to think about eternal things. M'Cheyne later wrote, "This day eleven years ago, I lost my loved and loving brother, and began to seek a Brother who cannot die."

M'Cheyne redirected his energies towards God and entered divinity school. At age twenty-three he answered the call to be a pastor at St. Peter's Church in Dundee, Scotland, "an honor to which I cannot name an equal." He involved himself heavily in the lives of the 4,000 souls of Dundee, preaching, writing, teaching and above all, praying for revival.

M'Cheyne believed the primary concern of a minister of God, or any Christian, was first their own soul. "Above all things, cultivate your own spirit," he wrote. "Your own soul is your first and greatest care. A word spoken by you when your conscience is clear, and your heart full of God's Spirit, is worth ten thousand words spoken in unbelief and sin. A holy minister is an awful weapon in the hand of God."

But how can Christians cultivate their own spirit? M'Cheyne believed that the answer was found in simple, unhurried communion with God. "The dew comes down when all nature is at rest—when every leaf is still," remarked M'Cheyne. "A calm hour with God is worth a whole lifetime with man. The work of God would flourish by us, if it flourished more richly in us." In a personal journal entry, he wrote, "February 23. Sabbath. Rose early to seek God and found Him whom my soul loveth. Who would not rise early to meet such company?"

Throughout his ministerial career M'Cheyne continued in intense study of the scriptures. His overwork contributed to ill health which included "violent heart palpitations" and subsequent weakness. Nevertheless, he continued his pastoral visits and evangelistic tours through rain and snow. As his health deteriorated, M'Cheyne saw in his physical condition a parable of the human condition. He told his people, "Every day that passes is drawing you nearer to the judgment seat. Not one of you is standing still." He became more urgent in his preaching, longing for a "deep, pure, widespread, and permanent work of God in Scotland."

Finally in the spring of 1843, he caught a fever. Many gathered outside St. Peter's church as he lay dying, and on March 25, 1843, he passed away. M'Cheyne was only 29 years old—"the candle that burns brightest burns shortest." But the impact of his calm hours with God is felt to this day.[1]

PRAYER: *Almighty God, let me be "an awful weapon in your hand." May all I do and say flow out of communion with you.*

DAY 142: LIKE AN EAGLE

Isaiah 40:31

"They will soar on wings like eagles" (Isa. 40:31).

Isaiah must have watched eagles closely to see the way they soar. As birds go, eagle's wings are big, but the muscles that make them flap aren't. Pound for pound, an eagle's strength is no match for the strength of a hummingbird and its thickly muscled chest and back. The strength of eagles is not in their flapping but in their soaring. An eagle will perch high atop a canyon wall and wait for the thermals—warm wind currents that rise up from the canyon below. When the rising wind is just right, the eagle will fold its wings to its side, literally cast itself into the chasm, and plummet into the abyss. Isaiah would not have known this in his day, but God has equipped eagles with tiny sensors in their beaks to let the bird know when it has reached the optimal speed. When it does, it will spread its wings, catch the thermals, climb up into the sky and soar. Isaiah didn't know the mechanism, but he could see the effect.

That is a great picture of hoping in God. Through no strength of our own, we cast ourselves upon God and fall into his mercy and soar on his promises. Our strength comes from trusting, not flapping.

To fully appreciate the power of this verse, read the entire fortieth chapter. The key sentence is, "To whom, then, will you compare God?" (Isa. 40:18). Isaiah's method is to use negative contrast to show God's incomparable majesty. He takes the things we already think to be great—the earth, the seas, nations, and the starry heavens—and shows them to be nothing compared to God. He has measured the waters in the hollow of his hand and held the dust of the earth in a basket. Before God, all the nations are like a drop in a bucket, and the stars trot out before him like obedient troops on the parade ground. This is the God into whose power we cast ourselves and soar, like an eagle!

PRAYER: *I hope in you, O Lord. Nothing can compare to you! In you I will trust and be strengthened and renewed. For you have promised this, and I believe your promise to be worthy of all my trust.*

DAY 143: CARPE DIEM

Isaiah 55

"Seek the Lord while he may be found; call on him while he is near" (Isa. 55:6).

"Seek the Lord while he can be found; call on him while he is near" (Isa. 55:6). Is there ever a time when you can't call on the Lord or when you don't find him near? No and yes. God's mercy is greater and wiser than we can ever imagine (No), but it is not infinite or indefinite (Yes). No one should presume to know when God's mercy has reached its limit; nor should anyone presume to say that it hasn't. Let God be God and the rest of us liars (Rom. 3:4); and let that make us humble and breathless with gratitude for the mercy we have known.

When Isaiah wrote this, it was a great moment in Judah's history, a window of opportunity, a *kairos* moment (see devotion on Day 80). The moment had come to them as an invitation to a banquet of gourmet food, something not to be missed (Isa. 55:1-2). But they might have missed it if they hadn't RSVP's the invitation. That's one way to think of prayer: as an RSVP. The meaning of the moment comes down to two Latin words: *carpe diem*—seize the moment. In other words, "Seek the Lord while he can be found; call on him while he is near."

For all of us who live between the times, in the *kairos* between the resurrection of Christ and the consummation of history, the message is the same: *carpe diem*. Call on the Lord while he may be found. "Now is the time of God's favor, now is the day of salvation" (2 Cor. 6:2). The great and gracious day will pass and with it our opportunity. Perhaps more to the point, our day will certainly pass too, our span of life, our moment to choose eternally. Death will come, and worse, we may die before we really live; our hearts may grow so dull and cold that we have all but missed the moment to choose God.

Prayer keeps you alive to the moment—God's moment for you. Calling on the Lord is not a one-time event, but an ongoing way of life. It is truly living in the moment, in the best sense of that phrase.

PRAYER: *Blessed Savior, thank you that this day and this season in the time of your favor. I rejoice in your grace and call on your name. Hallowed be your name.*

DAY 144: HE WON'T HEAR YOU

Isaiah 59:1-2

"Your sins have hidden his face from you, so that he will not hear" (Isa. 59:2).

"Your sins have hidden his face from you, so that he will not hear" (Isa. 59:1). "He can hear you, but he's not listening" is the way modern idiom might express this. The people have complained that God isn't answering their prayers. There are two schools of thought as to why this is so: One says he can't hear; the other says he can't do anything. Isaiah offers a third view: God won't hear. "Surely the arm of the Lord is not too short to save, nor his ear too dull to hear. But your iniquities have separated you from your God" (Isa. 59:1-2). God has heard everything they have to say, and he can do anything he wants, but he doesn't want to because of the way they are living.

Later in the chapter, to describe their condition, Isaiah nearly exhausts the Hebrew theological vocabulary for sin (Isa. 59:12). There are "offenses"—acts of rebellion that the Hebrews sometimes called "sins of the high hand." These are deliberate, "in your face," kinds of sin. There are simply "sins"—all the ways the people have fallen short and missed the mark including sins of weakness and of sloth. There are "iniquities"—wanton distortions and perversions of the true and the good. Sometimes these iniquities take the form of evil inversions where black becomes white, and upside-down becomes right-side-up. Together these three words make up a devastating indictment: the people have become so adept at all the ways of evil that they are sin-masters, experts in the art of living badly.

Therefore, when the people speak to God, he turns and looks the other way. "Your sins have hidden his face from you" (Isa. 59:2b). It is said that God hates the sin and loves the sinner. That is true, but with this important proviso: God loves the sinner, but he hates the sin the sinner does so much that he is offended by the sinner too. God's displeasure with sin goes beyond the grief that his beloved child is doing bad, self-destructive things. It includes grief, but it is also a holy anger at all that is repugnant to a holy God. His creature has committed treason; someone he made in his image has defiled his image. God is angry with the sinner.

This would be unbearably depressing were it not for God's eagerness to forgive those who confess and repent of their sins. "Christ died for sinners" means God turned his face from his Son, that he might once again turn his face toward us (2 Cor. 5:20-21).

PRAYER: *I have sinned against you, Holy Father. For the sake of your Son, turn your face back toward me. Forgive me and heal me, for Jesus' sake.*

DAY 145: THE LORD'S WATCH

Isaiah 62:6-7

"I have posted watchmen on your walls, O Jerusalem" (Isa. 62:6).

In prayer, God works on us by his grace, and allows us to work on him by our faith.[1] That he would give us this "dignity of causality"[2] is a mystery to make us rejoice, and above all, to pray. These verses add to the mystery: "I have posted watchmen on your walls, O Jerusalem: they will never be silent day or night. You who call on the Lord, give yourselves no rest, and give him no rest till he establishes Jerusalem and makes her the praise of the earth" (Isa. 62:6-7). God has posted his people like watchmen on the walls. He wants his watchmen to pester him until he gives them what he wants to give them.

The seventeenth century Moravians took this calling very seriously and established what they called, "The Lord's Watch," or *Herrnhut*, in German. It was a twenty-four-hour, seven-days-a-week prayer vigil that lasted, without interruption, for 100 years. During that time, this relatively small Christian fellowship sent out 2000 missionaries around the globe. It was at a Moravian prayer meeting that John Wesley felt his heart "strangely warmed" and came to know that he really belonged to Christ. The Wesleyan revivals owe much to persistent watchmen determined to pester God.

Beginning in the same century, a group of churches in Ipswich, Massachusetts also prayed without interruption for a century (see Day 120). It wasn't continuous around-the-clock praying, but it was a regular rhythm of weekly, monthly, and quarterly prayer meetings. During that period, most of New England's churches and seminaries became Unitarian. Under great spiritual pressure, the praying churches remained faithful to the historic Christian faith and experienced periodic revivals. The vigil ended during the Civil War. Less than five years later, the churches all lost their grip on the faith.

We are at war; the battle is spiritual. To not choose sides is to choose the wrong side. We fight it together on our knees. Edmund Burke's statement was about politics, but it applies to the Lord's watch too: "When bad men combine, the good must associate; else they will fall, one by one." God has posted us on the wall, has he not?

PRAYER: *Stir us to pray, Lord! Stir me, but also stir us—especially* us*—to give ourselves and you no rest until your kingdom comes and your name is revered in all the earth.*

DAY 146: COME DOWN, LORD!

Isaiah 64:1-12

"Oh, that you would rend the heavens and come down" (Isa. 64:1).

"We're in a terrible mess, it's all our fault and we're getting exactly what we deserve. But please Lord, come down and save us." That's the gist of the prayer in Isaiah 64.[1] It's a kind of prayer that appears many times in Scripture, perhaps also in your life. It's not that bad things are happening to good people, but that bad things are happening to bad people. Why even ask God to lighten up? We're bankrupt morally. We don't have a leg to stand on, so why not just suck it up and get into a stoic groove until the storm passes?

Isaiah doesn't do that. He does even more than ask God to lighten up; he prays, "Oh that you would rend the heavens and come down" (Isa. 64:1). And that's not all, he makes a strong case for why God should do this despite their guilt. Reason number one is that God has done it before: "Since ancient times no one has heard, no ear has perceived, no eye has seen any God besides you, who acts on behalf of those who wait for him" (Isa. 64:4). That may not seem a compelling reason for God to save them, except what God did in the past was his self-chosen way of showing his people the kind of God he is. Reason number two is that they are his people, in a very intimate sense: "Yet, O Lord, you are our Father. We are the clay; you are the potter; we are all the work of your hand. Oh, look upon us, we pray, for we are all your people" (Isa. 64:8-9). Again, as in reason number one, Isaiah is doing nothing more than remind God of his self-chosen relationship to his people: Father and potter. If they are ever to be good, it will be because he has shown the mercy of a father and the skill of a potter.

And here is something very important. Note that Isaiah's case for mercy has nothing to do with his or his people's good qualities or inner beauty. It is entirely about God's good qualities. He doesn't ask God to find the spark of good in them and to fan it into flame because there isn't any spark. The entire appeal is to God's goodness. It may seem a little audacious, but it is exactly the way God wants to be addressed for it is prayer in his name, according to his character.

PRAYER: *"We do not make requests of you because we are righteous, but because of your great mercy. O Lord, listen! O Lord, forgive! O Lord, hear and act! For your sake, O my God, do not delay, because your city and your people bear your Name" (Dan. 9:18-19).*

DAY 147: WRESTLING WITH GOD

Peter Taylor Forsyth (1848-1921)

"Then the man said, 'Your name will no longer be Jacob, but Israel, because you have struggled with God and with men and have overcome'" (Gen. 32:28).

The Roman Catholic writer Carlo Carretto did not trust theologians who do not pray; presumably because the great temptation of theological inquiry is to reduce Almighty God to an object for study. Prayer is the great antidote to this presumption because true prayer is loving, humble communion with a Person.

In this sense, Peter Taylor Forsyth was the ideal theologian for he was a theologian who loved to pray and who wrote lovingly and wisely about prayer.

Forsyth believed prayer was so central to the health of the Christian life that "The worst sin is prayerlessness. Overt sin… [is] the effect of this, or its punishment. We are left by God for lack of seeking him."[1]

Forsyth was also a pastor. He believed that one had to spend time with people in order to know their problems and to spend time with God in order to solve them. It is this combined perspective of pastor and theologian that make *The Soul of Prayer* so helpful. As theologian, Forsyth writes thoughtfully on the mysteries of prayer; as pastor, he speaks to hearts in meaningful and practical ways.

Only a pastor/theologian could have written as creatively as Forsyth did about what it means to wrestle with God in prayer. Forsyth hated resignation and fatalism in prayer, believing that sometimes to resist the will of God is to do the will of God if what we resist is what God has willed to be temporary and intermediary—poor health, a bad job, a difficult marriage, for instance. It may be God's will that you be in these circumstances but not that you stay in them. "He has a lower will and a higher, a prior and a posterior. And the purpose of the lower will is that it be resisted and struggled through to the higher"[2] Wrestling in prayer from the lower to the higher is one of God's chief means of educating our spirits.

"Resist God, in the sense of rejecting God, and you will not be able to resist any evil. But resist God in the sense of closing with God, cling to him with all your strength, not your weakness only, with your active and not only your passive faith, and he will give you strength. Cast yourself into his arms not to be caressed but to wrestle with him. He loves that holy war. He may be too many for you and lift you from your feet. But it will be to lift you from earth, and set you in the heavenly places which are theirs who fight the good fight and lay hold of God as their eternal life."[3]

PRAYER: *Dear Father, you are my only hope; I have no place to go but to you. Your Son said to pray and not give up (Luke 18:1). Jacob would not let go of you until you blessed him (Gen. 32:22-32). Strengthen me to pray this way—with tenacity, grit, and strong faith!*

Introduction to Jeremiah

DAY 148: "I HAVE MADE YOU AN IRON PILLAR."

"Why is my pain unending and my wound grievous and incurable?" (Jer. 15:18).

Jewish tradition has it that Jeremiah was stoned to death in Egypt. If he was, it could not have been a more fitting end to his career as a prophet: killed by his own people in a place he didn't want to be. From the beginning, Jeremiah struggled with his call to be a prophet, once even accusing God of bullying and seducing him into his service (Jer. 20:7). He was rejected by his own people in every way, from mockery, ridicule and slander to death threats and false imprisonment. Even his own family plotted against him (Jer. 12:6). God's words to Jeremiah, "before you were born I set you apart" (Jer. 1:5), were true in every way. He lived and died lonely and set apart.

Jeremiah was not like Jesus who lovingly embraced his Father's will all the way to the cross without bitterness and complaint. But Jeremiah suffered like Jesus who was a man of sorrows and acquainted with grief; one from whom men hide their faces. Jesus was rejected by his own, and his worst enemies came from his own household (Mark 6:1-6). Jesus was threatened with death by the priests of Jerusalem and led to the cross as a lamb to the slaughter. But through it all he knew how to weep and pray and cling to God in racking sorrow (Matt. 26:36-44; 17:46; Heb. 5:7). Jesus is our model of prayer in extremity, and Jeremiah is our mirror.

We should learn to pray like Jesus when in trouble. The truth is, we often pray like Jeremiah—angry, despondent, and despairing. But in his own way, Jeremiah gives us hope by showing us that God takes reluctant and morose people and does great things with them, even though for a season they see no great things for themselves (Jer. 45:5). Best of all, God hears their prayers.

PRAYER: *Gracious and compassionate Father in heaven, thank you for your servant, Jeremiah, but teach me to suffer less like Jeremiah and more like Jesus.*

DAY 149: DIVINE CONSTRAINT

Jeremiah 1:1-19

"Get yourself ready! Stand up and say to them whatever I command you. Do not be terrified by them, or I will terrify you before them" (Jer. 1:17).

Jeremiah did not look back on the day he was called to be a prophet with warm sentiment the way we might keep a photo or a copy of the church bulletin from the day of our baptism. Sometimes, he wished God's call to be a prophet had never happened. "O lord, you deceived me, and I was deceived; you overpowered me and prevailed.... The word of the Lord has brought me insult and reproach all day long" (Jer. 20:7, 8). Jeremiah's call was not the culmination of a career path he had been on since he began school. It was a matter of divine constraint.

Jeremiah's call wasn't his idea, but it was God's will even before Jeremiah was born. God formed Jeremiah in his mother's womb for this purpose. God's call was intensely personal: he reached out and put the word in Jeremiah's mouth. Jeremiah was a receiver like we all must be. Medieval artists often portrayed the impregnating Spirit entering the virgin Mary through her ear. It wasn't that they were naïve about the way women get pregnant. They were saying that the entrance of the life of God into a human heart always comes through hearing the word of God. Like Jeremiah, like Mary, like you. Once the word comes in, it must come out. Jeremiah had to speak what he heard, even when it made his life miserable. He couldn't hold it in even if he tried; and he tried to hold it in but couldn't. It was like a fire shut up in his bones: "I am weary of holding it in; indeed, I cannot" (Jer. 20:9).

At times, God seemed a bully to Jeremiah, but ultimately, he knew better. God was like the lion, Aslan, in C. S. Lewis' story. When Lucy first heard of him from Mr. and Mrs. Beaver, she wanted to know if he was safe. "'Safe?' said Mr. Beaver, 'Who said anything about safe? 'Course he isn't safe. But he's good. He's the King, I tell you.'"[1] To enter the communion of prayer with a God like this may sometimes soothe you, but don't be surprised if it sometimes upsets you. You may not always like what you hear—ask Jeremiah. God isn't safe, but he is good, and everything he does is good.

PRAYER: *Lord, I am not my own, for I was purchased by the precious blood of Christ. So even when I can't understand your commands, I'll trust your love anyway.*

DAY 150: WHEN GOD FORBIDS PRAYER

Jeremiah 7:16; 11:14; 14:10-17; 15:1-2

"So do not pray for this people, do not offer any plea for them or petition for them; do not plead with me, for I will not listen to you" (Jer. 7:16; 11:14; 14:11; 15:1).

Sometimes television ads for automobiles will show cars being driven recklessly through mountain passes and busy city streets to demonstrate what marvels of modern engineering they are in speed and handling. A caption will appear at the bottom of the screen indicating that the cars were driven by professional drivers. The message is "You shouldn't try to drive your car this way." Only the experts under carefully controlled situations may drive like this. This text from Jeremiah is like that. What are we to make of God forbidding Jeremiah to pray for the people, not once, but four times? Obviously, one should not carelessly and simplistically apply this command to just anyone. Whenever we meet some particularly vile and recalcitrant sinner, we might be tempted to write them off. Reading these texts raises a speculation: did the early church pray for the infamous Saul, their oppressor, or had they written him off their prayer lists—only to be amazed to see God make him Paul, the apostle?

The probable meaning of the command was for Jeremiah not to pray any longer that they be spared the Babylonian onslaught. The people were too far gone, and God had made up his mind about their punishment. Jeremiah wasn't to pray for that, but no doubt he could pray for other things: like the fulfillment of God's promise that they one day be restored under a new covenant (Jer. 31:31-34).

What's the point for us? God may reveal to you that you are to stop praying for something you have been specifically praying for. Maybe the prayer has been for a healing; although again, we should be very cautious about things like that. There are far more prayers cut short by impatience and lack of faith than prayers that were stretched out too long. The greater lesson is that prayer is not our attempt to get God to do what we want, but the means he has given to give us what he wants. Most of what Jesus has to say about prayer is to persist in prayer that God's will be done; not to stop praying since he's going to do what he wants to do anyway! Usually, we won't know what God's will is until we persist.

PRAYER: *Father, your will alone is good; may your good will be done. It is your will that I persist in prayer (Luke 18:1-8). So help me to keep on praying until you say otherwise.*

DAY 151: CORRECT ME, LORD

Jeremiah 10:23-25

"Correct me Lord, but only with justice" (Jer. 10:24).

Jeremiah prayed this prayer on behalf of his people. He said "me," but he meant "us." It's a good way to pray for other believers when they have sinned. Ezra did this, as did many of the pray-ers of the Old Testament (see devotion on Ezra 9:6-15). The sins and needs of others may not be exactly your own, or not at all your own, but we belong to each other as members of Christ's body. Praying this way reminds us of that solidarity. It is a concrete way to bear one another's burdens and so fulfill the law of Christ in prayer (Gal. 6:2). Many Jews around the world still pray these verses at Passover, speaking in the first person, but meaning everyone. Pray corporately in this way, and it will keep your prayers from condescension and pride. And who knows? You may need for yourself the very things you pray for others.

As you pray corporately, pray submissively: "I know, O Lord, that a man's life is not his own; it is not for a man to direct his steps" (Jer. 10:23). Praying submissively reminds us of whom our loved ones belong to as we pray for them. They are the Lord's, and not a hair can fall from their head without the will of their heavenly Father. Whatever he desires is best and it will be done. We go astray whenever we act as though we are the ones who direct our steps. The first step in being set straight is to let God do what only he can do well: direct our steps (Ps. 25:4-5).

Finally, affirm what God wills to do correct you (or those for whom you are praying). Jeremiah's prayer is sweet. He wants the Lord's correction, he really does, but he prays that it won't be too harsh to bear: "Correct me, Lord, but only with justice—not in your anger, lest you reduce me to nothing" (Jer 10:24). In praying this way, we aren't trying to get God to do something better or different. We are learning to pray in line with who God is—in his name and according to his character. We are learning to want better for others than we otherwise would have. God always tempers his justice with mercy, and he wounds only in order to heal. He is delighted when we pray this way for each other.

PRAYER: *Father, forgive us our debts as we forgive our debtors, for we do not live only unto ourselves, but unto you and each other.*

DAY 152: RUN WITH THE HORSES

Jeremiah 12:1-17

"Why does the way of the wicked prosper?" (Jer. 12:1).

A paraphrase of Jeremiah's prayer might go like this: "You're good, God, after all, you are God. So don't get me wrong. But I know a few things about goodness too, and there are some things I think you need to explain; like the way you seem to have blessed these scoundrels, and let me, your servant, suffer." Poet Gerard Manley Hopkins wrote a paraphrase of this prayer, too. One of his lines said something like, "With friends like you, who needs enemies?"

Wert thou mine enemy, O thou my friend,
How wouldst thou worse, I wonder,
than thou dost Defeat, thwart me?[1]

The glory of the gift of prayer is that God lets us speak to him that way! But the gift also includes the privilege of hearing him answer what we say. Prayer is a two-way conversation. God's answer to Jeremiah's complaint is to put it in perspective, and none too gently. The first perspective is, "You think this is bad? You haven't seen anything, yet." God says, "If you have raced with men on foot and they have worn you out, how can you compete with horses?" (Jer. 12:5). The message is: Jeremiah better brace himself for more of what he doesn't like. He will need encouragement from the next two perspectives to do that.

The second perspective is seeing God's own pain in the mess. "I will give the one I love into the hands of her enemies. My inheritance has become to me like a lion in the forest. She roars at me; therefore, I hate her" (Jer. 12:8). God's suffering is always greater and truer than ours because his love is greater and truer. The purer the love, the keener the pain when the beloved goes astray. Jeremiah's suffering is just a part of God's suffering. But if he chooses, his suffering can make him a participant, a partner with God in his (cf. Phil. 3:10).

The third perspective is the perspective of hope: "But after I uproot them, I will again have compassion and bring each of them back to his own inheritance and his own country" (Jer. 12:15). Things will get worse before they get better, but the worse is not worth comparing to the better (Rom. 8:18). Prayer is nourished in hope.

God's words to Jeremiah call us to a "muscular" faith that can "run with horses." But his words also remind us of who we run with and where we running to.

PRAYER: *Thank you, Lord, for listening to each of my complaints but not caving to them. Strengthen me to run with the horses.*

DAY 153: THE DIVINE AMEN

Jeremiah 16:19-21

"Then they will know that my name is the Lord" (Jer. 16:21).

This is a different kind of prayer than the one Jeremiah prayed in 12:1-4; and a different kind of answer from God. Jeremiah's prayer life is full of stops and starts, ups and downs. Prayer, like faith, is not a quiet, placid retreat into a quiet, little, happy place in your heart. It can be quiet, and it can be happy, but it is first a relationship of trust that is forged amid the pressure of a struggle against relentless enemies: the devil, the world, and our own sinfulness. Prayer is ever the same, ever changing.

Jeremiah continues to suffer under the hatred and rejection of his own people. Nothing has changed. His generation is doomed to destruction. But he is buoyed up by two great things. First, he knows God is his only hope, "my strength and my fortress, my refuge in time of distress" (Jer. 16:19a). Second, he has a bigger vision of God's purposes—and an older vision. "To you the nations will come from the ends of the earth and say, 'Our fathers possessed nothing but false gods, worthless idols that did them no good'" (Jer. 16:19b). As bad as things are now, there is a glorious future coming in which the nations, all the peoples of the earth will repent of their idolatry and come to the Lord. God's chosen people are now just like the nations, idolaters doomed to destruction. But God's promise to Abram to make his descendants a blessing to the world will come true (Jer. 12:1-2). In his prayer, Jeremiah is thinking God's thoughts after him.

And again, God comes right back at him as he did in 12:1-5, but not with a rebuke. This time. God says a kind of divine "Amen!" The Lord so thoroughly agrees with Jeremiah's hope he says, "Therefore I will teach them—this time I will teach them my power and might. Then they will know that my name is the Lord" (Jer. 16:21). This kind of praying is deeply satisfying. To hope in the Lord, to pray this hope, and to feel the divine "Amen," is a joy unparalleled and all too rare in prayer. God wants us to want what he wants. Then he wants us to ask for what we want; and he loves to say, "Yes! It shall be done."

PRAYER: *Great God, Almighty Savior! You are all I need, and the coming of your kingdom is all I want. Come, Lord, save your people and show us your glory.*

DAY 154: YOU LIED, LORD!

Jeremiah 20:7-18

"O Lord, you deceived me, and I was deceived; you overpowered me and prevailed" (Jer. 20:7).

Have you ever spoken to God this way, or were you tempted to and backed off for fear you might be struck by lightning? The verb translated "deceived" is literally "seduced," or "enticed." Other synonyms would be tricked, fooled, and misled. Is that what God did to Jeremiah?

Looking back at Jeremiah's call, God was quite frank with Jeremiah. He said it would be hard, and he would have to stand against the whole nation, but God would make him strong to stand (Jer. 1:17-19). There were no false pretenses there. Maybe what took Jeremiah by surprise was how it felt to stand against the whole nation. Maybe he wasn't ready for the ridicule and mockery (Jer. 20:8). It's one thing to suffer great hardship and to be thought of as brave and heroic; it's another thing to be considered a fool and made the butt of jokes. Jeremiah was ready to be hated as a warrior but not laughed at as a buffoon. Whatever the reasons, Jeremiah feels this is not what he had signed up for, and he wants out. But he can't get out. "But if I say, 'I will not mention him or speak any more in his name,' his word is in my heart like a fire, a fire shut up in my bones. I am weary of holding it in; indeed, I cannot" (Jer 20:9).

What are we to make of this prayer? One thing that stands out is how little God seems to be offended by it. At the very least, it must be permissible to speak to God this way. Jeremiah is wrong about the facts of the situation, but he is right about how he feels, and that is good enough reason to speak. What matters most to God is not that we address him "correctly," but that we speak honestly. It's the relationship that matters to Almighty God. The worst that can happen is that we go silent and cold with the Lord. He can hold his own with our anger, and when he deems the time to be right, he can set us straight. Look at what he did with Job (Jer. 38:1-2; 40:1-8). So, speak your mind, hang in with God, and know that he will not turn you away, even if you think he has turned you away.

PRAYER: *Dear Father, sometimes the things I feel about you aren't nice or right, but I feel them anyway. Thank you that I matter enough to you for you to allow me to say them. Thank you that you hang in with me, even when I don't want to hang in with you.*

DAY 155: GOD PLUS ONE

Mary Slessor (1848-1915)

"The angel of the Lord encamps around those who fear him, and he delivers them" (Ps. 34:7).

Mary Slessor, a single woman and a missionary to the Sudan, once put herself directly between two tribal armies about to fight and demanded that they lay down their arms. At the end of the day the determined, little redhead stood by a pile of weapons five feet high!

From childhood, the odds had been stacked against Mary Mitchell Slessor. Her mother worked long shifts as a weaver while her alcoholic father drank away the money and terrified the children with his unstable lifestyle. At age eleven, Mary was forced to leave school and begin working twelve-hour shifts in a factory. Yet the harsh conditions of her childhood didn't break her spirit. She volunteered her time teaching Sunday school in the slums, was active in the Presbyterian Church, and secretly dreamed of becoming a missionary. In 1874, the death of David Livingstone set off a wave of missionary zeal through Scotland, and Mary volunteered for missionary service in the Sudan.

Twelve years into her service there she discovered a horrifying practice of the Okyong people. The Okyongs believed that if a woman gave birth to twins, one of them was the result of intercourse with a demon. It was common practice to leave newborn twins outside the village in clay pots, to be eaten by ants or to die of neglect. There was only one thing to do. Mary built a hut for herself out of sticks and mud and immediately began caring for abandoned twins, sometimes pulling them right out of trash heaps outside the villages. Soon her hut became an orphanage, a tangled web of hammocks and cradles all connected with string so she could rock them all at once while she prayed or read.

Slessor saved the lives of hundreds of orphans. She eventually became a district tribal judge and was awarded the Order of the Hospital of St. John of Jerusalem. All this mostly embarrassed her, and she dismissed it as a bunch of "blarney." Mary died on January 13, 1915.

Among the many remarkable things in this remarkable woman's life is her attitude toward prayer. Though every inch an activist, she believed prayer was the foundation of all activity. She wrote,

> *My life is one long daily, hourly, record of answered prayer. For physical health, for mental overstrain, for guidance given marvelously, for errors and dangers averted, for enmity to the Gospel subdued, for food provided at the exact hour needed, for everything that goes to make up life and my poor service.... I can testify with a full and often wonder-stricken awe that I... know God answers prayer.... Prayer is the greatest power God has put into our hands for service. Praying is harder work than doing... but the dynamic lies that way to advance the kingdom... Pray on—power lies that way.*[1]

PRAYER: *Make this prayer of Mary Slessor your own: "God plus one is always a majority—let me know that Thou art with me."*

DAY 156: NOTHING IS TOO HARD FOR YOU

Jeremiah 32:1-44

"After I had given the deed of purchase to Baruch... I prayed to the Lord" (Jer. 32:16).

"Buy low, sell high," is a good rule-of-thumb for investors in stocks and real estate. Making more and losing less is the object of any wise purchase. Something like that is in the back of Hanamel's mind as he goes to Jeremiah's house with an offer that Jeremiah really can't refuse. According to the laws of ancient Israel (cf. Lev. 25:25-28), Jeremiah, as the nearest relative, must buy the property Hanamel wants to unload. Perhaps the impending Babylonian crisis has made real estate values drop in Jerusalem, and Hanamel wants to liquidate this asset before values get even lower. Whatever his reason, it's a mean thing, given Jeremiah's imprisonment, for Hanamel to put this kind of pressure on his nephew.

But what Hanamel means for evil, God means for good. The Lord reveals to Jeremiah what Hanamel is going to do, and he tells him to buy the property, seal the deeds, and put them in a clay jar so they will last a long time. This will be a sign of hope, says the Lord; for even though Jerusalem will be destroyed in judgment, the day will come when "houses, fields and vineyards will again be bought in the land" (Jer. 32:15). Jeremiah makes the purchase with joy and enthusiasm, praying, "Ah, Sovereign Lord, you have made the heavens and the earth by your great power and outstretched arm. Nothing is too hard for you" (Jer 32:17). God agrees and answers with a rhetorical question, "I am the Lord, the God of all mankind. Is anything too hard for me" (Jer. 32:26)? Jeremiah turns out to be the wiser investor. For a pittance of faith, and few shekels, he gained a goldmine of hope (1 Pet. 1:4-5).

"Nothing is too hard for you." The next time we hear this said in Scripture will be centuries later when the angel Gabriel appears to a teenage girl to announce that she is about to have a very unusual and difficult pregnancy (Luke 1:26-38). She will give birth to the Savior, and she will remain a virgin. When she wants to know how such a thing can possibly happen, the angel says, "Nothing is impossible with God" (Jer. 32:37). So it turns out in ways Jeremiah could never have imagined, that the only way to have hope is to know that nothing is too hard for God.

PRAYER: *What are facing today that cries out for hope? Pray about it the way Jeremiah prayed: "Ah, Sovereign Lord, you have made the heavens and the earth by your great power and outstretched arm. Nothing is too hard for you" (Jer. 32:17).*

Introduction to Lamentations

DAY 157: PRAYING IN ABJECT AFFLICTION

"Because of the Lord's great love we are not consumed, for his compassions never fail" (Lam. 3:22).

The Grand Canyon makes the Colorado River a more beautiful and powerful river. Further south, downstream, as it flows along the Arizona and California borders toward Mexico, its banks become indistinct, and it gets shallow and lazy and dirty. But upstream, through the Canyon, where the walls are high and the space narrow, the river is a glorious force. The boundaries and structures of the Canyon make the river a better river.

This is true of almost everything that is worthwhile, including grief. Lamentations is about grief, and the author speaks of grief like water. To pray through grief is to "pour out your heart like water in the presence of the Lord" (Lam. 2:19). But grief, like pouring water, can be very messy. There is nothing necessarily wrong with being messy. Childbirth is messy, surgical theaters are messy, life is messy, but these messy situations can produce life and healing. Good boundaries keep mess from turning to chaos or sloppy shallowness. Like the walls of the Grand Canyon, boundaries deepen grief and make it creative and healing—and a powerful force for prayer. Mere raw emotion has little value over time; but grief that is disciplined and instructed by hope turns despair to praise and ashes to beauty (Isa. 61:3).

Lamentations is a book about grief within boundaries. The grief it expresses is horrific, but its structure is studied and poetic. There are five laments, each with 22 verses, arranged according to the 22 letters of the Hebrew alphabet—except the third lament, which has 66 verses (22 times 3). To learn to pray like Lamentations demonstrates is to learn to grieve within creative and life-giving boundaries. Even the progression of the themes of the book teaches something. The book begins with lament, moves to hope (which is the center), and concludes with repentance. There are two kinds of grief: bad grief and good grief. Good grief leads to repentance by way of hope, as Paul described it in 2 Corinthians 7:9-10. Hope is the center, for without hope, grief leads only to despair.

PRAYER: *Pray the words from the great hymn, "How Firm a Foundation." Sing your prayer if you know the tune.*

When through the deep waters I call thee to go,
The rivers of sorrow shall not overflow;
For I will be with thee, thy troubles to bless,
And sanctify to thee thy deepest distress.
(from John Rippon's Selection of Hymns)

DAY 158: MAKE MEMORY A GOOD SERVANT

Lamentations 3:19-33

"I remember my affliction and my wandering, the bitterness and the gall.... Yet this I call to mind and therefore I have hope" (Lam. 3:19-21).

The value of memory, like intellect, is determined by what it serves. Memory in the service of despair is powerful to destroy. Memory in the service of hope is powerful to save. In *The Pilgrim's Progress*, Christian was locked up in Doubting Castle and beaten savagely with a club by Giant Despair. His club was made of memory. As Despair beat Christian, he was filled with memories of his sin and how many times he been warned not to sin but had sinned anyway. As he was clubbed by memory, he sank deeper and deeper into despair. But one night, the same memory that Despair had used for torture came to him and whispered something in his ear. Then Christian realized with joy that all along he had been carrying the key to unlock Doubting Castle. The key was in his heart, and it was Promise. He thrust it into the lock, and though it was hard to turn, the lock yielded, and he was set free.[1]

Sometimes praying about things like loss and disappointment and failure can leave you more despondent after you prayed than before you prayed. The memory, the recollection of these things, even though spoken to God, can be like Despair's club in Doubting Castle. The key is promise. Pray the promises of God into your despair. Make memory into a good servant. Remember God's love and faithfulness as well as you remember your own lack of love and faithlessness. "Yet this I call to mind and therefore I have hope: Because of the Lord's great love we are not consumed, for his compassions never fail" (Lam. 3:21-22).

The Lord wants your suffering to refine you, not consume you. You may think that you are getting exactly what you deserve for the wrongs you have done and bow your head in resignation. But you are wrong! We never get exactly what we deserve. Only one person got exactly what we deserve; and he died on a cross and was raised from the dead for our justification (Rom. 4:25). Our sin and guilt are real. But God's love is greater, and where once there was condemnation, now there is discipline.

PRAYER: *Pray this prayer from Lamentations thankfully: "Though he brings grief, he will show compassion, so great is his unfailing love. For he does not willingly bring affliction or grief to the children of men" (Lam. 3:32-33).*

Introduction to Ezekiel

DAY 159: WHEN THINGS GO BADLY

"They will know that I am the Lord,
when I disperse them among the nations" (Ezek. 12:15).

Why is it, there always seems to be more to talk to God about when things are going badly? Part of the answer to that question probably has something to do with how quickly we forget to be thankful. Man has been described as the "ungrateful biped." We need to pray what George Herbert prayed: "Thou that hast given so much to me, Give one thing more, a grateful heart."[1] The second part of the answer is that God is usually speaking to us in some new way when things go badly. It's not that he isn't speaking when they go well, but that he has something new to say when they go bad. When he takes something away from us, it's so he can give something better.

Like all the other prophets, Ezekiel prophesied during dark days, perhaps the darkest in Israel's history, and among the most difficult of people: a privileged upper class with a highly developed sense of entitlement and a shallow optimism. They were in exile, but they didn't expect to be there for long. They were convinced that soon they would be back in Jerusalem worshiping in their pride and joy: the Temple. Most of them would die before that happened. And when some did return, it would be to a city that had been razed and a temple that had been compromised (see Ezra and Nehemiah). When shallow optimism falls, it falls hard, and it doesn't always grow into something stronger and deeper. That false optimism would grow into real faith, was the burden of Ezekiel's prophecy.

God was giving something better to replace what he had taken away. He would be the sanctuary, and so would their hearts (Ezek. 11:16-25; 36:26-27). The future of the new temple ministry would be more glorious than the first. Ezekiel's vision is of a river flowing from south of the altar, first a trickle, then a stream, and then a torrent of water giving life to everything around it like the rivers in Eden (Ezek. 47:1-12). The great opportunity for prayer in hard times is to discern the new thing God is doing and to pray it into existence. The opportunity is to repent of our narrow loves and little desires and to see these expanded to cry out for the fullness of God's perfect and pleasing will.

PRAYER: *Read Ezekiel 47:1-12 and say or sing as a prayer the words of this classic hymn:*

Like a river glorious is God's perfect peace,
Over all victorious, in its bright increase;
Perfect, yet it floweth fuller every day,
Perfect, yet it groweth deeper all the way.

Refrain:
Stayed upon Jehovah, hearts are fully blest,
Finding, as He promised, perfect peace and rest.
(from "Like a River Glorious" by Frances Havergal).

DAY 160: HE IN YOU AND YOU IN HIM

Ezekiel 11:16-21

"Yet for a little while I have been a sanctuary for them in the countries where they have gone" (Ezek. 11:16).

What God says here is so startlingly uncommon in the Old Testament that it might as well be brand new. The sanctuary, the temple in Jerusalem had been the symbol of his presence among his people. Now they were in exile in Babylon, the home of other gods. Where could they go to meet with their God? God's answer is, "I've come to meet with you. I'm not in the sanctuary; I am the sanctuary!" By implication, God says, "you are in me." They couldn't get to the temple, so the temple came to them! The gospel pops up in the most unexpected places, doesn't it? It would be 600 years before the full implications of this act would be known—when Jesus named himself the new temple (John 2:19-20). It took the tragedy of the exile and separation from the temple for God to make the point he had been trying to make all along: that he wanted to live among them as their God.

But there was more that he wanted. He not only wanted them to be *in him* as their true sanctuary, but God wanted to be *in them* as his sanctuary. "I will give them an undivided heart and put a new spirit in them; I will remove from them their heart of stone and give them a heart of flesh" (Ezek. 11:19). He is more explicit later in Ezekiel: "I will put my Spirit in you and move you to follow my decrees and be careful to keep my laws" (Ezek. 36:27). The gospel appears where we would never look for it. Again, it would be 600 years before the full implications came to light—when Paul told the Corinthians, "Do you not know that your body is a temple of the Holy Spirit who is in you, whom you have received from God?" (1 Cor. 6:19).

Stated philosophically, this is the ontological basis, the relationship proper for prayer: In Christ, we are in God and God is in us. He is our sanctuary, and we are his as we enjoy every spiritual blessing in Christ—the chief blessing being Christ in us, the hope of glory (Eph. 1:3; Col. 1:27)! To speak to God and be heard you don't need to climb up to heaven, or cross the sea. No, he is very near you, in your heart and your mouth so you may speak (cf. Deut. 30:11-14).

PRAYER: *Precious Savior, thank you for how near you have come to me and how close you are. Hear me when I pray. Speak, for I am listening.*

DAY 161: IN THE GAP

Ezekiel 22:30-31

"I looked for a man among them who would build up the wall and stand before me in the gap" (Ezek. 22:30).

What is God looking for, if anything? Is there anything he seeks? Whenever the Bible speaks of God's search, it usually has something to do with prayer. Three examples will suffice. When Asa forsook prayer for a military alliance with Aram, God said, "For the eyes of the Lord range throughout the earth to strengthen those whose hearts are fully committed to him" (2 Chron. 16:9). God is on the hunt for people who will ask him for help. When Jesus discussed worship with the Samaritan woman, he said his Father sought those who would worship him in spirit and in truth (John 4:23). God is on a search, looking for true worshipers. Worship and prayer are integral to each other.

Then there is the passage before us: "I looked for a man among them who would build up the wall and stand before me in the gap on behalf of the land so I would not have to destroy it" (Ezek. 22:30). The picture is of a wall around a city broken down with an enemy army poised to rush in to destroy the city it once protected. They are savage and heavily armed, shouting and snarling, swords drawn, bows bent. The gap is small enough for one man to defend, but big enough for an army to rush through. Only a brave man would step into that breach to fight. And God is looking for that kind of person. Moses was such a man; he stood in the breach (Ps. 106:23). So was Jesus, who in his suffering and death made intercession for sinners (Isa. 53:12).

This is as vivid and dramatic a picture of intercessory prayer as you'll find anywhere in Scripture. It says the stakes are high in intercession: life and death, heaven and hell. It says it takes great faith and courage to pray. It says God's call for us to intercede is a call to great dignity and responsibility. It says prayer is a great mystery! We can only speculate as to why the sovereign, almighty God who needs no help from anyone would limit himself to our prayers. But that he has is clear from Scripture. If we won't intercede until we understand why, we will never intercede, and some will die (Ezek. 22:31). God is looking for people to stand in the gap.

PRAYER: *Here I am, Lord. I will stand before you in the gap for the sake of your holy name, and for the lives of those I pray for.*

DAY 162: SDG

J. S. Bach (1685-1750)

"Praise the Lord. Praise God in his sanctuary; praise him in his mighty heavens. Praise him for his acts of power; praise him for his surpassing greatness. Let everything that has breath praise the Lord. Praise the Lord" (Ps. 150:1-2, 6).

Johann Sebastian Bach was a musician of prodigious genius, in every way. On the one hand, the quality of his work has earned him universal admiration as one of the greatest composers of all time. On the other, the quantity of what he produced is breathtaking. In his lifetime he composed over 1000 musical pieces, including nearly 200 cantatas and pieces for violin, cello, lute, organ, music box, and timpani. He did all this in relative obscurity, working mainly as a church organist. It wasn't until Mendelssohn "rediscovered" Bach's music a generation later that he became a global name.

What is less understood and appreciated about Bach is the theological and spiritual depth of his work. Bach was a devout Lutheran and believed that the only legitimate reasons to write music were for the praise of God and what he called the "permissible" refreshment of the spirit. He strongly believed in creating "well-regulated church music to the glory of God." Bach was deeply affected by 1 Chronicles 25 which gives an account of the singers and musicians in charge of making music and prophesying in the Lord's temple. He penned in the margin: "This chapter is the true foundation for all God-pleasing music."

Bach is known for his cantatas—musical pieces written for Church services featuring biblical texts, hymns, and Christian poetry. These works were not simply biblical texts and Christian words arbitrarily put to music. The very structure and melody of the music expressed the thought of the lyrics. For example, in his *St. Matthew Passion*, Bach created a kind of halo around the words of Jesus on the cross by having the strings play long, quiet tones whenever his lines are sung. This ends abruptly with the line, "My God, my God, why have you forsaken me?" Here, at the moment of Christ's greatest cry of dereliction, the string halo is removed. The stark contrast creates a jarring emotional effect.

In a very real sense, Bach's works were bathed in prayer. He often penned the initials, JJ near the beginning of a score and SDG at the end. JJ stands for *Jesu Juva*, Latin for "Help, O Jesus"; SDG for another Latin phrase, *Soli Deo Gloria*, "To God Alone Be the Glory." Bach was clearly under the influence of the Reformation (and biblical!) insight regarding vocation and work. Though the work we do as Christians takes many shapes, we all have the same calling or vocation: "whatever you do, do it all for the glory of God" (1 Cor. 10:31). God can be glorified as much in the writing of a cantata, or the plowing of a field, as in the serving of Holy Communion—for artists, farmers, and clergy alike have the same call. Bach prayed that he would answer God's call in his work. Can you pray the same for yours?

PRAYER:

Teach me, my God and King,
In all things Thee to see,
And what I do in anything,
To do it as for Thee.[1]

DAY 163: CAN THESE BONES LIVE?

Ezekiel 37:1-14

"[He] set me in the middle of a valley; it was full of bones" (Ezek. 37:1).

It was a scene like the killing fields in the aftermath of the Khmer Rouge atrocities in Cambodia, dead bodies everywhere, nothing but sun-bleached bones. The Lord took Ezekiel to this deathly scene in Israel and asked him, "Son of man, can these bones live?" Since the Lord asked the question, Ezekiel didn't say the obvious: "No they can't." He said, "O Sovereign Lord, you alone know." God can do anything; the only question is what does he want to do? And in this case, how does he want to do it?

He wants to raise these bones to life as a symbol of what he wants to do for his people. How he intends to do it is very important for understanding how prayer, the word of God, and spiritual revival fit together. God tells Ezekiel to "prophesy to these bones." That means, preach to them. The message he is to preach is a message of hope: "I will make breath enter you, and you will come to life" (Ezek. 37:5). The message is powerful. The bones come together and are connected by tendons and covered by flesh, but the bodies are still dead—lifelike but lifeless. Then God tells Ezekiel to "prophesy to the breath." That means to pray for the Spirit to come into these corpses and give them life the way God first breathed into Adam, and he became a living being (Gen. 2:7). Spiritual revival will come through preaching the gospel of hope and praying for the Spirit of life.

Preaching and praying, praying and preaching—these are God's chief means for spiritual revival. Paul linked the two together when he told the Ephesians to take up the sword of the Spirit, which is the word of God, and to pray in the Spirit as they did: "on all occasions with all kinds of prayers and requests" (Eph. 6:17-18). The text is literally, take up the sword of the Spirit, "by means of all prayer and petition." The sword of the Spirit, the word of God, is wielded by prayer. God is still asking, "Can these bones live? Can the bones of a corrupt culture and a lukewarm church yet come alive?" His means haven't changed: Preach the word and pray for the Spirit to give life.

PRAYER: *O Holy Spirit, raise up a generation of Ezekiel's for our times. Make them—and make me—powerful to preach and faithful to pray.*

Introduction to Daniel

DAY 164: MONSTROUS NATIONS

"O Lord, the great and awesome God, who keeps his covenant of love with all who love him and obey his commands" (Dan. 9:4).

The book of Daniel can read like the greatest hits in a children's Sunday School curriculum. Daniel in the lion's den or Shadrach, Meshach, and Abednego in the fiery furnace—cartoons have been made of these stories. But the book deserves an R rating, not a G rating for violence. The nations of the earth are portrayed as monsters, rapacious and grotesque, devouring the weaker nations as prey and each other as competitors (Dan. 9:7). Even the children's story favorites end in bloodshed and gory death. The drama of Daniel is set amid intractable and callous forces of evil, as seen in nation states and empires. The message is that God is sovereign over these forces, and God's people are called to be humbly faithful as they wait for him to fulfill his purposes.

Because of this, Daniel contains some of the most exciting, mind-stretching teaching on prayer in the entire Bible. The courage of Daniel's prayer-life—his intercession for Israel and his collaboration with the angels in prayer—are remarkable for their vividness and for the theology that underlies them. Daniel is an extended version of the answer Psalm 11 gives to the question, "When the foundations are being destroyed, what can the righteous do" (Daniel 9:3)? The answer of the psalm and of Daniel is to know that "the Lord is in his holy temple; the Lord is on his heavenly throne" (Dan. 9:4) and to pray accordingly.

PRAYER: *Pray these words from Psalm 9:19-20, naming nations and peoples and institutions and media that oppress and lie:*

Arise, O Lord, let not man triumph,
let the nations be judged in your presence.
Strike them with terror, O Lord;
let the nations know they are but men.

DAY 165: DEFIANT PRAYER

Daniel 6:1-15

"Three times a day he got down on his knees and prayed" (Dan. 6:10).

It was quite a compliment that Daniel's enemies knew the only way they could get anything on him would be because of his faith, not for lack of morals (Dan. 6:5). Of course, the two are intertwined, but they can be separated. Too often it's the other way around: a leader's theology and religious practice will be sound, but his moral integrity will crack. So, the corrupt leaders duped Darius into passing a law forbidding prayer to any god or man but Darius. He was just enough of an egotist and a fool to pass such a law.

What would you do if such a law were passed? Keep your prayers silent? Prayer doesn't have to be public to be prayer, right? Prayer is a purely personal matter, right? What we do in the marketplace and what we do in the privacy of our homes are two different things, right? Daniel didn't think so. His prayers were a declaration of reverence and allegiance to a God whose name and kingdom were in direct conflict with Darius' pretensions. For him, to pray "may your name be hallowed" and "may your kingdom come," meant doing something about it in public. These prayers could not be merely inner dispositions. So, the first thing Daniel did when he heard about the edict was to go home to his upper room where he prayed, throw open the window toward Jerusalem, and pray three times daily, as he always had. He understood what we all must understand about prayer: that it is a radically subversive act. Whether silent or spoken, public or private, prayer is what theologian David Wells called, "the ultimate interference with the status quo." Darius' edict gave Daniel the opportunity to demonstrate that spiritual reality.

Some critics have deemed western Christianity privately engaging, but publicly innocuous, meaning we have compartmentalized our faith into the purely private realm. It feels good to pray in a small group or alone on a mountaintop. But it doesn't have a lot to do with what we do in the valley of schedules, deadlines, business, politics, and justice. Test yourself and ask, *do the things I pray for affect what I do out in the world?* Or do I even pray for things that have any meaning beyond my personal and private life? Then learn from and be encouraged by Daniel's prayer life.

PRAYER: *Sovereign Lord! Teach me to pray for things that will make a difference in the valley of schedules, deadlines, business, politics, and justice. Give me the courage to live publicly what I pray privately.*

DAY 166: A MODEL PRAYER

Daniel 9

"I prayed to the Lord my God" (Dan. 9:4).

Daniel's prayer is marvelous—another of the great prayers of Scripture. Its structure, content, and method are timeless and eminently worth imitating. It is a model prayer.

First, it is a biblical prayer. A careful study of this prayer would reveal the vast knowledge Daniel has of the Hebrew Scriptures. His prayer is laced with references and allusions and quotations from the Bible he knew. He doesn't just know the Scriptures, he breathes them in, and he breathes them out. George Herbert's great line about prayer, "God's breath in man returning to its birth,"[1] is true of Daniel in spades. When Daniel prayed, he breathed the same Spirit that Abraham, Moses, and Jeremiah breathed. He prayed what they prayed, and he prayed with them. Daniel is often seen as a solitary man of prayer, but even when he was most alone, he wasn't alone. He was with the faithful people who came before him.

Second, it is a liturgical prayer. The language of his prayer is overwhelmingly the language of the Bible, not necessarily the language of Babylonian exiles in the sixth century. It's not that using contemporary language was something he never did or that it was less spiritual than the Bible's language. It's just that the Bible's language dominated and informed the way Daniel prayed. The words of Scripture are not dead words; they are alive and active (Heb. 4:12-13). This kind of liturgical prayer can give new life and energy to our more spontaneous and extemporaneous prayers.

Third, it is a heartfelt prayer. Daniel prayed with passion. The strong biblical content and liturgical style of his prayer did not take away from his sincerity; they strengthened it. Heartfelt prayers come directly from the heart; but sometimes the heart needs to be carried along. This is where the Bible and liturgy can serve us so well. Powerful prayers come from a heart transformed by the word of God and informed by the distilled wisdom of the church through the ages. James Gilmour, a pioneer missionary to Mongolia, wrote about the role of the Bible and liturgy in his prayer life:

> *When I feel I cannot make headway in devotion, I open the Psalms and push my canoe and let myself be carried along on the stream of devotion that flows through the whole book. The current always sets toward God and in most places is strong and deep.*[2]

Pray like Daniel and you will pray with Christ and his people and from the heart.

PRAYER: *Sovereign Lord, open my ears to your word that I may open my mouth in prayer that is pleasing to you; through Jesus Christ my Lord.*

DAY 167: PRAYER AND POWERS

Daniel 10

"Your words were heard, and I have come in response to them" (Dan. 10:12).

The angel in this text should fire our prayer-imagination. True, some have let their imaginations get a little too fired up with these angelic beings, but we should not be so put off by their excesses that we fall into our own. Echoing C. S. Lewis's comment about devils,[1] Old Testament scholar John Duncan said talk about angels has tended to bounce back and forth between "vulgar credulity" and "presumptuous incredulity."[2] Angels are real, and they often play significant roles in God's dealings with his world. Maybe their role serves to remind us that God, though near, is also high and exalted; that though he is our friend, he lives in unapproachable light and cannot be seen (Isa. 57:15; 1 Tim. 6:16). Because he is exalted and unapproachable, God sends his servants, the angels.

The reality of the angels points to the greater reality of war in the heavenly realms, also known as spiritual warfare. There is always more going on around us in the unseen realm than we can ever see. "For our struggle is not against flesh and blood, but against the rulers, against the authorities, against the powers of this dark world and against the spiritual forces of evil in the heavenly realms" (Eph. 6:12). In Daniel's context, the names of some of these rulers and authorities are "the prince of Persia" and "the prince of Greece" (Dan. 10:13, 20).

Prayer plays a critical role in this conflict. Daniel's prayer triggers Gabriel's mission (Dan. 9:23). The fight between the angel Michael and the prince of Persia took place as Daniel engaged in a time of intense prayer and fasting (Dan. 10:3). It isn't only that our struggles on earth parallel cosmic struggles in the heavenly realms; our struggles in prayer actually participate in those unseen conflicts and affect their outcome. The messenger from heaven asked Daniel, "Do you know why I have come to you?" He explained, "Soon I will return to fight against the prince of Persia, and when I go, the prince of Greece will come.... No one supports me against them except Michael" (Dan. 10:20-21). The angel is clearly enlisting Daniel's prayer support for that conflict! And Daniel joins him: "In the first year of Darius the Mede, I took my stand to support and protect him (Michael)" (Dan. 11:1). Great is the mystery of prayer! Our prayers matter to the angels and actually affect the outcome of cosmic conflicts. We may never see the impact of our prayers this side of heaven, but until then we will walk and pray, not by sight, but by faith.

PRAYER: *Address the angels in your prayer, as in Psalm 103:20. "Praise the Lord, you his angels, you mighty ones who do his bidding, who obey his word." Father in heaven, strengthen your servants in the heavenly realms.*

DAY 168: THE REDEMPTION OF WORK

Brother Lawrence (1611-1691)

"Whatever you do, work at it with all your heart, as working for the Lord, not for men" (Col. 3:23).

"There is nothing more terrible than activity without insight." For many, these words of the historian Thomas Carlyle describe the miserable state of their daily work. A clumsy 17th century monk known as Brother Lawrence has much to teach us.

Nicholas Herman was born in 1611 in Lorraine France. He described himself as a "great awkward fellow who broke everything." After an unsuccessful career as a footman, soldier, and a brief stint as a hermit, Nicholas joined the Carmelite monastery as a lay member. He was given the name Brother Lawrence of the Resurrection and became a full member of the order in 1642.

From the beginning, Brother Lawrence was assigned kitchen duty, a job that no one wanted. For forty years, his daily routine remained the same: rising early to slice vegetables, cook soup, and pour wine, then scrubbing pots and pans after each meal. For the first ten years of his work, Brother Lawrence struggled. Then one day, quite unexpectedly, he experienced a change. "I suddenly found myself changed," he wrote, "and my soul, which up till then was always disturbed, experienced a profound interior peace."

What changed was that Brother Lawrence had begun to do his work "as unto the Lord" (Col. 3:23); or as he put it famously, to "practice the presence of God." The dishes were still dirty, the kitchen still loud and frantic, yet he maintained an inner communion with God that made his work bearable, even joyful. "The time of business does not with me differ from the time of prayer, and in the noise and clatter of my kitchen while several persons are at the same time calling me for different things, I possess God in as great tranquility as if I were upon my knees at the blessed sacrament." He enjoyed the practice of God's presence so much that at times he had to keep himself from visibly laughing in front of others.

Brother Lawrence's simple message of bringing insight to activity through continuous prayer—of practicing the presence of God—has helped to redeem the daily work of many thousands.

> *So think of God all the time—during the day, at night, in your daily work, even in your leisure time activities. He is always nearby. Don't ignore him. If you had a friend nearby, you would not ignore him when he came to visit. Why then would you neglect God? In short, do not forget him. Think of him often. Adore him continually. Live and die with him. As a Christian this is our job and calling. This is what we are here for. It is glorious!*[1]

PRAYER: *Lord, help me to work at all I do with all my heart as working for you, not for earthly masters (Col. 3:23).*

Introduction to Hosea

DAY 169: A MARRIAGE MADE IN HEAVEN?

"How can I give you up? How can I hand you over, Israel?" (Hosea 11:8).

Not all marriages made in heaven are happy. Ask Hosea. God himself had arranged Hosea's marriage to Gomer, but it was a disaster from the beginning, what with her constant affairs and all. But that was the point: Hosea's unhappy marriage was to be a living illustration of his prophetic message that God had an unhappy marriage to Israel. For Israel, like Gomer, had a "spirit of prostitution" (Hosea 5:4). She just wouldn't stay out of bed with other gods.

God's "marriage" to Israel was a marriage made in heaven because it was so one-sided. It was made in heaven only, originating with God alone. This is the way God loves. New Testament scholar Anders Nygren described God's love as *subject-centered*, as opposed to *object-centered*.[1] Object-centered love is love which springs up because the object of love, the beloved, is so irresistibly wonderful. This kind of love is more a reflex than a choice. It is the kind that "falls" in love. Subject-centered love is love that originates in the lover. It does not happen because the object, the beloved, is so lovable, but because the lover is so loving. This kind of love is clearly a choice, but to say it is a choice is not to say it is any less passionate. God's love for Israel let Israel break his heart. Though she deserved death because of her religious prostitution, God cried out, "How can I give you up? How can I hand you over, Israel? My heart is changed within me; all my compassion is aroused" (Hosea 11:8-9).

Though academic sounding, the very notion of something called subject-centered love speaks of the gospel. For the gospel, the good news, is not that we loved God, but that he loved us. We love him because he first loved us. It is also great news for prayer. We do not confess our sins to a God who loves us only when we are good. We confess our sins to a God who loves us good or bad. All our prayers are preceded by his prayer that we open our eyes and see the Love that has pursued us our whole life. We don't have to get God's attention because we already have it.

PRAYER: *Thank you, Father, that I may love you because you first loved me and gave your Son as an atoning sacrifice for my sins (1 John 4:10).*

DAY 170: ELOQUENT BUT INSINCERE

Hosea 6:1-3

"Your love is like the morning mist" (Hosea 6:4).

It's easy to pray more than you know and more than you mean. For instance, every time anyone prays the Lord's Prayer, they pray more than they know. Who can fully understand and appreciate the magnitude of praying for God's kingdom to come? Paul prayed that the Ephesians would know a love that was beyond knowing (Eph. 3:19), which presumably he didn't fully understand either, but he prayed for them to know it anyway. When we pray the big prayers of Scripture, our reach always exceeds our grasp. But that's OK.

But what about praying for things you don't really mean? Didn't Jesus roundly condemn that sort of thing when he said, "These people honor me with their lips, but their hearts are far from me" (Matt. 15:8)? Why would anyone want to pray that way? Maybe to sound good to others (which can be done), or even to sound good to God (which is the most foolish thing in the world). This is apparently what Israel was doing in the prayer they pray in our text. It is a model prayer, beautiful and thoughtful, expressive of the highest and best. God does wound to heal. He does revive and restore. His mercy is as reliable and refreshing as the winter and spring rains. Therefore, the people pray, "Come, let us return to the Lord." But God's response is less than enthusiastic. God is grief-stricken: "What can I do with you, Ephraim? What can I do with you, Judah? Your love is like the morning mist, like the early dew that disappears" (Hosea 6:4). He looked past their great words and saw their insincere hearts.

Their eloquent, but shallow, prayer is probably more common than we wish. The human heart is deceitful. Can any of us know our real motives in anything we pray? David understood this well and prayed, "Who can discern his errors? Forgive my hidden faults" (Ps. 19:12). When we doubt the purity of our motives in the things we pray, we can do three things. One, we can confess our sin. Two, we can pray that God will purify our motives: "Give me an undivided heart, that I may fear you name" (Ps. 86:11). Three, we can keep on praying good prayers until we do mean them!

PRAYER: *Father, you know all things. You know my heart better than I do. Forgive my insincerity and form my motives according to your truth, that I may honor you in my deeds, my words, and my thoughts.*

DAY 171: SINCERE PRAYER

Hosea 14:1-9

"Return, O Israel, to the Lord your God" (Hosea 14:1).

God wants his people back, the way a lover wants his beloved back. His promises are rich and extravagant: "I will heal their waywardness and love them freely" (Hosea 4). When Israel returns, she will have the splendor of an olive tree, the fragrance of a cedar, the fame of Lebanon's wine. The language God uses in verse five to describe what he will be to Israel is even strongly reminiscent of the Song of Songs. God will be like refreshing "dew" (Song of Songs 5:2), causing Israel to "blossom like a lily." In the Song of Songs, the verb "blossom" is used in the context of a lush, romantic setting for love (Hosea 6:11; 7:13). "Lily" is even more erotic, used of the bride's beauty, the couple's lips, and her silken breasts (Hosea 2:1-2; 2:16; 4:5). God's willingness to forgive and to bless is always greater than our desire to be forgiven and blessed.

But God's promise to pour out forgiveness and healing is contingent upon Israel praying a prayer Hosea told Israel to pray: "Take words with you and return to the Lord. Say to him, 'Forgive all our sins and receive us graciously, that we may offer the fruit of our lips'" (Hosea 11:2). What makes this prayer so remarkable is that it is merely a shortened version of the beautiful, but insincere, prayer of Hosea 6:1-3, the prayer God rejected. But this prayer is based on true repentance, for it renounces the false security of military power, confesses the sin of idolatry, and expresses a commitment to justice: "Assyria cannot save us; we will not mount war-horses. We will never again say 'Our Gods' to what our hands have made, for in you the fatherless find compassion" (Hosea 14:3).

Repentance and prayer go together. It's not that God doesn't like our words; he just doesn't like our empty words. When sincere and backed by our life, words can even be a kind of sacrifice of praise offered to God. The writer of Hebrews alludes to this prayer to make that very point. "Through Jesus, therefore, let us continually offer to God a sacrifice of praise—the fruit of lips that confess his name." Hebrews links this prayer to the same concern for justice that Hosea called for: "And do not forget to do good and share with others, for with such sacrifices god is pleased" (Heb. 13:15-16).

PRAYER: *Lord, make my life a sacrifice of praise, so the fruit of my lips will also please you. Forgive me and bless me and make me your own.*

Introduction to Joel

DAY 172: PRAYING FOR PENTECOST

"Return to the Lord your God, for he is gracious and compassionate, slow to anger and abounding in love" (Joel 2:18).

When called upon to explain the extraordinary events of Pentecost, Peter went to the book of Joel (Acts 2:14-21). There were at least two good reasons for doing this: the obvious being the fulfillment of the prophecy in Joel 2:28-32; the not-so-obvious being the overall point of view of the book. Joel's prophecies were aimed at expanding Israel's sense of the scope of God's sovereignty in history—that God's interests weren't confined to his dealings with Israel, but included all the nations. From the beginning, his interest in Israel had been for the sake of all the nations (Gen. 12:1-2). The popular idea in Israel was that "the great and terrible day of the Lord" (Joel 2:31) would mean the punishment of other nations only for their sin. Joel includes Israel in this punishment, too. But with repentance, restoration and blessing would come for Israel—and for all the nations. Joel is part of a vital body of Old Testament prophecy that lays the foundation for the Great Commission of Jesus in the New Testament (Matt. 28:16-20).

Exactly how this universal judgment and blessing will come about is not entirely clear in Joel. But what is clear is that it will hinge on an unprecedented outpouring of the Holy Spirit on all people. The New Testament admonition to "pray in the Spirit" (Eph. 6:18) has its roots in Pentecost and, centuries before Pentecost, in the prophecy of Joel. We pray for many reasons: for our own personal benefit and for the good of those we love. We also pray that God will pour out his Spirit on all people, so that "everyone who calls on the name of the Lord will be saved" (Joel 2:32).

PRAYER: *Pray for those you know who do not know the Lord, asking that he pour out his Spirit on them that they may call on the name of the Lord and be saved.*

DAY 173: I WILL POUR OUT MY SPIRIT!

Joel 2:28-32

"And everyone who calls on the name of the Lord will be saved" (Joel 2:32).

"I will pour out my Spirit." This is a striking picture—not a taste of the Spirit, not a bite or a bit, but poured out. How much of the Holy Spirit do you want? Jesus had promised the disciples that though John baptized with water, they would be baptized with the Holy Spirit. What would that be like; to be immersed in God, washed in God, drenched in God, brought completely under the influence of God? How much of the Holy Spirit do you want? Do you want God only in moderation and under your terms, or totally? People are inoculated against disease by getting a little dose of the virus which prevents them from getting the real thing. We can be inoculated against God by getting just enough of God not to get God. God is poured out, not sipped.

"On all people." The Spirit will be poured out regardless of gender or age and, by implication, ethnic or national background. To be baptized in the Spirit is to gain God's view of other people, for he won't come only to "us," but also to "them." When that happens, "they" must become "we." God's Spirit poured out can be a very personal experience for those he touches, but it is never private. The Spirit is given to the church, and the gift of the Spirit is to build the church with living stones drawn from every tribe and language and people and nation (Eph. 2:19-22; Rev. 5:9-10). To pray in the Spirit is to pray for the mystery of the gospel to be powerfully preached and made known to everyone (Eph. 6:18-20).

"And everyone who calls on the name of the Lord will be saved." The promise of the Spirit creates a crisis, a call for decision. It is not an indiscriminate, general pouring out. The Spirit must be prayed for. For those who know this, and have called on the name of the Lord, it creates a new crisis in prayer. Does it not follow that, if "everyone who calls on the name of the Lord shall be saved," then the greatest prayer we can pray, and must pray, is that everyone will!

PRAYER: *Holy Spirit! I don't want just a little of you, I want all of you. Pour yourself on me and fill me. And I plead with you to draw others to pray for the same.*

Introduction to Amos

DAY 174: LET JUSTICE ROLL!

"But let justice roll on like a river, righteousness like a never-ending stream!" (Joel 5:24).

The best-known line from the book of Amos is, "But let justice roll on a like a river, righteousness like a never-failing stream" (Joel 5:24). That was God speaking. To understand his great call to justice, we need to understand the enormous appeal of the religious alternative that beckoned to Israel on every side. The practice of Canaanite religion was basically the practice of sacred sex. The Canaanites believed that humanity was woven into a divine cosmos and that there was no qualitative difference between a human being and the earth. Therefore, to tap into the power of the universe, one needed to get in touch with the energy of one's body. What more powerful urge was there than sex? Sociologist Peter Berger put it bluntly: "the gods were as close as one's own genitalia; to establish contact with them, when all was said mythologically and all was done ritually, one had only to do what, after all, one wanted to do anyway." Prostitution wasn't legalized, it was solemnized. Baalism was a religion of self-centered pleasure.

If the gods of Canaan were encountered in carnal ecstasy, the true and living God was encountered in a covenant and a law. Canaanite religion was about power and how to get it. God was about love and how to live it. The religion of Israel was inescapably ethical. The Ten Commandments were structured around how one was to treat God and treat other people.

Amos' message of justice goes right to the heart of the difference between pagan religion and the religion of the true and living God. So should our prayers. Every petition of the prayer Jesus taught should be understood in light of justice, especially the first three: God's holiness, God's kingdom, and God's will. The scope of these petitions is not exhausted by the concerns of justice, but they cannot be understood apart from those concerns. It is a dangerous thing to pray the Lord's Prayer with your mouth in the right place, but your heart, your money, your time, and your vote in the other.

PRAYER: *Pray the message of Joel, naming names and places and situations, pleading that indeed God's "justice roll on like a river, [his] righteousness like a never-ending stream."*

DAY 175: LET'S ROLL

Amos 5:21-24

"Let justice roll on like a river" (Amos 5:24).

Human nature being what it is, it's easy to see why Israel was tempted in two directions: either to go all the way and look to Baalism for religious fulfillment or to waffle a bit and customize their faith—mix a little Baal with the Lord God, a little selfish pleasure with love. Most took this route. If one had to guess which path God hated more, it was probably the latter. It never worked since, then as now, no one could serve two masters. What so infuriated God was that his name was attached to things that clearly belonged to Baal. That is the background of the famous call for justice in verse 24. It was preceded by, "I hate, I despise your feasts. Away with all the noise of your songs!" (Amos 5:23). Read that as, "You can't mix and match."

Religious rituals and ceremonies are peculiar things; they can either delight God or disgust him. When the rituals are ends in themselves, they disgust him. When they are means to a holy end, they delight him. Religious rituals performed as ends are seen as things that in themselves satisfy God. The worshiper can do whatever he pleases most of the time, but do the religious thing some of the time, and get credit for being good all the time. Jeremiah's take on this was that it turned the house of the Lord into a den of thieves; a place where people went to hide from God, not meet with him (Jer. 7:11). Used as a means, religious rituals express true love for God and impress his love upon us. They give voice to what's already inside, and they speak to what should be inside. Used as an end, religion compartmentalizes; used as a means, it unifies.

The phrase, "But let justice roll on like a river," says a lot. God wants our religious lives to be like a river; a continual flow of justice and righteousness, nurturing human life the way a river nurtures a desert. People flourish in justice and righteousness, but they wither and die without them. God hates religious compartments because nothing flows out of them. They're like boxes of bottled water, sealed and unopened in a drought. He doesn't want to be sprinkled here and there or sipped and rationed. He wants his justice and righteousness to flow out of us like the living water Jesus promised would bubble up in those who believe in him (John 4:14). Are your prayers ends, or means? Do they delight or disgust God?

PRAYER: *Righteous Lord! May my life not be like bottled water, but like a river. Teach me your justice, that I may pray your justice and live your justice, as one flowing, rolling river.*

DAY 176: SO THAT YOU MAY KNOW ME

Elisabeth Elliot (1926-2015)

"'You are my witnesses,' declares the Lord, 'and my servant whom I have chosen, so that you may know and believe me and understand that I am he'" (Isa. 43:10).

The opportunity Elisabeth Elliot had long prayed for, and was sure would one day come, had finally arrived. She could now enter the village of the people who had murdered her husband two years before. Elisabeth's husband, Jim, was one of five young missionaries murdered by the Auca Indians on the banks of the Curaray River, deep in the Ecuadorian jungle. She wrote of the opportunity: "The decision to accept or not—ordinarily one I would have made quickly and without much difficulty—struck me this time as being rather an important one. I prayed about it... the answer was a strong affirmative—I should go."

Elisabeth Elliot journeyed to the Auca village with her young daughter Valerie and Rachel Saint, the sister of Nate Saint, another one of the other murdered missionaries. She and Valerie lived among the Aucas for two years, long enough to see many come to Christ. Elisabeth tells her story in *The Savage My Kinsman*. Today there is a thriving church among the Aucas.

During that time, and afterward, Elisabeth asked herself, "What is a missionary?" Her initial answer had to do with things that fall under the general heading of philanthropy—things like preaching, teaching, church-building, medical work, baptizing, catechizing, and social work. But as she reflected on her time with the Aucas, she realized that she couldn't do any of these things for them. Her questions took her back to the Scriptures, where the word missionary was nowhere to be found. What she did find, however, in many passages, was the word "witness." One passage, in particular, arrested her. It was Isaiah 43:10: "'You are my *witnesses*,' declares the Lord, 'and my servant whom I have chosen, so that you may know and believe me and understand that I am he'" (italics added). Here the purpose of a witness is, above all, to know and understand and believe God. Everything a witness does is a means to this end. "He will go to any lengths to teach us, and his manipulation of the movements of men—Aucas, missionaries, whomever—is never accidental. Those movements may be incidental to the one thing towards which He goads us: the recognition of Christ." Elisabeth knew that Jim and his friends went into harm's way because they believed God wanted them to do it—and that in order to know God, one must obey God. It was the knowing that made the obeying worthwhile. They took literally the words of 1 John 2:17, "The world and its desires pass away, but the man who does the will of God lives forever."[1]

Elisabeth's insight has profound implications for the meaning of prayer. Prayer is often thought of only as a means to an end: for guidance and healing, for evangelistic and missionary success. But if the ultimate meaning of these things is that Christ may be known, should we not also see the true end of prayer as the same thing? We pray that Christ may be known, and as we pray, we come to know him better. The greatest gift of prayer is not the answer, but the Answerer.

PRAYER: *Jesus, it is the pleasure of your company that makes all praying and service worthwhile. Make me aware of your sweet presence, that I may serve you with gladness all my days.*

DAY 177: THE MYSTERY OF PRAYER

Amos 7:1-6

"So the Lord relented" (Amos 7:3).

The mystery of amazing grace is: "So the Lord relented" (Amos 7:3, 6). If we all got what we deserved, we would be dead. Two vivid pictures of what Israel deserved are in this text. One is of swarms of locusts that strip the land completely bare; the other is of a fire that devours even the "great deep," probably the Mediterranean ocean. But the Lord relented! The thing that should mystify us is not that bad things sometimes happen to good people, but that such a good thing as mercy should happen to bad people. Whenever we pray for God to give us mercy, we do two things: we acknowledge that we have done something terrible, and we plead that, instead of responding in kind, God will do something wonderful.

God's relenting is the amazing mystery of prayer. We see this in Amos' prayer: "I cried out, 'Sovereign Lord, forgive!' So the Lord relented" (Amos 7:2-3). In order to draw Amos into prayer, the Lord showed him his will to destroy Israel. When Amos prayed, it then pleased God to relent. Destruction, prayer, mercy were all dimensions of God's will. The mystery of prayer is great because of a greater mystery: how God's sovereign and immutable will interacts with human freedom. How can it be that "all things have their will, yet none but thine?"[1] It is beyond understanding, but it is clear that somehow the two coexist. God can both propose prayer and answer prayer; declare his mind and change his mind. Through it all, he carries out his unchanging will through the prayers of the saints.

A key to this mystery, but only a key for the mystery has many doors, is the perspective Amos brought to his prayer for mercy. Amos was a typical prophet, gloriously unbalanced in his zeal for God's glory and like a magnifying glass concentrating the blazing light of holy truth on sin (See Introduction to Isaiah). The light can set things on fire and destroy them, so Amos pled for mercy—not as one who had a casual attitude toward truth, but as one who knew the consuming power of truth. In the same way, Jesus taught us to pray that God's name be hallowed before we ask for mercy.

PRAYER: *Lord, because you call me to come, I enter into the mystery of prayer. Give me the boldness and humility of Amos. Give me your perspective on the things I pray for. Let me pray always that your holy will be done, believing that somehow my prayers are part of getting your will done.*

Introduction to Obadiah

DAY 178: PRAYER AGAINST CALLOUSNESS AND BITTERNESS

"Because of the violence against your brother Jacob, you will be covered with shame" (Obad. 10).

The fact that Obadiah is the shortest book in the Old Testament in no way diminishes its importance. The bitter rivalry between Israel and Edom is more than a backdrop for a prophecy; it is a grim and vivid reminder that hatred and revenge are never healed by time, only intensified. Centuries later, Herod the Great, an Idumean and descendant of Edom, sought to destroy Jesus at his birth (Matt. 2:16). Only repentance heals the cancer of hatred. Obadiah's warnings were ignored, and a great many people suffered for generations to come.

Obadiah also warned against the danger of smugness. "Famous last words" is a phrase we use to speak ironically when things can turn out the opposite of how we thought they would. Falsely secure in high mountain fortresses, Edom's famous last words were, "Who can bring me down to the ground" (Obad. 3)? God was unimpressed: "'Though you soar like an eagle and make your nest among the stars, from there I will bring you down,' declares the Lord" (Obad. 4). God simply has no tolerance for smugness.

Smugness is deadly in prayer. Witness the two men in Jesus' parable who went to the temple to pray. One was quite confident that God would hear his prayers appreciatively. The other was afraid even to look up because he was so sure he deserved judgment. The first man looked for confirmation; the second man cried out for mercy. Jesus said the first man prayed only about himself and was therefore heard only by himself. The second man, though low, was brought high. He "went home justified before God. For everyone who exalts himself will be humbled, and he who humbles himself will be exalted" (Luke 18:14). Edom is more than a place and a nation; it is an attitude.

PRAYER: *Father in Heaven! Take away my stony heart and its bitter callousness toward those I resent—name a name or names. Put your Spirit in me and give me a tender, forgiving heart. Move me to forgive as you have forgiven me.*

DAY 179: FAMILY FEUD

Obadiah 1:12

"You should not look down on your brother" (Obad. 12).

When she fell in love with Romeo (a Montague), Juliet (a Capulet) mourned the ancient hatred between their two families. Mere family labels should mean nothing, especially if they keep star-crossed lovers apart:

What's in a name?
that which we call a rose
By any other name would smell as sweet.[1]

"Or as foul," an Edomite might add of an Israelite. The tragedy was that both belonged to the same family. Blood is not only thicker than water, but it can also be far more toxic. The rivalry between the two nations went back for centuries to the rivalry between the brothers Jacob and Esau. Over the years the hostility was embellished and inflamed by countless slurs and insults and acts of aggression. When Israel fell prey to foreign powers, Edom not only offered no help but also gloated when they saw their cousins fall (Obad. 10-14). God would punish Edom for this. No doubt God saw again in Edom's hatred the same evil that caused Cain to strike down his brother Abel. As with Abel, he had chosen to uniquely bless the line of Jacob, not Esau. He saw through Edom's animosity toward Israel to its real source: animosity toward God.

Look past the names of Edom and Israel and think of the names you know that are stained with bitterness in your own heart, especially in your own family. These hurts and hatreds can run deep. Their longevity can give them almost mythic power to shape perceptions. Obadiah's prophecy is a pointed reminder to repent of bitterness and callousness for its source is not ultimately in what you think others have done to you, but in whether you respect the way God runs the world. The implications for prayer are profound. You can't love a God you can't see if you won't love a brother or sister that you can (cf. 1 John 4:20).

PRAYER: *O Spirit of God, cleanse my heart of all bitterness. Forgive me for the ways I have grown hard toward others, especially family members. May I forgive as I have been forgiven, and may I be an instrument of peace in the world.*

Introduction to Jonah

DAY 180: GOD IS A MISSIONARY GOD

"I knew that you are a gracious and compassionate God" (Jonah 4:2).

At the 1976 Urbana Missionary Conference, Dr. John R. W. Stott addressed the 17,000 students gathered there on God's heart for missions. How much is missions a part of God's character and will? The titles of his addresses say it all:

"The Lord God is a Missionary God"
"The Lord Christ is a Missionary Christ"
"The Holy Spirit is a Missionary Spirit"
"The Christian Church is a Missionary Church"

Missions is of the very essence of who God has revealed himself to be. The eternal communion of Father, Son, and Holy Spirit has always been directed toward the whole world, not just a part. The church's mission is missions. In the words of Emil Brunner, the church exists by missions as a fire exists by burning.

The story of Jonah is one of the most engaging and theologically significant stories in the Bible. It satirizes and indicts Israel for its refusal to live up to its calling to be a blessing to the world (Gen. 12:1-2). Jonah, like the Israel he represents, is scandalized to learn that the God of Israel loves even Israel's worst enemies. His story turns on his reluctance to line his affections up with God's. *Reluctance* is weak. *Intransigence* is a better word for this man who never even prays for Nineveh, the people he is sent to preach to. Jonah the man has nothing to teach us about how to pray for the world God loves. But Jonah the book does, especially in God's answers to Jonah's complaints and self-pity.

PRAYER: *"Change my heart, O God; make it ever true. Change my heart of God, my I be like you" (lyrics by John Wimber and Eddie Espinoza).*

DAY 181: THE THINGS THAT GRIEVE GOD'S HEART

Jonah 4:9-11

"Should I not be concerned about that great city?" (Jonah 4:11).

In 1947, Bob Pierce was touring mainland China as an evangelist. After one of his services, a distraught mother pushed her way through the crowd surrounding Pierce, carrying in her arms her starving infant daughter, White Jade. She thrust the baby into his arms and disappeared. Pierce dug into his own pockets and gave money to help a missionary buy food for the child. After that experience, he was never the same. Three years later he founded World Vision. One year later, in 1951, he wrote a prayer in his Bible, which he kept till his death in 1978: "Let my heart be broken with the things that break the heart of God."

God's rhetorical question to Jonah was an invitation to pray the same prayer: "Should I not be concerned about that great city" (Jonah 4:11)? There were 120,000 people in Nineveh who didn't know left from right, right from wrong, up from down. They were utterly lost and confused, like sheep without a shepherd. And they were people, for heaven's sake—not some silly vine (see Jonah 4:5-10)! It was an invitation to be moved by something more than matters concerning his own comfort and to share in God's great and expansive love. American newspapers have a formula to gauge reader interest in stories: 10,000 dead in Nepal = 100 dead in Wales = 10 dead the other side of the country = 1 dead next door. God's invitation is to level the ground of our emotional playing field, so to speak. (Or should it be, *praying* field?) What percentage of your prayers are for the unreached peoples of the world? What proportion of your prayers are for the urban poor? Or widows and orphans? Racial reconciliation? Victims of HIV-AIDS?

God's drastic measure with Jonah fit his transgression. The belly of a big fish is a dark and constricted place. So is a heart that can't love beyond one's neighborhood and family.

PRAYER: *"Let my heart be broken with the things that break the heart of God" (Bob Pierce).*

DAY 182: THROUGH A MIGHTY STRENGTH

Magonus Sucatus Patricius (389-461)

"It is God who arms me with strength and makes my way perfect" (Ps. 18:32).

Magonus Sucatus Patricius, known to us as St. Patrick, was just a boy at the time. The son of a prosperous Roman official, he lived in relative ease on a little farm on the western coast of Britain. One night, everything changed. Pirates ransacked the family farm and carted Patrick back to Ireland as a slave.

He spent the next six years tending the flocks of a proud Irish territorial ruler named Miliucc. Deprived of education, warm clothes, and regular human contact, the heartbreak of his dismal situation would have done him in had he not begun to seek God in prayer. "I would pray constantly during the daylight hours," he wrote later. "The love of God and the fear of him surrounded me more and more—and faith grew, and the Spirit was roused, so that in one day I would say as many as a hundred prayers and after dark nearly as many again… through snow, frost, rain."

One night Patrick heard a mysterious voice, speak to him: "Your hungers are rewarded: you are going home. Look, your ship is ready." Shaken but excited, he miraculously escaped and made the 200-mile journey to the sea. Patrick found safe passage on a ship and returned home to an astonished family who received him as one brought back from the dead.

But home wasn't home anymore. Patrick was haunted by a sense of restlessness, and he couldn't find a place to settle down. One night he had a disturbing dream. He saw an Irish man he knew holding many letters, one of them with the heading, "The Voice of the Irish." Then Patrick heard the sound of many Irish voices crying out, "We beg you to come and walk among us once more." Patrick woke up, "Stabbed in the heart." He knew God was calling him back to Ireland.

In 432 Patrick sailed back to Ireland armed only with the gospel and prayer. His work was always dangerous—Ireland was a warrior culture. One account tells of how all the fires in Ireland were extinguished as a part of the Druid ritual of vernal equinox. When nightfall came, the Druids were enraged to find Patrick standing by a blazing fire in honor of Easter, which had fallen that year on the same day. He survived many confrontations like this.

Warrior prayers came out of his experience of violent opposition. Appropriately called "breastplate prayers," they are prayers for protection against the foes of the gospel.

PRAY THE BREASTPLATE PRAYER OF ST. PATRICK:

I arise today
Through God's strength to pilot me,
God's might to uphold me,
God's wisdom to guide me,
God's eye to look before me,
God's ear to hear me,
God's word to speak for me,
God's hand to guard me,
God's way to lie before me,
God's shield to protect me,
God's host to save me,
From snares of devils,
From temptations of vices,
From everyone who shall wish me ill,
Afar and near,
Alone and in multitude.[1]

Introduction to Micah

DAY 183: WHAT DOES THE LORD REQUIRE OF YOU?

"He has shown you, O man, what is good. And what does the Lord require of you? To act justly and to love mercy and to walk humbly with your God" (Mic. 6:8).

God is not vague. Though he is beyond us, he doesn't typically say things that are totally over our heads. He wants to be understood and known—not comprehensively, for that would be impossible for us, but enough that we can know what he wants us to do and be. We may never know the depths of God's truth, but he makes it accessible enough to wade in the shallows. How deep we go is a matter of grace and time and desire.

Micah contains one of the most famous summary statements in all the Bible of what God wants us to know. Micah 6:8 has been memorized, preached, and even sung for centuries: "He has shown you, O man, what is good. And what does the Lord require of you? To act justly and to love mercy and to walk humbly with your God." There is nothing vague about that. There are other things God is equally definite about. He hates—repeat—*hates* idolatry, injustice, rebellion, and empty formalism in religion. Open Micah randomly to just about any page and you will find expressions of God's loathing of these things. But he is just as definite about how much he loves to forgive the penitent. He loves to restore those who do what he hates. Micah exults in this: "Who is a God like you, who pardons sin and forgives the transgression of the remnant of his inheritance? You do not stay angry forever but delight to show mercy" (Micah 6:18). What could be better than to know exactly what God hates, what he loves, and what he expects of us?

God is not vague, but we are. Part of what it means to be a sinner is to know how to complicate the simple, to make the unambiguous ambiguous, and to qualify the unqualified. God responds likewise; to the pure he shows himself pure, to the shrewd he shows himself shrewd (cf. Ps. 18 25-27), and to the vague he will seem vague. Reading a prophet like Micah scrubs the vagueness out of your brain. It works like a dash of cold water on the face, or a compass in a dark forest pointing to true north. Read Micah and don't be vague; heartily agree with what God hates and loves; by praise, thanksgiving, petition—and confession.

PRAYER: *Father in Heaven! You have made it perfectly clear what you want me to do! Help me to love and know and joyfully do what you want!*

DAY 184: A SIGN ON THE RUBBLE

Micah 4:1-5

"The mountain of the Lord's Temple will be established as chief among the mountains; it will be raised above the hills, and peoples will stream to it" (Mic. 4:1).

Builders will often post a sign on a construction site telling passersby what they're building: a future restaurant or market or office complex, perhaps. This verse is like a sign on a building site, except the site will be a heap of rubble before it is a building. A modern-day equivalent would be a sign for a future terrorist resort and friendship center on the wreckage of the World Trade Center. God says, before Mount Zion is established as chief among all mountains, "Zion will be plowed like a field, Jerusalem will become a heap of rubble, the temple hill a mound overgrown with thickets" (Mic. 3:12). Other nations will do this to execute God's judgment on Israel; and one day those other nations will stream back to the place they once destroyed to learn about the Lord. The place of tragedy will become the place of joy.

God loves to turn ashes to beauty and mourning to joy. He makes things that are out of things that aren't. He raises the dead. The blind see, the lame walk, and infertile couples have babies in their old age. In the end, an old and corrupted heaven and earth will make way for a new heaven and earth. Where we see only rubble, God sees possibilities and building material. If your life is a mess, ask yourself—and ask the Lord—what sign has he posted on the rubble? What new thing is he building?

But take these thoughts back to the text and one step further. How can you pray for a world that has seen so much bloodshed and oppression? If God is indeed a God who makes the place of tragedy a place of joy, will you pray he will do that for the ancient hostility between Jew and Arab? For the deep hurt and bitterness of racism? For tribal and ethnic hatred that has poisoned lives for centuries?

PRAYER: *Come, Lord, and rule over us! Settle the disputes and discord among peoples; bring in your kingdom of peace. May we train no more for war.*

DAY 185: GOOD IN THE BEST SENSE OF THE WORD

Micah 6:8

"And what does the Lord require of you" (Mic. 6:8).

God works on us from both directions: inside-out and outside-in. In the Ten Commandments, he started with the deep things: no god but God, no idols, do not dishonor God's name, keep the Sabbath holy. These are first things, foundational principles, the building blocks for all the rest: honor your parents, don't murder, don't commit adultery, don't steal, don't lie, don't covet. A right relationship with God is the basis for a right relationship to people. The greatest command is to love God with your whole being. The second greatest command is like it: love your neighbor as yourself.

Micah's famous summary of God's requirements starts on the outside and works inward. "To act justly" is essential morality, introductory ethics, basic human decency, to give others their due. It's a good place to start, but not to end. For these acts must not be only external, they must come from the heart. Merely to do the right thing without love and understanding is to be a good person, but "in the worst sense of the word" (to borrow a phrase from Mark Twain). That's why Micah adds, "to love mercy" and "to act justly." Justice done only because it is right is better than no justice at all. It's like taking out the trash in a household; the house will be a lot worse if it's not done, but not a lot better if it is. But trash taken out for love can be almost sacramental in its impact, just as justice done for love of mercy can heal whole societies. Good laws alone can't make good people; but love can make good laws work powerfully to make people good.

Love is a matter of the heart. What if your heart doesn't love justice? How can you make your heart be what it is not? Only God can do that. So, Micah's list ends with "and to walk humbly with your God." Life with God enlivens life with others. "We love because he first loved us" (1 John 4:19), means that if we let him love us, we will love others too. To pray is to let God love you. Who you become in the presence of God will impact the world around you in love of mercy and acts of justice. It will make you good in the best sense of the word.

PRAYER: *Righteous Father! May your mercy and justice infect me with a love for mercy that is expressed in acts of justice.*

Introduction to Nahum

DAY 186: DANGEROUS OPPORTUNITY

"The Lord is slow to anger and great in power; the Lord will not leave the guilty unpunished" (Nah. 1:3).

It's the same God. Read Jonah and hear of God's love for the people of Nineveh; then read Nahum and hear of his plans to destroy them. It's the same God who does both. God himself is infinite, but his patience is not. There comes a time when his holy love and wisdom deem it time to stop being patient. The message of Nahum is that that time has come. Nineveh's unrepentant evil will bring God's righteous wrath to the city.

The Chinese word for "crisis" is made up of two characters: *wei* and *ji*. Each of these characters forms half the word; the first meaning *danger*, the second meaning *opportunity*. A crisis, by this definition, is literally a "dangerous opportunity." As with any proclamation of God's word, Jonah's preaching to the city brought a crisis, a dangerous opportunity to Nineveh. The opportunity was to live in the time of God's favor, the danger was not to. Otherwise, one day the preaching of a Jonah must give way to the preaching of Nahum.

All prayer for the lost is crisis prayer. There should be urgency to our intercession, for one day, time will run out and there will no more opportunity—only danger. "Now is the time of God's favor" (2 Cor. 6:2), doesn't necessarily mean that tomorrow will be.

PRAYER: *Pray for those who have not yet received Christ, and for those who have fallen away from the faith. Ask the Holy Spirit to open their eyes to what hangs in the balance, heaven or hell, life or death, forever.*

DAY 187: HOLY JEALOUSY

Nahum 1:1-8

"The Lord is a jealous and avenging God" (Nah. 1:2).

"The Lord is a jealous and avenging God" (Nah. 1:2). Really? The avenging part is more palatable to our religious sensibilities than the jealous part. Isn't envy a synonym for jealousy? It isn't if it applies to a husband who has been cuckolded. Jealousy is more than a morally legitimate word in love's vocabulary—it is a necessity. If promises were made to be faithful and loyal forever, no matter what, not to be jealous when those promises are broken would be morally reprehensible. "You say you're having an affair? How interesting. Let me know if you'll be in late tonight. I'll leave the porch light on." God's jealousy is his holy passion for his bride.

But it works a little differently in this context. God's passion for his people will show itself by avenging the evil the Assyrians have wreaked on Israel. There is an extremely important principle at work in this. Sometimes, when God's people are unfaithful to him, his jealousy for his people stirs him to anger against them. When this happens, he will sometimes use other nations as his instruments of justice. Unwittingly, Assyria was one of these nations. God used their evil, imperial schemes to conquer other nations and to punish his people for their unfaithfulness. But Assyria's schemes were still evil, so once the sovereign Lord used them to punish his people, he then turned to the Assyrians to punish them. In both cases it was his jealousy at work: in one case against his people with Assyria; in the other case against Assyria, for his people!

The point of all this is that God is supremely good. He will brook no rivals and will leave no sin unpunished. He will love his chosen ones with an everlasting love, but not a blind love. He will wound in order to heal (Hos. 6:1-3), and then he will wound those he used to do the wounding. "Nothing in all creation is hidden from God's sight. Everything is uncovered and laid bare before the eyes of him to whom we must give an account" (Heb. 4:13).

Sometimes it is good to simply pause and consider who this God is we sometimes speak to so glibly in prayer and to be moved to greater wonder and reverence for his holy love. "He is terribly tender and terribly demanding, terribly loving and terribly stern, terribly soft and terribly hard."[1] In other words, he loves us the way we all want to be loved, in our heart of hearts.

PRAYER: *Holy One, you are God, and I am not. Your thoughts are not my thoughts, and your ways are not my ways. I bless you that they are not.*

Introduction to Habakkuk

DAY 188: THE RIGHTEOUS SHALL LIVE BY FAITH

"But the righteous person shall live by his faithfulness" (Hab. 2:4).

The Talmud records the judgment of one rabbi that, "Moses gave Israel 613 commandments, David reduced them to 10, Isaiah to 2, Habakkuk to one: the righteous shall live by his faith" (Hab. 2:4).[1] It could be argued that Luther's apprehension of this same verse that Paul used it in his Romans epistle (Rom. 1:17) sparked the Protestant Reformation and changed the history of the world. It was a God-given insight that came to Habakkuk in a great crisis of faith.

The very thought that God would use a nation as evil as the Babylonians to punish his people Israel was unthinkable to Habakkuk (see yesterday's devotion), but that was exactly what God was doing. He said, "Look at the nations and watch—and be utterly amazed. For I am doing something in your days that you would not believe, even if you were told" (Hab. 1:5). That was certainly true! All Habakkuk could think to say in reply was, "Your eyes are too pure to look on evil; you cannot tolerate wrong. Why then do you tolerate the treacherous" (Hab. 1:13)? The Lord's reply was essentially "Wait and see what will happen; don't stop here, read the rest of the story. Judgment will come to Babylon too." Habakkuk 2:3 reads, "For the revelation awaits an appointed time; it speaks of the end and will not prove false. Though it linger, wait for it; it will certainly come and will not delay." It is after this reassurance that God tells Habakkuk, and all his people, that, "the righteous will live by his faith" (Hab. 2:4). In other words, "You don't see the whole picture, but I do, and I will do what is right. You're right: I cannot tolerate wrong. Trust me and wait and you will see just how true this is."

PRAYER: *The hardest part of prayer is the waiting and the disappointment. The faith of some has weakened and faltered in delay. But what was true for Habakkuk is true for all of us: We may pray with Habakkuk, "Though it linger, wait for it; it will certainly come and will not delay" (Hab. 2:3).*

DAY 189: FEET LIKE A DEER'S

Habakkuk 3:17-19

"Yet I will rejoice in the Lord" (Hab. 3:18).

It may be a little scary but make a list of the worst things you can think of that could happen to you. Read each of them to God, with the preface, "Though…" and the response, "Yet I will rejoice in the Lord, I will be joyful in God my Savior" (Hab. 3:18). When you are through the list, you should end with Habakkuk 3:19: "The Sovereign Lord is my strength; he makes my feet like the feet of a deer, he enables me to go on to the heights."

If you do this, you will do as Habakkuk did in this spectacular faith-text. In verse 17, he lists the kind of things that will probably come with a Babylonian invasion. Then he ends his worst-case scenario with, "yet I will rejoice in the Lord." There is more than meets the eye in, "he makes my feet like the feet of a deer, he enables me to go to the heights." The obvious is that God will make him sure-footed, no matter what high and dangerous places he may have to tread in the future. That's true, but he is saying more. "High places" in the Bible is usually a reference to places under the control of demonic forces, places of pagan worship. These high places were chosen for worship because they symbolized power—those who have the high ground in a battle control the battle. The faith of Habakkuk is that God may lead him to tread in dangerous and dark places—mountains, not valleys of the shadow of death. But his feet will not slip. In fact, he will take the high ground and, with it, possession of the land!

PRAYER: *A great parallel passage is Romans 8:37-39. It can be read and prayed antiphonally with Habakkuk 3:17-19*

Romans: "No, in all these things we are more than conquerors through him who loved us."

Habakkuk: "He makes my feet like the feet of a deer, he enables me to go to the heights."

Romans: "For I am convinced that neither death nor life, neither angels nor demons, neither the present nor the future, nor any powers, neither height nor depth, nor anything else in all creation…"

Habakkuk: "Though the fig tree does not bud…"

Romans: "Nothing will be able to separate us from the love of God that is in Christ Jesus our Lord."

Habakkuk: "Yet will I rejoice in the Lord."

This is the faith the righteous live by!

DAY 190: MAN OF PRAYER

E. M. Bounds (1835-1913) Man of Prayer

"Be joyful always; pray continually; give thanks in all circumstances, for this is God's will for you in Christ Jesus" (1 Thess. 5:16-18).

Bounds never forgot the men who had fought and died under his care. While serving as a chaplain in the Confederate army, he had won their respect, traveling with them, leading them in prayer and worship, and fearlessly braving the front lines in some of the bloodiest battles in American history.

For the rest of his days, he kept a list of their names in his wallet so he could pray for their families. The postwar south was in shambles, its people defeated and dejected. The chilling evidence of war was everywhere, from burned-out barns and houses to the common sight of men without arms, legs, and eyes. Bounds felt a deep love for the defeated people of Franklin, Tennessee, and he served as their faithful intercessor and preacher in a local pulpit.

Bounds strongly believed in the power of prayer. He gathered a group of men to pray with him every Tuesday night for revival, "until God answered by fire." A year passed, but the men continued praying. Finally, revival did come, and nearly 150 men and women "were gloriously converted."

After serving several years at churches in Alabama, Tennessee, and Missouri, he became editor of the St. Louis *Christian Advocate*. He spent his years with the *Advocate* calling the church to pray for revival while fighting the rising invasion of theological liberalism in America. "It is not new truth that the world needs," wrote Bounds, "so much as the constant iteration of old truths, yet ever new truths, of the Bible."

For the last seventeen years of his life, Bounds lived with his family in Washington, Georgia. His time was spent reading, writing, and praying. His habit was to rise every morning at 4am for prayer, breaking at seven o'clock for breakfast, and then spending the morning writing, only to return to prayer in the afternoon. On August 24, 1913, E.M. Bounds died—an old soldier of Jesus. A close friend received a postcard from Bounds written shortly before his death. It read: "Hold to the old truths—double distilled."

Bounds writings on prayer are imminently quotable. He was, at his best, speaking prophetically:

> *We are constantly on a stretch, if not a strain, to devise new methods, new plans, new organizations to advance the church and secure enlargement and efficiency for the gospel.... Men are God's method. The church is looking for better methods; God is looking for better men.... What the church needs today is not more machinery or better, not new organizations or more and novel methods, but men whom the Holy Spirit can use—men of prayer, mighty in prayer. The Holy Spirit does not flow through methods, but through men. He does not come on machinery, but on men. He does not anoint plans, but men—men of prayer.*[1]

PRAYER: *Spirit of God, I want to be a person of prayer. Use me, flow through me, anoint me—to be mighty in prayer.*

Introduction to Zephaniah

DAY 191: ONE DAY TIME WILL RUN OUT

"Seek righteousness, seek humility; perhaps you will be sheltered on the day of the Lord's anger" (Zeph. 2:3).

In Zephaniah 1:7, there is as grisly a picture of God's judgment as there is anywhere in the Bible: "The Lord has prepared a sacrifice; he has consecrated those he has invited." It's just one line, and there aren't any florid adjectives in it, but the picture is horrible. The sacrifice referred to is Israel, the "consecrated" ones (a term for priests) whom God has invited are the Babylonian conquerors. Every Jew knew what a sacrifice entailed: the slitting of an animal's throat, the butchering of the carcass, and the burning of the remains. That's what the pagan Babylonians—as God's priests or consecrated ones—were going to do to Israel. Descriptions of ancient battles from antiquity confirm the brutality these "consecrated" ones were capable of. The type of judgment is shockingly pertinent to Israel's sin: since they wouldn't offer themselves as living sacrifices to God in holy living, God himself will make a deadly sacrifice of them in judgment.

Zephaniah is absorbed by the theme of judgment generally—toward Israel and her enemies, but really toward the whole world. Zephaniah prophesied regarding the coming "Day of the Lord" that God told him, "I have decided to assemble the nations, to gather the kingdoms and to pour my wrath on them—all my fierce anger. The whole world will be consumed by the fire of my jealous anger" (Zeph. 3:8).

What does all this mean for those who pray that God's kingdom will come? It means that one day time will run out, and that those who refused to pray, will pray for the mountains and rocks to hide them from the wrath of God (Rev. 6:15-17). It means our prayers should be sober and urgent; for every prayer for Jesus to come implies a prayer for the great and final cosmic Day of the Lord to come—of which Zephaniah's prophecy was but a foretaste. Jesus and his apostles spoke frequently and pointedly of that day (Matt. 24:9-14; Rom. 2:16; 1 Cor. 1:8; Rev. 19:11-18).

PRAYER: *"Who knows the power of your anger? For your wrath is as great as the fear that is due you. Teach us to number our days aright, that we may gain a heart of wisdom" (Ps. 90:11, 12).*

DAY 192: MADE PURE BY FIRE

Zephaniah 1:1-7; 2:1-3; 3:9-20

"Then will I purify the lips of the peoples" (Zeph. 3:9).

A wedding ring is a splendid symbol of the marriage of a man and woman, and of God and his people. It is a circle, a symbol of eternity. Human love is beautiful, like the flowers in a wedding. But like the flowers in a wedding, it wilts and fades over time if it is uprooted from the soil of God's eternal love. To survive and flourish, our love must be planted in God.

A ring is also made of a precious metal. Precious metals are made more precious by fire since it is the fire that melts out the impurities. Marriages have their fire—both passion and disappointment, tragedies and misunderstandings. The fire need not destroy the marriage. It can make the marriage purer and more precious.

God is a husband to his people; he has married himself to us in covenant love. When we persist in sin like an unfaithful spouse, God brings the fire of judgment. Sometimes the fire is brutal and searing, like the Day of the Lord described in Zephaniah. But its purpose is for purity: "Then will I purify the lips of the peoples, that all of them may call on the name of the Lord" (Zeph. 3:9). The fire of judgment isn't God's last word; it's his next-to-last word. His last word is the redemption and restoration described at the end of Zephaniah's prophecy, and it is for the whole world, "that all of them may call on the name of the Lord." God doesn't enjoy judgment. It is work he must do, but Isaiah calls it his strange work… his alien task" (Isa. 28:21). "As surely as I live, declares the Sovereign Lord, I take no pleasure in the death of the wicked, but rather that they turn from their ways and live. Turn! Turn from your evil ways" (Ezek. 33:11)!

Knowing God's character gives us great hope to pray in the face of judgment. For we pray to a God who is not willing that any should perish, and who wills to turn the fires of judgment into the fires of purification. Even in the midst of Zephaniah's harshest words, we read this: "Seek the Lord, all you humble of the land, you who do what he commands. Seek righteousness, seek humility; perhaps you will be sheltered on the day of the Lord's anger" (Zeph. 2:3).

PRAYER: *Holy and merciful Father, if we got what we deserved we would all die as Jesus died. In your justice, please remember your mercy, and let your punishment be for our purification, not our destruction.*

Introduction to Haggai

DAY 193: THE SINS OF THE AFTERNOON

"Is it a time for you yourselves to be living in your paneled houses, while this house remains a ruin?" (Hag. 1:4).

The hardest part of a long-distance race is the middle. The beginning is flushed with excitement, and the end is animated by the hope of finishing, maybe winning. But the middle is in-between, where boredom and fatigue set in, and it can feel there has been no beginning and there will be no end—just pointless, weary effort. People can become self-absorbed when the race is life. Changing the metaphor, they become prey to the sins of the afternoon. "There comes an hour in the afternoon," wrote G. K. Chesterton, "when the child is tired of 'pretending'; when he is weary of being a robber or a cowboy. It is then that he torments the cat.... The effect of this staleness is everywhere."[1] Israel is in a time after the exile and their return to Jerusalem. All the hopes of a new beginning and the excitement of rebuilding have faded. It is the middle of the race, and the hour is 4:00 in the afternoon. They have turned inward to purely selfish pursuits for personal peace and affluence.

This is the situation the prophets Haggai, Zechariah, and Malachi spoke into. Each had a message of hope and warning to the bored and slothful. Their prophecies anticipate the fulfillment of all hopes. They provide glimpses into God's good future when the one comes who "will turn the hearts of the fathers to their children, and the hearts of the children to their fathers" (Mal. 4:6); when the "desired of all nations will come" (Hag. 2:7); when "they will look on... the one they have pierced, and they will mourn for him as one mourns for an only child" (Zech. 12:10); and when at last, "a fountain will be opened... to cleanse them from sin and iniquity" (Zech. 13:1).

Through the prophecies of these last three Old Testament prophets, a bright future invades the pallid present of Israel. As Chesterton put it, right in the middle of the staleness of the afternoon, "stands up an enormous exception. It is quite unlike anything else. It is a thing final like the trumpet of doom, though it is also a piece of good news, or news that seems too good to be true. It is nothing less than the loud assertion that this mysterious maker of the world has visited his world in person."[2] If that hope can't spur us to eager, faithful prayer, nothing will!

PRAYER: *Father in heaven! Give me grace to finish this life well, having fought the good fight, finished the race, and kept the faith (2 Tim. 4:7).*

DAY 194: MISPLACED PRIORITIES

Haggai 1:3-11

"Give careful thought to your ways" (Hag. 1:5).

After two years of falling profits, an expensive management guru was called in to help a large corporation streamline its operations and become more productive. After in-depth interviews with people at all levels of the organization, he submitted his report. His recommendation was, beginning with the president, to have each employee make a list each day of the things that need to be done. Then they were to assign numbers to each of the items on their list; number one for the most important item, number two for the second most important item, and so on. In other words, to improve productivity they were to set priorities: do first things first, and second things second.

Jesus said as much when he said, "But seek first [God's] kingdom and his righteousness, and all these things will be given to you as well" (Matt. 6:33). The "these things" are food, clothing, and shelter, the so-called basics, or necessities of life. But there is something more basic than the basics, more necessary than the necessaries: seeking God's kingdom. No matter how good the superstructure, the building will collapse if the foundation is missing.

Haggai was preaching kingdom priorities when he asked, "Is it a time for you yourselves to be living in your paneled houses, while this house remains a ruin" (Hag. 1:4)? The house in ruin was the temple, the place of worship. The "paneled houses" were their homes, which the people were building to look like palaces (cedar paneling was the preferred interior for king's dwellings). Clearly their priorities were upside down, and with them everything else. The economy was failing, and every effort they made to fix it seemed to do the opposite: "You have planted much but have harvested little. You eat, but never have enough" (Hag. 1:6). The way to fix all this was to stop trying to fix it and put God back in his proper place. The problem wasn't with their work, but with their worship.

How are your priorities relative to your work and your worship? Andrew Murray spoke much like Haggai, when he wrote, "Our true aim must not be to work a great deal and pray just enough to keep the work right. We should pray a great deal and then work enough for the power and blessing obtained in prayer to find its way through us to men."[1]

PRAYER: *Father, forgive me my misplaced priorities. Give me the faith to see that my salvation and strength is in repentance and rest, quietness and trust.*

Introduction to Zechariah

DAY 195: FAITH LIKE A FARMER

"Who despises the day of small things?" (Zech. 4:10).

The task at hand for the exiles was to finish rebuilding the temple. But the work had stalled more than once. Zechariah, like Haggai his contemporary, declared his prophecies into the indolence and torpor of Jerusalem in the late sixth century BC. Haggai's message was how the present could be transformed by faithfulness to the task (see yesterday's devotion on Haggai 1:3-11). Zechariah's instruction was to place the task under the light of a spectacular future. The most Messianic of the prophets, Zechariah is often quoted in the New Testament, especially in the passion narratives and in the book of Revelation. Through Zechariah, God asked the people rhetorically, "Who despises the day of small things?" (Zech. 4:10). If anyone in the nation raised their hands, they should put them back down. Paraphrased, the point was, "Things don't look great right now, but they will, so work as though you believed it."

Jesus said the kingdom of God is like a mustard seed (Mark 4:30-32). It starts tiny but grows into something huge. It is often God's practice to start small; like yeast in dough, like a seed in the soil, like a word spoken into nothing. Hope sustains work and prayer like nothing else can. The key is to think like a farmer and wait for the harvest, always watering and feeding and cultivating hope. No one who waits on the Lord will be disappointed.

PRAYER: *Father in Heaven! Give me faith to live now as though I have already received your promises.*

DAY 196: GOOD GRIEF

Zechariah 12:10—13:1

"And I will pour out on the house of David and the inhabitants of Jerusalem a spirit of grace and supplication. They will look on me, the one they have pierced, and they will mourn for him as one mourns for an only child" (Zech. 12:10).

Sometimes we have to hurt before we can heal; mourn before we can rejoice. This is the good grief Paul spoke of to the Corinthians: "For you became sorrowful as God intended.... Godly sorrow brings repentance that leads to salvation and leaves no regret" (2 Cor. 7:9-10). The "spirit of grace and supplication" that Zechariah prophesied God would pour out on Israel is also this good grief. This "grace and supplication" will come when they look "on me, the one they have pierced." Since it is God speaking, the one pierced is God! "And they will mourn for him as one mourns for an only child and grieve bitterly for him as one grieves for a firstborn son." The supplication will be prayers of sorrowful repentance. Zechariah is truly the most Messianic of the prophets.

This piercing of God's Servant and Son, by the very ones he loved, runs deep in the biblical witness to the Savior of Israel (cf. Ps. 22:6; Isa. 53:5; John 19:34-37; Rev. 1:7). Even his mother would feel the stab (Luke 2:35). To look to the Savior and mourn would be to acknowledge that they were the perpetrators of his wounds. Zechariah's prophecy peeled the bandages off a very deep and festering wound in Israel's relationship with God. It must do the same for all of us. The heart of our darkness is that we have pierced the heart of God. The heart of his love is that he has allowed us to do it. "But he was pierced for our transgressions, he was crushed for iniquities; the punishment that brought us peace was upon him, and by his wounds we are healed" (Isa. 53:5). We are healed by his wounds, but the healing cannot come unless we are wounded by his wounds; smitten by the godly grief that leads to repentance and salvation.

"God have mercy on me, a sinner!" is the most essential of prayers. It is the grace and supplication the Spirit brings to anyone who will look on the One who was pierced and mourn. When that prayer is prayed, "a fountain will be opened… to cleanse them from sin and impurity" (Zech. 13:1).

PRAYER: *"What Thou, my Lord, hast suffered, Was all for sinners' gain; Mine, mine was the transgression, But Thine the deadly pain." God have mercy on me, a sinner. (from the hymn "O Sacred Head Now Wounded")*

DAY 197: THE IMITATION OF CHRIST

Thomas A Kempis (1379/80-1471)

"Whom have I in heaven but you? And earth has nothing I desire besides you. My flesh and my heart may fail, but God is the strength of my heart and my portion forever" (Ps. 73:25-26).

The Imitation of Christ is considered by many to be second only to the Bible in its profound wisdom, clarity of thought, and converting power. The spectrum of its admirers is as broad as the church of Christ: St. Thomas More, General Gordon, St. Ignatius Loyola, John Wesley, St. Francis Xavier, and Dr. Johnson—not to mention countless other lay people who have acknowledged their debt to his book even though it was originally written by a monk for monks.

The common theme throughout the *Imitation* is our complete dependence on the love, mercy, and holiness of God, through Christ.

"Nothing is sweeter than love, nothing stronger, nothing higher, nothing wider, nothing more pleasant, and nothing fuller or better in heaven or earth; for love is born of God, and can rest only in God, above all created things."[1]

Moreover, in the personal nature of his dialogues between man and God in the *Imitation*, it is shown by A Kempis that Christ is not a static figure frozen in history, but a living and present reality. The risen Christ shapes the spiritual lives of his disciples today as decisively as the Christ of history shaped his disciples in the first century. Love is not an idea or abstract virtue, but a person. Ever the pastor, A Kempis can speak as mystic and scholar, but above all as guide to the practical issues of living the spiritual life. He tells us not only *why* we must imitate Christ but *how*.

The Imitation of Christ was finished in 1427, and hand-written copies were humbly circulated. In 1472, a year after A Kempis' death, the *Imitation* was set in type, and by 1779, 1,800 editions and translations were spread across Europe.

PRAYER:

O Lord, what can I trust in this life? And what is my greatest comfort on earth? It is you, O Lord, whose love is without limit. When have I ever done well without you? When have I ever been harmed when you are present? I would rather be poor with you, than rich without you. I would rather be a wanderer on the earth with you, than to be in heaven without you. For where you are, there is heaven. And where you are not, there is death and hell. You are everything that I long for; therefore, I will earnestly pray to you. There is no one who can help me except you alone, O my God. For you are my hope, you are my assurance, you are my strength, you are my comfort, and my most faithful helper in every need.[2]

Introduction to Malachi

DAY 198: PRAYER IN TIME OF DISAPPOINTMENT

"'I have loved you,' says the Lord. But you ask, 'How have you loved us?'" (Mal. 1:2).

The book of Malachi opens with a sad poignancy. God says to his people, "I have loved you." But they ask, "How have you loved us?" Their question seems to say, "All this talk about your love is just that—talk." That's the way we feel when we are disappointed with God. Whatever the let-down—broken health, financial loss, wayward children—it can seem that he just didn't come through with what he promised.

That's the state of Israel's psyche when Malachi delivers his prophecy. In a sense, the glorious prophesies of Haggai and Zechariah had come true: the exiles had returned to the land, rebuilt the temple, and repaired the wall in Jerusalem as predicted. Israel was a nation again. But nothing about it seemed very glorious. Israel was still a third-rate power, a nobody on the margins of the Persian Empire. Jerusalem's temple had once been "beautiful in its loftiness, the joy of the whole earth" (Ps. 48:2). What a joke those words seemed now as the people looked at a city and temple that were bare sketches, little stick figures of what they once were.

Disappointment with God takes us to very predictable places. Bitterness sets in, and we think thoughts that were once unthinkable: "All who do evil are good in the eyes of the Lord" (Mal. 2:17). Worship becomes so listless as to disgust God: "Oh, that one of you would shut the temple doors, so you would not light useless fires on my altar! I am not pleased with you…" (Mal. 1:10). We hold so tightly to whatever security we think we have, especially money, that we rob God: "Will a man rob God? Yet you rob me… In tithes and offerings" (Mal. 3:8). Even marriages suffer. Hearts that grow cold toward God will soon grow cold to those nearest us: "You have broken faith with her, though she is your partner, the wife of your marriage covenant" (Mal. 2:14).

Malachi provides an agenda for prayer in a time of disappointment with God. First, praise God for his faithfulness in the past and his promises for the future. Remember to "guard yourself in your spirit" by remembering that "I the Lord do not change" (Mal. 2:16; 3:6). Second, get back into conversation with God. Throughout the book, God structures his message in the form of an invitation to a dialogue (Mal. 1:2, 6-7; 2:17; 3:7-8, 13-14). Talk to God more than you talk about him.

PRAYER: *Father! Make me alert to guard my spirit. Save me from my tendencies toward self-pity, bitterness, and ingratitude!*

DAY 199: PRAYER AND MONEY

Malachi 3:8-12

"Will a man rob God?" (Mal. 3:8).

The accusation that they were robbing God had to grate on the conscience of Malachi's hearers—and their patience. Crops had been bad, cash was scarce, and now they were being pressured to give. But robbing God was a serious offense that could not be sloughed off simply by complaining about how little they had. They knew about the tithing laws, and they knew they hadn't been tithing. The prophecy would have sent them into angry despair if they didn't hear why God was so insistent about their giving. He wanted to bless them: "Test me in this… and see if I will not throw open the floodgates of heaven and pour out so much blessing that you will not have room enough for it" (Mal. 3:10). Storing up their treasures in heaven (Matt. 6:20) would actually increase their treasures on earth!

What we do with our finances has a direct bearing on our prayer life. Certainly, robbing God puts a strain on the relationship. But there is a deeper reason for its importance: Jesus said giving was a form of investment, of storing up treasures in heaven, and added, "For where your treasure is, there your heart will be also" (Matt. 6:21). That is where money and prayer intersect. Prayer is a matter of the heart; a bad heart makes for bad prayer, and a good heart makes for good prayer. If your heart is somewhere other than with the Lord, then your prayer life will suffer. Put your treasure with God and your heart will be there too. It's that simple. "'Return to me and I will return to you,' says the Lord Almighty" (Mal. 3:7).

We can come closer to God by what we do with our money, but it isn't because we really give anything to him. Whatever we give to God, he gave us in the first place. What happens is that, when we give, we imitate God. By acting like God, we form a deeper fellowship of love. We become a little more like his beloved Son: "For you know the grace of our Lord Jesus Christ, that though he was rich, yet for your sakes he became poor, so that you through his poverty might become rich" (2 Cor. 8:9).

PRAYER: *Gracious and generous God, you are my treasure. If giving you my money brings me closer to you, then no amount of giving is too much.*

Introduction to Matthew

DAY 200: THE SPREADING CIRCLE

"All authority in heaven and on earth has been given to me. Therefore, go and make disciples of all nations" (Matt. 28:18).

Matthew's gospel starts off as Jewish as can be but ends up as global as can be. Its first words are, "A record of the genealogy of Jesus Christ the son of David, the son of Abraham" (Matt. 1:1). The first thing Matthew wants to do is establish Jesus' credentials as the promised Jewish Messiah, the sum of a particular people's identity and hopes. Many have recognized Matthew as the most Jewish of the gospels. But by the end of the gospel, the thing Matthew wants to leave us with is an identity and hope as big as the world. Jesus' parting words to his disciples are, "All authority in heaven and on earth has been given to me. Therefore, go and make disciples of *all nations*" (Matt. 28:18-20, italics added).

Along the way, hints of where Matthew is heading appear frequently. In Jesus' infancy, there is the visit of the Magi, men from the other nations, who come to worship the "king of the Jews" (Matt. 2:2). Other precursors include the preaching of John the Baptist whose call to baptism, in effect, ex-communicates the entire Jewish nation, putting them on the same footing as every other nation (Matt. 3:1-12). Matthew describes the exemplary faith of the Roman centurion, earning Jesus' most glowing accolade: "I tell you the truth, I have not found anyone *in Israel* with such great faith" (Matt. 8:10, italics added). Matthew also relates the parable of the field which is the world (Matt. 13:38) and the tenacious faith of another non-Jew, a Canaanite woman (Matt. 15:21-28).

St. Matthew's overriding passion is to show Jesus to be the fulfillment of all of God's promises in Old Testament Scripture. The word "fulfilled" appears twelve times in the gospel, but the idea is implicit throughout. Jesus fulfills, or "fills-full," all God did and said before. Matthew shows the hope of Israel to be far more than Israel ever hoped. He is the hope of all the nations of the earth! Surprisingly then, the very Jewishness of Matthew serves as a bridge linking God's promises to a particular people with his intentions for all peoples. The son of David (Matt. 1:1), it turns out, was all along really the Son of God, the second person of the Trinity (Matt. 28:19).

When we pray as Jesus taught, we always pray for more than we understand. The kingdom is better and bigger than we can imagine. Even the bread we are commanded to pray for (Matt. 6:11) is but a sign of "the food that endures to eternal life" (John 6:27). God fulfills our prayers in ways that no eye has seen, no ear has heard, and no mind has conceived (1 Cor. 2:9). As Luther was fond of saying, we ask for silver, but God gives us gold instead.

PRAYER: *Thank you, Father, that you had the whole world in mind when you gave one couple, and one people, a son though whom you would bless everyone.*

DAY 201: HE'S BEEN WAITING FOR YOU

Matthew 1:1-17 (Luke 3:21-38)

"A record of the genealogy of Jesus Christ" (Matt. 1:1).

This is one of two passages that many people skip over when reading the gospels. The other is Luke 3:21-38. Both are genealogies—lists of obscure people with hard to pronounce names that serve as a kind of family tree or pedigree for Jesus. Both include names of people who can be described as good, bad, ugly, surprising, and obscure. Look the names up sometime; it's worth the effort.

When did God start thinking about Jesus? Matthew's list says it began at least with Abraham, 2000 years before Jesus was born. Luke's list goes back even further to Adam, the first human. The orthodox and correct answer is, God never started thinking about his Son. He was always with God the Father.

Maybe a better question is: When did God start thinking about us? The genealogies tell us that God has been thinking about saving us for a very long time. These names are like synapses in the mind of God leading up to the great name he will speak in Jesus. A synapse is the point in the brain where a nervous impulse passes from one neuron to another. These people are the connections in God's thought about his plan to save the world through his Son. Actually, his thoughts began even before these people. "For he chose us in [Christ] before the creation of the world" (Eph. 1:4).

When you pray, you are not interrupting God, you are joining God! Before you spoke to him, he was speaking to you. To pray is to enter into the conversation. Jesus said our Father knows what we need before we ask him (Matt. 6:8). That is because he knew us before we knew him. There is nothing you can say that can possibly surprise God—no sin to confess, no need to express. He has been waiting for you to speak for a very long time.

PRAYER: *Father in Heaven! I come to you today, knowing you were here before I got here. Thank you that I am part of your eternal plan, and that I join you in your grand purposes as I pray.*

DAY 202: AT EASE WITH GOD

Matthew 6:5-8

"And when you pray, do not be like the hypocrites" (Matt. 6:5).

"Hypocrisy is the homage that vice pays to virtue," wrote La Rochefoucauld in his *Maxims*; and with some cynicism added, "Our virtues are frequently but vices disguised." The point it seems is that the good is enormously attractive, even to those who are bad. If they won't be good, they at least try to look good. To whom do they look good? They look good to those who can see only the exterior of their lives and maybe to themselves. Hypocrites aren't usually strong in self-awareness.

The problem with praying as a hypocrite is that God can't be fooled. With God there is no exterior and interior, no public me and private me. There is only me. If I pray to look good to others and pull it off, Jesus said I will get my reward all right; the thing I really wanted. But it will be my only reward. I may pray and be well thought of by others, but I pray impoverished, because I pray without God.

Pagans aren't totally unlike the hypocrites. Their babblings may be sincere, but they are sincerely wrong in the same way hypocrites are insincerely "right." Both pray to a false god. The hypocrite thinks God doesn't see; the pagan thinks he doesn't know. Jesus assures us that God both sees who we are on the inside and knows what we need before we ask.

The good news here is that we can be completely at ease with a God like this. There is no way we can surprise or shock him. So why try? It is futile. He loves us as much before we confess our sins as he does after we confess them. He knows better than we do what we need. We don't need to impress him with eloquence or theological depth in our prayers, because frankly, we can't! The sincere lisp of a child means as much to him as all the poets have ever attempted.

PRAYER: *Father, you know me inside and out. May that knowledge encourage me to greater intimacy with you.*

DAY 203: THE SUM OF ALL PRAYERS

Matthew 6:9-13 (Luke 11:2-4)

"This, then, is how you should pray" (Matt. 6:9).

Thomas Aquinas believed everything we need to know is found in three things. We know what to believe from The Apostles' Creed; what to do from The Ten Commandments; and what to pray from The Lord's Prayer.

The Lord's Prayer is like a compass. It points to true north, and from there east, west, and south. In other words, when we are clear on God's priorities, all other concerns find their proper place. The Lord's Prayer washes and dresses and sanctifies our longings and desires, and it gives them their proper expression. And what it does for us it does for all the prayers of the Bible, implicit and explicit. All the truth of Holy Scripture can be hung on the pegs of its petitions.

Clearly Jesus meant for it to be repeated, not as meaningless repetitions (Matt. 6:7), but as meaningful repetitions—to be whispered tenderly and often the way lovers speak to each other. The Lord's Prayer can be like a Christmas tree on which we hang our own decorations, our own prayers. Or it can be like a map. The directions, the guidelines, are there, but we must take the trouble to travel, to pray them.[1] Each direction, each guideline says, "pray this way."

First, we pray that God's name be hallowed, revered, respected, held in awe, and adored. The beginning of wisdom, after all, is the fear of the Lord (Ps. 11:10; Prov. 1:7).

We also pray that God's kingdom will come and that he will sovereignly bring about the glorious day when the earth will be as full of the knowledge of God as the waters cover the sea (Isa. 11:9). We pray that every knee will bow, and every tongue confess that Jesus Christ is Lord (Phil. 2:10-11).

We pray that he will be our food and drink as we work and wait for his kingdom (John 4:34) and that, in the meantime, God will provide our bread, whatever we need to persevere (Matt. 6:19-34).

We pray that God will forgive our sins. Isn't it lovely that Jesus teaches us to wait before we talk to God about our sins—to speak first to God about God before we speak to God about us?

Finally, we pray that we will be protected from every test and from evil as we struggle in this spiritual warfare for God's rule on earth (Eph. 6:10-20).

Pray these petitions as you read your Bible. The possibilities and variations are endless.

DAY 204: FORGIVE AS YOU HAVE BEEN FORGIVEN

Matthew 6:12-15

"But if you do not forgive [others] their sins, your Father will not forgive your sins" (Matt. 6:15).

It is possible to be in prayer and far from God. When Cain brought his offering to God, his heart was full of anger and hate; revealed by what he did later to his brother Abel when Abel's offering was accepted, and Cain's was refused (Gen. 4:1-8). Clearly, the Pharisee praying alongside the tax collector was also far from God, though he imagined himself to be standing in God's presence (Luke 18:9-14).

That's because there is a direct connection between our relationship to others and our relationship to God. If things aren't right between others and us, we can be sure they aren't right between God and us.

This is especially true in the area of forgiveness. Jesus is alarmingly blunt: forgive others and God will forgive you; refuse them forgiveness and God will refuse you forgiveness. There is a profound logic to this principle. It goes like this. Question: what do you most need from God? Answer: his mercy. Question: what do others most need from you? Answer: your mercy. Question: how can you expect to receive what you most need from God, if you refuse others the thing that they most need from you?

And what are we saying to God if we refuse to forgive others? Do we think their sin against us is so bad that it is beyond his mercy? Or worse, do we think the sin God forgave us wasn't really so bad after all—that we in some way deserved his forgiveness? Either way, the cross is emptied of its power. God's mercy is trivialized, and we make ourselves little gods.

To be forgiven is very humbling. John Newton, the author of the hymn "Amazing Grace," was a slave trader and libertine before his conversion. He never forgot what it meant for God to forgive him, and what that forgiveness meant in his attitude toward others. He wrote, "A man, truly illuminated, will no more despise others, than Bartimaeus, after his own eyes were opened, would take a stick, and beat every blind man he met."[1]

PRAYER: *As you pray, forgive those who have sinned against you. If need be, ask God to forgive your lack of forgiveness.*

DAY 205: ALWAYS READY TO LISTEN

Matthew 7:7-11 (Luke 11:9-13)

"How much more will your Father in heaven give good gifts to those who ask him?" (Matt. 7:11).

Considering how much stock Jesus put in prayer, it's a little surprising how little he had to say about how to pray. He said nothing about techniques or mechanics of prayer. About all he had to say about how to pray is to keep at it, to persist and persevere (Matt. 7:7-8). His silence on techniques probably stems from the fact that prayer is a heart matter and more about who we are than what we do. Prayer is not so much about communication as communion with God.

But Jesus had a lot to say about why we should pray and persist in prayer because God is always ready to listen and incredibly generous with his gifts (Matt. 7:9-11).

Jesus reasoned this way: Good parents are good only insofar as they are like the Father in heaven. He isn't like a good parent; good parents are a little like him. One of his great qualities is his generosity and kindness. In this sense, even bad people can be pretty good parents because even they know how to give good gifts to their kids. Everyone knows this. So how much more will the Father in heaven, of whom even the best parents are but rough copies, give good things to those who ask him?

Luke's version of this saying tells us that Jesus summed up the "good gifts" as the Holy Spirit. "How much more will your Father in heaven give the Holy Spirit to those who ask him" (Luke 11:13)! Here is an even more profound reason to trust God's good intentions for us: not only does he want to give us good gifts, but he also wants to give us himself. Even his gifts would no longer be good if they did not lead us to his heart.

So, we persist and persevere in prayer not because God is reluctant to give, but because he is so very ready to give! "Perseverance is the rope that ties the soul to the doorpost of heaven," wrote Frances Roberts.[1] But we would not have the rope unless God had first thrown it down to us.

PRAYER: *Father, you have commanded this, so I will seek your gifts. I will ask you to meet my needs and those of the world, but above all I will pray for your presence, seek your face, and not let go until you bless me.*

DAY 206: NOT TYPICAL

Pandita Ramabai (1858-1922)

"He has shown you, O man, what is good. And what does the Lord require of you? To act justly and to love mercy and to walk humbly with your God" (Mic. 6:8).

By any standard, Pandita Ramabai was not a typical Indian woman. Born in 1858 to a wealthy Hindu Brahmin family, her father insisted that she be educated in classic Sanskrit literature. As a young woman, she so impressed the pundits (scholars) of Calcutta with her knowledge that they called her "Pandita," a feminized version of their title. She broke tradition by marrying a man who belonged to a caste lower than her own, and she further rankled Indian custom by speaking out in favor of female emancipation. Her book, *The High-Caste Hindu Woman* (1887), was a pioneer work of its kind, and brought in income and interest in her cause from the West. She founded a boarding school for girls and labored tirelessly for education and welfare for widows and orphans. A tour of the United States in 1883 brought in enough income for her to fund a program to educate high-caste widows. As if all this were not enough, she converted to Christianity, which sealed her rejection by Hindus. The only thing worse would be to share her faith in Jesus as the means of salvation for everyone, which she began to do in 1891. After this, Pandita became a passionate evangelist and social worker, leading many young women to Christ.

The land in Kedgaon, near Poona, became the location for Pandita's greatest life work. There she formed a center for orphans and widows called "Mukti," meaning "salvation" or "deliverance." At Mukti, hundreds of women and girls were rescued from a famine that struck in 1896-97. Pandita longed for Christ's transforming power to revive the helpless widows and orphans of India. This desire was intensified in December 1904 when she got word of the Welsh revival. Thrilled by reports of mass conversions in Wales, Pandita organized the girls into prayer circles of ten girls each, urging them to pray for the salvation of nominal Christians everywhere, not just in India. At first there were seventy praying. Then she sent out a call for other prayer circles to be formed and gave each group a list of ten unsaved girls or women to pray for. Within six months there were 550 at Mukti gathering to pray twice daily for revival.

On June 29-30, 1905, God answered their prayers, and the Holy Spirit fell on the Mukti community. Everywhere women and girls began to weep and confess their sins and cry out to God for empowerment. Classes were suspended, and many of the students spent hours in intercessory prayer for strangers they had never even met. Some of the prayer meetings lasted 15 and 17 hours. The emotions were powerful, and the fruit of revival was lasting. Twenty years later, to the surprise and delight of those who experienced the revival, it was discovered that those whose experience of God was most extravagantly emotional at the time were still living godly and sober lives.

The Mukti Mission later grew to 1300 women. After the revival, Pandita threw herself into the translation of the Bible into Marathi, a project that took 18 years. Though she died in 1922, Mukti still had 649 students in 1971. Pandita Ramabai is remembered as a woman of prayer and great courage.

PRAYER: *Lord, send me to proclaim freedom to captives, good news to the poor, healing for the brokenhearted, and the day of the Lord's favor! (Isa. 61:1-2).*

DAY 207: HOW TO ASTONISH JESUS

Matthew 8:5-13 (Luke 7:1-10)

"When Jesus heard this, he was astonished" (Matt. 8:10).

It should be very hard to impress the one who spoke the universe into existence, much less astonish him. But twice in the New Testament it is said that Jesus was *astonished*. Matthew 8:10 is one of those situations. What makes Jesus' astonishment even more astonishing is that it was not addressed to a Jew, one of God's chosen people, but to a Gentile, an outsider, an officer in the Roman army of occupation. And the thing Jesus is impressed with is a religious quality, something the Jews were supposed to be experts at. Jesus is delighted and amazed at this man's faith.

Jesus appreciates faith because faith lets God be God as nothing else can. It is God's nature to give, to overflow. Faith is about receiving. Faith opens our hands and lets God give.

Read Psalm 104 and see how God rejoices to feed and water his creation. It grieves God when we won't receive. He even pleads, "If you would but listen to me, O Israel. Open wide your mouth and I will fill it. If my people would but listen to me" (Ps. 81:8, 10, 13). The very pinnacle of God's revelation of himself to us was in his Son Jesus, who broke bread and said, "Take and eat; this is my body" (Matt. 26:26).

So, faith fits perfectly what philosopher Peter Kreeft called "the grammar of existence." In language, grammar has to do with the proper relationships between words—nouns and verbs and predicates and articles. If the grammar of a sentence is bad, the meaning is lost or confused. In existence, grammar is the proper relationship between humans and God. The grammar of existence is, "God is God, and you are not." Forget this and everything gets confused. Faith lets God be God and you be you. Without faith it is impossible to please God (Heb. 11:6). With faith, you may not astonish him, but you will certainly please him.

Tell him what you need today, and as you do, thank him that it is his pleasure to give it.

PRAYER: *Thank you, dear Father, that it so pleases you when I open my hand to receive your good gifts.*

DAY 208: WHY EVEN TRY?

Matthew 9:35-38

"Ask the Lord of the harvest, therefore, to send out workers into his harvest field" (Matt. 9:38).

So many people, so much need, so few resources, you might as well give up. That's one way to look at the crowds that Jesus saw. No amount of love and food would be enough to meet their needs, so why even try?

But Jesus tells us to pray, anyway. It's the first thing he tells us to do. Prayer is primary because only God is big enough to do this impossible thing. Only God, the Great Shepherd of the sheep, can marshal the resources and the people—especially the people—necessary to care for the helpless and harassed. Prayer is not the last resort; it is the first. It is not something to be done instead of compassion, it is the beginning of compassion. Jesus' heart goes out to these lost ones, so he prays.

Prayer is the beginning of compassion, but not the end of it. Authentic prayer is always ready to be the answer for the thing prayed for. Jesus urged his disciples to pray for the Lord of the harvest to send out workers, and in the very next verse (Matt. 10:1), he equipped them to go out and be the workers they prayed would come! True prayer comes from love and leads to more love. Watch out for what you pray for!

True prayer comes from compassion and leads to hope. It opens our eyes to see the possibilities. We see a crowd of hopeless and lost people. God sees a harvest of souls for eternal life. To pray with Jesus for the lost of the world is to put our love and hope to work.

Let your mind range far and wide around the world. There are nations and peoples and tribes with no knowledge of the Savior. The AIDS pandemic rages across Africa and Asia. Poverty grinds children into the dust. Oppression and injustice hold billions in their grip. Take heart, be strong, and pray to the Lord of the harvest to send people—to send you!—to do his great work. There are strongholds to bring down (Matt. 16:18) and harvests to reap.

PRAYER: *Lord of the harvest, Shepherd of the sheep, because of your great love, send people to love the harassed and helpless in your name. Send me.*

DAY 209: KNOW YOURSELF

Matthew 11:25-30

"I praise you, Father... because you have hidden these things from the wise and learned, and revealed them to little children" (Matt. 11:25).

The sixteenth-century theologian and reformer John Calvin began his monumental *Institutes of the Christian Religion,* with an assertion that sounds startlingly modern, even psychological: "Without knowledge of self, there is no knowledge of God. Without knowledge of God there is no knowledge of self."[1] That certainly makes sense on a human level: a man cannot be a husband unless he has some idea both of what a husband is and what a wife is. The two kinds of knowledge go together, of the self and the other. It is no different with God, because our relationship with God is just that—a relationship between an I and a Thou, a self and an Other.

In order to pray, what do you need to know about yourself and God? Jesus tells us about both. Of himself, Jesus says that he is gentle and humble in heart and that he offers rest for our souls. Notice what he is not. He is not a dictator or a slave driver or a project manager trying to get the most out of you. He doesn't want to burn you out. He won't add to the burdens you bring him in prayer. "A bruised reed he will not break, and a smoldering wick he will not burn out" (Matt. 12:20). That's very good news about Jesus. It gives you confidence to come to him, doesn't it?

What do you need to know about yourself? In a word, Jesus says you need to know you are a little child. In this context, to be a child is to be the opposite of proud. The proud are those Jesus calls "wise and learned" whose confidence is in themselves, not in God or anybody else. The proud cannot really pray because, "A proud man is always looking down on things and people: and, of course, as long as you are looking down, you cannot see something that is above you" (C. S. Lewis). Naturally, God resists the proud, but he gives grace to the humble (1 Pet. 5:5). That's good news about you too, very good news. You don't have to be anyone important or holy or super-spiritual to come to Jesus. All you need to be is yourself—his child—in need of love and mercy. Does that not also give you confidence to pray?

PRAYER: *Father, dear Father, I happily renounce all my pretensions to strength. My only hope is in the gentle mercy of your Son. Teach me your way, Jesus.*

DAY 210: STRIKE UP THE BAND

Matthew 18:19-20

"If two of you on earth agree about anything you ask for, it will be done for you by my father in heaven" (Matt. 18:19).

It could be argued that these verses changed the course of American history. The imagination of the brilliant theologian Jonathan Edwards had been fired by the word "agree" in the text. The Greek word is *sumphoneo*, from which we get "symphony." Taking his cue from this word, Edwards wrote a long pamphlet calling the churches of New England to see prayer as a kind of concert in which they would pray in agreement for two things: the revival of religion in the church and the spread of God's kingdom in the world. Many churches prayed this way, and the Great Awakenings of the eighteenth and nineteenth centuries sprang from this kind of prayer. The spiritual renewal and profound social and political reform that came out of these revivals has been well-documented. America was not the same after its churches prayed this concert.

In all honesty, we must admit that these verses are not about prayer, necessarily, but about church discipline. Jesus promises to be present with the church when its people gather in his name to discipline recalcitrant members.

But the principle applies equally to prayer because Christ is present with his people in a special way when they are unified. That was his prayer for the church—the last thing John's gospel tells us he prayed before he was arrested. He asked his Father to make his people one, just as he and his Father are one. That way the world would believe in Jesus and know the church to be a uniquely blessed community (John 17:23)—the very thing that happens in a spiritual awakening. That is because when we agree in Jesus' name, the Maestro has struck up his band, and the music is beautiful.

Most of the prayers of the Bible were originally prayed by groups, not by individuals. It is the same for most of the Bible's instructions on prayer: they were given to groups, to churches, not merely to individuals. God puts great stock in corporate prayer. We should too, for it requires and creates a level of Christian community that speaks powerfully to the world of the reality of God. If you haven't already, find people who will covenant to pray with you in the symphonic way Jonathan Edwards called the churches in New England to pray. Christ has promised great things to those who pray this way.

PRAYER: *Holy Spirit, you have made us one in Christ. Awaken us to that reality, and teach us to pray together, as one, for God's kingdom to come.*

DAY 211: SOMETHING BEAUTIFUL FOR GOD

Matthew 26:6-13

"She has done a beautiful thing to me" (Matt. 26:10).

She went way over the line of social nicety and religious propriety when she, a woman, entered a room of men and poured on Jesus' head a jar of perfume worth a year's wages. The disciples certainly thought so. "Why this waste?" they asked. "This perfume could have been sold at a very high price and the money given to the poor." Clearly this emotional creature had lost her perspective.

But Jesus didn't think so, and he defended her. What she did was entirely appropriate, even beautiful. "She has done a beautiful thing for me," he retorted. The Greek word translated "beautiful" means fine, beautiful, elegant. In the Greek Old Testament, the Septuagint, it is a word used to describe the things that please and delight God. What makes Jesus' response so remarkable is that it is preceded, in chapter 25, by some of his strongest words about caring for the poor. He so identified with them that he said, "Whatever you did for the least of these brothers of mine, you did for me" (Matt. 25:40).

Why then, did he so willingly—even enthusiastically—accept for himself what could have been given to the poor? It is because the adoration of God is supreme and leads to every other kind of love. Before our faith is anything else, it is adoration. There can be such a thing as good works without love, but never love without good works. Without love, even the good works will sputter and die. So, when Paul commended the Macedonians for their generosity, he wrote, "they gave themselves first to the Lord and then to us in keeping with God's will" (2 Cor. 8:5). Beware of a religion that is overly practical.

Martin Luther called worship the "bridal chamber." The qualities natural to the bridal chamber are extravagance, passion, intimacy, and exuberance. "How beautiful you are and how pleasing, O love, with your delights!" says the Song of Songs (7:6). Dare we take those qualities to our worship of God? Dare we not? Have you ever abandoned yourself to worship God the way this woman did?

PRAYER: *Precious Lord, how beautiful, how pleasing, you are! You deserve my best and my all. May my worship be exuberant, passionate, and extravagant.*

DAY 212: WE THANK YOU, O GOD, FOR YOUR FAITHFULNESS

Sei and Yah Buor

"Those who sow in tears will reap with songs of joy" (Ps. 126:5).

You probably haven't heard of Yah Buor. That's okay because God has. He's heard from her many thousands of times. The little Saturday night prayer group that met with her and her pastor husband Sei, during the winter of 1995 in Holland, Michigan, will never forget her.

When she joined the group, she and her four children had been reunited with Sei after many months of separation. A nightmarish civil war was sucking the life out of their beloved Liberia. Everywhere there was mayhem, murder, and rape. Mere children with assault rifles were swaggering through streets and into villages. The Buors fled their homeland to seek sanctuary, first in neighboring Sierra Leone and then in Kenya. When the opportunity presented itself for Sei to come to Western Seminary in Michigan for theological training, they prayerfully decided that it was a door opened by God and that he should go even though they didn't know how the rest of the family could join him. The war had already separated Yah from her mother for years, and now she had to say goodbye to her husband and find her way as a mother of four and as a refugee in a foreign country. It was a great day of rejoicing when she and the children arrived at the Grand Rapids airport in the frigid winter of 1995.

How to describe her? Picture a short woman with a round, richly black face from which dazzling white teeth beam whenever she smiles or laughs—which is often. Picture her in prayer. The layers of clothing she wears indoors for her West African body to be comfortable in a western Michigan winter give her the appearance of a child from a Charlie Brown comic bundled up for a snow day. Look at her sweet, ebony face barely exposed above the wool turtleneck, and see it glow as you hear her say to the Lord, "We thank you, O God, for your faithfulness." "Thank you" is the most natural response in any language to the goodness of a faithful God.

Picture Yah standing for so many others. She is a representative of the millions who are displaced and oppressed and persecuted but who have put their hope in the living God. See especially a humble faith that can give thanks in every circumstance.

Pray with Yah in eager expectation for the day when her prayers will be answered, and they will return to their native land. Cry out day and night for God's justice (cf. Luke 18:1-8). Believe that God is faithful and that there will again be laughter in the Liberias of this life. We thank you, O God, for your faithfulness.

PRAYER: *"Restore our fortunes, O Lord, like streams in the Negev. Those who sow in tears will reap with songs of joy. He who goes out weeping, carrying seed to sow, will return with songs of joy, carrying sheaves with him" (Ps. 126:4-6).*

Introduction to Mark

DAY 213: MAN ON THE MOVE

"'Come, follow me,' Jesus said, 'and I will make you fishers of men.' At once they left their nets and followed him" (Mark 1:17-18).

Mark is the fastest paced of the gospels, and its perspective on Jesus is that he is a strong man of great energy, constantly on the move, and God's conquering Son. Miracle stories make up the bulk of the gospel. Exorcisms are common. Words like "amazed" and "astonished" are the words Mark often uses to describe people's reactions to him. Even his own disciples will sometimes say, with a kind of holy terror, "Who is this?" Mark's narrative style is almost childlike and breathless. Fond of the historic present, he tells past events as if they were happening in the present. His favorite words are "and" and "immediately." In the third chapter alone 34 clauses or sentences are linked together by nothing more than a principal verb and the word "and."

Yet it is Jesus the activist, who in this respect lived a life not unlike our own, whom Mark shows to also be a man of prayer. Jesus rises very early to pray the morning after an exhausting day, not in spite of his schedule, but because of it. To pray through Mark is to learn to pray amid the tyranny of the urgent and the busy.

The first words out of Jesus' mouth in this gospel are, "The kingdom of God is near. Repent and believe the good news!" (Mark 1:15). This is essentially the topic sentence of the book. True to his style, Mark proceeds, not so much by telling us what Jesus said about the kingdom, but by showing us what he did about it. What emerges is a picture of God's rule that is a mystery. The kingdom is present and future, already and not yet, a reality to be received but also hoped for. In the three seed parables of Mark 4, Jesus says the kingdom is like a tiny seed planted in the soil. Though it begins in secrecy and weakness, it grows inexorably into something glorious and universal.

Thus, Mark's gospel shows us that prayer, like the kingdom, is a mystery. We pray for the kingdom of God to come (Matt. 6:10; Luke 11:2), and we pray in the kingdom of God that already has come. Though for the time being we live by unseen realities, the day is coming when faith will become sight. Therefore, all prayer is ultimately a kind of joyful yearning. We are glad for what is and hungry for what will be. By faith, prayer sows in apparent weakness and hopes for what will be raised in strength (1 Cor. 15:42-44).

More to the point, prayer is like Jesus as Mark describes him. Though Jesus is God's strong man, the Messiah, and the Son of God, his mission was to die the death of a common criminal (Mark 8:31-38). From the world's perspective, Jesus was a failure, but he lived by unseen realities. His "failure" was in fact the liberation of many (Mark 10:45), and one day his triumph will be plain for all to see. To pray the gospel of Mark is to pray with this Jesus.

PRAYER: *Today is the day to hear your voice and follow you, Lord Christ. Help me to obey without delay.*

DAY 214: THE FIRST THING

Mark 1:35

"Very early in the morning, while it still dark, Jesus got up, left the house and went off to a solitary place, where he prayed" (Mark 1:35).

It had been a very full and demanding day in the life of Jesus, beginning on the Sabbath as he taught in the Capernaum synagogue. When a demonized man interrupted him in his teaching, Jesus delivered him. Then he went home with Peter and Andrew and healed Peter's mother-in-law who was sick and in bed with a fever. Word of his miraculous powers spread throughout the region, and when the Sabbath ended that evening, people came from miles around to be healed (see Mark 1:21-34). Jesus must have been exhausted when he finally went to bed late that night, but he was up very early the next morning to pray.

Question: Was he up early to pray in spite of what he had been doing the day before or because of what he had been doing? Clearly, he got up early to pray *because* of what he had been doing. There was too much at stake for Jesus to risk losing communion with his Father. To pray was to be restored and refocused. He had done his Father's will the day before. What was his Father's will for today? If he didn't listen carefully, he might succumb to someone else's will. (Mark 1:37).

What about you? Does your schedule determine your prayer life, or does your prayer life determine your schedule? Do you sometimes think yourself too busy to pray, or too busy not to pray? Who sets your priorities? Jesus played before an audience of One (John 5:19-20, 30). Who or what is your audience? If Jesus, the sinless Son of God, found it necessary to be diligent in prayer, how much more should we? Make communion with your Father in heaven the first and foundational thing you do each day.

PRAYER: *Jesus, sometimes I am pulled this way and that, from daylight to dawn. There are so many voices asking, inviting, demanding, pleading, for my attention. Clear my mind, focus my thoughts, order my priorities, for the sake of your name. Amen.*

DAY 215: THEN HELP ME, LORD

Corrie ten Boom (1892-1983)

"Keep me as the apple of your eye, hide me in the shadow of your wings" (Ps. 17:8).

Her prayer was simple and desperate: "Lord Jesus, protect me!" It was all she could gasp out as the Gestapo beat her, demanding to know where she and her family had hidden the Jews. Corrie ten Boom kept her secret. That night in the jail, her father led the family in devotions from Psalm 91: "He who dwells in the shelter of the Most High will rest in the shadow of the Almighty" (Ps. 91:1). The Ten Boom family had hidden the Jews from the Nazis; surely God would shelter and hide Corrie and her family, too. In the months that followed, Corrie's father died in prison, and she and Betsie, her sister, were sent to the infamous *Ravensbruck*, where Betsie also died after months of intense suffering.

Corrie had grown up in a family that was famous for its hospitality. After World War I, Germany was filled with thousands of deprived and malnourished people. Though the Ten Booms lived in The Netherlands, Corrie's father, as president of International Watchmakers, arranged for many of these needy Germans to be taken into the homes of the members of his organization. Four young children came to live in the Ten Boom's home. The family reached out into their community in similar ways. Corrie even started a youth club, with its first law, "Seek your strength through prayer." She could not have known then how prophetic that law would be for her personally.

It was only natural that the Ten Booms would open their home to hide fugitive Jews. It was also only natural that she would find strength in prayer to endure the awful punishment the Nazis wreaked when they caught her. The story of her struggles in Ravensbruck about the faithfulness of God in a hellhole and the grace of God to forgive is a classic tale of the power of believing prayer.

Years after the war, Corrie had spoken at a church in Germany, telling again of God's amazing faithfulness in dark places and the need to forgive enemies. After the service, to her surprise and profound discomfort, she saw a former SS guard from Ravensbruck walking her way, his face beaming, his hand extended. "Thank you for the message," he said. "Isn't it wonderful that Jesus has washed my sins away?" His hand was still extended as hers hung limply at her side. He was the one who had stood by leering as she and Betsie and other women were forced to strip naked to enter the showers. Rage rose up inside. "I can't do it, Lord. Don't ask me for this, it's too much." Then Corrie remembered the message of forgiveness she had preached all over the world—and in that place just moments before. She also remembered the many times the Lord had answered her simple, desperate prayer. "Then help me, Lord," she prayed silently. She felt a power rush through her arm, and a warmth enter her mind as she extended her hand and eagerly shook his. Once more she had cried out for Jesus to help her, and once again he had given her strength.[1]

PRAYER: *"Keep me safe, O God, for in you I take refuge" (Ps. 16:1).*

DAY 216: DEATH, BE NOT PROUD

Mark 5:22-23

"My little daughter is dying, please come and put your hands on her so that she will be healed and live" (Mark 5:23).

On the wall of the cancer ward was a picture, drawn by a dying child. A giant military tank filled the paper with its big gun pointed down at a tiny little girl holding a tiny little sign with the barely discernible word, "stop."

No one can stand before death. It is a cold, remorseless monster with an insatiable appetite. Death is the great leveler, swallowing up young and old, high and low, alike (Ps. 49:14; 69:15; 141:7). No one escapes it. Our mortality rate is 100%. All are helpless before death.

And yet, this time it is a little girl! Again! And there is a father for whom all this helpless and hopeless talk about the mortality rate is unacceptable. He will pray. He will present his case before Jesus. And what a "case" he makes! He falls at Jesus' feet and pleads earnestly for him to put his hands on the girl and heal her. And tender Jesus, who loves a broken and contrite heart, who lives with the lowly (Is. 57:15), and who delights in faith (Mark 5:36), finds his argument compelling.

Death is helpless before Jesus. In him, death is swallowed up in victory. Faith is the victory that overcomes the world, not because faith itself is so strong, but because the one faith trusts is so powerful (1 Cor. 15:54; 1 John 5:4). Bring your helpless hopelessness to Jesus as tenaciously and passionately as Jairus brought his daughter to Jesus. Bring the dying and those dead in sin to him. What Jesus did for this little girl and for her father he has pledged to do for all who believe, whether now or when he returns. He will gather all his lambs to his great heart of love, and not one will be missing (John 10:27-29).

PRAYER: *Father in heaven! You have conquered our great enemy, death. May I live this day with hope and thankfulness that nothing can separate me from your love.*

DAY 217: CHUTZPAH!

Mark 7:24-30 (Matthew 15:21-28)

"Yes Lord," she replied, "But even the dogs under the table eat the children's crumbs" (Mark 7:28).

Coming from the Hebrew, *chutzpah* is a Yiddish word for the quality of nerve and brazen temerity that won't take no for an answer. Although the Canaanite woman in this story is most certainly not a Hebrew, she has plenty of chutzpah. Jesus came to her region to get away from the crowds and doesn't want to be seen. So, what's the first thing she does when she discovers he is in her neighborhood? She goes to see him! Not only that, but she falls at his feet and begs him to deliver her daughter from demon possession. No apologies for interrupting his plans from this lady. In Matthew's account (Matt. 15:21-28), we are told that, at first, Jesus answers her with silence. What does she do then? She keeps coming at him so hard that the disciples urge him to send her away. Then, when Jesus finally does speak, he playfully rebukes her—the Greek for "dogs" is "little dogs" meaning a household pet—and lets her know that he has different priorities for the time being. But she doesn't break character for a moment. She says, "Yes Lord, but even the dogs under the table eat the children's crumbs." In other words, "Whatever it takes to get what I need for my daughter, I aim to get it from you, and I won't go away until I do."

And Jesus gives this "little dog" something he doesn't give to any of the "children." Not only does he deliver her daughter, but he says, "Woman, you have great faith!" The only other person to get this commendation was also a "dog," a Gentile, a Roman centurion (see Matthew 8:10-13). Content to receive from Jesus only "crumbs," she wins "best of the show" in faith.

Speaking of dogs, Luther was watching his dog beg for food and said, "If only I would pray that way." That's the kind of faith the Lord looks for in prayer. It is not the capacity to believe something will happen, but the tenacity to keep coming to him until it does. Jesus loves a faith that will wrestle as much as he loves one that will rest. His greatest promises are for those who will keep on asking, seeking, and knocking (Luke 11:9-10). Holy chutzpah.

PRAYER: *Gracious Master! I know more of your love than the Gentile woman probably understood when she came to you. Yet sometimes I hesitate. May I come to you with persistence and with the boldness of holy chutzpah.*

DAY 218: I BELIEVE, HELP MY UNBELIEF!

Mark 9:17-18

"I do believe; help me overcome my unbelief" (Mark 9:24).

How do you come to Jesus? What do you expect from him?

Some of us come like this father, thinking that Jesus is probably willing to help but not sure he is able: "But if you can do anything..." (Mark 9:22b). Others are like a leper who came to Jesus, thinking he was able, but wondering if he was willing: "If you are willing, you can make me clean" (Mark 1:40). Both kinds of people believe in half a God: either a deity with lots of love but limited power, or a god with plenty of power but limited love. Neither god is the God and Father of Jesus Christ. The God we pray to in the name of Jesus is perfect both in power and in love.

The Lord shows remarkable patience with those who believe in these half-gods. To those like the father, Jesus laughs and says, "'If you can?' Everything is possible for him who believes" (Mark 9:23). To those who are like the leper, he is "filled with compassion" and smiles as he says, "I am willing" (Mark 1:41).

Healing faith, or for that matter, any kind of faith, is not an either/or, but a both/and. It is not, either you have it all or you don't, but a little bit of this and a little bit of that. Both the father and the leper, with their puny, little faith, came away from Jesus blessed. That's because our faith is not *in faith*, but in Jesus. He said it only takes a little bit of faith, a mustard-seed-sized faith (Matthew 17:20), for him to laugh or smile and do for us what we need. Thanks be to God, it is enough to say to him, "I do believe; help me overcome my unbelief" (Mark 9:25)!

PRAYER: *Blessed Father, I believe everything you have said is true—most of the time. Please be patient with me and grow my faith. I believe, help me when I don't.*

DAY 219: PRAY FOR THE CHILDREN AND PRAY LIKE THE CHILDREN

Mark 10:13-16 (Matthew 19:13-15; Luke 18:15-17)

"And he took the children in his arms, put his hands on them and blessed them" (Mark 10:16).

Jesus paid a lot of attention to children in his prayers, and so should we. The things that angered Jesus are not often mentioned in the gospels, but this is one of them. He was indignant when his disciples tried to keep the children away from him. Perhaps they thought he had more important things to do than to pray for children. He didn't. Even their parents didn't understand how important they were to Jesus. They wanted him to touch them, but Jesus went further. "He took them in his arms, put his hands on them and blessed them" (Mark 10:16).

Jesus also thought the children had a lot to teach us about prayer. Not only should we pray *for* children, but we should pray *like* children. He said the kingdom belonged to such children, and those who will not receive the kingdom like children will never enter it (Mark 10:15). In prayer, we speak to God as Father. Who is better able to understand calling out to a father than a child? Think of it, trust and receptivity come naturally to children. Grace is a given. Love is expected. Nothing is complicated. They give their hearts willingly and uncritically.

Maybe that is why Jesus so wants us to bring the children to him. It is their nature to trust. If they don't have him to trust, they will trust something else. How vulnerable they are to those whose only desire is to steal, kill, and destroy them (John 10:10)! Unless they are brought to Jesus, their very strength of faith becomes their fatal weakness. Those who think children should be left alone to decide for themselves about Jesus don't understand children or Jesus. Children need his touch and blessing.

Pray for children. Pray like children.

PRAYER: *Kind and merciful Jesus, bless these children I know (say their names to him), and bless me to know how to be like them in simple trust.*

DAY 220: HOLY EXCAVATION!

Mark 11:22-24

"Whatever you ask for in prayer, believe that you have received it, and it will be yours" (Mark 11:24).

The setting for this saying made it even more dramatic for Jesus' disciples than it is for us. From the Mount of Olives (near where he said it), the Dead Sea could be clearly seen. Picture it this way: perhaps Jesus was pointing down at where they stood as he looked eastward into the distance and said, "If anyone says to this mountain, 'Go throw yourself into the sea.'"

It may have been more dramatic for them than for us, but it was probably less difficult to understand. Jews were used to hearing their rabbis speak proverbially. To make a point, the teacher would often use "blacks and whites" and hyperbole to make a point. For instance, Jesus said, "If anyone comes to me and does not hate his father and mother, his wife and children, his brothers and sisters—yes, even his own life—he cannot be my disciple" (Luke 14:26). The point is not that we should hate these people, but that our love for Jesus should be so much greater that our love for them that it looks like hate. His Jewish audience understood what he meant about the mountain and the sea in the same way.

The point is, prayer works wonders, like throwing a mountain into the sea! Of course, this proverb must be interpreted wisely and soberly. God is not a machine—put in a nickel of faith and you get a nickel's worth of wonders, put in a million dollars and you get a million dollars' worth. He knows what is best and will always do what is best. We mustn't ask for things that are sinful. We should also consider our station and calling, knowing that the needs of a Moses or Elijah for the miraculous may not be the same as our need.

Nevertheless, prayer is powerful, and Jesus wants us to pray with confidence. He wants us to pray as Andrew Murray urged us to pray, claiming "every promise God has made, in its largest and fullest meaning."

PRAYER: *Almighty God, you are a great God; nothing is too hard for you. Give me a faith worthy of your greatness.*

DAY 221: PLEASE TAKE IT AWAY, PAPA!

Mark 14:32-42 (Matthew 26:36-46; Luke 22:40-46)

"'Abba, Father,' he said, 'everything is possible for you. Take this cup from me. Yet not what I will, but what you will'" (Mark 14:36).

Jesus has his Father's full attention, because nothing so seizes a father's attention like hearing his child cry out, "Papa!" That's a rough equivalent of the extraordinary intimacy and urgency implied by "Abba, Father." His son is in distress and the Father can fix it. Everything is possible for him, everything. He can cancel the mission to the cross, he can take away the bitter cup his son wants him to take away. He can do it, he really can. Jesus is prostrate, pleading, "Please take it away, Papa."

Gethsemane is the place. Gethsemane means "olive press," after the crude device by which olives were crushed under the weight of a big stone, their oil flowing into a receptacle, the way Jesus' sweat falls like drops of blood to the ground (Luke 22:44). Jesus is being crushed by the weight of his Father's will which is that he carries the load of our sorrows and sins to the cross.

Three times Jesus asks if he may be excused from his assignment. But three times he adds, "Yet not what I will, but what you will." As hard as it is, his Father's will is his will too. Sometimes the only way for a cup to pass is to drink it to the dregs. Fully confident of God's power ("everything is possible for you") and love ("Abba, Father"), Jesus willingly submits to his wisdom.

Thus, in his submission and extreme weakness, Jesus was never more powerful. The cross looked like weakness, but it was in reality God's mighty strength to save. By the world's standards, a premature and ignominious death looked silly, but it was in reality God's profound wisdom (1 Cor. 1:18-25). Because of this, every knee will bow and every tongue confess that Jesus Christ is Lord (Phil. 2:10-11).

What about you? The most powerful words you can ever say to God are the same as Jesus' words: "Yet not what I will, but what you will." Become God's captive and then you will be free.

PRAYER: *Dear Father! Not what I will, but what you will. Make me your captive, and I will be free.*

DAY 222: WHY HAVE YOU FORSAKEN ME?

Mark 15:33-34

"And at the ninth hour Jesus cried out in a loud voice…
'My God, my God, why have you forsaken me?'" (Mark 15:34).

It was suffering like this that moved Bernard of Clairvaux to write, "What language shall I borrow to thank Thee, dearest Friend, for this Thy dying sorrow, Thy pity without end?"[1] Who indeed can understand, much less speak of the suffering of the Son of God that made him feel such dereliction? Was he indeed, abandoned by his Father at this moment of bearing and dying for the sins of the world? There is a profound mystery here that no one should dare to explain with confidence.

But there is something to be learned here about prayer. Jesus was quoting the first lines of Psalm 22, a psalm that would become the most quoted psalm in the New Testament. Those Jews who heard him would have recognized the source and context of his words. First century Jews were biblically literate in a way that is hard for modern Christians to fathom. Jesus too, of course, knew the source and context of his words and would not have torn a line of Scripture out of its context just to express his emotions at the moment. His cry of abandonment pointed beyond itself to something glorious and wonderful because Psalm 22 is a psalm that begins with despair but ends with soaring hope. The sufferer will be so overwhelmingly vindicated by God that, "All the ends of the earth will remember and turn to the Lord, and all the families of the nations will bow down before him" (Ps. 22:27).

We too can pray like Jesus in our sufferings. We too can pray appropriate Scripture to give words to what we feel. We too may pour out our hearts in grief and anguish, as Jesus and the psalmist did. There need be no reticence to our cries. But we must also affirm the hope that we nevertheless have. Oswald Chambers wrote, "when a man gets to despair, he knows that all his thinking will never get him out, he will only get out by the sheer, creative effort of God; consequently, he is in the right attitude to receive from God that which he cannot gain for himself."

PRAYER: *My God and my only hope, when I run out of options, you remain with me, and you are all I need. When I seem to have many options, you are still my only hope and all I really need.*

DAY 223: BY PRAYER ALONE

Hudson Taylor (1832-1905)

"'Not by might nor by power, but by my Spirit,' says the Lord Almighty" (Zech. 4:6).

Hudson Taylor made a vow before he left England to go to China as a missionary: "When I get out to China, I shall have no claim on anyone for anything. My only claim will be on God. How important to learn... to move man through God by prayer alone."[1] The enormity of what Taylor saw when he stepped off the boat in Shanghai, made it clear his vow would be tested severely, many times over.

Shanghai was a war zone under siege from the North. He watched in horror as stretcher after stretcher of wounded and dying men were bought into the marketplace. From his tiny, bedroom window, he witnessed the torture and execution of many prisoners and the casual attitude of the populace toward death and suffering. And he felt as never before the staggering burden of a great people without the hope of the gospel. His work would be evangelizing "a parish of a million." Who was equal to such a task? Certainly, no mere human effort would ever be sufficient to open their eyes.

Then there were his personal limitations. He had no experience or social standing, only a tenuous grasp of the language and barely enough money to afford the lowest living quarters. Taylor did not fit in socially with the missionary community and disagreed with the way they lived; sequestered in European-style colonies, with servants and afternoon tea. His decision to wear his hair in a long ponytail and to dress and eat like the Chinese was a scandal to them all, and further isolated him.

But Taylor pressed on "by prayer alone" and saw the power of God amid war, death threats, and the loss of a wife and two children to disease. Once, a Chinese businessman heard Taylor speak about Jesus. He approached him and said, "I have long sought the Truth, as did my father before me, but without finding it out. In Confucianism, Buddhism, Taoism, I have found no rest, but I do find rest in what we have heard tonight. Henceforward I am a believer in Jesus." The businessman then asked Taylor how long England had had the light of Christ. Taylor replied that it had been several hundred years. "What," cried the businessman, "several hundreds of years! Is it possible that you have known about Jesus so long, and only now have come to tell us? My father sought the truth for more than twenty years and died without finding it. Oh, why did you not come sooner?"

When Taylor first arrived in Shanghai, the eventual founder of the China Inland Mission knew of only 300 believers in China. By the time of his death in 1905, the number had grown to 100,000. He prayed for God to send more missionaries—100 was his request, but 600 came. Taylor once described his work: "Envied of some, despised by many, hated perhaps by others; often blamed for things I never heard of, or had nothing to do with... often sick in body as well as perplexed in mind and embarrassed by circumstances... but the battle is the Lord's and He will conquer."

PRAYER: *Faithful Savior, you are everything I will ever need. Teach me to pray and live in that truth.*

Introduction to Luke

DAY 224: THE GOSPEL OF PRAYER FOR THE WORLD

"The Spirit of the Lord is on me, because he has anointed me to preach good news to the poor. He has sent me to proclaim freedom for the prisoners and recovery of sight to the blind, to release the oppressed, to proclaim the year of the Lord's favor" (Luke 4:18-19).

Luke's gospel has been rightly called the gospel of prayer. At every decisive moment of Jesus' life, Luke shows him praying. He prays at his baptism, before his first conflict with the Pharisees, before choosing the Twelve, before asking his disciples who they think he is, before he predicts his death; and on the Mount of Transfiguration. Luke also contains material on Jesus' prayer life and his teaching on prayer that the other gospel writers do not. Luke gives us Jesus' prayer for Peter's crisis of faith and the parables of the midnight visit and the unjust judge. The phrase "praising God" occurs more times in Luke's gospel than in all the New Testament books combined. Luke contains three great hymns the church has sung for centuries. To read Luke thoughtfully is to have one's spiritual acuity sharpened and to be led to pray as Jesus did.

Luke's gospel has also been called the universal gospel, rightly so. Jesus is shown to be a man for all seasons and all peoples—especially for the outcast, the poor, the disenfranchised, and the non-Jew. The instances are too numerous to list, but one example that is unique to Luke's gospel is the parable of the Good Samaritan. For the typical Jew of Jesus' day, a good Samaritan was an oxymoron. Luke also shows the special place women have in Jesus' respect and affections. Luke alone tells of the thief's prayer on the cross, and only Luke tells of the traitor tax collector Zacchaeus.

With his emphasis on prayer and the universality of the gospel, no other gospel writer shows the scope and depth of intercessory prayer as Luke does. Bob Pierce, the founder of World Vision, once prayed that his heart would be broken with the things that break the heart of God. That is a good prayer, but Luke's gospel takes a different approach: it simply invites us to have our hearts expanded and enriched to include in our love and our prayers all those whom God loves.

Christianity may no longer require the defense it needed in the first century. But the church always needs Luke's unique perspective on Jesus.

PRAYER: *Thank you, thank you, thank you, Father, for the good news!*

DAY 225: SCARS FROM AN OLD WOUND

Luke 1:8-20

"How can I be sure of this" (Luke 1:18).

It was the biggest day of his life. Many priests in Israel would live an entire lifetime and never get this opportunity. At long last he would enter the Holy of Holies. There he would burn incense as the congregation waited outside to see the smoke rise from the holy place. The smoke symbolized the prayers of the people, and when they saw it, they would fall on their faces and offer up their prayers and thanksgivings. In a sense, Zechariah was standing as close to God as a man could, leading his nation in prayer. So, he shouldn't have been all that surprised when he saw an angel standing there with him.

He was surprised. He was not only surprised, but unbelieving. When he heard the angel speak those thrilling and comforting words, "Do not be afraid, Zechariah; your prayer has been heard," all the old man could muster was, "How can I be sure of this?" One who stood in the very presence of God had told the old man that he and his barren wife would finally have the son they had so long prayed for. But it wasn't enough.

How could that be? Zechariah's faith was suffering from scars from an old wound. Faith is like a hand that grasps the promise of God like a gymnast grasps a bar. But if wounded in the palm, it can be hard to hold on. Fearing disappointment, you can prefer the safety of doubt to the risk of believing.

Is that you? Do you find yourself hanging back where you would most like to move forward, shrugging your shoulders when everything in you wants to embrace God's love for you? Is your prayer life stuck in a rut because of a frightened and weakened faith? Remember, the only difference between a rut and a grave is in their dimensions.

Jesus' greatest promises are for those who keep on seeking and asking in faith. But he is merciful even to those who don't do this so well. Zechariah and his wife will still get their baby even though Zechariah will undergo a season of divine discipline. His faithfulness is greater than your doubt and fear. Don't ask God in unbelief, "How can it be?" Ask him in wonder and gratitude, "Amazing love! How can it be?" (from the hymn "And Can It Be that I Should Gain" by Charles Wesley)?

PRAYER: *Faithful Father, teach me to expect great things from you, and to ask great things from you.*

DAY 226: HOLY EXAGGERATION

Luke 1:46-55

"My soul glorifies the Lord" (Luke 1:46).

What do people do when they have been touched by God's salvation? Whatever else they may do, they start moving. Our word *ecstasy* comes from two Greek words, *eks*, meaning out of, and *stasis*, or place. To be ecstatic means quite literally, to be moved. Mary is ecstatic after the angel tells her she will be the mother of the Son of God. She cannot just sit still in Nazareth, so she packs up and travels to Elizabeth's house. Elizabeth herself is miraculously pregnant, and when Mary arrives, the baby in her womb gets ecstatic too and leaps in her womb for joy. And when the two women meet, can you picture them doing anything else but clasping each other's hands and dancing a little jig right there in the doorway and into the street?

Then Mary's ecstasy finds a voice, and she sings a song the church has sung for centuries. It is traditionally known as The Magnificat from Latin which means to glorify or magnify. "My soul glorifies (or magnifies) the Lord." The word "glorify" in the NIV is perfectly accurate but "magnify" offers some refreshment to the imagination and understanding. Think of it this way—there are two kinds of magnification: the kind that makes the small seem big, as in a microscope; and the kind that shows what seems small to actually be big, as in a telescope. This world's glories are of the microscopic variety. What is really tiny is made to look big. God's glory is of the telescopic variety. As with the pinpoints of light in the night sky, so with the embryo in Mary's womb, what seems small is discovered to be gigantic—when seen through the lens of faith.

G. K. Chesterton defined a saint as one who exaggerates what the world neglects.[1] That is what Mary did that day as she sang her praise to God. And it's clear from her song that God also exaggerates what the world neglects, and neglects what the world exaggerates. The lowly will be lifted up, and the high and mighty will be brought down. Praise is the great corrective lens of existence. To learn to glory in what God glories is to see things as they really are and to be made ecstatic. Praise God and be moved!

PRAYER: *Open my mouth to praise you, God of wonders! You are worthy of extravagant praise. Teach me to "exaggerate" what the world neglects, to maximize what sin minimizes.*

DAY 227: TO KNOW WHO AND WHOSE YOU ARE

Luke 3:21—4:13

"You are my Son, whom I love; with you I am well pleased" (Luke 3:22).

This was an intensely personal moment for Jesus, and very sweet. Hearing his Father say, "You are my Son, whom I love; with you I am well pleased," was something Jesus would have to cling to for dear life in the days ahead. For the meaning of his identity as God's Son would be tested severely in the desert and on his way to the cross. He must not forget who and whose he was. It was a matter of life or death.

What did it mean for Jesus to be God's Son? On the one hand, it meant that he was—and is!—related to God as no one else can be. He was of the same stuff, the same nature, the same genetic endowment, if you will, as God the Father. He was "God of God, light of light, very God of very God" (The Nicene Creed). On the other hand, it meant that Jesus was God's Son not only by his nature, but by his obedience. "The Son can do nothing by himself; he can only do what he sees his Father doing, because whatever the Father does the Son also does" (John 5:19). Obedience is particularly what the Jordan River experience is all about.

Jesus' Father was thrilled with him at his baptism, for there he stood in the muddy waters of the river, among sinners, in perfect obedience to his Father's will. If he would lead them into his Father's kingdom, he would have to do it his Father's way—by becoming one of them and by suffering with them and for them. The cross must precede the crown. Jesus knew this, his Father knew he knew this, and the Father was delighted with his Son.

In the wilderness, the Devil would challenge the Father's will and test Jesus' identity at every point. The challenge, "If you are the Son of God…" was Satan's attempt to redefine Jesus' mission on his terms. He failed because Jesus knew who and whose he was.

Jesus told us to address his Father as *our* Father when we pray. It's different for us, because who he is by nature, we become through faith, by adoption (John 1:12). But we share this with Jesus: our identity is also revealed by our obedience. "We are yours by adoption," prayed Thomas Wilson, "make us yours by the choice of our will." To pray this way is to delight and please our Father.

PRAYER: *"We are yours by adoption; make us yours by the choice of our will."*

DAY 228: IF YOU ARE WILLING

Luke 5:12-14

"Lord, if you are willing, you can make me clean" (Luke 5:12).

Some come to Jesus the way this leper did, convinced he was able to heal him but afraid he didn't want to. "Lord, if you are willing, you can make me clean." They believe in Jesus, but don't think he believes in them. It's a terrible feeling to be powerfully drawn to someone you think may be repelled by you. Do you feel that way sometimes?

Leprosy is a disease that disfigures and cripples. It also contaminated according to first century beliefs. Lepers were legally required to stay away from healthy people and to issue dire warnings if approached: "Unclean! Unclean!" This leper had to break the law to even come to Jesus. But leprosy was more than a disease, it was a metaphor. It stood for all that separates people from God and makes us unfit to be in his presence. Luke had this in mind when he positioned the story of Peter and Jesus just before this story. When it dawned on Peter just how good Jesus was, he fell at his knees and said, "Go away from me, Lord; I am a sinful man!" (Luke 5:8). Peter was a leper too, on the inside.

To pray is to stand naked before God. We're all naked anyway, whether we pray or not, because God sees through all pretense and deception into the depths of our heart. But to pray is to really feel that unsettling truth. If you think God is disgusted by what he sees inside, you're not likely to pray. If that's you, watch what Jesus does with this leper: he touched this untouchable and said, "I am willing, be clean" (Luke 5:13). To Peter, he said, "Don't be afraid; from now on you will catch men" (Luke 5:10). In other words, "Not only am I not disgusted by you; I want you to be my partner."

Jesus touched the unclean because he was first touched by the unclean. He came not to condemn sinners, but to bear their sin. Spurgeon wrote, "The heart of Christ became like a reservoir in the midst of the mountains. All the tributary streams of iniquity, and every drop of the sins of his people, ran down and gathered into one vast lake, deep as hell and shoreless as eternity. All these met, as it were, in Christ's heart, and he endured them all."[1] That's how much he wants us to come in prayer.

PRAYER: *Loving Father, you know me inside and out; to you my darkness is as day. Yet you look at me with pity and forgiveness. I humbly receive your unconditional love!*

DAY 229: PRAYER AND DECISION-MAKING

Luke 6:12-13

"Jesus spent the night praying to God" (Luke 6:12).

All night is a long time to pray, especially if alone, as Jesus was. Why would he do such a thing? The obvious answer is that Jesus was making one of the biggest decisions of his life. The next day he was to select the men who would be his apostles, the inner circle of leaders to whom he would entrust so much. A lot was riding on his choices, so, of course, he would want to consult his Father. From even before the time of his temptation, Jesus' guiding principle was, "The Son can do nothing by himself; he can only do what he sees his Father doing, because whatever the Father does the Son also does" (John 5:19). Jesus knew the Scriptures well. He knew how badly things had gone with the Gibeonites when Joshua had not inquired of the Lord (Josh. 9:1-27) and how well things went for David when he did (2 Sam. 5:17-25).

The more pressing question for us is not why Jesus prayed all night, but how. It's not hard to imagine working all night, or watching movies all night, or even reading all night if the book is really fascinating—but praying all night? How does one do that? Did Jesus just ask, over and over again, "Who should be among the Twelve?" That's highly unlikely, not only because it would be incredibly boring, but because Jesus was against that sort of thing in principle (Matt. 6:7-8).

Jesus probably spent the night doing the kind of thing David asked the Lord to let him do forever: "One thing I ask of the Lord, this is what I seek; that I may dwell in the house of the Lord all the days of my life, to gaze upon the beauty of the Lord and to seek him in his temple" (Ps. 27:4). Since God knows what we need before we ask, prayer is more about communion than communication (Matt. 6:8). Jesus knew that, and therefore, he knew that what he needed most in order to make good decisions was not information, but a refreshed fellowship with his Father. His night was spent doing all the things that genuine prayer does: asking and listening, inquiring and praising, thinking and thanking, meditating and singing, in silence and in speech. It wasn't a few minutes of prayer stretched out over a night, but a lifetime of prayer compressed into a few hours.

Making good, prayerful decisions is not about a moment's effort, but a lifetime of prayer. God is more interested in us becoming the right people, than in us making the right decisions.

PRAYER: *Jesus, teach us to pray!*

DAY 230: BEING AND DOING

Luke 10:38-42

"But only one thing is needed" (Luke 10:42).

Martha may be one of the most "modern" of all the characters in the Bible. The reason? She is so busy. Other times and cultures have had their own besetting sins; one of ours is undoubtedly our busy-ness. The thing that makes it so subtly pernicious a sin is that we are often busy doing good things. For so many, the great enemy of God's best is not the worst—the classically venal sins like lust, greed, and gluttony—but the good. The Devil knows this. Goethe's Faust was a quintessential modern man, translating John 1:1, "In the beginning was the Act."[1] We've made activity an idol.

Luke describes Martha's busy-ness as distraction. There's an irony! Martha thinks she is attending to the matter at hand, but she has really been drawn away from the matter at hand. Jesus expanded on this and said, "Martha, Martha, you are worried and upset about so many things, but only one thing is needed" (Luke 10:41-42). Her distraction is her confusion over the distinction between the many and the One, the good and the best. She's lost her bearings on the sea of possibilities. She's buried in the details.

Jesus shows the way out of Martha's muddle by pointing to Mary. The way out is to listen at the feet of Jesus in obedient attentiveness. Jesus is not a project manager, a slave driver, trying to squeeze every ounce of work out of us he can get. He says his purpose is not to add work to our lives but to show us how to carry it. He is gentle and humble at heart; his yoke is easy, and his burden is light (Matt. 11:28-30). It isn't that God is against doing, it's that he wants us to understand that being always precedes doing. Who we are with him is more important than what we do. Take care of the being and the doing will take care of itself. Let Mary's posture at Jesus feet be a picture of prayer and work, being and doing. "You can do more than pray, after you have prayed," wrote A. J. Gordon, "but you can never do more than pray until you have prayed."[2]

PRAYER: *I confess, Lord, that I am easily distracted—even as I pray. Make me like Mary; teach me to sit at your feet and listen quietly, to be your child so I may be your joyful servant.*

DAY 231: HEAVEN'S JOY

Luke 15

"In the same way, I tell you, there is rejoicing in the presence of the angels of God over one sinner who repents" (Luke 15:10).

One of the Bible's most compelling descriptions of what it means to pray is to stand before God in "the Most Holy Place by the blood of Jesus" (Heb. 10:19). What do we find in the presence of the Holy One? Truth? Mystery? Blinding light? Ineffable goodness? A party? All of the above! But it's the party part we need to get our minds around now. Because Jesus said there is a party going on in heaven whenever a sinner repents and comes home.

Luke 15 has been called the "gospel in the gospel." In three short stories, Jesus describes God's attitude toward sinners. First, Jesus describes what it means to be a sinner. It's like being a lost sheep who stupidly wanders from patch of grass to patch of grass, living for the moment, and becoming easy prey for wolves. Or being a sinner is like being a lost coin in a dark house, as helpless as an inanimate object. Or it is like a rebellious son who can only blame himself as he deliberately takes the fast track to destruction, never looking back and laughing all the way. Stupid, helpless, and bull-headed—that's how God sees sinners. The one word that describes them all is *lost*.

On the other hand, God also loves sinners even in their stupidity, helplessness, and rebellion. When a sinner is found or comes home, God's joy is so great there has to be a party. As the waiting father told the callous and unforgiving older son, "we *had* to celebrate and be glad, because this brother of yours was dead and is alive again; he was lost and is found" (Luke 15:32, italics added). Joy is a divine necessity.

Thank God that you were once lost and are found; helpless and now recovered; a rebel that has come home. And if the joy has left you, pray that God will restore in you the joy of his salvation. Ask yourself if your prayers for the lost match God's passion for them. Pray that his Spirit will expand your compassion until your prayers are worthy of his love. Enter the Most Holy Place. Come into the joy of heaven.

PRAYER: *"I thank thee, who hast overthrown my foes and healed my wounded mind; I thank thee whose enlivening voice bids my freed soul in thee rejoice." (from the hymn, "Thee Will I Love, My Strength, My Tower" by Johann Schleffer and translated by John Wesley)*

DAY 232: PERSISTENCE AND HUMILITY IN PRAYER

Luke 18:1-14

"Then Jesus told his disciples a parable to show them that they should always pray and not give up" (Luke 18:1).

Martin Luther is credited with two word-pictures of prayer that capture what Jesus was teaching in these two parables on prayer. The first picture was of a dog begging for food with eyes burning, ears perked, and tail wagging. "If only I would pray that way," Luther observed. That's what Jesus meant when he taught his disciples to pray and not give up (Luke 18:1). The widow was dogged, like a dog who knows where the food is.

Luther's second picture was of a beggar. Just before his death, Luther wrote on a scrap of paper, "We are beggars. That is the truth."[1] That's what Jesus meant when he said, "For everyone who exalts himself will be humbled, and he who humbles himself will be exalted" (Luke 18:14). We all come to God needy and unworthy. Beware of praying to God like the self-righteous, self-sufficient Pharisee. Instead, pray like the tax collector.

These prayer parables gain strength if seen against the background of what precedes them. In chapters 16-17, Jesus challenged his followers to live their lives with eternity in view. In the story of the dishonest steward (Luke 16:1-15), he urged them to invest in heaven by the way they handle money on earth. In the parable of the rich man and Lazarus (Luke 16:19-31), he said essentially the same thing but with a sober reminder that the stakes are life and death or heaven and hell. Then Jesus teaches at length about the coming of the end (Luke 17:20-37). Through all of this he warns: things aren't what they appear to be. What you now see is temporary; what you don't yet see is eternal. The temporary is passing away, the eternal is coming. Be alert and be prepared. Everything depends on it.

But how does one live wisely and alertly in these deceptive and unstable times? Jesus' answer is in these two parables. We remain ready by staying closely connected to God through persistent, humble prayer. Ninety percent of prayer is just showing up persistently, day in and day out. We are like children crossing a busy highway whose attention wanders. We lose our focus, and we make bad choices. We need to hold on to our Father's hand to keep safe. One hundred percent of prayer is knowing your deep need of God. Of course, it only follows that if we know how much we need God, we won't find it hard to persist. Humility is the root of persistence.

PRAYER: *Keep before me my need, Father. Don't let anything distract me from the absolute of staying closely connected to you. Strengthen me to pray and not give up.*

DAY 233: BATTER MY HEART

John Donne (1572-1631)

"No discipline seems pleasant at the time, but painful. Later on, however, it produces a harvest of righteousness and peace for those who have trained by it" (Heb. 12:11).

Though better known now as a poet than as a preacher, Donne was considered the most eloquent preacher of his time, and served as chaplain to James I, King of England, and as Dean of St. Paul's Cathedral. One of his most famous sermons was the one he preached for his own funeral, entitled, "Death's Duel." He left his sickbed to preach it, returned home to pose for a portrait in a funeral shroud, and died a few weeks later.

Imminently quotable, some of Donne's lines—such as, "No man is an island" and "Death, be not proud"—have become part of common discourse down to the present. The *Oxford Dictionary of Quotations* has 79 entries from Donne's writings. His work is a brilliant example of the power of a "baptized imagination." When pressed into the service of God, a vivid imagination and a powerful intellect can produce works of beauty that are powerful to both commend and illumine the truth of the gospel. The following are examples of the power of his craft to encourage and enlighten.

Like Jacob and the apostle Paul, Donne agonized over the surrender of his will to God's will, and he prayed for God to do whatever it took to bring him to submission, even violence:

Batter my heart, three person'd God; for, you
As yet but knock, breathe, shine, and seek to mend;
That I may rise, and stand, overthrow me, and bend
Your force, to break, blow, burn and make me new.

He cried out that he was like a walled city held by God's enemy, or worse, a bride betrothed to God's enemy! Would God divorce him from their common foe?

I, like a usurped town, to another due,
Labor to admit you, but O, to no end,

He prayed that God would work in him the paradox of true freedom (cf. Luke 9:24):

Take me to you, imprison me, for I
Except you enthrall me, never shall be free,
Nor ever chaste, except you ravish me.[1]

PRAYER: *Lord, take me to yourself and imprison me! For if you do not enthrall me, I will never be free; nor will I ever be chaste, unless you ravish me.*

DAY 234: FOR THE SAKE OF ITS NON-MEMBERS

Luke 19:46 (Matt. 21:12-13; Mark 11:15-18)

"My house will be called a house of prayer for all nations" (Mark 15:17).

What Jesus saw that day sent him into a fury. Jesus didn't usually act this way, so we would do well to pay close attention to whatever it was that led him to knock over tables, kick over benches, and generally wreck the whole place.

Let's be clear about what didn't upset him. It wasn't that business was being conducted in the temple since the selling of animals for the sacrifice was official temple business. The problem was *where* the business was being done—the outer court which was "The Court of the Gentiles." This place was reserved for non-Jews to come and pray, but it had become a noisy, smelly marketplace. There was no room for prayer! It wasn't so much what *was* happening there, as what *wasn't* happening.

The temple was meant to be, above all else, a place to pray. It was not just for the "chosen," but it was to be a place of prayer for all the peoples of the earth. Jesus cited Isaiah 56:7, "My house will be a house of prayer." Mark, in his gospel, completed the quotation with the phrase "for all nations." Jesus was furious that the very place reserved for all peoples to encounter God was shut off to them. The "business" of the temple was keeping the temple from its true business.

The church, the community of Christ, is the new temple (see Eph. 2:19-22). How much more might Jesus be upset if his church, which he also calls his body, forgets its true business? William Temple, a former Archbishop of Canterbury, said the church is the only institution in the world that exists for the sake of its non-members. The future of the church lies in a great celebration in which people from east and west and north and south will come and sit at God's table in his kingdom. Woe to his people if they forget God's purposes (Luke 13:28-30)!

Pray for your church. Pray that its business will be God's business, not ecclesiastical clutter. Pray that your church will be a place where all peoples can feel welcome and where all peoples are lifted up to God in prayer. Make it a personal habit to pray for all the peoples of the earth; especially those who have little or no gospel witness.

PRAYER: *"May the peoples praise you, O God; may all the peoples praise you" (Ps. 67:5).*

DAY 235: BUT I HAVE PRAYED FOR YOU

Luke 22:31-32

"But I have prayed for you, Simon, that your faith may not fail" (Luke 22:32).

Satan already has Judas in his hip pocket (Luke 22:3), now he wants the rest of the disciples. He "has asked to sift you as wheat," Jesus told them. The "you" is plural, referring to all the disciples, and Satan's goal is to make them like sheep scattered by fear, disillusionment, and disunity who are ready to be picked off one-by-one by a predator. This scattering is the very thing that will happen to them. In Matthew's gospel, Jesus spoke of the aftermath of his arrest and crucifixion and quoted the prophet Zechariah. "I will strike the shepherd, and the sheep of the flock will be scattered" (Matt. 26:31).

Significantly, Jesus' prays specifically for Peter. He says, "But I have prayed for you." Here the "you" is singular. Note the Lord's priorities. When the sheep are scattered, he prays first for the shepherd, the leader. Peter's leadership role will be critical in the restoration of the disciples. When he is restored, he must strengthen his brothers (Luke 22:32). Jesus knew how important shepherds are for his sheep because he is the Good Shepherd. When the shepherd goes down, the sheep suffer. Jesus saw it coming.

What a vivid picture of Jesus' love for his church, and for its shepherds and pastors. Even on the eve of his execution, he was thinking of their welfare. No, he thought of them *especially* on the eve of his execution. After all, his death was for the sake of the church (Eph. 5:25).

We should pray for pastors and leaders with the same tender compassion that Jesus prayed for Peter. When they fail in their calling to care for the sheep, our response should not be to scorn or to leer cynically at the sight. We should pray for their restoration, and the restoration of the sheep scattered by their fall. We may imagine Jesus interceding for his church right now, at the right hand of the Father (Heb. 7:25). We may also picture him praying especially for the leaders of his church. Let us join Jesus in our prayers.

PRAYER: *Lord Jesus, you are the great and good shepherd of the sheep. You have appointed some to be your under-shepherds—to serve you by serving your people. Bless and keep your shepherds. Restore them when they sin and strengthen them to be faithful. I pray especially for* ______________________ .

DAY 236: IT'S NEVER TOO LATE OR SIMPLISTIC

Luke 23:32-43

"Jesus, remember me when you come into your kingdom" (Luke 23:42).

Two lives were lived badly, but one ended well. One man went to his death cursing Christ, the other reached out to him in faith. That is one way to read this brief encounter between Jesus and the penitent thief as they both hung dying on a cross. There is great hope here for all who have wasted their lives and who wonder if there is any hope for them. Be assured that there is hope, the story says. This latecomer was given an insight into Jesus that even his disciples didn't have. When he prayed, "Jesus, remember me when you come into your kingdom," he confessed faith in Jesus' victory over death. Even the apostle despaired of such hope at the moment. The thief is like the men in Jesus' parable who get a full day's wages for an hour's work (Matt. 20:1-16).

His prayer was a model prayer in simplicity. The thief prayed, "Remember me!" What could be more elemental? The two irreducible minimums of all true prayer are, (1) you must know your need, and (2) you must know the only one who can meet your need. All genuine prayer is rooted in humility and hope—humility about yourself and hope in the Savior who "was numbered with the transgressors… and made intercession for the transgressors" (Isa. 53:12).

Jesus' answer to the thief's prayer was a paradigm of God's eagerness to answer prayer. The response was immediate—"today you will be with me in paradise." The response was also gracious. One might even say Jesus over-answered when he added "in paradise." The thief wanted simply to be remembered, Jesus promised that he would be by his side in paradise. The word "paradise" is synonymous with "Abraham's side" or bosom, the place reserved for people the quality of Abraham (cf. Luke 16:22-23). It was also a Persian word for the king's walled, private garden—a place of special honor reserved for a favored servant or subject to be with the king. Jesus usually gives more than we ask, and better than we ask.

Know this: It is never too late or too simplistic to cry out, "Remember me!" Know also that God is more ready to hear your prayer than you are to pray it.

PRAYER: *O Lover of my soul! You know my folly and my rebellion. You know the time I have wasted. Be merciful to me for your name's sake, as I pray with that dying criminal, "Remember me!"*

DAY 237: INTO YOUR HANDS

Luke 23:46

"Jesus called out with a loud voice, 'Father, into your hands I commit my spirit.' When he had said this, he breathed his last" (Luke 23:46).

What a way to go. What a way to pray as you go: "Father, into your hands I commit my spirit." The prayer is taken from a line in Psalm 31:5. Some scholars believe "into your hands I commit my spirit" was the first prayer every Jewish mother taught her child to pray before going to sleep at night. When Jesus prayed this prayer, he added "Father" to it. Jesus died then, the way a child falls to sleep in his Father's arms.[1]

Right up to the very end of his life, Jesus drew on the Scriptures to shape his prayers. Charles Spurgeon remarked with admiration how even the incarnate Son of God, the grand original thinker, prayed from the Scriptures.

> *How instructive is this great truth that the Incarnate Word lived on the Inspired Word! It was food to him, as it is to us; and... if Christ thus lived upon the Word of God, should not you and I do the same? Oh, that you and I might get into the very heart of the word of God and get that word into ourselves! As I have seen the silkworm eat into the leaf, and consume it, so ought we do to the Word of the Lord—not crawl over its surface, but eat right into it till we have taken it into our inmost parts. It is idle merely to let the eye glance over the words.... But it is blessed to eat into the very soul of the Bible until, you come to talk in Scriptural language, and your very style is fashioned with Scriptural models... [as with] John Bunyan... Prick him anywhere; his blood is Bibline [or biblical]. I think it well worthy of your constant remembrance that, even in death, our blessed Master showed the ruling passion of his spirit, so that his last words were a quotation from Scripture.*[2]

If this is the way Jesus prayed, how much more should we? May it be said of us, "Prick them anywhere; their blood is Bibline."

PRAYER: *Lord Jesus, teach me to pray as you taught your disciples, and as you taught us when you hung dying on the cross. Let your word find a home in my heart, mind, and mouth. Teach me to pray as you prayed—from and through the Holy Scriptures.*

DAY 238: THE FELLOWSHIP OF THE BURNING HEART

Luke 24:13-32 (John 5:39-40)

"Were not our hearts burning within us while he talked with us on the road and opened the Scriptures to us?" (Luke 24:32).

We all need a companion or a guide when we read the Bible just as the disciples did on their way to the village of Emmaus on resurrection Sunday. They were confused about a lot of things. Then Jesus came along and explained the Scriptures to them, and their lives made sense again. Jesus demonstrated how he was both the subject of the whole Bible and its authoritative interpreter. "Beginning with Moses and all the Prophets, he explained to them what was said in all the Scriptures concerning himself" (Luke 24:27). When he finished, they looked at each other and exclaimed, "Were not our hearts burning within us while he talked with us on the road and opened the Scriptures to us?" (Luke 24:32).

Nothing could be better than that! Wouldn't you give anything to have Jesus himself at your side, explaining the meaning of the Bible as you read? He promised something like that when he promised the gift of his Holy Spirit, whom he appropriately called the Counselor. "But the Counselor, the Holy Spirit, whom the Father will send in my name, will teach you all things and will remind you of everything I have said to you" (John 14:25).

Just as Christ is present in Scripture, his Spirit is present alongside Scripture, revealing its truth to us. This doesn't guarantee theological precision to a prayerful reader or make every Christian an infallible interpreter of the Bible. But it does assure us that God will reveal the truth of Scripture to us if we ask him to. He never disappoints those who earnestly seek him the way Jesus said to pray—asking, seeking, and knocking continually (Luke 11:9-10; Heb. 11:6).

The Bible has been called God's love letter to us. It's better than that because the Lover is himself breathed into the book (2 Tim. 3:16). Happy are those whose hearts burn within them as they find in the Bible not only God's expression, but also his very presence.

PRAYER: *"Open my eyes, that I may see wonderful things in your law" (Ps. 119:18).*

Introduction to John

DAY 239: OF THE FATHER'S LOVE BEGOTTEN

"The Word became flesh and made his dwelling among us. We have seen his glory, the glory of the One and Only, who came from the Father, full of grace and truth" (John 1:14).

William Barclay thought each of the four Gospels could be symbolized by one of the four marvelous and mysterious creatures that surround the throne of God in the book of Revelation (see Revelation 4:7).[1] Stained glass windows in many churches follow the same idea. The man stands for Mark because his is the most human of the Gospels. The lion stands for Matthew because his Gospel shows Jesus as the Messiah, the Lion of the tribe of Judah. The ox stands for Luke because Luke shows Jesus, like the ox, to be the universal sacrifice and servant of humankind. The eagle stands for John because it was believed that the eagle is the only creature that can look directly into the sun and not be blinded. John's Gospel is like the eagle because it looks deep into the heart of Jesus and leaves the reader illuminated, but not blinded. For this reason, it has been called "the intimate Gospel."[2] John even describes himself as "the disciple whom Jesus loved" and who reclined at the table beside Jesus in a place of intimacy (see John 13:23; 19:26).

There is no better picture of the purpose and pleasure of prayer than the image of John communing with the Savior and seeking his face as we would a friend's (see Exod. 33:11; 2 Cor. 3:18). The book of John is the product of a lifetime of unity with Jesus us and reflection upon that experience. John records fewer events than the other three Gospels but gives much more commentary on what Jesus thought, felt, and said about the events. In a sense, the very content of this Gospel is like prayer.

Perhaps John's greatest contribution to the life of prayer is his record of what Jesus says about the tender and loving relationship between the Father and the Son (see John 5:19-20). Jesus regularly spoke of God as "my Father," and he tells us to address God as "our Father" (Matt. 6:9; see John 20:17). What Jesus is naturally by birth, we may become by new birth through faith in him (see John 1:12-13; 3:3-8). The result is that we share in the rights and blessings of the Father's Son when we become his Father's children.

Because of our status as God's children, we can have great confidence and expectation in prayer. Jesus prayed that we would enter into the same fellowship of love he has with God (see John 17:20-21, 23). To pray from such a privileged position of love and inclusion—to be part of the Father and the Son's relationship—is to be sure that whatever we ask in the Son's name will be given to us (see John 14:13-14; 16:24). To believe this is to breathe the atmosphere of prayer.

PRAYER: *Thank you, Jesus, for this staggering promise: "I will do whatever you ask in my name, so that the Son may bring glory to the Father" (John 14:13).*

DAY 240: IT'S ALL IN THE FAMILY

John 1:10-13

"…children born not of natural descent, nor of human decision or a husband's will, but born of God" (John 1:13).

Jesus taught his disciples to start their prayers with "Our Father" (Matt. 6:9). What a wonderful place to begin! To pray to the true and living God is not to address a vague and distant deity but to speak as a child to one's Father.

But wait! How can any mere human presume to be called a child of God? There are some sentimental—and blasphemous—views of God that reduce him to be more like us and to make us all his children. But the God that John speaks of is the Holy One of Israel, whom no one can see and live (John 1:18: Exod. 33:20). The God of the Bible lives in unapproachable light (1 Tim. 6:10). A miracle must take place, and a gracious gift must be given to humans for any of us to speak to God as Father. The miracle and the gift are spoken of in these stunning words: "Yet to all who received him, to those who believed in his name, he gave the right to become children of God, children born not of natural descent, nor of human decision or a husband's will, but born of God" (John 1:12-13).

We may become God's children, not by natural birth, but by new birth—or to use one of Paul's concepts, by the miracle of adoption. This is God's gift to us in Christ. Adoption is to be received by faith—not achieved by human effort but received by simply trusting in God's promise that all who believe will receive the gift and the miracle.

How should we then pray? Start with the most sublime of all relationships. Say "Father." Or, if you have never asked God to become your Father through faith in Christ, start there. Ask him; trust him; receive the gift and miracle of new birth. Then say "Father." Say it over and over again and let it sink into the depths of your soul and thrill you with its possibilities. St. Teresa of Avila said she found it difficult when she prayed to get past the word "Father." It was to her like a beautiful land that she wanted to live in forever. She will live there forever, and so will we.

PRAYER: *Our Father, who art in heaven—in whom we live, and move, and have our being: grant that I and all Christians may live worthy of this glorious relation, and that we may not sin, knowing that we are accounted as yours. We are yours by adoption, make us yours by choice of our will.*[1]

DAY 241: PRAYING WHEN JESUS PERPLEXES

John 4:43-54

"He went to him and begged him to come and heal his son, who was close to death" (John 4:47).

This is Jesus' second miraculous sign as recorded in John's Gospel. The first happened in the same town in Galilee, Cana, and involved the rescue of a wedding party. The wine had run out, and Jesus provided more wine—over 120 gallons more of even better wine than they had before (John 2:1-11). The second sign is the healing of an official's son.

Both signs in Cana were homey and personal, sharp contrasts with Jesus' massive, public acts of mercy such as feeding the crowds. With these first signs, only a limited number of people were involved. If these miracles were all Jesus ever did, they may have been forgotten within a couple of generations—like the people they touched. That fact alone is blessing enough for those who pray. Most of us are average citizens, of no significance in the world's grand schemes. Yet the Father hears our prayers. Our weddings and children, hopes and dreams, lives and deaths may be negligible in the world's eyes, but not in our Father's eyes.

As small as we are, it is our Father's good pleasure to teach us great lessons about prayer (Luke 10:21). There are two lessons to be learned here. The first is about our credentials. What do we possess that we can bring to Jesus to recommend ourselves to Him? Our need is our only credential. In the story of the official's son, the boy's father begs. He grovels. Knowing Jesus is all he has to base his hope upon. He is poor in spirit, a blessed and basic condition for prayer (Matt. 5:3). If Jesus doesn't hear and act, the man's son will die. The only credential we need to bring to Jesus in prayer is our need.

The second great lesson about prayer here is that Jesus often responds to our prayers in ways we find perplexing, even discouraging. Jesus initially responds to the father with a rebuke, though his remark is probably directed more to the Galileans, in general, who are listening. "Unless you people see miraculous signs and wonders, you will never believe" (John 4:48). Then Jesus refuses the father's request for him to come to his son's bedside (John 4:49-50). But what Jesus does, he does out of his great wisdom and love. The rebuke focuses the father's faith on higher things than even his son's recovery. The refusal shows Jesus to be even more powerful than the man thought. Jesus doesn't need to be physically present to be powerfully present. Through it all, the father clings tenaciously and tremblingly to Jesus, despite what he doesn't understand. In the end his faith is rewarded and strengthened.

PRAYER: *"Other refuge have I none, hangs my helpless soul on Thee; leave, ah! Leave me not alone, still support and comfort me. All my trust on Thee is stayed, all my help from Thee I bring, cover my defenseless head with the shadow of Thy wing" (from the hymn "Jesus Lover of My Soul" by Charles Wesley).*

DAY 242: BLESSED ARE THE PEACEMAKERS

Elias Chacour (born 1939)

"Blessed are the peacemakers, for they will be called sons of God" (Matt. 5:9).

When he was a boy, Elias Chacour prayed a prayer that changed his life forever. Elias was born into a Palestinian Christian family in 1939. When he was eight, he and his family were displaced by the Israelis to the village of Gish. He was awakened one night by the sound of angry voices blaring over loudspeakers: "Come out of your houses. We want all men to come out and give themselves up. You are leaving here at once." That night Elias' father and brothers were arrested and taken away.

In the months that followed, something peculiar began to stir in the young boy. He began to crave solitude. Sometimes while playing a game, his eyes would gaze off into the surrounding hills and he would wander away to be alone. One hot day, as he sat under an olive tree, aching for his father and brothers, he remembered words of Jesus his mother would recite as he lay in her lap: "Blessed are those who mourn, for they will be comforted." Then he imagined Jesus walking toward him, saying those words. For the first time, the words made sense, and Elias began to pray.

> *Almost without thinking, I began innocently pouring out my heart. "Mother has your comfort. I can see that. But can't you just speak a word and make all this trouble go away? Do you want us to be your lips and hands and feet—as Mother prays—to bring peace again? If that's true, you can use my hands and feet. Even my tongue," I added, thinking of my usually fiery words."*[1]

Elias also prayed that the Lord would bring his father and brothers home. He was thrilled to be reunited with them three months later. But there was much more to come.

Not long afterward, Israeli soldiers roared into Gish again, looking for the thief they believed had cut a piece of telephone wire from the new kibbutz they were building. They grabbed any children who were nearby and began to savagely beat them and accuse them of the crime. Elias was among the victims. As he was being beaten, he could hear their words: "You are worth nothing... thieves... dirty Palestinians." But he heard another voice too, speaking more of the words of Jesus he had heard in his mother's lap: "Peace, be still," and "Blessed are you when people falsely say all kinds of evil against you... for in the same way they persecuted the prophets who were before you." A few days later the wire was found. It had been cut accidentally by a wagon wheel on the hard ground. Elias remembered his prayer under the live tree: "You can use my hands and feet. Even my tongue."

As an adult, Elias Chacour was ordained a Melkite priest and has served Christ for years in a little church in Ibillin, Galilee. The recipient of many international peace awards, he has also traveled the world preaching the gospel and speaking on peace and justice, leading non-violent demonstrations, and working for reconciliation between Palestinians and Israelis. His favorite term for Israelis is "brothers and sisters."

PRAYER: *My Creator and Savior: You have given me everything I am and have. I belong to you, body and soul, in life and in death. You can use my hands and feet. Even my tongue.*

DAY 243: YOU ARE MORE THAN YOUR BELLY

John 6:25-69

"I am the bread of life" (John 6:35).

The crowd prayed a good prayer, although they didn't realize they were voicing a prayer. "Sir, from now on give us this bread" (John 6:34). Who wouldn't make this kind of request. Jesus had just said that this "true bread from heaven... gives life to the world" (John 6:32-33).

But the crowd prayed for far more than they knew. They were still thinking that what Jesus offered was some kind of super-bread—a new manna (Num. 11:7-9)—that would cure forever an empty stomach. But the bread Jesus was offering was himself, and the satisfaction was eternal. "I am the bread of life. He who comes to me will never go hungry" (John 6:35). They were looking for less than what they asked. That's usually the way it is with God and us. "We ask for silver," said Luther, "and God gives gold." And he pays us a great compliment as he does. He tells us we are more than our bellies and fleshly appetites. We were made for eternity, for God.

But sometimes the "more" God gives seems to us like less. In John 6, we see that many were deeply offended by Jesus' offer. Wasn't he just Joseph's boy, one of the locals? How can he make such an incredible offer (John 6:42)? You can see their eyes rolling as they speak. Then offense turned to disgust. "How can this man give us his flesh to eat?" (John 6:52). When all was said and done, Jesus' "hard teaching" (John 6:60) marked a mass deflection of disciples: "From this time many of his disciples turned back and no longer followed him" (John 6:66). Beware! Don't get so focused on what you ask of God that you no longer see God. The Giver is always better than the gift—infinitely better. In order to give you the very best, he may have to refuse you the good you ask for.

After his amazing offer, Jesus found himself standing rejected, looking at a greatly diminished crowd, and asking the Twelve, "You do not want to leave too, do you?" (John 6:67). May Peter's answer be ours, "Lord, to whom shall we go? You have the words of eternal life. We believe and know that you are the Holy One of God" (John 6:68-69).

PRAYER: *Lord Jesus, "From the best bliss that life imparts, we turn unfilled to Thee again" (from the hymn "Jesus, Thou Joy of Loving Hearts" by Bernard of Clairvaux)*

DAY 244: DRINKABLE LIGHT

John 7:37-39

"If anyone is thirsty, let him come to me and drink" (John 7:37-39).

In C.S. Lewis's story *The Voyage of the Dawn Treader*, the pilgrims sailed to the very edge of the world, to the utter East, and discovered that the water there is no longer salty. It is sweet. More amazing was the effect the water had on all who drank it. When Caspian drank, "His face was changed. Not only his eyes but everything about him seemed to be brighter" Caspian said the water was more like light than anything else. "That is what it is," said the mouse, Reepicheep, "drinkable light." In the days that followed, everyone on the ship "drew buckets of dazzling water from the sea, stronger than wine and somehow wetter, more liquid than ordinary water.... And one or two of the sailors who had been oldish men when the voyage began now grew younger every day."[1]

On the last and greatest day of the Feast of Tabernacles, Jesus loudly invited all who heard to come to him and to drink water like that described in Lewis's story. John added that this living water was the Holy Spirit (John 7:39). The occasion made the offer dramatic. The Feast of Tabernacles celebrated God's gracious provision for Israel in their wilderness wanderings, including the provision of water. For each of the seven days of the Feast, water was carried from the pool of Siloam to the temple to remind the people of how God had never failed to quench their thirst during those long years in the desert. It was on the last day of the feast that Jesus made his announcement. He said, in effect, "I am the greater water, the fulfillment of all God has ever done to satisfy your thirst."

There may be another layer of meaning in Jesus' words. The feast was marked by a lot of feasting, or partying, as we might say. A lot of food and wine had been consumed by this time. Jesus' words may have sounded like. "Are you still thirsty after all that? Then come to me and be satisfied."

Like his teachings about bread in chapter six, the Lord is again offering to fill us with something better than food and water, something our physical hunger and thirst can only point toward. Jesus is offering himself by the work of the Holy Spirit. Of all the good gifts God gives us in prayer, he is the greatest (Luke 11:13). He is "drinkable light."

PRAYER: *Christ, you are the light of the world and the water of life. Fill me till I thirst no more. Give to me what you promised: the fullness of your Spirit.*

DAY 245: EVERYTHING DEPENDS ON THE ONE TO WHOM YOU PRAY

John 10:1-18, 27-30

"I am the good shepherd" (John 10:11).

If you are a sheep, everything depends on whom you have for a shepherd. There are hired hands who are in it only for the money. The moment being a shepherd gets a little inconvenient or dangerous, they resign, and the sheep are left to wolves and thieves. A question worth asking is: Which is worse—hired hands or wolves. Wolves are "honest" they only do what comes naturally. Hired hands are pretenders (Isa. 56:9-12; Ezek. 34). There can be any number of wolves licking their chops, wanting to eat the sheep, but if the shepherd is good, the sheep will be safe. If the shepherd is bad, it only takes one wolf to destroy the whole flock.

Jesus is the Good Shepherd. In every way he is the opposite of the hired hand. Jesus is the gate. He keeps the sheep secure, and no one can get to them except through him. He makes the sheep free so they can "come in and go out, and find pasture" (John 10:9). The Good Shepherd knows the sheep by name, each one of them, and every one matters (John 10:14). Above all, Jesus is good because he lays down his life for the sheep (John 10:11, 15).

When you pray, everything depends on the One to whom you pray. What is God like? Can you trust him? Will your life be safe in his hands? Does he love you? Put him to the test: Does God listen? He does, for he is the Good Shepherd who knows your name! Does God care about you? He does, for he laid down his life for you! Does God have good plans for you? He does, for his purpose is to give you life in its fullness (John 10:10). God is no pretender; he hates pretenders. He is the real thing. Come to him with confidence and joy.

PRAYER: *Protect and guide me, Good Shepherd. Forgive my sins, heal my wounds, and refresh me, not because I deserve it, but because you are the Good Shepherd.*

DAY 246: BECAUSE HE LOVES US SO

John 11:1-44

"Jesus wept" (John 11:35).

This story has a spectacular ending! A dead man gets raised, and later his sister pours out her love for Jesus in a way that Jesus said will never be forgotten (John 11:2; 12:1-8; Matt. 26:13). The story is short, spanning only about four days, but it is packed with meaning. It is a case study in how death can affect us and how our prayers affect God.

Our prayers always affect God, and he always responds—not according to our power, wisdom, or love, but according to his. When Jesus received the message from Mary and Martha that his friend Lazarus was sick, he didn't leave immediately to go to them. Instead, he waited two more days, even though he knew Lazarus would die (John 11:11-15). Either Jesus was negligent, or he was divinely in charge. Either he let things get out of control, or he was so in-control that no turn of circumstances could thwart his purpose. Clearly it was the latter, and this story encourages us to pray with our eyes not on our frightening and discouraging circumstances, but on his unseen power.

Jesus' power served his wisdom. He saw that it would be better for all involved for Lazarus to die because God would get greater glory from raising Lazarus from the dead than from healing him (John 11:4). And when God gets glory, everything else get glorious—like people's faith: "Lazarus is dead, and for your sake I am glad I was not there, so that you may believe" (John 11:14-15).

The range of loving emotions Jesus expresses in this story is amazing, especially given the fact that he was so confident of this power and wisdom. He was "deeply moved in spirit and troubled," and he "wept" (John 11:33, 35, 38). The word translated "troubled" is used two other times of Jesus in John's Gospel. Jesus was "troubled" when he spoke of his impending death (John 12:27) and when he announced that one of the disciples was going to betray him (John 13:21). But why should Jesus be upset about anything at all since he knew everything would turn out so wonderfully? He was troubled because God's children were suffering, and it is his nature to suffer with them. Our prayers affect God because he loves us so. When we grieve, he grieves too—not because he is helpless, but because he loves.

PRAYER: *Thank you, dear Jesus, that you are moved by my tears, but unmoved by anything I might ask that would be less than your perfect will. Give me faith to trust you when you seem unresponsive.*

DAY 247: FATHER! GLORIFY YOUR NAME!

John 12:23-28

"The hour has come for the Son of Man to be glorified" (John 12:23).

What do you pray when you are in trouble? You pray, "Help!"—right? It's instinctive and reflexive and to want to get away from trouble unless, of course, you are being urged on by some other principle—some higher purpose, like Jesus was. The only way to understand his words is in light of this higher purpose. Jesus said, "Now my heart is troubled, and what shall I say? 'Father save me from this hour'? No, it was for this very reason I came to the hour, Father, glorify your name!" (John 12:28). Gaining the Father's glory was greater to Jesus than avoiding his own pain, so Jesus prayed, "Father, glorify your name!"

Yet Jesus' glory was involved too. In verse 23 he says, "The hour has come for the Son of Man to be glorified." Jesus will be glorified, but by a strange route. Jesus' glory will come through his death. Jesus' heart was troubled because he was in "big trouble" from a worldly perspective. But the trouble Jesus faced was the kind a seed undergoes when it is buried in the soil. "Kill" the seed, and it will come back better and stronger than it was before.

God's glory is his infinite inestimable worth—his "weight," as the Hebrew word for glory, *kabod*, suggests. The heavens declare God's glory, and he made us in his image, in part, to show his glory. Our glory is borrowed glory and is fading away. God's glory is eternal. When we make his glory our goal, we will share in it forever. There is no higher prayer to pray, no prayer more beneficial to our own good, in trouble or out of trouble, than to pray that God's name be glorified. In the prayer that Jesus taught his disciples, it is the first thing to pray for: "Hallowed be your name" (Matt. 6:9).

Missionary Helen Roseveare saved hundreds of lives by faithful service in the Belgian Congo. During the Simba rebellion, however, she was captured by the rebels and beaten and raped repeatedly. Later she was asked if her accomplishments offset the pain she suffered. Her answer was an unsentimental, "No." Then the Lord spoke to her and said, "Helen, the question is not, 'Was it worth it?' but 'Am I worthy?'" She answered, "Of course you are, Lord." Her glory, her accomplishments, were not enough to satisfy her. But God's glory was.

PRAYER: *Father in heaven! Your glory is my greatest good. Whether by dying or by living, may your glory be my highest goal.*

DAY 248: MAXIMUM LOVE, NOT MINIMUM LOVE

John 13:1-17

"Having loved his own who were in the world, he now showed them the full extent of his love" (John 13:1).

The disciples were in no mood for what Jesus did at dinner that night. Their mood was competitive. Still glowing from the enthusiastic reception that the crowds had given them the Sunday before, they were arguing with each other about the rank they would get when their master's kingdom was established (Luke 22:24).

Jesus' mood was very different. He was clear about what lay ahead. He knew he would soon die. There was glory and a kingdom, but the path ahead was through suffering. As the disciples chattered, Jesus looked at how dirty their feet were, and he loved them by serving them.

According to some ancient Jewish sources, the task of foot-washing was regarded as so menial that slaves couldn't be forced to do such demeaning service. It was up to the individual slave's discretion whether to wash the guests' feet, which appears to be the point here. The men in the room were a collection of mere individuals, arguing about what belonged to them and relating to each other in a *minimal* way.[1] There was no breach of etiquette, nor was there any love. They weren't brothers; they were associates.

And Jesus loved them. So, he sought them out. Without fanfare, he got up and began to relate to his men in a *maximal* way. As he washed their feet, he practiced the opposite of what they were practicing. They weren't in the mood for this sort of thing, and Peter's response summed up their feelings: "No! Never!" But it was too late, for Jesus had already broken down their defenses. When Jesus said, "Unless I wash you, you have no part with me." Peter could only reply, "Then, Lord, not just my feet but my hands and my head as well!" (John 13:8-9).

Jesus had made his point visually, but lest they miss it, he made it verbally. "I have set you an example that you should do as I have done for you" (John 13:15). A little later Jesus said that this kind of love will inform and enlighten the world (John 13:34-35). In other words, Jesus tells them, "You must seek each other out as I have sought you. You dare not be mere individuals, getting along politely and minimally. The world must see clearly that you belong to me. The only way it will know this is if you belong to each other in the same way you belong to me."

PRAYER: *Jesus, you have commanded it, so we pray it: May we love one another as you have loved us.*

DAY 249: THE POWER OF THE NAME

John 14:12-14; 15:7; 16:23-24

"You may ask me for anything in my name, and I will do it" (John 14:14).

There is something here that Jesus absolutely does not want us to miss. He says it six times over three chapters, the first in John 14:13, "I will do whatever you ask in my name." Then he says it five more times (John 14:14, 15:7, 16; 16:23, 24). Read each of these passages and be duly impressed with how strongly the Lord wants us to remember the power of praying in his name. Not only will he and his Father do what we ask in his name, buy praying this way will give God great glory and us great joy (John 15:8; 16:24).

"What a deal," some have thought, "just use his name, and he'll do whatever I ask." They say this because they don't understand the significance of the name. A lot of materialistic self-promotion has been justified by this misunderstanding. And the faith of many has been damaged when the use of Jesus' name did not achieve the desired results.

In the Bible, a name is not a label; it is a person or the character and nature of that person. To pray the name of Jesus is not to use his name as a mantra, but to submit to his will as one would to a master. Jesus is saying, "Whatever you ask *according to who I am* will be done for you." The "whatever" is conditioned by the "name," not the other way around. To pray in the name of Jesus is just another way of saying, "Your will be done on earth as it is in heaven" (Matt. 6:10).

Should we be encouraged or discouraged by this qualification? Will our prayers shrink or expand according to this knowledge? They must become bigger and better! What Jesus desires and wills is glorious and beautiful. In contrast to his, all our desires are cheap and tawdry. When our prayers are aligned with his name, we are better people, and our prayers take on divine power in a way very much like what Dante described as what happened to him when he looked into the face of God. He wrote, "But now my desire and will were revolved, like a wheel which is moved evenly by the Love which moves the sun and the other stars."[1] Now that is power in prayer!

PRAYER: *Holy Jesus, teach me your ways, that I may revere your name. Teach me the power of wanting to want what you want, that I may have the joy of answered prayer in your name.*

DAY 250: OF FRUIT AND PRAYER

John 15:1-17

"I am the true vine" (John 15:1).

Some scholars believe that Jesus' words in John 14:31 signal that he and the disciples left the upper room at that point. In that case, the group was walking as Jesus spoke to them. Their walk that night would likely have taken them past the temple, on which was a golden vine and clusters of grapes. The historian Josephus said the clusters were "as large as a man."[1] The moment was perfect for the point Jesus wanted to make: He is the vine; his disciples are his branches. The goal of the disciples' lives, as with a branch, is to be fruitful. The way to be fruitful is to be a branch that is vitally connected to the vine.

What is the fruit? It is the fruit of the Spirit (Gal. 5:22-23), of which Jesus singles out joy and love for special mention (John 15:11, 17). Pause and let that sink in. God's great purpose for your life is not to make you more productive (as in achieving goals and getting a lot of work done), but more fruitful (as in taking delight in the intimate relationship of branch to vine). Jesus gives us a powerfully inviting image of the Christian life: It's like a cluster of juicy, sweet grapes! The productivity will come not as a cause, but as an effect. Jesus came that we may have life to the full (John 10:10).

The place of prayer in this economy is very interesting—and thrilling. We may think prayer will make us fruitful. Jesus thinks it is the other way around: being fruitful will lead us to prayer. "You did not choose me, but I chose you and appointed you to go and bear fruit—fruit that will last. *Then* the Father will give you whatever you ask in my name" (John 15:16, italics added). The source of all prayer is not in the branch, but in the vine. The energy motivating and sustaining prayer is the life of Jesus coursing in us, leading us to cry out, "Abba, Father (Rom. 8:15-16). To be sure, prayer that originates in Jesus will soon die if it is not expressed back to Jesus. But the critical truth here is that prayer is a gift, not an achievement. We pray for the same reason we love—because he first loved us (1 John 4:19). Prayer is so much more than a duty—it is the life of Jesus flowing through us. We *must* pray because, as branches in the vine, we *may* pray.

PRAYER: *Jesus, you are the vine, and I am but a branch—but a grateful branch! Make me fruitful so that I may pray more and cause me to pray more that I may be more fruitful.*

DAY 251: WITH HIS DYING BREATH

Blind Chang (Died 1900)

"I will sing to the Lord all my life; I will sing praise to God as long as I live" (Ps. 104:33).

The Boxer Rebellion of 1900 saw the death of 32.000 Chinese Christians and 188 missionaries and their children. Among them was a powerful evangelist known as Blind Chang. His death was no more remarkable than the many others who sealed their testimony for Christ by laying down their lives. But the privilege granted him of publicly praising God to his very last breath is.

Before his conversion, Chang was so reprobate a sinner he was nicknamed in Chinese "One without a particle of good within him." One day in a rage, this thief, gambler, and womanizer even threw his wife and daughter out of their home. When he suddenly lost his eyesight at the age 30, many of his neighbors were sure it was God's judgment that had made him blind.

Chang heard of a missionary hospital, hundreds of miles from his home, where surgeries were being performed that could restore his sight. Somehow, he got to the hospital, only to be told that all the beds were filled and that he could not be admitted as a patient. But when the hospital evangelist gave him his bed and Chang's sight was partially restored, he received the gospel with great joy and expressed a fervent desire to be baptized and follow Christ. James Webster, one of the missionaries at the hospital, told Chang he would not baptize him until he showed evidence of the genuineness of his faith by returning to his village and living out his faith with the people who had given him his nickname. When Webster later visited his village, he was thrilled to see that Chang's testimony had led over 400 people to faith in Christ.

Though Chang eventually lost his sight again due to a botched medical procedure, he never lost his faith. Instead, he became a powerful evangelist, memorizing most of the New Testament and large portions of the Old. When the Boxers tried to stamp out Christianity in China, Chang became their prime target. To capture him, they held fifty Chinese Christians prisoner and threatened to kill them all if someone did not reveal Chang's whereabouts. When Chang heard of this, he turned himself in.

Blind Chang was to be executed by decapitation. Unafraid, he sang the first Christian song he had ever learned as his captors took him to the place of execution. "One without a particle of Good within Him" had made peace with his Judge and Maker, and he knew God's face would be the first he would see.

Jesus loves me, he who died, Heaven's gate to open wide;
He will wash away my sin, let his little child come in.
Jesus loves me, he will stay, close beside me all the way;
If I love him when I die, He will take me home on high.

As the executioner's sword flashed in the sun and came down, Chang prayed, "Heavenly Father, receive my spirit."[1]

PRAYER: *Almighty and merciful Father, grant me grace to glorify you in life and in death.*

DAY 252: THE "REAL" LORD'S PRAYER

John 17:23

"I in them and you in me. May they be brought to complete unity" (John 17:23).

People lean close to hear the words of a dying person. Last words carry great weight. When life is all said and done, what was most important to this person? The last things said and prayed can be an important clue to what a person's life was all about.

How important was it to Jesus that Christians get along with each other? It was one of the last things he prayed for before he was arrested and crucified.

But greater than the timing of his prayer was the depth of the unity for which Jesus prayed. His passion for unity was so intense that he asked his Father to make us *one as he and his Father are one* (John 17:21, 23). Jesus wanted his church to be a living demonstration of the love and oneness of the Godhead—the Three in One and the One in Three!

There is more: The claim Jesus made for the power of Christian unity is unparalleled in all his teachings. He said it would convince the world that he was sent by God (John 17:23). Jesus believed that the greatest argument for the truth of his unique and divine identity would come not from theologians and philosophers, but from simple believers living together in the kind of love he prayed for that night. He said this of nothing else. This is the Lord's great prayer. Clearly, Christian unity mattered greatly to him.

Does it matter that much to you? Christ died for individuals, but the New Testament's favorite way of speaking of individuals is as God's people, his body, his bride, the temple of the Holy Spirit (1 Corinthians 12:27, Ephesians 5:25-33; 1 Corinthians 3:16-17). There can be no place for individualism in the church, for "The man who seeks God in isolation from his fellows," wrote R. H. Tawney, "is likely to find, not God but the devil, who will bear an embarrassing resemblance to himself."[1] Pray the "real" Lord's Prayer, pray that we will be one as he and his Father are one. Pray that you will be an answer to his prayer in the care you give to his body, the church.

PRAYER: *Heavenly Father, as Jesus prayed, so I pray: Bring us as believers to complete unity, that the world may know that Jesus came from you, and that you love us as you love your Son.*

Introduction to Acts

DAY 253: THE CONTINUING WORDS AND DEEDS OF JESUS

"They all joined together constantly in prayer" (Acts 1:14).

The real action in the book of Acts is not exactly the acts of the apostles as is commonly thought. The apostles are very busy, to be sure, but the book is more interested in who is busy through them. Luke opens the second book of his two-volume work by saying, "In my former book, Theophilus, I wrote about all that Jesus *began* to do and to teach until the day he was taken up to heaven, after giving instructions through the Holy Spirit to the apostles he had chosen" (Acts 1:1, italics added). The clear implication is that Luke's second book was a continuing record of the things Jesus was doing before his Ascension, and now would continue to do by his Spirit, through his apostles. John Stott proposes that a more accurate, though cumbersome, title of the book would be, "The Continuing Words and Deeds of Jesus by his Spirit through his Apostles."[1]

If Acts is about what Jesus is still doing, then much depends on the church obeying Jesus' command to "wait for the gift my Father promised" (Acts 1:4)—the gift of the Holy Spirit. One way to read this exciting book is from the perspective of how the church waits on God, receiving his power, and then doing his will. Repeatedly, the church waits in prayer (Acts 1:14; 2:42-47; 4:23-31; 12:5; 13:2-3). Repeatedly, the mission of Christ is advanced as they do. Acts calls and encourages us to do Jesus' work in Jesus' way, through prayer and the word of God (Acts 6:2-4, 7).

PRAYER: *Thank you, Lord, that all I do, I do in and through you. With your help, O Holy Spirit, I will therefore breathe out prayer, without interruption.*

DAY 254: BEING A PRAYER MEETING

Acts 1:1-14

"They all joined together constantly in prayer" (Acts 1:14).

"The early church didn't have a prayer meeting," said Armin Gesswein, "the church was a prayer meeting."[1] Prayer wasn't a specialized ministry, it was the very life of the church. They joined together in prayer constantly (Acts 2:42).

Why was this so? It was their direct response to the Lord's direct command to "wait for the gift my Father promised" (Acts 1:4, 5, 8). To wait was to pray, to pray was to wait. Waiting is not passively passing the time until the promise comes. It vigorously lays hold of what is promised and lives accordingly into the future. This is what prayer is. To pray is to do what watchmen do as they wait for the morning, eyes fixed on the horizon, straining to see the sun. "My soul waits for the Lord more than watchmen wait for the morning, more than watchmen wait for the morning" (Ps. 130:6).

Prayer is fueled by hope. We don't pray to get God's attention; we pray because he has ours. His promises are wonderful and sure. He commands us to wait for them, actively and prayerfully. We have not because we ask not, or because we ask badly, with base motives, says James (Acts 4:2). But there is another reason: we have not because we wait not, like these Jerusalem believers. Those who wait receive and are strengthened as they wait. "Wait for the Lord; be strong and take heart and wait for the Lord" (Ps. 27:14). Let the church stop having prayer meetings, and start *being* a prayer meeting! That is where the power lies.

PRAYER: *You have my attention, Lord! You are faithful to hear us. May I, and all my church family, constantly plead and claim your good promises in prayer.*

DAY 255: VITAL SIGNS

Acts 2:42-47

"They devoted themselves to the apostles' teaching and to the fellowship, to the breaking of bread and to prayer" (Acts 2:42).

The church waited for Christ's extraordinary promise, the baptism of the Holy Spirit, and their waiting was rewarded. The extraordinary happened, and Christ's community was immersed in the very life of God. What came next? More waiting, more praying. Luke says the church was devoted to four things: teaching, fellowship, the breaking of bread, and prayer. The extraordinary was to be lived out in the ordinary patterns of life. The church continued the way it began—waiting. Waiting was becoming a habit.

Prayer is one of the four vital signs of a healthy church—like a heartbeat. If the pulse is weak and erratic, the body is sick. If it is strong and steady, the body is healthy and strong. Look at the health of the Jerusalem church. There was a pervasive sense of awe as the people saw wonders and miraculous signs. There was great joy as they shared their money, their time, and their homes. Outsiders wanted to be on the inside as "the Lord added to their number daily those who were being saved" (Acts 2:47).

What the church needs today is what it has needed from the beginning: more and more of the presence of Jesus. We don't need more programs and meetings; we need more of the Lord. When Jesus shows up, remarkable things happen. Just look again at what was happening in Jerusalem.

God comes to churches and individuals who wait for him. To wait is to pray, to pray is to wait. Prayer is not an occasional, extraordinary thing, but a pattern, a habit, of life.

PRAYER: *Lord Jesus, we need you so desperately! Form within me and my church, a deep devotion to waiting on you in prayer!*

DAY 256: EARTHSHAKING PRAYER

Acts 4:23-31

"When they heard this, they raised their voices together in prayer to God" (Acts 4:34).

Their prayer time ended with a kind of earthquake. How did that happen? It began with the church praying a classic biblical prayer, which is to say they proceeded the way so many of the psalms and other great prayers of Scripture do. It is a prayer worthy of imitation.

They rehearsed before God all that he had done and said in history (Acts 4:24-26, 28). He had always been the Sovereign Lord, creator of heaven and earth, King of kings, and ruler of the nations. Read—or better, pray—this prayer thoughtfully. You will get a crash course in a sound biblical theology of creation, revelation, and history. This theology is summed up in the verbs used of God—he made (Acts 4:24), he spoke (Acts 4:25), and he decided beforehand what would happen (Acts 4:28).

In the light of the past, they recounted what was going on in the present (Acts 4:27). God already knows these things, of course, but it is a key part of the communion of prayer for God's people to lay their circumstances out before God anyway. According to Jesus, God's comprehensive knowledge of all things gives us greater reason to speak our needs, not less (Matt. 6:8).

Finally, the saints made their requests (Acts 4:29-30). The order of the prayer is important: first the rehearsal and praise, then the requests. The requests come a lot easier when we are reminded who we are speaking to! We are speaking to the Almighty, and nothing is too hard for him.

The saints in Acts ask that God do what only God can do—healing and miracles. For themselves, they ask that God will help them do what they are supposed to do—be bold in their speaking. It's a great arrangement: May God be who he is, powerful and wise. May his people be who they are supposed to be, bold and faithful witnesses.

This kind of prayer moves the earth, not usually as the shaking they experienced, but in more important ways. Kingdoms rise and fall, and history unfolds as the prayers of the saints are presented before the throne of God (Rev. 8:1-5).

PRAYER: *Sovereign Lord, you are the God of creation, revelation, and history. I know that nothing is too hard for you! So do whatever you desire to do in and through my life!*

DAY 257: KEEPING THE FIRST THINGS FIRST

Acts 6:1-7

"We will turn this responsibility over to them and will give our attention to prayer and the ministry of the word" (Acts 6:3-4).

It took a crisis for the church to realign its priorities. It usually does. Spiritual euphoria had carried the young Christian community along up to this point. Growth was bursting out everywhere, in conversions, in favor with the people—and in widows and orphans needing practical help. In that day there was no governmental safety net to catch widows and orphans. If their family and friends couldn't provide for them, they fell—hard. It was up to the church to obey God's clear mandate to care for these people (James 1:27).

But it was a huge job, and there were complaints—serious complaints. Some were accusing the church of racism for giving preferential treatment to Hebraic Jews over Grecian Jews. Something had to be done. The apostles were so involved in the controversy that they were spending less time praying and teaching the Word of God. They were in a quandary. The widows and orphans must be cared for, racism (if the charge was true) must be eradicated, and they must tend to the ministry of prayer and the Word. "It would not be right for us to neglect the ministry of the word of God in order to wait on tables." But the tables still needed waiting, and it was clear they couldn't do everything.

So, they delegated. Some of the saints were set apart to be table-waiters. The Greek word used for their job is the word behind our English word *deacon*. The first deacons were waiters! Significantly, all the surnames of the deacons were Greek. Along with neglect of the poor, there could be no room for racism in the church.

Two things precious to the integrity of the church were preserved in this bold move. The widows and orphans got what they needed; and the church got what it needed—a leadership that was devoted to prayer and to the Word of God. These two were not seen as either/or choices, but as both/ands. If the church loses either prayer and the Word or care for the poor, eventually both will be undermined, and the church will be weakened.

PRAYER: *I pray for my church, Father, that we all will do our part so that spiritual and physical needs are met. Lead us as we lay our priorities before you.*

DAY 258: THE BREATH OF THE SOUL

Acts 7:54-60

"While they were stoning him, Stephen prayed" (Acts 7:59).

Stoning to death, though quicker than crucifixion, is as ghastly a way to die as there can be. Typically, the victim was stripped then knocked off a 9-foot scaffold by one of the witnesses to the crime. If he survived the fall, another witness would drop a stone on his chest. If he survived that, others would pelt him with stones until he was dead. Stephen's death was something like that, though probably not as deliberate. It had all the markings of a lynching in its spontaneity.

While all this was going on, Stephen, the church's first martyr, prayed. It has been said that prayer is the breath of the soul. How fitting since the first thing we do when we come into the world is breathe, and the last thing we do as we depart is breathe. In between, the Bible says, "Let everything that has breath praise the Lord" (Ps. 150:6). Stephen's last breath, like his Lord's, was the breath of his very soul. He prayed for himself, "Lord Jesus, receive my spirit," and he prayed for his murderers, "Lord, do not hold this sin against them."

How could he breathe such prayers in that horrific moment? No doubt it was because he was allowed to see something of the glory of God and of Christ standing at his right hand (Acts 7:55-56). Although his exclamation at what he saw probably pushed the angry judges over the edge. It only hastened what was inevitable. But the glorious immensity of what he saw made the inevitable suffering, grisly as it was, seem small in comparison. This has been the experience of many martyrs over the centuries. Often, but not always, their troubles are made to seem light and momentary in the light of God's glory (2 Cor. 4:16-18).

Christians of other generations used to pray for what they called a "good death." Stephen died a good death. We could experience something like that by learning to pray Stephen's prayer *before* we die in the hope that we may pray it *when* we die. We can pray now, "'Lord Jesus, receive my spirit.' I'm not in control, but you are; I leave myself in your hands." We can pray now, "'Lord, do not hold this sin against them.' Let me live forgiven and forgiving, without bitterness." Good living makes for good dying.

PRAYER: *Lord Jesus, I'm not in control, but you are. I leave myself in your hands. Help me live forgiven and forgiving, without bitterness.*

DAY 259: "THE MOST DEJECTED AND RELUCTANT CONVERT"

Acts 9:1-19

"He fell to the ground and heard a voice say to him, 'Saul, Saul, why do you persecute me?'" (Acts 9:4).

C. S. Lewis described himself at his conversion as, "the most dejected and reluctant convert in all England."[1] Paul was no doubt the most surprised (and surprising) convert in all history. On his way to imprison and kill Christians, he became one.

Blinded by the light, Paul asked, "Who are you, Lord?" It was a prayer, truly! The answer he got was the last he expected. The voice from the light was Jesus, the very one whose name he despised. How could he possibly have known that one day he would say, "I consider my life worth nothing to me, if only I may finish the race and complete the task the Lord Jesus has given me" (Acts 20:24).

God is always the initiator in prayer. "Our prayer is the answer to God's," wrote P. T. Forsyth.[2] Therefore, Paul responds to God's initiation, "Who are you, Lord?" The life of prayer is filled with many such surprises. Sometimes the circumstances and events of life come at us with the force of a blinding light, and the God we thought we knew is really very different than we imagined—very different, unsettlingly different. And we kick against the light, as God told Paul he did: "Saul, Saul, why do you persecute me? It is hard for you to kick against the goads" (Acts 26:14). God's mercy is severe, but it is still mercy. His hardness is really his kindness.

In later years, Lewis's memory of his reluctant conversion, like Paul's, had served to underline for him the amazing grace of God: "The prodigal Son at least walked home on his own feet. But who can truly adore that Love which will open the high gates to a prodigal who is brought in kicking, struggling, resentful, and darting his eyes in every direction for a chance of escape? The hardness of God is kinder than the softness of men, and His compulsion is our liberation."[3]

PRAYER: *Your grace is truly amazing, Father! Thank you for your everlasting mercy and kindness—even when it comes in surprising and severe ways.*

DAY 260: A CASTLE AND A GARDEN

Teresa of Avila (1512-1582)

"How lovely is your dwelling place, O lord Almighty! My soul yearns, even faints for the courts of the Lord; my heart and my flesh cry out for the living God" (Ps. 84:1-2).

Teresa of Avila was a woman who possessed what we would call "grit." She and others like her needed a lot of grit to navigate their way spiritually through the tumult of sixteenth century Europe. The Protestant Reformation had ushered in a new age of religious freedom with an emphasis on biblical, personal faith—an idea embraced by many. Teresa, and others like her (among them her friend St. John of the Cross), agreed with some of the reformers' critique of the Roman Catholic Church, but she remained within the church as a Carmelite nun to work for internal renewal.

Teresa is best known for her work, *The Interior Castle*, an allegory in which the soul moves from the outer courtyard to the innermost sanctuary of the castle's seven mansions. Along the way, prowling beasts (symbolizing the hindrances to prayer) seek to waylay the pilgrim. Each mansion is a stage along the way to union with Christ, which is beautifully pictured as the emergence of a silkworm from a cocoon to the life of a white butterfly. Beyond the mansion of union with Christ is the dark night of the soul and, finally, spiritual marriage to Christ.

Though a mystic, Teresa was very practical and uncomplicated in her advice about prayer. She compared the cultivation of prayer to the cultivation of a garden in which Christ himself must pull up the weeds, and we (with his help) water the flowers so they will delight our Lord with their fragrance. "Pray as you can," she advised, "for prayer doesn't consist in thinking a great deal, but of loving a great deal." She believed God could lead the simplest Christian, using only the words of the Lord's Prayer, into the heights of contemplation. For her the bottom line was that we must "Never, for any reason whatever, neglect to pray."[1]

By the time of her death, Teresa had founded twenty new Carmelite convents and had spread mysticism as a practical method of reform throughout Spain. She and her friend, St. John of the Cross, were criticized and even imprisoned by the church they loved for their reform efforts. Today they are considered by many Christians of diverse traditions to be the preeminent authorities of the theology of spiritual life.

PRAY A PRAYER OF TERESA'S: *Govern all by your wisdom, O Lord, so that my soul may always be serving you according to your will, and now as I desire. Do not punish me, I pray, by granting what I want and ask, if it offends your love, which would always live in me. Let me die to myself, that I may serve you, let me live to you, who in yourself are the true life.*[2]

DAY 261: GOD'S WEAKNESS IS STRONGER THAN HUMAN STRENGTH

Acts 12:1-24

"But the word of God continued to increase and spread" (Acts 12:24).

Acts 12 begins with a sword coming down on the neck of James (Acts 12:2) and ends with Herod, the man who ordered it, being eaten by worms (Acts 12:23). There is a beheading and a consumption—a study in grisly contrasts.

More elegant and instructive is the contrast between methods and audiences. Herod's audience is the Jewish leaders who were pleased with his execution of James. His method is more of the same: arrest another apostle, Peter this time, and kill him. If one execution advanced his power so much, then a second execution will double it (Acts 12:3-4). Herod's audience is those with power. His method is coercion and intimidation—the tried-and-true way to succeed in a world hostile to God.

The church, on the other hand, has God as its audience and prayer as its method (Acts 12:5). Prayer is the only means the church has to accomplish anything because God is all the church has. If bets were placed on the outcome, the worldly wise would put their money on Herod. Set next to Herod, the church looks weak and silly.

But God's "weakness" is stronger than human strength, and God's "foolishness" is wiser than human wisdom. The outcome is almost comedic. Herod's plans are thoroughly frustrated, and in the end, he is dead. The church is stunned with amazement and joy. Herod can't keep Peter in jail, and the church can't believe he's out. Peter must knock on the door a long time before the little prayer meeting will believe its prayers have really been answered. Instead of being squelched, "the word of God continued to increase and spread" (Acts 12:24).

Prayer can look rather foolish and weak to some, even to the people of God. However, prayer moves mountains and kingdoms—to the laughter of heaven and eventually the church. God loves it when his people pray, and the powers of darkness tremble.

PRAYER: *Forgive me, Lord, for the times I doubt the power and effectiveness of my prayers. Keep reminding me that true strength and wisdom reside with you and are unleashed when your people pray.*

DAY 262: THE FUEL AND THE GOAL OF MISSIONS

Acts 13:1-3

"So after they fasted and prayed, they placed their hands on them and sent them off" (Acts 13:3).

The demise of Herod marks also the demise of Jerusalem as the center of action in the book of Acts. There is a saying, he who marries the spirit of this age will be a widow in the next. Jerusalem's leaders had committed themselves to the likes of Herod and what he stood for. His time was up, and so was theirs. The catastrophe Jesus had wept over (Luke 19:41-44) was coming. Jerusalem no longer plays a significant role in the advance of the kingdom of God. The center of kingdom activity has moved to Gentile cities, like Antioch.

Once again, the real action is happening in a prayer meeting: "While they were worshiping the Lord and fasting, the Holy Spirit said, 'Set apart for me Barnabas and Saul for the work to which I have called them'" (Acts 13:2). The work is to take the gospel to the peoples of the earth, beginning with an evangelistic outreach on the island of Cyprus. World missions are launched, not in Jerusalem, but in a Gentile city as believers worship and pray.

That it should begin in a service of prayer and worship is highly significant. Why? The missionary movement of the church must begin as the church does what missions are ultimately for: the worship of God. "Missions is not the ultimate goal of the church. Worship is," writes John Piper.

> *Missions exist because worship doesn't.... When this age is over, and the countless millions of the redeemed fall on their faces before the throne of God, missions will be no more. It is a temporary necessity. But worship abides forever.... Worship, therefore, is the fuel and goal of missions. It's the goal of missions because in missions we simply aim to bring the nations into the white-hot enjoyment of God's glory.... But worship is also the fuel of missions. Passion for God in worship precedes the offer of God in preaching. You can't commend what you do not cherish.*[1]

The better we learn to cherish God in prayer, the more passionate, and empowered we will be to commend him in missions. After Antioch, the rest is history.

PRAYER: *"Sing to the Lord, all the earth; proclaim his salvation day after day. Declare his glory among the nations, his marvelous deeds among all peoples" (1 Chron. 16:23-24).*

DAY 263: UNSTOPPABLE JOY

Acts 16:16-40

"About midnight Paul and Silas were praying and singing hymns to God" (Acts 16:25).

The whole idea of a flogging was to beat a person within an inch of his life and to stop just before the victim expired. Presumably, the purpose of being "severely flogged" (Acts 16:23), as Paul and Silas were, was to beat them nearly to death. Whatever it was, it was awful. It was made even worse by fastening their feet in stocks and making it impossible for them to lie on their stomach and protect themselves in any way.

But there they stiffly sat, backs raw, praying and singing hymns at midnight. Luke adds dryly, "and the other prisoners were listening to them" (Acts 16:25). No mystery that! Of course they were listening. You can be sure the prisoners had never heard flogging victims in stocks singing at midnight. What kind of joy is that?

It was a joy grounded, not in the present moment, but in the big picture. Clearly the present moment was terrible, but it was also temporary. What would remain would be everlasting joy for a moment's misery on earth. Everything that mattered was guaranteed for Paul and Silas. Their sins were forgiven, and they were assured of an eternity with God. Everything was fundamentally sound; just a few passing details were askew.

Theirs was a joy nurtured by rejoicing, that is, by praying and singing. *Joy* is a noun. It is what you experience when your life is fundamentally sound. Joy is like health. *Rejoice* is a verb. It is what you do when you express gratitude for health. It is declaring to yourself and to others, but above all to God, that you are glad everything is so ultimately good. To fail to rejoice is to stifle joy. To rejoice is to reawaken the soul's perception of how fundamentally great things really are. Paul spoke with great authority when he later commanded the church which was founded that night to "Rejoice in the Lord always. I will say it again: rejoice!" (Phil. 4:4).

PRAYER: *I do rejoice in you, Lord! Free me from the prison of having my joy determined by circumstances. Thank you for your care and provision for everything that truly matters, for my eternal safety.*

Introduction to Romans

DAY 264: "THE CHIEF PART OF THE NEW TESTAMENT"

"Oh, the depth of the riches of the wisdom and knowledge of God!" (Rom. 11:33).

Some of the most spectacular views in the Rocky Mountains can be found in the Grand Teton range in Wyoming. At a point just south of the Grand Teton itself, the great peak that gives the mountains their name, one can look east down into the city of Jackson Hole and Jenny Lake, in Wyoming; and west into the town of Pierre's Hole in Idaho. Straight north is the great peak, usually shrouded in clouds and mystery, terrifying in its splendor. Other peaks and ranges stretch out in every direction. Standing there on a clear day gives you the sensation of being on top of it all and of seeing everything in God's good creation.

The book of Romans has this effect on the rest of the Bible. "If we have gained a true understanding of this Epistle," wrote John Calvin, "we have an open door to all the most profound treasures of Scripture."[1] No other book in the Bible states so cogently and profoundly the meaning of the gospel and its implications. Luther believed it to be the "chief part of the New Testament, and... truly the purest gospel." He preached that every Christian should "know it word for word, by heart," and "occupy himself with it every day, as the daily bread of the soul."[2]

To know Romans is to know the great themes of Scripture—and therefore how to pray with understanding the great things Jesus told us to pray for: the hallowing of God's name, the coming of his kingdom, and the doing of his will. Moreover, to read Romans 8 is to begin to probe the mystery and miracle of prayer *to* God and *in and through* God—Father, Son, and Holy Spirit.

Though Romans is grand in its sweep, it is also very practical. The movement in thought from Romans 11:33-36 to 12:1-2 is a model of how much earthly good can come from being heavenly-minded. In just six verses, with a few deft strokes, Paul shows us how to move from contemplation to action, from prayer to work, from singing of the "depth of the riches of the wisdom and knowledge of God" to the offering of our "bodies as living sacrifices." Instructions will follow on how to pray for everything from governments to taxes to diet to unity with other believers to the evangelization of the Gentiles. Understanding and praying the book of Romans is having your mind in heaven and your feet planted firmly on the earth.

PRAYER: *Great God and Father! Help me to anchor my prayers in the grand sweep of your purposes in history.*

DAY 265: PAUL, THE PRAYING ACTIVIST

Romans 15:30

"Join me in my struggle by praying for me" (Rom. 15:30).

Are you too busy to pray—or to pray very much? Don't answer that question until you consider the prayer life of a very busy, real-life activist—the apostle Paul. Paul's great ambition in life was to preach the gospel where it had never before been preached, no matter the cost (Rom. 15:20; Acts 20:22-24). He did this vigorously and unstintingly, traveling from Syria to Rome, through deserts and over mountain passes, on foot and by sea. You can read about some of Paul's efforts in 2 Corinthians 11:22-29. His adventures included multiple imprisonments and floggings, several brushes with death, three beatings with rods, one stoning, three shipwrecks, regular harassment and humiliation, sleepless nights, hunger, thirst, cold, nakedness and the daily pressure of his concern for all the churches.

Yet Paul described himself as a man who prayed constantly (Rom. 1:9; Col. 1:9; 2 Thess. 1:11; 2 Tim. 1:3). Instead of making him pray less, his busy schedule drove him to pray more. The more there was to do, the more there was to pray about. This was because of how Paul saw reality. He knew the real issue in life was not his to-do list, but the spiritual significance of the list. The real struggle was not about what needed to be done, but the spiritual realities behind what needed to be done. So, this man of action prayed, constantly (Eph. 6:11, 18-20).

Perhaps the root of our problem with prayer and busy-ness is in how we see reality. Paul knew the real battle was spiritual, sometimes we don't. Many modern Christians have been secularized, a process by which "religious" things like prayer lose their practical social significance. It's not that we think spiritual reality does not exist; it's just that on some level we come to believe that it doesn't make a lot of difference in how things get done on earth. Nothing could be farther from the truth.

Dr. A. J. Gordon described perfectly the relationship between prayer and work when he wrote, "You can do more than pray, after you have prayed; but you can never do more than pray until you have prayed."[1] There are a lot of important things to do besides pray, but we won't get to them until we pray. In the same vein, Andrew Murray laid out a fundamental principle of Christian priorities: "Our true aim must not be to work a great deal and pray just enough to keep the work right. We should pray a great deal and then work enough for the power and blessing obtained in prayer to find its way through us to men."[2]

PRAYER: *Father forgive my laziness and inconsistency in prayer.*

DAY 266: A MODEL PRAYER

Romans 1:8-12

"I thank my God through Jesus Christ for all of you" (Rom. 1:8).

To learn to pray well, we don't need manuals, we need models. We need to pray with the great people of prayer more than we need to read about another formula for prayer. This prayer of Paul's is a wonderful model. Try praying for others the way he prayed for the Romans.

Pray *thankfully* as Paul did (Rom. 1:8). Thankful intercession does good things for the intercessor—you! It can keep you from condescension in your prayers for others. Sometimes when we pray, a little superiority can creep in, especially if the ones we pray for have wandered far from God. We feel that we are the doctors, and they are the patients. To thank God for the people you are interceding is to acknowledge that the Lord is already at work in their lives. Thanking God acknowledges that we can't tell him anything he doesn't already know, and that our loved ones are beloved of the Father. It's impressive how often Paul's prayers for others are thankful prayers, even when the people he prays for are in trouble spiritually, like the Corinthians (1 Cor. 1:4, and Eph. 1:16, Phil. 1:3, Col. 1:3, 1 Thess. 1:2, 2 Thess. 1:3, 2 Tim. 1:3, Philem. 4).

Pray *constantly* as Paul did (Rom. 1:9). This may seem impossible, but it isn't. The sense of the Greek is that his prayers were repeated and frequent. Paul probably turned his every thought and memory of others into short "bullet" prayers—expressions of longing and love to God for their blessing and peace. Sometimes his prayers were long discourses, but more often they probably were phrases. You can do the same as you go about your daily activities. For some, a prayer can be simply a mental image of God's light and truth flooding into the person prayed for.

Pray *expectantly* as Paul did—that somehow you might be an answer to your prayers (Roman 1:10-12). Paul wanted to be with people to encourage them and for them to encourage him. Always be willing to let God use you to do the thing you ask him to do. "Prayer and labor ought to go together. To pray without laboring is to mock God; to labor without prayer is to rob God of his glory. Until these things are conjoined, the gospel will not be extensively successful."[1]

PRAYER: *Think of those who need your prayers and pray for them, giving thanks for each one as you do—especially those who are difficult people.*

DAY 267: FATAL OMISSION

Romans 1:18-32

"Although they knew God, they neither glorified him as God nor gave thanks for him" (Rom. 1:21).

Sin has a history, with a beginning, a middle, and an end. The end is death (Rom. 6:23), the middle is the history of humankind, and the beginning is described right here in these verses. It is the fatal omission of giving God his due: "For although they knew God, they neither glorified him as God nor gave thanks to him" (Rom. 1:21). The essence of sin is ingratitude which deliberately debases God's glory. What follows is devastating: thinking becomes futile, the heart is darkened, and—worst of all—God steps back and lets sin take its course. Three times Paul says, "God gave them over" (Rom. 1:24, 26, 28). To what? To the things that inevitably come from refusing to reverently and joyfully acknowledge that God is God. Ingratitude has a trajectory that leads to all the awful and sordid things detailed in verses 24-32. Fatal *omission* leads to fatal *commissions*.

Sin has a history in the world and in your personal history. Here Paul describes sin's birth and growth along predictable lines from ingratitude to a confused mind to a darkened heart to immoral and appalling behavior. Other passages in Scripture do the same (Gen. 3; James 1:12-15). A good exercise in self-awareness and confession is to examine a particular personal sin according to how it has grown.

Examining the history of our sin does not remove the possibility of repeating the same sin in the future. But repeatedly dragging our sin into the light begins to cut off sin at its source. Tracing sin to its origin is a significant, practical step on the sacred journey of holiness.

PRAYER: *Go back over the "history" of what you did wrong. Ask some hard questions: Where did my fatal omission begin? When did I fail to be grateful and give God glory? What influenced me to forget him? How did my thinking get confused? In what ways has my heart been blinded?*

DAY 268: CRYING AND GROANING AND LEARNING TO PRAY

Romans 8:15-27

"We do not know what we ought to pray for, but the Spirit himself intercedes for us with groans that words cannot express" (Rom. 8:28).

"And by him we cry 'Abba, father.' The Spirit himself testifies with our spirit that we are God's children" (Rom. 8:15-16). Praying is the most natural thing in the world for a Christian to do. It is as natural as a baby learning to say "Daddy" or "Mommy." That's what prayer is at its core; simply crying out to God as a child would to a trusted and loving father. Prayer is a thrilling privilege. It is made even more remarkable by the fact that God goes out of his way to assure us that he really listens and understands even when we can't find the right words. God gives us his Spirit to testify with our spirit that we are indeed his children and that he hears us.

Prayer is natural for a Christian, but it doesn't always come easily. Sometimes the problem is that our understanding of God's purposes is limited, and we just don't know what to pray for (Rom. 8:26). Sometimes the difficulty is part of a much larger struggle—the groaning of the created order as it waits to be "brought into the glorious freedom of the children of God." The creation groans, and we do too as we wait for our freedom. Paul says the pain we feel is like the pangs of childbirth, and the best prayers we can utter are no more than inarticulate groans. Again, the Holy Spirit is our helper, translating as it were, our prayers to the Father (Rom. 8:22-23, 27).

James Boice says learning to pray, with the help of the Holy Spirit, is a little like a man learning to play the violin with virtuosos. No instrument sounds worse in the beginning stages of learning, it's all screech and scratch. But the student is determined to play well, so he checks the program guide for the classical music station and notes when the violin concertos will be aired. He buys the music for each concerto and does his best to play along with the orchestra. At first he sounds terrible. But as time passes, he begins little by little to sound more and more like the orchestra. But all along, as he groans on his instrument, the orchestra plays the music beautifully. The student's poor performance is caught up and completed in the music of the masters.

Praying with the help of the Holy Spirit is like that. As God conducts the orchestra flawlessly, his Spirit patiently teaches us until one day we play with the Master himself.[1]

PRAYER: *Abba, Father! Thank you for giving me your Spirit to pray for me and with me when I don't know how to pray.*

DAY 269: PASSION FOR ONE'S PEOPLE

Romans 9:1-5—10:1

"My heart's desire and prayer to God for the Israelites is that they may be saved" (Rom. 10:1).

Here is love of unimaginable proportions! So great is his love for his people that Paul would be eternally removed from Christ whom he loves, if it would mean his people would turn to Jesus. That is what the word "cursed" means. It is English for the Greek *anathema* which means to be given over to God's wrath for eternal destruction. Only one other person in Scripture prayed with this kind of love. It was Moses, who prayed that if God would not forgive the sin of his people, "then blot me out of the book you have written" (Exod. 32:32).

That's not exactly true. There was one other person who prayed and acted with even greater love. Jesus was actually given over to God's wrath for the sake of the whole world. His words on the cross—"My God, my God, why have you forsaken me?" (Matt. 27:46)—were more than an emotional expression. They were descriptions of fact. Jesus who knew no sin became sin for our sake and was, in fact, cut off from the presence of God (2 Cor. 5:21).

Amazing love! how can it be
That Thou, my God, shouldst die for me![1]

Love like this can be hard to receive—it is so vast, so unimaginable. It is even harder to identify with this kind of love and to practice it. Who can love this way but Jesus, and perhaps a few super-saints? There is a way to love like this—the only way. Through the power of his Spirit, Christ can live in your heart through faith and so root and establish you in his love that you can "know this love that surpasses knowledge" (Eph. 3:14-21). It's not an overnight process, this miracle of being made like Jesus. It takes place over a lifetime of spending time with him and gazing at his love through the eyes of faith.

PRAYER: *Dear Jesus, through your Spirit strengthen me with your love, that I may know this love that surpasses knowledge. Then may my heart be broken in loving intercession for the salvation of my people!*

DAY 270: THE TRUE SEMINARY

John Sung (1901-1944)

"He talked least, preached more, and prayed most."

John Sung's zeal for Christ landed him in a mental hospital when the authorities of New York's Union Theological Seminary didn't know what to do with a student who suddenly became so joyful in his faith that he would sometimes weep and shout for joy on campus. Since his behavior didn't fit their theology, they had him committed to a mental hospital. Incarcerated for 193 days with only a Bible and a fountain pen, Sung devoted himself to Scripture and prayer, reading his Bible front to back forty times. Sung referred to his time of quiet solitude in the asylum as his "true seminary," for it prepared him for the role he would play in one of the mightiest revivals of the twentieth century.

A native of China, Sung came to Union Seminary with impressive academic credentials, having completed three degrees within five years and two months of entering college in the United States: a Bachelor of Science, a Master of Science, and a Doctor of Philosophy. But his immersion in the world of academia had left him empty spiritually, backslidden, and doubting everything he believed. Seminary made matters worse until he experienced the dramatic renewal of his faith that got him into so much trouble.

After his discharge from the mental hospital, Sung boarded a ship and returned to China. All his degrees and honors would have given him much prestige in his homeland, but as he neared Shanghai, he took literally the words of Paul in Philippians 3:7—"Whatever was to my profit, I now consider loss." Sung dumped all his diplomas and honors overboard, except his doctoral diploma, which he kept for his father's sake.

In the years that followed, Sung organized a team of evangelists, which he named the "Bethel Evangelistic Band," and preached all over China. Wherever they went, people responded to their message in droves with tears streaming down their faces as they publicly confessed their sins. Though he was a quiet man, Sung would transform in the pulpit, preaching fiery sermons proclaiming the tender mercy of God and the need for complete repentance from sins.

Sung urged people to give themselves to prayer as the first priority of the believer's life. He let nothing hinder his own prayer life and rose every morning at 5:00 to pray for two to three hours. He liked to have small pictures of the people he interceded for, so he could pray for them with a "deeper burden." Many were healed, and many more converted through his prayers. It was said of him that he talked least, preached more, and prayed most.

Sung died young, at age forty-three, of intestinal tuberculosis. But his ministry continued long afterward. Some of the evangelistic groups he founded were still in operation 50 years later—not bad for a man who got his seminary education by being kicked out of seminary.[1]

PRAYER: *Lord, I want to know you, and the power of your resurrection and the fellowship of sharing in your sufferings, even becoming like you in your death—as your servant John Sung did—that I may attain to the resurrection from the dead.*

DAY 271: OPEN YOUR MOUTH

Romans 10:8-13

"It is with your mouth that you confess and are saved" (Rom. 10:10).

Open your mouth. Go ahead, just do it. Open your mouth and say simply, "Jesus is Lord!" Whisper it, say it out loud, try shouting it some time. For, "it is with your mouth that you confess and are saved." And "everyone who calls on the name of the Lord will be saved" (Rom. 10, 13). Your salvation depends on proclaiming Jesus as Lord. So does your prayer life.

Salvation and prayer are both inward and outward. Both involve heart and mouth—inward belief and outward confession. The inward expression of faith depends on the outward expression, and each is incomplete without its counterpart. To have a mouth without a heart is to be a hypocrite. To have a heart without a mouth to express it is... impossible. It is like having a baby without a birth. Prayer is more than what you do with your mouth, but it is not less than that.

Sometimes the hardest part of prayer is just opening your mouth to speak. Strong feelings and longings may well up inside the heart, but they get stuck in the throat. So, open your mouth and begin to speak. Don't worry about the spiritual depth of your words or whether they are worthy of what is inside you. The Holy Spirit will dress and translate your words to the Father (Rom. 8:26-27). God promises wonderful things for those who will simply open their mouths and call to him. He says, "Open your mouth wide and I will fill it" (Ps. 81:10).

PRAYER: *Say this aloud: "Jesus, you are risen from the dead, and you are my Lord. Be my Lord in all I think say and do."*

DAY 272: WITH OUR LIVES AND WITH OUR LIPS

Romans 11:33—12:2

"From him and through him and to him are all things" (Rom. 11:36).

Chapters 9-11 of Romans is one of the most wondrously amazing passages in all the Bible, capping off eight previous chapters that set forth the essence and global implications of the Christian message. This passage is also one of the thorniest and hardest to understand in all the Bible. Subjects like divine election and predestination, God's sovereignty and human freedom, the destiny of Israel and the peoples of the world all appear in their bewildering and breathtaking glory. Coming to the end of chapter 11, one doesn't know whether to gasp or to sing.

Paul chooses to sing. We are but flecks of foam on the ocean of God's grandeur. No one can give to, advise, or second-guess God. Everything, all there is, comes from him. As awesome and intimidating as a God like this can be, there is deep comfort in his greatness. Who really wants a God who is easily understood and manageable? If God is only a human writ large, then there is cause for great worry in this chaotic drama we know as human history. In the final analysis, a god we can "relate to" is in the same mess we are in. Thank God that he is not a God we can "relate to."

But there is even greater cause for comfort and joy in this awesome and frightening God. He has chosen to relate to us! He so loves the world that he gave his only Son for our salvation (John 3:16). Though we are nothing before his awesome glory, he has counted the hairs on our heads, and we may call on his name and be heard and saved (Rom. 10:13).

There is nothing left to do but sing, not only with our lips, but also with our lives by offering them as living sacrifices. The command of Romans 12:1-2 is matched by the old prayer from *The Book of Common Prayer*, known as "The Great Thanksgiving." Say it aloud and keep saying it till you mean it.

PRAYER: *"And, we pray, give us such an awareness of your mercies, that our hearts may be sincerely thankful, and that we may show forth your praise not only with our lips, but in our lives, by giving up ourselves to your service, and by walking before you in holiness and righteousness all our days; through Jesus Christ our Lord. Amen."*

DAY 273: DANCING TO THE MUSIC OF THE FUTURE

Romans 12:12

"Be joyful in hope, patient in affliction, faithful in prayer" (Rom. 12:12).

Joy, hope, patience, and faithfulness—taken together—are a powerful prescription for spiritual health in hard times. Joy is an obvious ingredient. What could be better in a difficult marriage or a terminal illness or an oppressive job than to somehow be fundamentally glad in spite of it all and through it all! Joy is linked with hope, something Rubem Alves said is the "music of the future." He wrote, "Faith is hearing the music of the future, faith is to dance to it." The joy—the dancing—is the effect of hope in our lives. Knowing that God's good promises for the future are sure sets us free to be glad in the midst of a suffering present.

Patience in affliction is possible only if there is hope. Without hope, there is only despair. With hope there is the confidence, the dancing confidence, that whatever we may have to go through now is nothing compared to the glorious future God has planned for us (Rom. 8:18). We can wait patiently because our wait, no matter how hard, is light and momentary compared to eternity (2 Cor. 4:17).

Prayer plays a pivotal role in the prescription. On the one hand, hope nurtures prayer. No one will pray without hope. What's the point if there is no possibility of things ever being better? But on the other hand, prayer nurtures hope because hope is a miracle that the Holy Spirit produces in our heart. We cannot force ourselves to hope. Paul prayed for the Ephesians that the eyes of their heart would be opened, "in order that you may know the hope to which he has called you" (Eph. 1:18). There is a symbiotic relationship between prayer and hope. We pray because of hope, and we have hope because of prayer. Each is the cause and the effect of the other.

Ask God to open your spiritual eyes to see the hope to which he has called you. Pray the promises of Scripture as you do. Don't be surprised to feel your spirit start to dance.

PRAYER: *God of all hope, tune my ears to hear the music of your future; and strengthen my faith to dance to it now.*

DAY 274: UNITY, NOT UNIFORMITY

Romans 15:5-6

"May the God who gives endurance and encouragement give you a spirit of unity" (Rom. 15:5).

The 17th century, German theologian, Rupertus Meldenius, had a grand way of summarizing the intent of this prayer of Paul's. Paraphrased, it was unity in essentials, freedom in nonessentials, and love in all things. Essentials are the things all Christians must agree on to be Christians: things like the divinity of Christ, the triune nature of God, salvation by grace through faith, and the resurrection of Jesus. Nonessentials are the things Christians may legitimately disagree about even as fellow members of the body of Christ. In this passage the issue had to do with dietary practices that separated Jewish and Greek Christians. "Love in all things" is the attitude Christians must take toward one another, especially in those matters about which they disagree.

Paul's prayer that God give the Romans "a spirit of unity" concerns this last category of beliefs—"love in all things." Unity does not require them to agree on everything, it asks that they lovingly make allowance for each other in the areas where they disagree. In a section extending back to the beginning of chapter fourteen, Paul repeatedly urges them to welcome weaker Christians. They are not to judge, despise, or offend each other over matters of individual conscience. Paul summarizes his argument just before this prayer: "We who are strong ought to bear with the failings of the weak and not to please ourselves. Each of us should please his neighbor for his good, to build him up. For even Christ did not please himself" (Rom. 15:1-3a).

Paul's prayer is not that all Christians think the same, but that they all have the mind of Christ (Phil. 2:1-11). Absolute uniformity of thought belongs to cults where doctrines and opinions become more important than love. Unity belongs to the mind of Christ, because it springs from a love that seeks the good of others. Uniformity is a dull, deadening thing. Unity is lively and life-giving. Uniformity is easy to achieve simply by narrowing the standards of membership to exclude all who disagree! Unity is hard because it requires that people lay down their "rights" in order to serve others. God gets great glory when his people lay down their rights. When they do, they imitate Christ. "Accept one another, then, just as Christ accepted you, in order to bring praise to God" (Rom. 15:7).

As you pray for unity in your church, ask God where he may be asking you to make allowance for those with whom you disagree.

PRAYER: *Lord God, you are the Three-in-One, and the One-in-Three: Father, Son, and Holy Spirit. Make us one as you are one. Remove from me any action or attitude that disturbs the unity of your body, the church.*

DAY 275: GOD'S "YES," "NO," OR "YES, BUT..."

Romans 15:30-33

"I urge you… to join me in my struggle by praying to God for me" (Rom. 15:30).

To be a Christian is to take a side in a cosmic conflict—a spiritual struggle that engages body, mind, and spirit in a fight for the kingdom of God. Eternity hangs in the balance for all involved—and all are involved, whether they know it or not.

Knowing that the struggle is spiritual, Paul asks the Romans to join him by praying for him and his work. Spiritual warfare requires spiritual weapons (Eph. 6:10-20). Prayer is a critical weapon in this battle, not because prayer itself is powerful, but because prayer calls upon the name of God who is powerful and who can make us strong in the strength of his Spirit.

Prayer also provides fellowship in the fight. That's why Paul asks the Romans to join him in his struggle by praying for him. We need God's help, but we also need each other as we stand and fight. We pray for each other, not as a substitute for other forms of help, but as the fount of help, the foundation. The kingdom and the power and the glory are all God's, but he gives his kingdom and power and glory to his church when we ask in the unity of the Holy Spirit.

To pray is to fight, but finally, it is also to surrender—to God. When we pray, we do not bend God's will to ours; we rather align our wills with his. We cannot conquer in his name unless he first conquers us. Paul's requests are very specific: that he be rescued from unbelievers, that his service be acceptable to the church, and that he be able to visit the Romans. As for acceptance, God's answer was probably "Yes." What about rescue? The answer was more like "Yes and no." Paul was arrested, tried, and imprisoned in Jerusalem. However, he was also rescued three times from lynching, once from a plot to kill him, and once from flogging. The trip to Rome? That was more like "Yes, but…" When Paul did finally get to Rome, it was as a prisoner!

We may ask God to do things in a way we think best, but he always reserves the right to be God and do them in the way *he* thinks best. His "Yes and no" and his "Yes, but" are as wise and good as his "Yes."

PRAYER: *Lord God, I surrender my requests to your perfect and creative will whether it is "yes," "no," "yes and no," or "yes, but."*

Introduction to 1 and 2 Corinthians

DAY 276: EXASPERATING SAINTS

"The greatest of these is love" (1 Cor. 13:13).

If Paul kept a prayer list for the Corinthians in his journals which you could peak at, you might be surprised to discover how very contemporary it looked. His concerns for these people included things like quarrels and cliques, sexual immorality, grace taken for granted, false teaching, and narcissistic religious experience. Paul was concerned with resistance to authority on the one hand, and a cult of leadership on the other. The church was a mess. Its people were shallow, arrogant, and self-absorbed.

Yet they were a people holy to God and called by God to be holy—"sanctified in Christ Jesus and called to be holy." They were also a people of prayer, part of the worldwide communion of those "who call on the name of the Lord" (1 Cor. 1:2). Paul prayed for the Corinthians, with fear and trembling, from the beginning (1 Cor. 2:1-5). The alternative was to despair. He couldn't rely on personal charisma to persuade them to do the right thing, because many in the church thought he was a pretty unimpressive apostle. Paul knew they held him in contempt (2 Cor. 10:10). His singular hope and only boast was in the power of Christ.

So, the Corinthian correspondence is great encouragement to obey Jesus' command to pray and not give up (Luke 18:1). Despite their immaturity and resistance to the Holy Spirit, two of the greatest chapters in the Bible came out of Paul's struggle with the Corinthians: the hymn of love in 1 Corinthians 13 and the resurrection manifesto in chapter 15. Out of a man's deep hurt and discouragement in ministry came a witness to the power of God perfected in human weakness (2 Cor. 12:7-10).

PRAYER: *Father in heaven! Help me to see how much you love the difficult people you have entrusted to me to care for.*

DAY 277: "I'D RATHER LEARN HOW TO PRAY"

1 Corinthians 2:1-5

"I did not come to you with eloquence or superior wisdom as I proclaimed to you the testimony about God" (1 Cor. 2:1).

It's not hard to guess why Paul would have felt weak and fearful as he preached to the Corinthians. He knew the message and the messenger were not tailor-made to the tastes of these Greek city dwellers. Quite the contrary, the message of a crucified Savior cut across the grain of Greek intellectualism and Corinthian Greek ideas of success—radically so.

As for the messenger, Paul's speaking abilities did not match the Greek ideal of the orator. The most powerful and influential people in that culture were those who could use words with dramatic and rhetorical flair. Later, even after the Corinthian church was established, there were those in the church who complained that his speaking "amounts to nothing" (2 Cor. 10:10).

Humanly speaking, it was impossible for these people to be impressed with this unimpressive apostle and his bizarre message, so he didn't try. It would be a miracle if they believed his message. But then, it always is a miracle when anyone believes for, "The god of this age has blinded the minds of unbelievers so that they cannot see the light of the gospel of glory of Christ" (2 Cor. 4:4). Paul's only hope for success would be the empowerment of the Holy Spirit. So, he preached with great simplicity and humble reliance on the power of God to open the eyes of these pagan nonbelievers. And God answered his prayer.

Which is harder, anyway? To dazzle the ears and impress the mind or to see human hearts changed? No argument or orator has ever changed a heart. Only God can change a heart. So, Paul rejoiced that the faith of the Corinthians was real because it did not rest on, "wise and persuasive words, but with a demonstration of the Spirit's power, so that your faith might not rest on men's wisdom, but on God's power" (1 Cor. 2:4-5).

That is why prayer is so important for the advancement of the kingdom. When we pray, we are asking God to do what only God can do—open eyes and change hearts. And that is why the great evangelist, Dwight L. Moody, impressive preacher that he was, said, "I'd rather learn how to pray than preach. Jesus' disciples never asked him to teach them how to preach, but how to pray."

PRAYER: *Almighty God, the things I need most are the things only you can give: forgiveness and understanding, faith, hope and love. I cry out to you to give me these things, for in myself I can do nothing.*

DAY 278: YOU ARE GOD'S TEMPLE

1 Corinthians 3:1-17

"You are God's field, God's building" (1 Cor. 3:9).

Paul says something here that would stun King Solomon and the architects of the great Jerusalem temple. Despite all its grandeur and glory, there was a greater glory yet to come when the people of God would be the temple of God. It can never be said of any precious stone, fine wood, or beautiful design that it was made in the image of God. Not even the brightest star can be spoken of this way. Only people are made in the image of God. Human beings reflect the glory of God as nothing else in creation can. Therefore, the church is made of the very finest materials, and it is constructed in the very finest design.

The church must have a very lofty purpose in God's economy. The first temple was built to be a house of communion with God, or as Jesus put it, "a house of prayer for all nations" (Mark 11:17). The first temple was a place of prayer. The new temple is not a place, but a community of prayer—a fellowship of "pray-ers" who by their life together in the world invite all the peoples of the earth into a glorious communion.

Paul's great concern is that he, as an apostle, will build the church well. It also matters greatly to him that the people of the church will not damage what is being built. The Corinthians are damaging the church with divisions, a serious crime indeed. "If anyone destroys God's temple, God will destroy him; for God's temple is sacred, and you [the people of the church] are that temple" (1 Cor. 3:17).

The implications for prayer are direct and devastating. How can God's people have fellowship with him if they can't have fellowship with each other? How can they pray to God for others if they won't pray with each other? The church can't be a house of prayer for all nations if it can't be a community of prayer in the neighborhood or city it meets in. Pray for your church—pray that it be united in the Spirit and that its people will unite in prayer for the peoples of the earth.

PRAYER: *Father in heaven! Thank you for including me in your church, the assembly of your holy people. Unite us in your Holy Spirit so that we may be united in prayer for the peoples of the earth.*

DAY 279: THE JOY OF A MELANCHOLY MAN

David Brainerd (1718-1747)

"Why are you downcast, O my soul? Why so disturbed within me? Put your hope in God, for I will yet praise him, my Savior" (Ps. 42:5).

Though first in his class, David Brainerd was kicked out of Yale in 1743. Just four years later, he died of tuberculosis at age twenty-nine, after preaching alone among the Mohican and Delaware Indians in the dangerous wilderness that was then the western frontier of the American colonies. Brainerd was melancholy in the extreme, and his diaries are filled with references to dejection and self-doubt. Yet his diaries are still in print and have exerted enormous influence down to the present. Often discouraged himself, his personal testimony to God's grace has encouraged people of the stature of Henry Martyn, William Carey, Adoniram Judson, and Jonathan Edwards (who edited his diaries).

Brainerd's natural bent was toward dejection, but his delight in God and faith in prayer sustained him supernaturally during his arduous years on the frontier. On his first visit among the Mohicans, he was secretly tracked by hostile warriors. As the moment to kill him drew near, the warriors suddenly held back at the sight of a rattlesnake coiled on the ground beside Brainerd, ready to strike him. But the snake miraculously uncoiled and slithered away. Astonished, the warriors took this as a sign that the Great Spirit was with Brainerd, and they left him unharmed.

Reading Brainerd's diaries makes one long to know the God he knew:

> *Tuesday, July 3 [1744]. Was still very weak. This morning, was enabled to pray under a feeling sense of my need of help from God, and, I trust, had some faith in exercise. Blessed be God, was enabled to plead with Him a considerable time. Truly God is good to me. But my soul mourned and was grieved at my sinfulness and barrenness, and longed to be more engaged for God. Near nine, withdrew again for prayer and through divine goodness had the blessed spirit of prayer. My soul loved the duty and longed for God in it. Oh, it is sweet to be the Lord's, to be sensibly devoted to Him! What a blessed portion is God! How glorious, how lovely in Himself! Oh, my soul longed to improve time wholly for God! Spent most of the day in translating prayers into Indian. In the evening, was enabled again to wrestle with God in prayer with fervency. Was enabled to maintain a self-diffident and watchful frame of spirit in the evening, and was jealous and afraid lest I should admit carelessness and self-confidence.*[1]

PRAYER: *Pray this prayer of David Brainerd's: "Lord, to Thee I dedicate myself! Oh, accept of me and let me be Thine forever. Lord, I desire nothing else; I desire nothing more. Oh, come, come, Lord, accept a poor worm. 'Whom have I in heaven but Thee? And there is none upon earth, that I desire besides Thee.'"*

DAY 280: SPIRITUAL DISCIPLINE

1 Corinthians 9:24-27

"Everyone who competes in the games goes into strict training" (1 Cor. 9:25).

There is a poster of a wrestler working out with weights, his face wrinkled in a sweaty grimace, veins bulging in his neck and biceps. It is a picture of pain and determination. The caption of the poster reads, "There are two kinds of pain; the pain of discipline and the pain of regrets." To be alive is to experience pain. We have no choice in the matter. But when it comes to discipline, we can choose the kind of pain we want. Discipline hurts, but so does the lack of discipline. The wrestler was in pain, but it was a good pain; better by far than the pain of regrets, the pain of losing to his next opponent.

This clearly was the apostle Paul's take on the discipline of living the Christian life. He committed himself to the great goal of winning the prize for which God called him heavenward in Christ Jesus (Phil. 3:14). Sure, Paul's life of faith was unpleasant at times, but that was nothing compared to missing the prize, especially given that Paul was urging others to run toward the same goal. Dallas Willard was thinking like Paul when he wrote about the costs of *nondiscipleship*:

> *Nondiscipleship costs abiding peace, a life penetrated throughout by love, faith that sees everything in the light of God's overriding governance for good, hopefulness that stands firm in the most discouraging of circumstances, power to do what is right and withstands the forces of evil. In short, it costs exactly that abundance of life Jesus said he came to bring (John 10:10).*[1]

But discipline is not so much a negative quality as a positive refusal. Discipline says no to something lesser in order to say yes to something greater. Cultivating a life of prayer can be costly and inconvenient, but how much greater the value! And as with all disciplines, when pursued over time, the duty will become delight.

PRAYER: *Father, help me to see the big picture of my life, to look beyond momentary pleasures to the really great pleasures, to say no in order to say a greater yes to the abundant life you promised. Amen.*

DAY 281: A DIFFICULT PASSAGE ON PRAYER

1 Corinthians 10:31—11:16

"Whatever you do, do it all for the glory of God" (1 Cor. 10:31).

Paul's words about head coverings and men and women in prayer are one of his more difficult sayings. There have been four broad ways to read this passage:

1. Skip over it, put it out your mind, and move on to things that are easier to understand and seem more relevant to our times.

2. Assume that what Paul said had relevance for that time and place, but only for that time and place. Then move on to more relevant concerns.

3. Be offended by it, conclude that Paul was displaying a kind of male chauvinist, cultural myopia, and read no further. If he was wrong about this head covering business, he must be wrong about other things too.

4. Take Paul's words about head covering as timeless divine truth to be followed today. Some sincere Christians have taken this fourth option.

As important as these debates may be, one doesn't have to consider and critique the merits of the four approaches to appreciate the important truth that lies behind Paul's instructions. His reason for giving the instructions is help the Corinthians apply the truly timeless principle of doing everything for the glory of God. This section actually begins in 10:31: "So whether you eat or drink or whatever you do, do it all for the glory of God." Paul then uses his own life to underline the principle, and he urges the Corinthians to follow his example: "even as I try to please everybody in every way. For I am not seeking my own good but the good of many, so that they may be saved. Follow my example, as I follow the example of Christ" (1 Cor. 10:32).

The principle is simply, glorify God in all you do. The flipside of the principle is, don't seek to please yourself but please God by "pleasing" others. Fit into the norms of your culture (whether timeless or not) so the attention will be on God when you pray, not on how you are dressed when you pray. Remember all prayer, but especially public prayer, is not about self-expression, but about the glory of God. Surely this is one thing all four positions can agree on! It's not about us, it's about God.

PRAYER: *Dear God, unite your people in worship. Help us to lay aside all arguments about propriety and seek to glorify you with one voice.*

DAY 282: PRAYER, EXPERIENCE, AND THE TRUTH

1 Corinthians 12:1-3

"No one who is speaking by the Spirit of God says, 'Jesus be cursed'" (1 Cor. 12:3).

Of course, the Spirit of God would never prompt someone to say, "Jesus is cursed." It's ridiculous. Why state the obvious? Because Paul wants to use the obvious to make a not-so-obvious point.

First, a brief word about the pagan religious background of many of the Corinthian believers. They were surrounded by a variety of Greek mystery religions that placed a premium on religious experience as the test of being touched by God. It was assumed that the practice of a religion would cause one to be "moved" by the deity being worshiped. Ecstasy and trances were the rule, and everybody expected them. The Greek word translated "influenced" in our text can also be translated "moved." Paul here is reminding the Corinthians that they were once "moved" in bad directions, "influenced and led astray to mute idols" (1 Cor. 12:2). To be "moved" is not necessarily a good thing.

The not-so-obvious point for the Corinthians is, "Be careful that you do not import your old pagan assumptions into your newfound faith in Christ." Just because you feel something strongly in your heart does not mean God is speaking to you. Simply being "moved" in prayer to is not self-authenticating. To challenge these notions, Paul says the obvious. One may be "moved" very strongly to say something foolish or evil, like "Jesus be cursed." But being "moved" would not make it true! The real test of prayer is not whether it is "moving," but whether it is in "Spirit and in truth" (John 4:24)?

Christian spirituality embraces both objective truth and subjective experience, but truth must govern experience. The apostles understood this when they insisted that they must be devoted not only to prayer, but to both prayer and the word of God (Acts 6:2, 4).

It is also significant that Paul makes this critical point before he launches into a discussion of spiritual gifts. The overarching theme will be the purpose of spiritual gifts, which is for the common good of the church (1 Cor. 12:7). God doesn't give a Christian a spiritual gift so he or she can have a great religious experience. He gives the gift so all the people in the church can have a great experience—of encouragement and ministry. The real test of prayer, as with all of God's gifts, is its faithfulness to the truth and its contribution to the building up of the church.

PRAYER: *Lord, be Lord of my experience. Teach me to care more about you when I pray, than how I may feel when I pray. Be the center of all my experience.*

DAY 283: LOVE, THE HEART OF PRAYER

1 Corinthians 13

"The greatest of these is love" (1 Cor. 13:13).

If Scripture were the Himalayas, this chapter could qualify as Mount Everest. By any reckoning, it is one of the highest points in all the Bible, a place to stand and understand all the rest. What Paul says in this passage is true. There are "three great lasting qualities"[1] in this life—faith, hope, and love—but the greatest of these is love.

Some scholars believe 1 Corinthians 13 was originally a song and that Paul inserted it in his letter to move his readers to sing. These words have since been put to music. If you know a tune to sing it to, thank God that you do, because singing can be another way to pray. This passage is especially important to prayer for love is the fuel and goal of prayer.

Prayer is fueled by appreciation for the God to whom we are speaking. Try reading this chapter aloud, substituting "God" for "love." Windows and doors can fly open in your mind as you do. You may find yourself exclaiming, "So this is the God I'm speaking to! How wonderful he is! Who wouldn't be delighted to speak with him for hours?" Our minds can do funny things and imagine God to be an abstraction or a peevish old man. Neither image inspires prayer. 1 Corinthians 13 is the antidote to a shrunken imagination.

Or take this exercise a step further. Add the phrase "with me" or "to me." For instance, instead of praying "Love is patient," pray "*God* is patient *with me*." Do you sometimes come to prayer feeling dull and cold inside, fearful and apprehensive? God is patient with you. He is not irritated that you are dull and lifeless. Let him love you for a while. Don't try to speak until you've let his love warm your heart and banish your fear. God is patient with you. He is not easily angered. He keeps no record of wrongs.

Love is the goal of all prayer. Jesus told us to pray that God's name will be hallowed and that his rule will be established on earth. How do we hallow his name? By loving him with our whole being and by loving our neighbor as ourselves. 1 Corinthians 13 describes what this love looks like. What does God's kingdom look like? And what is his will for all the earth? Again, 1 Corinthians 13 will tell you how to pray for these things.

Open this chapter and use it as a prayer agenda. Pray the qualities of love into the people you pray for, into your church, your neighbors, and the world. Ask God to accomplish the greatest thing in the world in the lives of those for whom you pray—that they will know and demonstrate God's love.

PRAYER: *Gracious Father, warm my heart to your tender love. Work in us your love. Let your love reign overall the earth.*

DAY 284: PRAY ALSO WITH YOUR MIND

1 Corinthians 14:13-17

"I will pray with my spirit, but I will also pray with my mind" (1 Cor. 14:15).

Bertrand Russell, the atheist philosopher, said, "Most Christians would rather be caught dead than thinking, and most are." That's unfair, but there is enough truth in it to cause us to pause and consider what Paul meant when he wrote, "So what shall I do? I will pray with my spirit, but I will also pray with my mind; I will sing with my spirit, but I will also sing with my mind" (1 Cor. 14:15).

What was the apostle driving at? At the very least, he was trying to be obedient to the Lord Jesus' command to love God with all his heart, soul, and mind (Matt. 22:37). A mind is a terrible thing to waste which we do by restricting its use to the things of this earth. Employ your mind in the greatest of uses—the worship of the God who made the mind!

Paul was also addressing the Corinthian's over emphasis on the ecstatic and non-rational experience in worship. Some of these beliefs were a holdover from their pagan past in the Greek mystery cults (see devotional on Day 281). But some of the confusion was just plain selfishness and laziness.

The selfish part was their absorption in private, subjective experience. In a service of worship, a few individuals might be experiencing profoundly moving intimations of the presence of God. But the church is not a collection of individuals, it is the body of Christ. If the private experience of an individual doesn't ultimately go public and build up others, then it is selfish experience and perhaps not of God at all. It can even be an abuse of God's gifts.

This where the mind is so important. Good thinking leads to clear communication. If private experience is going to go public and encourage others, it must be spoken. Language means logic and syntax, words and ideas. Paul said what he said about praying and singing with his mind in the context of public worship (1 Cor. 14:5, 12, 19, 26). One of the ways we can love our neighbor is to think well about our faith, so we can speak well about our faith. Anything less is laziness, and not love at all.

PRAYER: *Father in heaven! I will praise you with my mind, too. Teach me to think well so that I can speak well, to your greater glory and the encouragement of your people.*

DAY 285: THE GOD OF ALL COMFORT

2 Corinthians 1:3-7

"For just as the sufferings of Christ flow over into our lives, so also through Christ our comfort overflows" (2 Cor. 1:5).

What a friend we have in Jesus,
All our sins and griefs to bear!
What a privilege to carry
Everything to God in prayer!

Take all your troubles to God, for he is the "Father of compassion and the God of all comfort" (2 Cor. 1:3). Compassion is his nature; to comfort is his pleasure. And know, as you pour out your heart, what he will do with your troubles. Sometimes he will take them away, but not usually. He has a greater purpose. God will redeem your suffering from meaninglessness by making it useful for others, "so that we can comfort those in any trouble with the comfort we ourselves have received from God" (2 Cor. 2:4). The worst thing that suffering can do to us is isolate us. God's comfort turns our suffering into a bond with others who suffer.

O what peace we often forfeit,
O what needless pain we bear,
All because we do not carry
Everything to God in prayer.

What is needless pain? It is unnecessary pain. It is burden enough to carry the troubles of life which are a given. But our burden becomes intolerably heavy when we add to it the needless pain of isolation. Take your troubles to God, and he will turn your suffering into fellowship by leading you to comfort others with the comfort he has given you. You probably already know this is true. Have you not met people whom you went to comfort but who, instead, comforted you? God had been there ahead of you to comfort them. He made their trouble a means to comfort you.

Let God do this with your troubles and behold a miracle: there emerges within your pain an inexplicable joy. Your suffering isn't just yours anymore—it is Christ's, too! "For just as the sufferings of Christ flow over into our lives, so also through Christ our comfort overflows" (2 Cor. 1:5). Let your trouble forge a bond with Jesus.

Can we find a friend so faithful
Who will all our sorrows share?
Jesus knows our every weakness,
Take it to the Lord in prayer.[1]

PRAYER: *"Whom have I heaven but you? And earth has nothing I desire besides you. My heart and my flesh may fail, but God is the strength of my heart and my portion forever" (Ps. 73:25-26).*

DAY 286: OUR TRUE CONFIDENCE IN PRAYER

2 Corinthians 3:4-6

"Such confidence as this is ours through Christ before God" (2 Cor. 3:4).

"Who do you think you are?" That was the kind of mocking question implicit in the words of Paul's critics at Corinth. He spoke to them as though he thought he was somebody, but he seemed like a nobody. It's not a bad question. Who do any of us think we are when we claim to have a message from God that will change human lives? "Who do I think I am?" That is the question every Christian should ask. Do we really believe we have any authority or power to speak so confidently of God?

Paul was very clear about this issue. He had no confidence in himself, but every confidence in "Christ, before God" (2 Cor. 3:4). As for competence, the question of whether he had any was irrelevant because whatever competence anyone has comes from God alone. In his first letter, Paul put the question of competence back in the lap of his critics: "For who makes you different from anyone else? What do you have that you did not receive? And if you did receive it, why do you boast as if you did not" (1 Cor. 4:7). Everything we have comes from God—every ability, every gift. We came into the world naked; we will leave the world naked. The Lord gave whatever we have, and we will have to give it back—all of it. Blessed be the name of the Lord. Yes, blessed be *the name of the Lord*, not the name of some apostle or evangelist or religious authority.

We pray because our confidence and competence come from God alone. Even the gifts and abilities we were given at birth, or through education and life experience, are of no use without God's blessing. We pray because our very life comes from the Spirit (2 Cor. 3:6). Given this spiritual reality, we have no cause for confidence in ourselves, on the one hand, and no cause for fear, on the other. But we have every cause to pray because our confidence and competence comes from God alone.

PRAYER: *Almighty God, yours alone is the kingdom and the power and the glory. My confidence and competence are in you alone. May it always be so—that you, not I, should receive all the glory for the great things you have done through me.*

DAY 287: THE GLORY OF PRAYER

2 Corinthians 3:7-18

"We all reflect the Lord's glory" (2 Cor. 3:18).

There is an old children's Sunday school song that goes, "Climb, climb up sunshine mountain, faces all aglow." The theology of the song was better than anyone knew, or even intended. For that was exactly what happened to Moses whenever he climbed up Mount Sinai to meet with God. When he came back down the mountain into the Israelite camp, "his face was radiant because he had spoken with the Lord" (Exod. 34:29). This phenomenon frightened the people, so Moses put a veil over his face. That was the way it was in the days of the Old Covenant, before Christ.

Now the veil is off! And not just off the face of Moses, but off the face of every believer! Through Jesus, we all have the privilege of standing in the presence of the living God. As we stand in God's presence, we reflect his glory, and we "are transformed into his likeness with ever-increasing glory" (2 Cor. 3:18). Our "glow" is better than Moses' because his faded and ours won't.

This is a great passage on prayer even though the actual word "prayer" doesn't appear in it. The Bible says that when Moses went up Mt. Sinai, "he entered the Lord's presence to speak with him" (Exod. 34:34). In comparing our experience of the Holy Spirit with Moses' experience on Sinai, Paul makes a powerful connection with prayer and its effects on those who pray.

What are the effects of prayer? In the words of John Piper, "seeing is becoming." We become what we attentively and lovingly gaze at. When what is gazed at is someone as brightly glorious and splendid as God, we cannot help but be changed by what we see. This is the secret of prayer and of Christian growth: 90% is just showing up. Simply coming into God's presence in the name of his Son deeply affects us. Archimedes said, "Give me a place to stand, and I will move the world." Prayer is the place to stand! The world is changed by those who are transformed by the glory of God.

PRAYER: *"My heart says of you, 'Seek his face!' Your face, Lord, I will seek" (Ps. 27:8). Make your face shine on me. Change me, with ever-increasing glory to be more like your Son.*

DAY 288: THE WORLDVIEW OF PRAYER

2 Corinthians 4:16-18

"For what is seen is temporary, but what is unseen is eternal" (2 Cor. 4:18).

G. K. Chesterton wrote a parable about what it means to be converted. He said the unconverted are like a man born with his head stuck in the earth. He is upside down, and the earth seems to be the only solid thing while the heavens feel airy, insubstantial. When he is converted, he gets set right side up. His feet are placed on the ground where they belong, and his head is in the heavens where it belongs. Now he can walk the earth and not stumble because he sees where he is going.[1] Have you heard the saying, "too heavenly minded to be any earthly good"? Don't believe it. The only way to be of any earthly good is to be heavenly minded.

That is the worldview of prayer. There are two realities, earthly and heavenly. Both are real, but the heavenly reality is much larger than the earthly. It is determinative, while the earthly is not, and it is permanent, which the earthly is not. We pray because we know this to be the case. Prayer keeps one's head in Heaven because prayer is conversation with the King of Heaven. No matter how badly things may be going presently, we keep praying and don't lose heart as Jesus told us to (Luke 18:1).

Paul's words in 2 Corinthians 4:16-18 are his way of saying the same thing: "Therefore we do not lose heart. Though outwardly we are wasting away, yet inwardly we are being renewed day by day. For our light and momentary troubles are achieving for us an eternal glory that far outweighs them all. So we fix our eyes not on what is seen, but on what is unseen. For what is seen is temporary, but what is unseen is eternal."

For many of us, our problem with prayer is a worldview problem. On some deep level of our consciousness, we have become secularized and no longer believe that heavenly realities have anything to do with earthly matters. Nothing could be further from the truth.

PRAYER: *Open my eyes to see things as they are, Lord. Strengthen my heart to pray without giving up until the world of the seen has passed away and the kingdom of the unseen is here to stay. Come, Lord Jesus.*

DAY 289: A DIARY OF PRIVATE PRAYER

John Baillie (1886-1960)

John Baillie was one of the leading theologians of his time, holding teaching posts in Edinburgh, Toronto, and at Union and Auburn Theological seminaries in the United States. His two most important theological works were *The Knowledge of God* (1939) and *The Sense of the Presence of God* (published posthumously in 1962). But what he is more likely to be remembered for is his little *Diary of Private Prayer* (1936), a book which inspired a chain of prayer around the globe. Baillie's *Diary of Private Prayer* is a twentieth century devotional classic.

Baillie said there was never a time, from his childhood in Northern Scotland on, when he did not know the presence of God. Indeed, even the titles of his academic works show the impact of this lifelong gift. As a result, Baillie was one of those rare persons who combined faith and reason with grace and ease. His facility with the English language also made him an eminently quotable author:

> *The evidence for Christian truth is not exhaustive, but it is sufficient.... Christianity has not been tried and found wanting—it has been found demanding, and not tried.*
>
> *The final reality, and the ultimate fact of our total situation to which we need to be adjusted, is God. That indeed would be my definition of God: God is He with whom we have ultimately to do, the final reality to which we have to face up, and with whom we have, in the last resort, to reckon.*[1]

The prayer below is taken from Baillie's diary which is arranged in pairs of prayers, one for morning and one for evening, each day for thirty-one days. It is the prayer for the morning of the fifth day. Read it slowly and pray it as though it were your own.

PRAYER:

God of my forefathers, I cry unto Thee. Thou hast been the refuge of good and wise men in every generation. Through all ages Thou hast been the Lord and giver of life, the source of all knowledge, the fountain of all goodness.
The patriarchs trusted Thee and were not put to shame:

The prophets sought Thee and Thou didst commit Thy word to their lips:
The psalmists rejoiced in Thee and Thou wert present in their song:
The apostles waited upon Thee and they were filled with Thy Holy Spirit:
The martyrs called upon Thee and Thou wert with them in the midst of the flame:
This poor man cried, and the Lord heard him, and saved him out of all his troubles.

Forbid it, Holy Lord, that I should fail to profit by these great memories of the ages that are gone by, or to enter into the glorious inheritance which Thou hast prepared for me, through Jesus Christ my Lord. Amen.[2]

DAY 290: SPIRITUAL WARFARE

2 Corinthians 10:1-6

"For though we live in the world, we do not wage war as the world does" (2 Cor. 10:3).

God often tears things down before he builds them up. Paul calls these things which are opposed to God, "strongholds… arguments and every pretension that sets itself up against the knowledge of God" (2 Cor. 10:4-5). Such beliefs must be demolished for they are the very essence of evil. These deeply entrenched attitudes and ways of thinking keep us from God who is "the spring of living water" (Jer. 2:13). Strongholds don't exist "out there" independent and detached, but inside our minds and our thoughts. The mere thought of their existence should give us a chill, but sometimes false beliefs have such a strong place in our minds that we don't even notice them.

That's the point. When we are held in a spiritual stronghold, we usually don't realize it. We cannot set ourselves free, much less anyone else. It takes "divine power to demolish strongholds" (2 Cor. 10:4). That is what spiritual warfare is all about. It calls on the power of God to set yourself and others free, using what Paul calls earlier the "weapons of righteousness" (2 Cor. 6:7). The list of these weapons is expanded in Ephesians 6:10-20. Prayer is not the only weapon of righteousness, but it is by prayer that the other weapons are wielded, including the Word of God. We are at war in this world, but our weapons are not the weapons of this world.

One more very important point is that it is no fun bringing down a stronghold, especially if the stronghold is in you. The very nature of a spiritual stronghold is that it is a "pretension" set up against the knowledge of God. That word suggests it has to do with pride, self-sufficiency, and ignorance—none of which surrender willingly or quietly. But before God can build, he must destroy. "No man will ever reach the heights to which Christ can lift him," wrote Alexander Maclaren, "who does not begin his upward course by descending to the depth into which Christ's Gospel begins its work by plunging him."[1] Pray earnestly for God to tear down the strongholds for others, as you plead for him to do the same with you.

PRAYER: *Holy Spirit, do your powerful work to bring down the strongholds in my life and in the lives of others. Bring down my pride and self-sufficiency. Take captive every thought and make it obedient to Christ.*

DAY 291: GOD'S GRACIOUS REFUSAL

2 Corinthians 12:7-10

"My grace is sufficient for you, for my power is made perfect in weakness" (2 Cor. 12:9).

Paul begged like Jesus begged in Gethsemane—three times he pleaded with God to take a "thorn" away. And three times he got the same answer Jesus got: "No" (Mark 14:32-42). The fact that neither Paul nor Jesus were finally disappointed in God's refusal is one of the greatest lessons one can learn about prayer, especially prayer for the things we want the most.

What did Paul beg for God to take away? No one knows what it was exactly. All we know for sure is that he was content with God's refusal because it was to keep him humble. God had given Paul a vision that could only be described as "inexpressible" (2 Cor. 12:4). This religious experience of Paul's was an advantage in Corinth because the Corinthians were very impressed with visions and those who had them. In Corinth, supernatural manifestations and experiences were regarded as validations of an apostle's authority (see devotion on Day 276). Apparently, some in Corinth saw themselves as so heavily "validated" that Paul sarcastically called them "super-apostles" (2 Cor. 11:5). Their pride in their religious experiences had taken the focus off God and his glory and put it on them and theirs. Pride is a terrible thing—an aggressive and terminal cancer in the soul—something to be avoided at all costs because God resists the proud but gives grace to the humble (1 Pet. 5:5).

Therefore, Paul welcomed anything that kept him from robbing God of his glory. If a frustrating and debilitating "thorn" was what it took, then it was just fine with him. If less comfort meant more of God, then let there be less! Weaknesses, hardships, insults, and persecutions are transformed into delight. "For when I am weak, then I am strong" (2 Cor. 12:10).

Here we find a great lesson in prayer. Learn to trust and appreciate the wisdom of God's gracious refusals. If he says "No," it is because he wants to say a greater "Yes." John Calvin pointed out that God may sometimes grant the end we desire, but not the means we think necessary to achieve it. Paul desired God's glory, a worthy goal. For a while, he thought the best means to that end was by healing. In the end, Paul got nothing he asked for, but everything he hoped for.

PRAYER: *Dear Father, if your "Yes" to my request would mean less of you, then say "No." Your love is better than life.*

Introduction to Galatians

DAY 292: PRAY AGAINST HERESY

"The righteous will live by faith" (Hab. 2:4; Gal. 3:11).

Paul's language in Galatians is among the strongest in the New Testament: "But even if we or an angel from heaven should preach a gospel other than the one we preached to you, *let him be eternally condemned!*" (Gal. 1:8, italics added). He says it again in the next verse: "let him be eternally condemned!" The Greek for "condemned" is *anathema* which is used in the Greek Old Testament to describe anything cursed by God and consigned to destruction. That's the curse Paul solemnly utters on anyone who would preach a gospel other than the one he preached to the Galatians. That awful imprecation sets the tone for the rest of the book as Paul defends the integrity of Christ's message against false teaching. If not addressed, the confusion in the Galatian church could hinder the advance of the gospel and the ultimate fulfillment of God's covenant with Israel.

Paul's letter to the Galatians bids us to pray for matters of the utmost importance. So much is at stake. Jesus said, "I will build my church, and the gates of Hades will not overcome it" (Matt. 16:18). The ultimate outcome of the struggle is guaranteed, but there can be many casualties along the way. Christ will build his church and his kingdom will come, but what will happen to the Galatians and those influenced by their heresy? Will they be lost? What will happen in your church? Pray with Paul and with Jesus that his church will be built successfully in your congregation.

PRAYER: *Remind me, Holy Father, that what is at stake in the gospel is nothing less than the difference between life and death—heaven or hell—forever.*

DAY 293: ABBA!

Galatians 4:1-10

"So you are no longer a slave, but a son; and since you are a son, God has made you also an heir" (Gal. 4:7).

"Daaaa...da! Maaa...ma!" It doesn't usually come out smoothly the first time, but there's great celebration when an infant first says "Mommy" or "Daddy." With the development of language, the relationship between parent and child enters a new phase. The two can communicate on a new level, and there's a heightened awareness and delight in who the other is. Now the child can call for the parent when afraid or excited or lonely. There is nothing that gets a parent's attention like the sound of a child calling, "Daddy!" or "Mommy!" God is the same way.

The ability to call out "Father" is exactly what Paul says the Holy Spirit gives the believer. The noun, "Abba" comes close to our "Dad," an intimate word of affection and confidence—but also of awe and respect. The verb, "calls out" is a word for strong emotion or a stammering cry. It is as primal as a child's cry for mom or dad. This is where all prayer begins—with the witness of God's Spirit prompting and freeing our hearts to cry, "Abba!" That the Holy One of Israel, the Creator of heaven and earth, should bid us call him "Father" is stunning and even difficult to believe. Whether whispered or shouted, spoken quietly, or sung, an exclamation point always belongs with "Father!" Are you still amazed and grateful?

All the things that preceded this unprecedented privilege were "basic principles of the world" (Gal. 4:3). These were the fundamental principles of religion for both Jew and Gentile (Gal. 4:8-9). At best, the practices served only as preparation for the real thing. At worst, they were substitutes for the real thing. The real thing was a relationship of awe, love, and trust embodied in the cry, "Abba!" Ultimately, all spiritual disciplines, even the disciplines of reading Scripture and prayer, are to lead us to a face-to-face encounter with our Father, God. Has the practice of your faith led you closer to the Father, or farther away?

PRAYER: *Father in Heaven! I both tremble and am at peace when I speak to you this way. Thank you that one as great and awesome, as worthy of fear and reverence as you are, should bid me cry out, as a child, "Father, Dear Father!"*

DAY 294: INTERCESSION IS LIKE CHILDBIRTH

Galatians 4:19-20

"My dear children, for whom I am again in the pains of childbirth until Christ is formed in you" (Gal. 4:19).

Out of his frustration with the Galatians, Paul used a remarkable metaphor to describe his work among them. He said he was like a mother "once again" in labor for the birth of her child! In other words, he thought the child was birthed, but it is still in the birth canal, and the outcome is still in question. Supreme frustration, but profound insight into the nature of intercessory prayer for difficult things and hard-hearted people.

The metaphor shows us the love that moves one to intercede. Like a pregnant mother's expectant love for her unborn child, the love of the intercessor "always protects, always trusts, always hopes, always perseveres" (1 Cor. 13:7). No one is more hopeful and passionate for the future than a pregnant woman. No one is more given to her task as a mother's body is no longer her own but is pressed into the service of another. What love! What a way to pray.

The metaphor also shows us the work of intercession. It can be like childbirth: hard, exhausting, but full of hope. Some see prayer primarily as a path to relaxation and inner quiet. It can be that way, but for serious intercession, it is anything but. It will end in the joy of birth, but the process is never relaxing. Paul told the Romans that to pray this way is to be part of a cosmic effort he described as "groaning" (Rom. 8:22-24).

Finally, the metaphor shows us the end of intercession. Its purpose, its telos, is nothing less than a fully functioning, healthy child. The final goal goes way beyond the moment of birth—it extends to the end of life. No good mother is content with merely a baby, as delightful as a baby is. She wants her child to grow up into maturity. The idea of childbirth echoes in Paul's statement of his goal in ministry which is "to present everyone perfect in Christ." He said, "to this end I labor" (Col. 1:29). His labor was more than intercession, but it was never less. His labor of love was a labor of intercession for those whose lives God had entrusted to him.

PRAYER: *Lord, teach me to pray the way a mother gives birth to her child—passionately, determinedly, unselfishly—with the same love, the same labor, and the same goal.*

DAY 295: PRAYING FOR THE FRUIT OF THE SPIRIT

Galatians 5:22-23

"But the fruit of the Spirit is love, joy, peace, patience, kindness, goodness, faithfulness, gentleness and self-control" (Gal. 5:22).

This list of "fruit" makes a wonderful list to pray for yourself and others. Since there are nine listed, one is tempted to say, "nine fruits," but the word is singular in the text and for good reason—the source is singular. The source of spiritual fruit is the Holy Spirit. Think of these nine as descriptions of the qualities that emerge in the character of a man or woman filled with the Spirit. Or think of them as the fruit of the same Spirit who moves us to pray (Gal. 4:6; Rom. 8:15). Or you may think of them as the fulfillment of Jesus' promise: "I am the vine, you are the branches. If a man remains in me and I in him, he will bear much fruit" (John 15:5).

You could also think of these as love in all its glory. Love is the greatest of Christian virtues, "the most excellent way" of all (1 Cor. 12:31). Dr. Kenneth Moynagh, has summarized the glory of love in the fruit of the Spirit:

Joy is love exulting, and peace is love at rest;
Patience, love enduring in every trial and test.
Gentleness, love yielding to all that is not sin,
Goodness, love in actions that flow from Christ within.
Faith is love's eyes opened the living Christ to see;
Meekness, love not fighting, but bowed at Calvary.
Temperance, love in harness and under Christ's control,
For Christ is love in person, and love, Christ in the soul.[1]

That last line is the best of all: think of the fruit of the Spirit as a sketch of the character of Jesus. The more we exhibit these traits, the more we look like our Lord. And the more we *look at* our Lord, the more we will exhibit these traits. What is prayer but gazing at the glory of Jesus, through the lens of Scripture, and becoming what we behold? Spiritual growth comes by letting the light of Christ into our soul the way a shutter lets the light into a camera. The image will be impressed on the light-sensitive heart—the picture taken—and we will begin to look like Jesus. Memorize the list and pray daily for each fruit.

PRAYER: *Lord, I want to be like Jesus in my soul. In all that I think, say, and do today, grant that I will show love, joy, peace, patience, kindness, goodness, faithfulness, gentleness, and self-control.*

DAY 296: POUR OUT YOUR HEART

Fern Nichols (1945-)

"Arise, cry out in the night, as the watches of the night begin; pour out your heart like water in the presence of the Lord. Lift up your hands to him for the lives of your children, who faint from hunger at the head of every street" (Lam. 2:19).

The original context of these words from Lamentations was the terrible siege and destruction of Jerusalem in the sixth century BC. During this time, Jerusalem saw, among many other horrors, starving children and their starving mothers being reduced to cannibalism. But the call to "pour out your heart like water... for the lives of your children" is universal. Parents in every time and place have been moved to pour out their hearts like water and cry out to God for the sake of their children's lives.

Fern Nichols was moved to pray in the fall of 1984 when her two oldest children were about to go off to what she called the "jaws of junior high peer pressure" in Abbotsford, British Columbia. At first, Fern asked a friend to pray with her, but soon five other mothers were gathered around her kitchen table to pray. They prayed that God would protect their children spiritually and physically. They prayed for the teachers. They also prayed that anyone trying to sell drugs on campus would be caught. Three months later three men were arrested for selling marijuana, and a house only a block from the school was found to be a main distribution center for marijuana in the area.

Word got out about the dramatic success of their prayers, and by the end of the year, there was a group of mothers pouring out their hearts for the lives of their children at every school in the district. The ministry took on the name Moms in Touch, and when the Nichols moved to Poway, California the next year, it spread to the high school there. Since then, Moms in Touch has added the word "International" to its name and can be found in 90 countries. In North America there are at least 150,000 moms in 25,000 groups praying for children in 34,000 schools. Without political agitation or public confrontation, the lives of thousands of students have been quietly and gently changed—as have many of their schools.

Part of the power of this ministry is in its simplicity and grounding in Scripture. Prayer meetings are to start promptly on time and to last an hour. Most important, they are to be for prayer only. No refreshments are to be served to distract the participants from the precious time allotted for prayer. The pray-ers learn to pray Scripture into the lives of their children and their schools.

So many prayer meetings end because there is no vision, no clear sense of purpose, and therefore, no strong motivation to pray. Who could be more motivated, passionate, and visionary for the well-being of their kids than mothers are?

PRAYER: *Holy Father! We love because you first loved us; and whatever love we have for our children is but an imperfect reflection of your love. So, we cry out for you to keep them safe from all evil and to make them secure in your powerful, saving love.*

Introduction to Ephesians

DAY 297: ASKING FOR GOD'S GLORIOUS RICHES

"I pray that out of his glorious riches he may strengthen you with power through his Spirit in your inner being" (Eph. 3:16).

The dad wanted to read the newspaper, but his five-year-old daughter wanted him to read to her from her book. She kept pestering him until he came up with a plan to put her off a little longer. To keep her busy, he devised a puzzle from a full-page picture of the earth in the newspaper. Thinking her ignorance of the world would make it impossible to solve, he cut the image up into little pieces and said to her, "As soon as you put the world together, honey, I'll read to you." She looked at the heap of newspaper pieces on the floor, groaned with frustration, but dove into the project. Pleased with himself, the father smiled and settled into his chair to read the rest of the paper. Not more than five minutes later he heard her squeal with delight and shout, "I'm done, Daddy!" He looked down, and to his astonishment, saw that she was.

"How could you do such a hard puzzle so quickly?" he asked her.

"It was easy," she replied. "There was a big picture of a man's face on the back of the world. When his face came together, the world came together."

We may not be able to see it now, but one day the world, and all its bloodstained history, will look like the face of Christ. That is the heart of the message of Ephesians. God's purpose in Christ is "to bring all things in heaven and on earth together under one head, even Christ" (Eph. 1:10). All the division and warring factions will one day be united in Christ. The church is the prototype of what this will look like. For "God placed all things under [Christ's] feet, and appointed him to be head over everything for the church" (Eph. 1:22). For the church? Yes. Ephesians is the premier book in the New Testament on the church.

As such, Paul's prayers for the church are unparalleled in their depth, elegance, and eloquence. Ephesians 1:15-23 and 3:14-21 should set the prayer agenda for any church that seriously wants to fulfill God's purpose. Pray with Paul for the church, for your church, and you may discover that what you thought the church was all about was far too small. It is Christ's "body, the fullness of him who fills everything in every way" (Eph. 1:23).

PRAYER: *Gracious God! By the power of your Spirit, teach me to pray God-sized prayers!*

DAY 298: EVERY SPIRITUAL BLESSING IN CHRIST

Ephesians 1:3-14

"Praise be to the God and Father of our Lord Jesus Christ" (Eph. 1:3).

These first fourteen verses of Ephesians are one, long, breathless sentence in the Greek. The passage reads like a psalm, worthy of comparison with the greats, like Psalms 23, 103, 139 and 145. And this passage is packed theologically. It is dense! The reality of the Trinity is clear in references to the Father (Eph. 1:3), the Son (Eph. 1:4-13), and the Holy Spirit (Eph. 1:13-14). Many of the great ideas of the gospel are also highlighted: God's people are chosen, predestined, forgiven, and redeemed.

This is a song to personalize. Read it through slowly and prayerfully, substituting the first-person singular for all the second persons plural. For instance, instead of "us" say, "who has blessed *me* in the heavenly realms." Do this repeatedly, over a week or a month, until you really mean what you read, and the apostle Paul's words become your own. Expect your outlook to brighten as you do.

Personalize the passage by understanding it deeply. Get a good commentary or Bible dictionary and familiarize yourself with the big theological concepts. As your understanding increases, so will your wonder and praise for our great God. That, after all, is the purpose of the gospel celebrated by this New Testament psalm—"that we, who were the first to put our hope in Christ, might be for the praise of his glory" (Eph. 1:12).

Let your understanding give you a new perspective on your life. Paul says we who know Christ understand something no one else can grasp—the meaning of history—God's purpose "to bring unity to all things in heaven and on earth under Christ" (Eph. 1:10). In other words, a child, an aborigine barely out of the stone age, or an illiterate farmer in Appalachia can know the secret of history while a PhD in history may not! The point is that our little lives are part of something unimaginably great. We can rest secure in the present because we know the one who holds the future. And he who holds the last hour is in control of the next moment—"to the praise of his glory."

PRAYER: *You are the God and Father of my Lord Jesus Christ! Praise be to you, for blessing me with every spiritual blessing in Christ.*

DAY 299: A PRAYER FOR ILLUMINATION

Ephesians 1:15-23

"I pray also that the eyes of your heart may be enlightened" (Eph. 1:18).

Søren Kierkegaard told a parable about a poor peasant who could never afford to buy a pair of shoes. One day he went to the city and earned enough money to not only buy shoes, but to get drunk too. That night he got drunk and passed out on the street. The next morning, as he slept, a wagon drove up and the driver shouted to him to move or he would run over his legs. The badly hung-over peasant woke up, raised his head, and looked at his legs. But he didn't recognize them because they were wearing shoes and stockings. He laid his head back, closed his eyes, and shouted back to the driver, "Drive on, they're not my legs."[1]

Lest we suffer the same thing spiritually, Paul prays, "I pray that the eyes of your heart may be enlightened" (Eph. 1:18). The magnitude of the spiritual blessings described in verses 1-14 are to our spiritual consciousness what shoes were to that poor peasant—times 10,000. The gap between what we were apart from Christ and what we are in Christ is too great for our little minds to comprehend (Eph. 2:1-3). We need more than data and information about the transformation; we need enlightenment. Therefore, Paul prays for the Ephesians, and we must pray for ourselves and others, that we may....

Know Christ: "I keep asking that the God of our Lord Jesus Christ, the glorious Father, may give you the Spirit of wisdom and revelation, so that you may know him better."

Know our hope: "I pray that the eyes of your heart may be enlightened in order that you may know the hope to which he has called you, the riches of his glorious inheritance in his people."

Know our power: "...and his incomparably great power for us who believe. That power is the same mighty strength he exerted when he raised Christ from the dead and seated him at his right hand in the heavenly realms."

These are stunning things to pray, much less to experience and understand. But knowing Christ and our hope and our power are nevertheless things we must ask God to help us comprehend. Otherwise, we will be like the peasant who didn't recognize his own legs.

PRAYER: *Oh, Holy Spirit! Open the eyes of my heart! I want to see you and know the hope and power I have in Christ.*

DAY 300: THE FULFILLMENT OF ALL DESIRE

Ephesians 3:14-21

"I pray that out of his glorious riches he may strengthen you with power" (Eph. 3:16).

Question: Does God think that you want too much or that you are satisfied with too little? Before you answer this question, do two things. First, hear the answer C. S. Lewis gave:

> *Indeed, if we consider the unblushing promises of reward and the staggering nature of the rewards promised in the Gospels, it would seem that our Lord finds our desires, not too strong, but too weak. We are half-hearted creatures, fooling about with drink and sex and ambition when infinite joy is offered us, like an ignorant child who wants to go on making mud pies in a slum because he cannot imagine what is meant by the offer of a holiday at the sea. We are far too easily pleased.*[1]

That's one way to answer the question. Now, do the second thing: measure your desires for yourself against the prayer Paul prays here for the Ephesians and for all who follow Jesus, including you! Do you desire anything like this:

> *Christ making his home and setting up permanent residence in your inner being? "That Christ may dwell in your hearts through faith" (Eph. 3:17).*

> *Knowing the full dimensions of Christ's love—knowing, in a sense, the unknowable? "to grasp how wide and long and high and deep is the love of Christ, and to know this love that surpasses knowledge" (Eph. 3:18-19a).*

> *Being as full of God as you can be and still be you? "that you may be filled to the measure of all the fullness of God" (Eph. 3:19b).*

Can anyone pray for these things and fully understand what it means? Probably not even the apostle Paul fully comprehended what he was praying for. But no matter, we should pray for these things anyway. It's OK if our reach exceeds our grasp. For, as Robert Browning asked, "what's a heaven for" if not for that?[2]

PRAYER: *Lord, my heart is narrow and my vision shortsighted. Expand me, open me, fill me to the measure of yourself.*

DAY 301: A CULTURE OF PRAYER AND PRAISE

Ephesians 5:19-20

"Speak to one another with psalms, hymns and spiritual songs" (Eph. 5:19).

Cultures have tremendous influence on how people think and behave. A violent culture tends to produce violent people. A culture of peace tends to do the opposite. The word "culture" comes from the Latin, *colo,* which means "to cultivate." A culture nurtures people the way soil, sun, water, and food do a garden. A good garden is well-cultivated; a bad garden is badly cultivated.

In the same way, a family, a church or gathering of Christians, even a workplace can become cultures of prayer and praise. This kind of culture is what Paul recommends in Ephesians 5:19-20. "Speak to one another with psalms, hymns and spiritual songs. Sing and make music in your heart to the Lord, always giving thanks to God the Father for everything, in the name of the Lord Jesus Christ." Prayer and praise don't automatically flourish in a church any more than a flower automatically grows in a garden. Flourishing requires planting and cultivation. The growth and health of prayer and praise must be intentional.

What conversation typically takes place in your church gatherings? It has been said that, although there is more to life than news, weather, and sports, a person might never know it by the conversation that takes place before and after a church service. The problem is not that these topics are unworthy of Christians; it's just that other things are so much more worthy. Speaking to one another with hymns, psalms, and spiritual songs should always characterize Christian conversation. Without being stilted or mechanical about it, we can be more intentional about the things we talk about in church and with fellow Christians. A culture of praise and thanksgiving nurtures faithful, wise, and happy people.

Maybe verse 18 gives us a clue as to how life should be in a culture of prayer and praise. It says, "Do not get drunk on wine, which leads to debauchery." Alcohol is a powerful and pervasive influence. It can lead people in certain definite directions. "Instead, be filled with the Spirit." The Holy Spirit should be the most powerful and pervasive influence in Christian fellowship. The Spirit also leads people in certain definite directions—toward "psalms, hymns and spiritual songs."

PRAYER: *Father in heaven! Open my mouth to sing your praise to my heart and to those I am with.*

DAY 302: GOD'S ARMOR

Ephesians 6:10-20

"Put on the full armor of God" (Eph. 6:11).

"Don't take it personally." That was the advice a retiring pastor gave to a young pastor. "Don't take what personally?" the younger man asked. "Don't take it personally when you are attacked and opposed in the ministry. It's not about you. You're in a battle, it goes with the territory." That advice is relevant for all believers. A soldier in a war gets shot at. His feelings don't get hurt when that happens. He doesn't take it personally because he knows it comes with being in a battle.

Paul assumed his readers knew that they were in a battle, but he reminded them that the battle was spiritual. It wasn't against the things their physical senses could perceive—the things they could taste, touch, hear, smell, and see. The battle was against the powers of the unseen realm—things seen only through the eyes of faith. Spiritual warfare calls for spiritual weapons.

Worldly weapons are useless in a spiritual conflict and using them is like hunting a lion with a squirt gun. Spiritual armor and spiritual weapons, which include the helmet of salvation, the breastplate of righteousness and the shield of faith, are essential. But how does one put on a "helmet of salvation," for instance? We put it on by prayer. At the end of the list of spiritual armor, Paul describes the "sword of the Spirit, which is the word of God" (Eph. 6:17). The next verse reads, "And pray in the Spirit." The Greek is something like, "by means of prayer." The idea is that the armor is donned by prayer, and the sword of the Spirit is wielded by prayer.

Paul applies prayer comprehensively with four "alls." We are to pray on *all* occasions, with *all* kinds of prayers, with *all* perseverance, and for *all* the saints. Prayer is the one weapon that fits every circumstance of spiritual warfare. It is always appropriate. But how we pray in spiritual warfare is also significant. Paul wants the Ephesians to pray that he would be fearless and wise ("that... words may be given to me"). These are the essential qualities of any good soldier: courage and good judgment. It isn't enough to have the heart to charge the enemy. A soldier must also have the head to know when and how.

Paul's instructions to the Ephesians are a critical briefing for any soldier of Christ fighting the good fight.

PRAYER: *Father, give me the heart and the head I need to fight the good fight. Give me courage and teach me wisdom.*

Introduction to Philippians

DAY 303: GRATEFUL, JOYFUL PRAYER

"Rejoice in the Lord always. I will say it again: rejoice" (Phil. 4:4).

One way to look at this remarkable letter of Paul's is to see it as a missionary update and a thank you letter to his supporters (Phil. 4:10-19). The notion that the canon of Holy Scripture includes a thank you letter is a delightful thought!

Of course, Philippians is much more than just a thank you letter. As Paul gives his thanks, he delivers one of the classic formulations of Christian doctrine regarding the incarnation of Christ (Phil. 2:6-11). Scholars call it the *kenosis* passage from the Greek word which means "to empty." The letter to the Philippians is also known for its emphasis on joy. The words "joy," "joyful," "rejoice," or related ideas appear again and again. The emphasis on joy is not incidental to the letter's purpose of giving thanks. When we are filled with thankfulness for the grace we've received, we are also filled with joy. Theologian Karl Barth said grace evokes gratitude like the voice of an echo and that gratitude follows grace like thunder follows lightning.[1]

Reference to thankfulness and joy is everywhere in Philippians. Are the people fighting amongst themselves? Paul appeals to gratitude and joy. Their experience of God's grace in the Incarnation and in union with Christ should motivate them to get along. Because of all the grace they have received, they should make joy complete by being like-minded and having the same love (Phil. 2:1-11). It isn't that the Philippians are forced to live in love or be punished; it is that their knowledge of God's goodness should make it impossible not to love one another. It is their joy to do so.

Maybe the book of Philippians isn't much more than a thank you letter. Letters and lives can't have a much better purpose than giving thanks. Joyful gratitude sustains the prisoner (Phil. 1:18-26), unifies congregations (Phil. 2:1-11), calms the worrier (Phil. 4:4-7), and makes a poor man content (Phil. 4:10-13). We can never pay God back for his goodness to us. What we can do is pray and live, "Thank you!" joyfully (Ps. 116:12-14). Is there any other way to be thankful?

PRAYER: *Father in heaven! You have given me so much. Give one thing more, a thankful and joyful heart.*[2]

DAY 304: INDEFATIGABLE PRAYER

Philippians 1:3-11

"I thank my God every time I remember you" (Phil. 1:3).

The problem with prayer is not that it is boring, but that our way of going about it is—at least sometimes. Paul's prayer for the Philippians is a great prayer and worth repeating word-for-word, but it is also a model of how to revitalize prayer.

First, look at *how* Paul prayed for the church—joyfully (Phil. 1:4). His joy came from two things: his memory of the past and his confident hope in the future. The past was full of great memories of their "partnership in the gospel" and the ways they had shared in God's grace with him. All of these memories added up to a longing in his heart for them "with all the affection of Christ Jesus" (Phil. 1:4, 5, 7, 8). When you pray for the people you love, take the time to remember the good and happy history you have had with them. Consider keeping photos nearby when you pray as a way to add color to your intercession. It helps us pray for others when our memory of them is vivid and loving.

Paul's prayers were joyful because he was also very confident that he need not worry about the Philippians as he prayed for them. Sometimes intercession becomes heavy, even depressing, because of our concern. Joy and a certain lightness of heart come when we remember that "he who began a good work will carry it to completion" (Phil. 1:6). We are not praying upstream, or against the grain, but with a God whose purposes for those we love will be fulfilled. God is more willing to answer prayer than we are willing to pray.

Second, look at *what* Paul prayed for the church—love. He prayed, not just for any kind of love, but for wise love—love that is filled with knowledge and depth of insight. This love can sort out from many options the one thing that is needed. When love is directed toward our neighbor, it always wants what is best for the beloved. When love is directed toward God, it wants to do what God thinks best. In both cases, love is happiest when it knows what is best. Prayer for what makes love happiest is happy prayer. When God answers this prayer in those we love, there is simply no telling what wonderful surprises lay ahead. And we can be sure that God most assuredly will answer prayer flowing from wise love (James 1:5).

PRAYER: *Faithful God, strengthen my hope and awaken my memory that I may pray for others with confidence and joy.*

DAY 305: LONGING

Philippians 3:3-14

"Whatever was to my profit I now consider loss for the sake of Christ" (Phil. 3:7).

Prayer, as in every aspect of life in the Spirit, has a beginning, a road, and a destination. It begins with a vision of something—or of Someone—of inestimable worth. Jesus said the kingdom of God is like a man who found a treasure buried in a field and who joyfully went off and sold all he owned to buy the field and get the treasure (Matt. 13:44). Some might watch the man liquidate his assets and wonder about his sanity in betting everything he owned on a field. But the man knows better. Paul was like that man. When he saw Christ, he looked at everything he had ever gained and saw it as loss compared to knowing Jesus. It was worse than loss, it was rubbish! The desire to pray is directly proportionate to our sense of the preciousness Christ.

The road of the spiritual life is strenuous and hard. Paul said, "I press on to take hold of that for which Christ Jesus took hold of me" (Phil. 3:12). The sense of the Greek for "press on" is of a hunter pursuing a quarry, or a runner running for the gold medal. "Take hold," a wrestling term, is even more vigorous. The Greek is literally, "I grasp, inasmuch as I was grasped by Christ." Picture Paul's conversion on the road to Damascus this way: He was on a mission to persecute Jesus, "breathing out murderous threats" (Acts 9:1). Jesus met him on the way and "grasped him"—he wrestled Paul to the ground and pinned him! Everything changed for Paul. From then on, the purpose for which Christ wrestled him to the ground was the same purpose for which Paul would wrestle to the ground and pin every obstacle to knowing Jesus. The same qualities that make for a great athlete, make for a great pray-er, including a vision of glory and a sober estimate of what it will take to get there.

The goal or destination of prayer is also its beginning. What makes us want to pray in the first place is a vision of the inestimable worth of Christ. The goal then is to know him and the power of his resurrection and even to share even in his sufferings if it means fellowship with the one we so desperately want to know.

PRAYER: *Dear Jesus, I want to know you and the power of your resurrection, to share even in your sufferings, and to become like you in your death if it means fellowship with you.*

DAY 306: A DEMONSTRATION OF THE SPIRIT'S POWER

Samuel Chadwick (1860-1932)

"My message and my preaching were not with wise and persuasive words, but with a demonstration of the Spirit's power, so that your faith might not rest on men's wisdom, but on God's power" (1 Cor. 2:4-5).

Samuel Chadwick's preaching took on a supernatural power after he set all his sermons on fire. One night as he prayed, Chadwick's conscience was stricken about his self-reliance. For months he had labored day and night preparing catchy, exciting, and pertinent sermons, but the congregation remained unmoved. "[There was a] false aim in my work," Chadwick later recalled. "I lived and labored for my sermons and was unfortunately more concerned about their excellence and reputation than the repentance of the people."[1] Though revivals were happening in surrounding villages, Chadwick's small congregation was untouched. Lack of success slowly wore down his confidence in himself. "The demands of the impossible task [of converting the congregation] awakened me to a sense of need. I had neither power nor might in either service or prayer."[2]

So it was with trembling hands that he pulled out his precious collection of sermons and set them on fire. Almost immediately he experienced an inner change: "I could not explain what had happened, but it was a bigger thing that I had ever known.... There came into my soul a deep peace, a thrilling joy, and a new sense of power."[3]

The next Sunday seven people were converted. Revitalized, Chadwick called the entire congregation to prayer. Soon afterward, his church experienced a revival that spread outward. Hundreds were converted, including Robert Hamer, a.k.a. "Bury Bob," a man notorious for his drunken violence and brawling. "God led us to Pentecost," Chadwick later wrote. "It awakened my mind as well as cleansed my heart. It gave me a new job and a new power, a new love and a new compassion. It gave me a new Bible and a new message. Above all else, it gave me a new understanding and a new intimacy in the communion and ministry of prayer, it taught me to pray in the Spirit."[4]

For the rest of his life Chadwick preached the necessity of the power of the Spirit through prayer. "Prayer is the test of faith and the secret of power.... The energy of the flesh can run bazaars, organize amusements, and raise millions, but it is the presence of the Holy Spirit that makes a temple of the Living God."[5]

PRAYER: *Come, O Holy Spirit! Better one word spoken in your power than a thousand spoken with human eloquence. Teach me to be slow to speak, and quick to pray before I do.*

DAY 307: PEACE OF MIND PRAYING

Philippians 4:4-9

"Do not be anxious about anything" (Phil. 4:4).

Have you ever tried to stop worrying by stopping worry? It doesn't work, does it. It's like deciding not to think about something. The more you think about not thinking, the more thinking you do.

The best way not to worry is by redirection. Do something else, preferably something that is the opposite of worry. The opposite of worry is thankful prayer: "Do not be anxious about anything, but in everything, by prayer and petition, with thanksgiving, present your requests to God. And the peace of God, which transcends all understanding, will guard your hearts and minds in Christ Jesus" (Phil. 4:6-7). What is it about prayer that is so effective against worry?

The Latin words for prayer and anxiety offer a good picture of how it works. The Latin word for anxiety is *curare*, a word used also to name a poison some South American tribes would put on the tips of their arrows. The poison works like anxiety by constricting the muscles of the body, especially the throat, until the victim suffocates. Isn't that the way worry feels? It is like hands around the throat or a weight on the chest. The Latin word for prayer is *orare*, which means essentially to open the mouth and speak. *Orare* works against *curare*, by opening us up and letting in the oxygen.

That's a picture of how it works, but here is how it works practically. Tell God everything you're worried about, but as you tell him, give thanks. Give thanks that he hears you and answers prayer. Give thanks that your sins are forgiven and that you will spend eternity in heaven. Give thanks that nothing can separate you from the love of Christ. In short, give thanks that everything which really matters has already been taken care of. All the rest is details—like the things you're worrying about as you pray.

And try this little spiritual discipline: When you are worried, and someone asks you how you are, say something like, "I'm fundamentally sound." Or if you want a little laugh, say, "Other than the fact that my sins are forgiven and I will spend an eternity of joy with God, I'm not doing too well."

PRAYER: *Dear Father! Thank you that all these things that nag at my peace of mind have no power to separate me from your love.*

Introduction to Colossians

DAY 308: THE POINT OF CONVERGENCE

"He is before all things, and in him all things hold together" (Col. 3:17).

Why do people climb mountains? The best answer to that question is Sir George Mallory's. When asked why he climbed the Matterhorn, he replied, "Because it is there!" Willi Unsoeld, a mountaineer and a philosopher, didn't like that answer. He thought there was a deeper reason: "People climb mountains because of a universal desire to find the point of convergence."[1] If you are standing on a mountain peak, the world below does seem to converge. Geographical features, cities and forests and rivers and hills, all come together and converge at the peak. Imagine if there were one place to stand where all the complexity of life would truly come together as from a mountaintop!

There is such a place in the person of Jesus Christ. He is, in his own words, "the First and the Last," the beginning and the end (Rev. 1:17). No book in the Bible states this more powerfully than the book of Colossians. "[Jesus] is the image of the invisible God, the firstborn over all creation… all things were created by him and for him. He is before all things, and in him all things hold together" (Col. 1:15-17). A. T. Robertson said Colossians gives a "full length portrait of Christ."[2] In so doing, this letter shows Jesus to be the point of convergence we all long for.

The church in Colossae was in danger of losing its grasp of Christ's supremacy. Instead of being the integrator of all things, he was being integrated into other schemes for convergence. Instead of Christ alone, it was Christ-plus or Christ with supplements. Paul wanted the Colossians to know that Jesus isn't one of the treasures of wisdom and knowledge. He isn't even the greatest of the treasures of wisdom and knowledge. He is the one "in whom are hidden all the treasures of wisdom and knowledge" (Col. 2:3).

The book of Colossians calls us to pray and to do everything in the name of a great Christ. Paul's prayer for these people is a model of pastoral concern coupled with theological acuity (Col. 1:9-14). He knows that ideas have far reaching consequences for good or for bad; and there is no idea more determinative of everything else than our understanding of Christ. Our faith—and our prayers—will be as big, or as small as our grasp of his greatness.

PRAYER: *My great and marvelous Lord, you are able to do far more than I ask or even imagine! Then do it! For your great name's sake!*

DAY 309: PLEASING GOD

Colossians 1:9-14

"And we pray this in order that you may live a life worthy of the Lord and may please him in every way" (Col. 1:10).

Ever since the publication of the 19th century bestseller, *In His Steps*, Christians have had their imaginations fired by the question, "What would Jesus do?" It can be helpful to project Jesus into a situation we are facing and imagine how he would act. However, if we are not careful, this practice can also be limiting. We can mistakenly attribute to our imaginary Jesus all kinds of things that aren't true of Jesus or that he wouldn't do. The Jesus of our imaginations may have nothing to do with the real Jesus.

A better approach is to pray what Paul prayed for the Colossians, asking "God to fill you with the knowledge of his will through all spiritual insight and understanding" (Col. 1:9). This request goes far beyond imitating what you think Jesus might do. It asks God to give you the mind and attitude of Jesus. This knowledge is more than accurate information; it is a living, breathing knowledge of God's will. Being filled with this understanding of God's will is similar to an athlete who has mastered all of the techniques so that performance becomes art.

The purpose for Paul's prayer gives an important clue as to how this knowledge comes. He prayed that they would know God's will so they could, "live a life worthy of the Lord and… please him in every way" (Col. 1:10). The sense of the Greek word translated "please" is to anticipate every wish the way a slave anticipates his master's every wish. In classical Greek, this attitude was never considered a good thing. The desire to please connoted servility and obsequiousness. It lacked dignity; it belonged to the weak. It was the attitude of a slave, and no free person would want to be that. Precisely. Only those who want to be God's slave will know God's will. "Obedience is the opener of eyes," wrote George Macdonald. In other words, we can only know what we will do. Obedience opens the door to deeper knowledge of God's will and to "all spiritual insight and understanding."

As you pray for this marvelous revelation, pay close attention to the ways it shows itself: "in every good work… growing in the knowledge of God… strength… endurance… patience… joy… thanksgiving" (Col. 1:10-12).

PRAYER: *Dear God, in the name of your Son, I ask you to fill me with the knowledge of your will through all spiritual insight and understanding that I may live a life worthy of your name and please you in every way.*

DAY 310: THE STILL POINT IN THE TURNING WORLD

Colossians 3:1-4

"Set your hearts on things above, where Christ is seated at the right hand of God" (Col. 3:1).

There is such a thing as a praying imagination. This passage is a prime example. Picture yourself walking through a shopping mall fashioned after John Bunyan's Vanity-Fair, the town given over completely to worldly pursuits and pleasures. All around you are shopkeepers and street vendors hawking their wares—drink, sex, success, wealth, power, beauty. Lights flash, music blares, and a loud calliope plays crazily. Hands reach for you, and strangers whisper in your ears. But your heart is still. It is fixed on Christ, "the still point of the turning world" (T. S. Eliot).[1] You are not touched by what clutches at you. Your heart is set on things above, "where Christ is seated at the right hand of God… on things above, not on earthly things" (Col. 3:1-2).

There is no getting through Vanity Fair without prayer. To be sure, praying is not all there is to be done; but you won't get to anything else until you pray. Prayer sets your compass on heaven and keeps you on track through the trackless wastes of the world.

Walking through this world with your heart set on heaven is not an easy journey, but it's not as hard as it sounds, either. In this text, Paul uses one of his classic formulations which is known by scholars as the "indicative and imperative." The indicative is an objective truth, or it is what is. The imperative is what must be done based on the truth of the indicative. In these verses the indicative is that you died with Christ, you are raised with Christ; and your true life is hidden with Christ in God. Therefore, the imperative which follows is to set your heart on things above, not on earthly things. The indicative makes the imperative possible. The point is, you can live your life differently in the world because your true life is hidden with Christ in heaven. The journey may be hard, but it can be done. It may stretch you, but it is a stretching toward (not away from) your true self. Prayer can feel unnatural on earth, but it is the most natural thing in heaven; and that is where you belong.

PRAYER: *Father in heaven! Give me a praying imagination. Open my eyes to heaven's realities, close them to the pretensions of the world.*

DAY 311: MUSCULAR PRAYER

Colossians 4:2-4, 12-13

"He is always wrestling in prayer for you" (Col. 4:12).

Epaphras prayed like a fighter. The expression is, "he is always wrestling in prayer for you" (Col. 4:12). The Greek for "wrestling" is the word behind our English word "agony." Originally, it was a noun, referring to the place where people went to watch wrestlers and boxers. Later, it came to mean, not only where they went, but what they went to watch. By Jesus' day, the same word was also used to describe the activity of attorneys in court! It is a muscular word, a vigorous word. That is how Epaphras prayed. He went to the mat for the churches at Laodicea and Hierapolis.

Concentration of the mind is essential in any athletic endeavor. But it is critical in boxing and wrestling! Lose your focus and you may get a black eye or be pinned to the mat. That image gives a particular vividness to Paul's words about prayer earlier in the chapter: "Devote yourselves to prayer, being watchful and thankful" (Col. 4:12). A lot depends on watchful, muscular prayer—the effectiveness of gospel preaching, for example. Paul wants the message to go out to an unbelieving world with clarity, vigor, and supernatural power (Col. 4:4-6). So, he urges us to wrestle with God in prayer; to speak to God about people before we speak to people about God.

Thankfulness in this intense kind of prayer keeps it from becoming exhausting. When you wrestle in prayer for souls, give thanks for them. Repeatedly express gratitude for the glorious gospel. It will keep the duty of prayer delightful.

This is a high calling, more worthy of concentrated devotion than the Olympic games. Why do we hold back? "What makes us Christians shrug our shoulders when we ought to be flexing our muscles?" asked Billy Graham. "What makes us apathetic in a day when there are loads to lift, a world to be won and captives to be set free? Why are so many bored when the times demand action?"[1]

Pray like Epaphras. Why not start a prayer group named "The Epaphras Fellowship"?

PRAYER: *Father in heaven! Your Son wrestled in Gethsemane for the sake of our salvation. Teach us to wrestle in prayer for the salvation of others.*

Introduction to 1 and 2 Thessalonians

DAY 312: PRAYER AND THE PAROUSIA[1]

"For you know very well that the day of the Lord will come like a thief in the night" (1 Thess. 5:2).

If you know how a book or movie is going to end, it impacts how you read all of the preceding scenes or events. The future has a way of invading and altering the present in a way the past never can.

Question: If you knew Christ were returning tomorrow, would you live any differently today? Stated differently, since you don't know whether Jesus is or isn't returning tomorrow, should his return somehow affect your living? Both questions should have the same answer. We should live every day in the light of the possibility of the Lord's return. Knowing that he *will* return should keep us on our toes. Not knowing *when* he will come should keep us on our toes even more. That future should invade and alter our present.

Paul's letters to the Thessalonians were written to a people keenly aware that the Lord was coming back—someday—whether tomorrow or next year, it didn't matter. Everything they did was to be done in the light of Jesus' return: evangelism, ministry, behavior, community life. Paul wrote to urge the church to live out, in very practical ways, an ethic of hope.

What could be more encouraging than to know the things we pray for will one day become reality. God's name will be hallowed, his kingdom will come, and all that is wrong will be set right! How happy we will be if, when he returns, Jesus finds us crying out for him to come (Luke 18:1-8)!

PRAYER: *Lord keep my feet planted firmly on earth, but my eyes on heaven expecting the coming of the Lord.*

DAY 313: THE CAUSES OF HAPPY EFFECTS

1 Thessalonians 1:2-3

"We always thank God for all of you" (1 Thess. 1:2).

Good roots make for healthy trees and good fruit. They are the cause of a happy effect. As Paul prayed for the Thessalonians, he thanked God for their good roots and excellent fruit. Their roots were faith, hope, and love—what theologians have called the three theological virtues. These theological virtues are to moral virtues what roots are to fruit.

Paul is writing to Christians whose faith produced work. One could say their faith *worked*—as faith always does and must. Faith without works is dead. It appears from this passage that the faith of the Thessalonians inspired service (1 Thess. 1:9), loving labor (1 Thess. 1:3), and a vibrant witness to the power of the gospel (1 Thess. 1:7-8). The Christians accomplished these things because of their trust in the Lord. William Carey said we should believe great things of God and attempt great things for God. The two go together.

Note that it was their *love* which prompted labor. Love makes you work hard. Faith that believes a great thing must include a love that will work hard for it. The old adage that genius is 10% inspiration and 90% perspiration is another way of saying it takes love to get the job done. The work of the Thessalonian church was about people. People can be notoriously difficult and ungrateful even while they are being served. Only love will put up with that.

Similarly, their *hope* inspired endurance. One of the devil's greatest weapons is discouragement. Fatigue is soil for discouragement. The weary are prone to think there is no hope: "Why bother? What difference does it make anyway?" Hope inspires endurance because it assures us that what we do will make a difference if we just keep at it.

We can pray for others and for ourselves that we would attempt great things for God, work hard at them, and keep at it. Or we might pray that God would build our faith, hope, and love. The second prayer might be better, for then we would be cultivating the roots of good fruit—the cause of a happy effect. We wouldn't just *do* good, we would *be* good.

PRAYER: *Holy Spirit of God! Strengthen my faith, deepen my love, and broaden my hope so that I might attempt great things, labor in love, and persevere in hope.*

DAY 314: PRAYER, PRAISE, AND PERFECTION

1 Thessalonians 5:16-18, 23-24

"Be joyful always, pray continually, give thanks in all circumstances" (1 Thess. 5:16-18).

Paul gave three short commands to be joyful always, pray continually, and give thanks in all circumstances. William Law spoke from the heart of these commands when he wrote:

> *"Would you know who is the greatest saint in the world? It is not he who prays most or fasts most, it is not he who gives most alms or is most eminent for temperance, chastity, or justice; but it is he who is always thankful to God, who wills everything that God wills, who receives everything as an instance of God's goodness and has a heart always ready to praise God for it.... Could you therefore work miracles, you could not do more for yourself than by this thankful spirit, for it... turns all that it touches into happiness."*[1]

These are extravagant claims, but true. Why is continual thanksgiving so important to spiritual health? Because it comes from an attitude toward God that is so healthy—the confidence that God is perfect in love, wisdom, and power. He always wills what is best, always knows what is best, and is powerful enough to always accomplish what is best. Continual thanksgiving practices this life-giving perspective. It says, "Father, even though I can't see your love, wisdom, and power in these circumstances, I believe you are bigger than what I can see. I will praise you for your power and for your goodness in every circumstance of my life."

Thanksgiving is a spiritual discipline. So, thank God for all you see (which usually isn't very much!). Then, when you run out of things to thank him for, thank him for what you cannot see (which is infinitely greater!).

Thanksgiving should be unstinting; and if it is, it will lead to indefatigable joy. As Law says, it "turns all it touches into happiness."[2] Nothing can stop our God! He will sanctify us through and through, no matter what. He will present us blameless at his coming, no matter what. He is faithful and he will do it (1 Thess. 5:23-24)—no matter what. So, thank him, no matter what.

PRAYER: *Father, even though I can't see your love, wisdom, and power in these circumstances, I believe you are bigger than what I can see. I will praise you that you are powerful, and you are good in every circumstance of my life.*

DAY 315: OF SPARROWS AND STUFFED ANIMALS

Ben Patterson (1942-)

"Are not five sparrows sold for two pennies? Yet not one of them is forgotten by God. Indeed, the very hairs of your head are all numbered. Don't be afraid; you are worth more than many sparrows" (Luke 12:6-7).

I regretted praying the prayer the moment I prayed it; but it seemed to jump out of my mouth. After tucking in my eight-year-old son, Andy, I was saying a goodnight prayer at his bedside. He had been disconsolate for a week over the loss of his little stuffed animal, a gray wolf he named "Wolfie." Andy's grief would escalate at bedtime since Wolfie had been his sleeping companion. Seeing his furrowed little brow and moist eyes every night broke my heart. I had prayed for God to comfort him, and I had prayed that we would find Wolfie, but in that moment my spontaneous, non-premeditated prayer was, "Father, please show us where Wolfie is, so Andy will know how much you love him."

My first thought after the "Amen" was, What if I just wrote a check God won't sign? What if we don't find Wolfie? Will Andy now conclude that God doesn't love him? I resisted the urge to throw in a caveat and add, "But if we don't find Wolfie, help Andy to know you still love him anyway."

I got up from my knees and walked out Andy's bedroom door. Suddenly, a picture popped into my mind: it was Wolfie in a sleeping bag in a box in our attic. Was that where he was? There had been a sleepover for Andy's friends last week.... I climbed up into the attic and crawled through the dust to the box with the sleeping bags. I pulled one out, opened it, and there was Wolfie! I scrambled out of the attic and ran to Andy's room with the proof of God's love in my hand. Though he wasn't in the mood for theological reflection on the event, Andy was very grateful and held Wolfie to his chest as we thanked God for his goodness.

Had I engaged in a little theological reflection before my prayer, I probably wouldn't have prayed it. I probably would have dismissed it as trivial and selfish. I would have wanted to hedge my bets and not put God on trial lest the Almighty come up short in Andy's eyes. But having prayed the prayer, quite by accident—no, not by accident—I later engaged in a different kind of theological reflection. If our Heavenly Father notices sparrows and counts hairs, he knows where the "Wolfies" of our lives can be found. If God became a human to show us his face, he certainly must care about a child's face creased with sadness. Nothing is too hard, too big, or too small for his love.

PRAYER: *Gracious and tender Father in heaven! You know how we are formed. You understand that we are little and afraid and confused. Show us your tender mercy. Stoop down, Almighty One, take us by the hand, and take us home.*

DAY 316: PRAY FOR THE SUCCESS OF THE GOSPEL

2 Thessalonians 3:1-5

"Brothers, pray for us" (2 Thess. 3:1).

Napoleon said, "An army marches on its stomach." He knew the chow line was the backbone of the front line. The church, however, advances on its knees, by prayer. We stoop to conquer. With this truth in mind, Paul asked the Thessalonians to pray three things for his work as a church-planting apostle. (These three requests are also a great way to pray for every missionary, preacher, and teacher you know. Wait!—it is a great way for you to pray for your own efforts to speak the Word of God into the lives of others.)

First, pray that the Word of God will spread rapidly (2 Thess. 3:1a). The image is athletic and robust. We are not to pray merely for the Word of God to be listened to and considered, or for it to be given a fair hearing in the marketplace of ideas. We pray that the Word of God will bound into the minds and hearts of hearers like a runner sprinting down a track leaving all other ideas in the dust (Ps. 19:4b-6; 147:15)!

Second, pray that the Word of God will be honored (2 Thess. 3:1b). The Greek is literally, "run and be glorified." Maybe the picture here is of a victorious runner being crowned on the victor's stand. It is a prayer that what happened when the Thessalonians heard the Word of God would happen again and again: "you accepted it not as the word of men, but as the Word of God, which is at work in you who believe" (1 Thess. 2:13).

Third, pray that you will be delivered from "wicked and evil men" (2 Thess. 2:3). The sad truth is that sometimes those most in need of a doctor are those who least want one. They not only resist the Word of God themselves, but they also work to keep others from hearing it. Paul knew what he was talking about from personal experience (2 Cor. 11:23b-26). As we pray for the Word of God to run forward and to be honored, we must also pray for its messengers to be protected from evil.

PRAYER: *Dear Holy Spirit, anoint your messenger and your Word so that Truth might run and win and be crowned—and so that your messenger will be kept safe.*

Introduction to 1 and 2 Timothy

DAY 317: THE LEGACY OF AN OLD WARRIOR

"Fight the good fight of the faith" (1 Tim. 6:12).

A man's office has a wall covered with pictures of Martin Luther, C. S. Lewis, Flannery O'Connor, Dietrich Bonhoeffer, Francis Schaeffer, and others. He calls it his "Wall of Those Who Have Finished Strong." A friend was looking at the wall and joked, "Why isn't my picture there?" The man replied, "You have to be dead to get there." The race isn't over until it is over. We won't know how well we finished until we finish.

The drama of Paul's letters to Timothy is that he is near the end of his life, and Timothy is near the beginning of his. Athletic and military metaphors abound as Paul strives to finish well and encourages Timothy to do the same. There is a fight to fight, a race to run, a prize to take hold of. Paul knew that for him to finish well, it would involve not only how he finished, but also how Timothy finished. The race is a relay; its success depends on how well he passes the baton to the next runner. None of us is really finished, until everyone is finished (Heb. 11:39—12:1).

The passionate prayer of a faithful soldier of Christ to see the next generation take up the same cross and be found faithful is woven throughout these letters. Paul's prayer might well have been the prayer of another old man in the Bible: "Even when I am old and gray, do not forsake me, O God, till I proclaim your power to the next generation, your might to all who are to come" (Ps. 71:18). Read these letters and pray with Paul for the next generation.

PRAYER: *Lord, you promised that the righteous will, "still bear fruit in old age, they will stay fresh and green" (Ps. 92:14). Grant that because of the righteousness of my Lord and Savior Jesus Christ, I will approach my last days faithfully and fruitfully.*

DAY 318: GUILT, GRACE, AND GRATITUDE

1 Timothy 1:12-17

"Christ Jesus came into the world to save sinners—of whom I am the worst" (1 Tim. 1:15).

Just how bad a sinner was Paul before his conversion? Wrong question. Paul spoke in the present tense when he said to Timothy, "Here is a trustworthy saying that deserves full acceptance: Christ Jesus came into the world to save sinners—of whom I *am* the worst" (1 Tim 1:15, italics added). It's true that there was a past tense to Paul's sinfulness. He described himself as a blasphemer, persecutor, and a violent man (1 Tim. 1:13). That word "violent" is particularly shameful. It is a word that describes one who took a sadistic pleasure in humiliating and inflicting pain on wrongdoers. Paul may have been keeping the letter of the law, but he went way beyond its spirit. That part of his life was over, but he still believed himself to be a great sinner. Paul's attitude toward himself is not unique among the great men and woman of God over the centuries. The closer they came to God, the more vividly they became aware of their sinfulness.

There is great value in this perspective, despite what we may think of its effect on self-esteem. Acknowledging our own sinfulness can keep us humble as few things can. A Russian proverb says nothing ages faster than memory. If we lose our memory of what we were, we lose our gratitude for what God has forgiven. Humility erodes quickly. What is left is a kind of amnesic pride. We reason subconsciously that we are not really that bad. This forgetfulness and self-satisfaction is fatal to the life of the Spirit because it implies that Christ didn't really have to be beaten and to die nailed to a cross to secure our freedom. All we ever needed was some good advice, not radical redemption. That last line is the creed of the lukewarm church.

Instead of making one morose, a good memory of what Christ forgave keeps joy alive. John Newton had been a slave-trader before his conversion. Throughout his life, he never forgot that fact. Nevertheless, he was the most gentle and cheerful of men, not in spite of his memory, but because of it. He wrote as his own epitaph: "John Newton... once and Infidel and Libertine... was by the Mercy of our Lord and Savior Jesus Christ, Preserved, Restored, Pardoned and Appointed to Preach the faith he had so long labored to destroy."

PRAY THIS PRAYER OF KIERKEGAARD: *"Father in Heaven! Hold not our sins up against us but hold us up against our sins, so that the thought of Thee when it wakens in our soul, and each time it wakens, should not remind us of what we have committed but of what Thou didst forgive, not of how we went astray but of how Thou didst save us!"*[1]

DAY 319: FIRST PRIORITY

1 Timothy 2:1-8

"I urge, then, first of all, that requests, prayers, intercession and thanksgiving be made for everyone"(1 Tim. 2:1).

One New Year's Day, the whole Tournament of Roses parade ground to a halt when a beautiful float sputtered and stalled. It had run out of gas, and the whole parade had to wait until it was refueled. The amusing part of the incident was that the float represented the Standard Oil Company! As large as its oil resources were, they were of no use to the float unless someone remembered to fuel the vehicle. That huge, lovely, immobile float on Colorado Boulevard in Pasadena is a picture of a prayerless church—blessed with all the vast resources of God but going nowhere. Paul urged Timothy to not let this happen to the church he pastored by reminding him of four things about prayer:

1. Prayer is urgent and of primary importance (1 Tim. 2:1a). "I urge, then, first of all..." Prayer should demand our immediate and frequent attention.

2. Prayer is all-inclusive (1 Tim. 2:1b-6). There are seven Greek words for prayer used throughout the Bible. Four of them are used in this passage. We are to pray in all ways, always, for all people—even people like the godless Nero, the king mentioned in verse two. Prayer is one of the great, multi-purpose "alls" of Scripture.

3. Prayer is founded on God's great passion to save people (1 Tim. 2:4a). The God we address in prayer "wants all men to be saved," so we must pray to him for their salvation.

4. Prayer is intimately linked to Jesus' great prayer for the church to be one, so the world will know God sent him (John 17). Paul's instruction that people pray together without anger or disputing is another way of praying for the church to be one (2 Tim. 2:8).

The fourth point raises a very important issue. It is significant that Paul's concern in this passage was for the prayer life of the gathered church—or corporate prayer. The recovery of this vital practice may be the greatest need in the modern church. When most people think of prayer, they think of individual, private prayer. As valuable as that is, when the Bible speaks of prayer, it is most often about corporate prayer. As Jesus said, "where two or three come together in my name, there am I with them" (Matt. 18:20).

PRAYER: *Lord, teach us to always pray, as of first importance, in all ways, for all people.*

DAY 320: PRAY TO FIGHT A GOOD FIGHT

1 Timothy 6:11-16

"Fight the good fight of the faith" (1 Tim. 6:12).

The language in this passage calls for strong exertion or a "muscular faith." We encounter words like "flee," "pursue," "fight the good fight," "take hold," and "I charge you." Jesus was clear that we have no strength in ourselves (John 15:1-5). However, we are not to think of ourselves as powerless—quite the opposite. We are to be strong in the grace of God, exerting ourselves in the strength of the Holy Spirit, living and praying with the focused aggressiveness and passion of a fighter (see devotional on Colossians 4:2-4; 12-13).

Why? We are faced with a great and challenging choice—an either/or. On the one hand, there could be great loss; on the other, great gain (1 Tim. 6:6-12). There is something to fear greatly and something to desire greatly. The choice is literally between "ruin and destruction" (1 Tim. 6:9) and "eternal life' (1 Tim. 6:12). To make matters worse, the enemy of our souls would deceive us into fearing what we shouldn't fear; and not fearing what we should. The gravity of the choice we face is not always apparent to us.

We need prayer to match the weight of such a choice. We need a powerful God to make us strong enough to see the choice for what it is—destruction or life—and to choose life. He is, "God, the blessed and only Ruler, the King of kings and Lord of lords, who alone is immortal and who lives in unapproachable light" (1 Tim. 6:15, 16). We need to cultivate such a clear vision of this God in adoring prayer that we readily flee from what obscures his glory, and we pursue what reveals it. We need to delight in God, the way an athlete delights to run a race.

It is not enough to fear evil; we must develop what Thomas Chalmers called "the expulsive power of a new affection." In the Greek myth, when Ulysses passed the Isle of the Sirens, he tied himself to the mast and stopped his ears with wax that he might not hear their song and be destroyed. His was a negative goodness. Orpheus, however, sat on the deck, and survived by playing his own music, a music far more beautiful than that of the Sirens. His was a positive goodness—a muscular faith.

PRAYER: *Father in Heaven! Take away anything that dims my vision of your glory or dulls my appetite for the Scriptures or distracts me from prayer so that I may fight the good fight and take hold of eternal life.*

DAY 321: FAN THE FLAME

2 Timothy 1:1-14

"Fan into flame the gift of God" (2 Tim. 1:6).

Service to Christ is carried out the same way a fire burns: by building it, lighting it, feeding it, poking it, stirring it, and fanning it. Paul told Timothy to "fan into flame the gift of God" (2 Tim. 1:6) by reminding him of how the fire was first built in his heart. He said, "Remember the kind of man your mother and grandmother made you" (2 Tim. 1:5). Their sincere faith had been passed on to him. Theologian Karl Barth was once asked if he could summarize everything he had learned about theology over a lifetime of study. He responded, "Yes, I can. In the words of a song I learned at my mother's knee: 'Jesus loves me, this I know, for the Bible tells me so.'"[1] Barth's answer wasn't flippant. The power of parents to build a fire in a man or woman is inestimable.

The power of trusted and wise mentors is also powerful. Paul reminded Timothy of how the wood was stacked and arranged in his heart by Paul's example (2 Tim. 1:10-11). There is a saying worth putting into practice: Everyone needs a Timothy, a Paul, and a Barnabas in their life—someone to mentor, someone to be mentored by, and someone to walk with as a peer. These relationships keep the fire burning.

But a fire must be lit to burn. That is the meaning of the reference to the laying on of Paul's hands (2 Tim. 1:6) and to the kind of spirit God gave Timothy: "not of timidity, but of power, of love and of self-discipline" (2 Tim. 1:7). Like stacking word for a fire, the bones can be assembled in the valley of dry bones, but the Spirit must be blown into them for them to live (Ezek. 37:1-14). So, Paul also reminded Timothy of the kind of man God had made him through his Spirit.

A fire must be fed. That's the importance of knowing the word of God (see the next devotional on 2 Timothy 3:14-17). Christ's servants must remember what the word of God has made them and is continuing to make them. Then the fire must be poked and stirred and fanned again and again. Left alone, a fire will die. Christian service must be continually cultivated by the Scriptures, the memory of what others have made us, and the knowledge of what God has made us.

PRAYER: *Dear Lord: You have given me your Spirit and the Holy Scriptures. Give also a love for your Word and for the people, as well as the memory I need to keep the fire burning in my heart.*

DAY 322: GOD'S BREATH IN MAN RETURNING

2 Timothy 3:16-17

"All Scripture is God-breathed" (2 Tim. 3:16).

The twenty-nine words that comprise 2 Timothy 3:16-17 are nothing short of remarkable. They are the most carefully considered, precise, authoritative, and balanced statement of the origin, use and purpose of the Bible that is in the Bible. Paul even coined a word to accomplish this: "God-breathed."

These words also give the best rationale in Scripture for praying Scripture, especially given that they were written to people experiencing persecution (2 Tim. 3:10-12) and apostasy (2 Tim. 3:1-5, 13). Paul's assessment of the world we live in is sobering: "everyone who wants to live a godly life in Christ Jesus will be persecuted, while evil men and impostors will go from bad to worse, deceiving and being deceived" (2 Tim. 3:12-13). It's not easy to be a follower of Jesus as there is pressure on all sides to go the world's way. We need the strength of God to stay faithful. As P. T. Forsyth put it, "If we find nothing over us, we succumb to what is around us."[1] The Scriptures give that strength. But it comes not from merely knowing the data of Scripture, but from knowing the God who breathes his breath in them.

The word Paul coined, "God-breathed," gives a beautiful picture of what it means to pray the word of God. George Herbert's poem, "Prayer (1)" describes prayer as "God's breath in man returning to his birth."[2] In other words, the breath of God that gives us life (Gen. 2:7), we breathe back to him in prayer. Paul's word suggests that in the Bible we meet God again, as in creation, and we are renewed and revived as we "inhale" the truth of God and "exhale" that truth back in prayer. In God-breathed Scripture, we encounter afresh the breath of God; and when we pray Scripture, we breathe back what is breathed into us!

Paul used four precisely chosen words to describe how God's breath is breathed in Scripture. He said the Bible is useful for teaching, rebuking, correcting, and training in righteousness. Paraphrased, the Bible teaches us what is true, rebukes us for what is false, sets us on the right path, and conditions our spiritual muscles to stay on the right path. Pray the word of God! Pray to understand it, pray back to God what you understand, and then pray for more understanding.

PRAYER: *"Breathe on me, Breath of God, / Fill me with life anew, That I may love what Thou dost love, / And do what Thou wouldst do" (from the hymn "Breathe on Me, Breath of God" by Edwin Hatch).*

DAY 323: FINISHING STRONG

2 Timothy 4:1-8

"I have fought the good fight, I have finished the race, I have kept the faith" (2 Tim. 4:7).

"The whole trouble in life today is that people only look at the beginning," wrote Martyn Lloyd-Jones.[1] He called this the "cinema" or "film" view of life. We could add that it is also the celebrity and glamour magazine view of life. Everybody looks so young and fresh and beautiful and cool. It is easy to think that this is *la dolce vita*, the good life. But the real question is not, *where are these people now?* The question should be, *where will they be?* The pressing concern is not where people begin, but where they end. What is the trajectory of their lives? Will they finish strong? Wesley boasted of the early Methodists, "Our people die well." *Will they? Will you?*

This is a tender passage. An old man, a father in the faith who is near death, is giving some parting words of encouragement to a young man, his son in the faith. Paul's words to Timothy are stirring and "muscular" in their impact: "In the presence of God and of Christ Jesus, who will judge the living and the dead, and in view of his appearing and his kingdom, I give you this charge… keep your head in all situations, endure hardship, do the work of an evangelist, discharge all the duties of your ministry" (2 Tim. 4:1, 5). Paul seals his encouragement to faithfulness in the strongest possible way—by his own example. He writes, "For I am already being poured out like a drink offering, and the time for my departure is near. I have fought the good fight, I have finished the race, I have kept the faith" (2 Tim. 4:6-7).

Timothy is at the beginning of his life, and Paul is near the end of his. Will Timothy finish well like Paul? Will you? The only way to finish strong is to do now what you want to be found doing at the end. The road before Timothy, and before all of us, calls for "a long obedience in the same direction" (Nietzsche). The Christian life is a marathon, not a sprint, and the crown of righteousness belongs to those who persevere. Persevere in prayer, that you may persevere in life.

PRAYER: *O Righteous Judge: May I, by your grace, die well. Strengthen me to live in such a way now that at the end of my life I can say, "I have fought the good fight, I have finished the race, I have kept the faith."*

DAY 324: A GREAT AND HUMBLE MIND

Samuel Johnson (1709-1784)

"For the foolishness of God is wiser than man's wisdom, and the weakness of God is stronger than man's strength" (1 Cor. 1:35).

When a man who had been very unhappy in marriage, immediately remarried after the death of his wife, Samuel Johnson described his act as "the triumph of hope over experience."[1] Johnson was easily amused and inflamed by his own and other's foibles, and he could express either sentiment with elegance, biting wit, and devastating sarcasm. He was greatly to be feared as an opponent in an argument. Once when insulted, he replied, "A fly, Sir, may sting a stately horse and make him wince; but one is but an insect, and the other a horse still."[2] After an evening of conversation marked by spirited debate and repartee, Johnson remarked to Boswell, his biographer, that the conversation had been good. Boswell agreed, and said, "Yes, Sir; you tossed and gored several persons."[3]

But his sharpest jabs were directed at those skeptics who ridiculed the Christian faith he so cherished. The eighteenth century, like the twentieth, was a time when intellectuals and aesthetes treated the faith with contempt. Joseph Butler said it was, "an agreed point among people of discernment" that the faith was worthy only "as a principle subject of mirth and ridicule, as it were by way of reprisals, for so long having interrupted the pleasures of the world."[4] Of these skeptics, Johnson wrote, "Truth is a cow which will yield such people no more milk, and so they are gone to milk the bull."[5]

But the man with the proud and formidable intellect before people was a child before God. His great mind was humbled before a greater God. Johnson's prayers reveal a man with a deep, even tortured, sense of his own sinfulness. Trust in God's mercy did not come easily to Johnson, but it did come. He was always grateful and humbled that it did.

PRAY THIS PRAYER OF SAMUEL JOHNSON'S: *O merciful God, full of compassion, long-suffering, and of great pity, who sparest when we deserve punishment, and in thy wrath thinkest upon mercy; make me earnestly to repent, and heartily to be sorry for all my misdoings; make the remembrance so burdensome and painful, that I may flee to Thee with a troubled spirit and a contrite heart; and, O merciful Lord, visit, comfort, and relieve me; cast me not out from Thy presence, and take not thy Holy Spirit from me, but excite in me true repentance; give me in this world knowledge of thy truth, and confidence in thy mercy, and in the world to come life everlasting, for the sake of our Lord and savior, thy Son Jesus Christ. Amen.*[6]

Introduction to Titus

DAY 325: HOW TO PRAY FOR THE CHURCH

"Teach what is in accord with sound doctrine" (Titus 2:1).

The saying, "It's hard to fly like an eagle when you are surrounded by turkeys," is a humorous way of describing how our community or close relationships can hold us back. It can also be an excuse. Far more powerful than the people we live with, is the culture we share with them. These common beliefs, attitudes, and values (often assumed and unexamined) come to us, as it were, with our mother's milk. Or, to change the metaphor, you don't ask a fish to tell you what water is like. Some things we don't understand because they are too distant, others because they are too close. Whether we fully understand it or not, our culture has a powerful influence, for good or for bad.

Crete, the Mediterranean island where Titus was a pastor, was renowned for its culture of avarice and greed. The Greek poet Epimenides, whom Paul quoted in the letter, expressed a widely held opinion when he wrote, "Cretans are always liars, evil brutes, lazy gluttons" (Titus 1:12). To "Cretanize" meant to lie and cheat. According to William Barclay, "to cretize against a Cretan," meant to match lies with lies. The very phrase "Cretan church" is almost an oxymoron.

If this was the culture the Cretan church was planted in, how could the church be in the world, but not of it? Paul's letter to Titus proposed a strategy for how to do this and a way to pray for any church—especially a church planted in a culture as virulent as Crete's.

1. Pray for the leaders of the church (Titus 1:5-9). A church will go no further spiritually than its leaders have gone.
2. Pray for the church to know and do what is good. Paul underlined the need for this kind of moral vision (Titus 1:16; 2:7, 14; 3:1, 8, 14).
3. Pray for the church to understand the distinctiveness of the faith it professes. Compared to other books of the New Testament, Titus has a disproportionate number of classic creedal summaries. Each one is crystalline in clarity and beauty (Titus 1:1-3; 2:11-14; 3:3-7).

PRAYER: *Lord, renew my mind—renew* our *minds so that we will no longer be conformed to the pattern of this world, but transformed by the mind of Christ (Rom. 12:1, 2).*

DAY 326: GOOD SHEPHERDS

Titus 1:5-9

"Appoint elders in every town" (Titus 1:5).

No one is surprised when a wolf behaves like a wolf. It's a different matter altogether when a shepherd doesn't act the way a shepherd is supposed to act. Wolves naturally want to eat sheep. They are carnivores, it's the way they are made. Shepherds are appointed to protect sheep, but it's not their nature—it's their choice and their responsibility. Wolves can be wolves, but as long as a shepherd chooses to be a shepherd, the sheep will be safe. Jesus had some pretty strong opinions about how this ought to be (John 10:11-15).

Paul advised Titus on the qualities of a shepherd and the choices a shepherd (or elder) must make to be a good leader. It is a total package, involving family (Titus 1:6), personal and social qualities (Titus 1:7-8), and belief (Titus 1:9). Family, personal, and social qualities are as important as belief. But it should be kept in mind that belief plays a pivotal role in the mix. Most people are worse than their principles; but their behavior reflects on the person, not the principles. The point is that the elder's confession of faith should be as orthodox and pure as the church expects their lives to be. It is significant that this short letter has three summaries of Christian theology that are gems of gospel truth (Titus 1:1-3; 2:11-14; 3:3-7). Paul establishes a vital connection between faith and morality.

A good elder should think like Jesus and behave like Jesus, the Good Shepherd. In the early days of telescopes, the image of the heavenly body being observed came through the lens to a mirror which reflected the image to the eye of the astronomer. The leaders of the church have the great duty and privilege of reflecting the image of Christ to the people of the church. They, along with all believers, have the awesome responsibility of making "the teaching about God our Savior attractive" (Titus 2:10). The job is everyone's in the church, but if the elders fail at it, the chances that the others will succeed are greatly diminished. Do you pray for your leaders according to the Bible's profile of their character and faith?

PRAYER: *Make verses 6-9 a prayer for your churches' leadership. Pray something like, "Dear Lord, may ____________________ be faithful in marriage, blameless in public life, not overbearing, not quick tempered..." and so on.*

DAY 327: FROM SLAVES TO CHILDREN

Titus 3:3-8

"He saved us, not because of righteous things we have done, but because of his mercy" (Titus 3:5).

Jesus said no one can serve two masters; for we will always hate one and love the other. That's the way God made us. We are naturally monotheists. No matter how many gods we think we have, we end up worshiping either the true and living God or some substitute god—an idol. The great German theologian, Helmut Thielicke, commented that everyone must serve one of two masters—the choice is not whether, but who. One master, however, will make us slaves; the other will make us children. God's servants are his children who serve him freely, out of love and gratitude. Actually, Thielicke was only summarizing things Jesus and the apostles had already said (Matt. 5:16; Rom. 8:15).

The structure of this confession of faith in Titus 3:5 is consistent with Jesus' warning about two masters. It provides a "before and after" picture. Before we were "enslaved by all kinds of passions and pleasures"—things like malice, envy, foolishness, disobedience, deception, and hatred (Titus 3:3-4). Paradoxically, we were enslaved to pleasures and couldn't stop having "fun." What was touted as freedom was really slavery. This situation is like the depressed woman who went to a New York psychiatrist complaining of the effects of her lifestyle of sex, drugs, and partying. When he asked her why she didn't just stop living that way, she looked puzzled and said, "You mean, I don't have to keep doing what I want to do?"

After such slavery, we were saved, washed, reborn, renewed, justified, and made heirs of eternal life (Titus 3:5-8). What a list! A new relationship was established. Formerly we were slaves, but now we are devoted "to doing what is good" (Titus 3:8). "Devotion" is a word related to love. "Good" means "excellent and profitable for everyone" (Titus 3:8). "Devotion to good" is the loving obedience of beloved children. It is the response of men and women who are glad and grateful for the grace of God that set them free.

Enslaved or devoted—take your pick. But if you have been set free, let your devotion begin with frequent prayers of praise and thanksgiving. Recite today's passage using your own name for "we" and "our." Be amazed at God's goodness. Let the liberated of the Lord say so! (Ps. 107:1-2)

PRAYER: *"O for a thousand tongues to sing, My great Redeemer's praise, The glories of my God and King, The triumphs of his love" (from the hymn by Charles Wesley).*

Introduction to Philemon

DAY 328: A PRAYER FOR JUSTICE AND RECONCILIATION

"I appeal to you on the basis of love" (Philem. 9).

Recognizing who others are in the sight of God is the foundation of true justice. As valuable as laws and social programs are, they cannot replace this fundamental shift in human consciousness. When Paul urged Philemon to forgive and receive his runaway slave, Onesimus, "no longer as a slave, but better than a slave, a brother" (Philem. 16), he sowed a seed that would ultimately destroy the very basis for slavery. To call for the abolition of slavery in that time would have been to perform a radical act—and to fail. But to invite a Christian slave owner to see his slave as a brother was to do something even more radical, and subversive. For Philemon to do this would mean a change in his heart. The human heart is the wellspring of life (Prov. 4:23) and the place where the most radical of changes begin.

Prayer for justice and reconciliation is a radical act too for it takes a changed heart to pray for these things. As Paul's prayer for Philemon shows, it also looks for a changed heart in others.

PRAYER: *Father in heaven! Open my eyes to see people as you see them.*

DAY 329: DO WHAT IS GOOD TO KNOW WHAT IS GOD

Philemon 6

"I pray that you may be active in sharing your faith" (Philem. 6).

A lawyer wanted to know how to get eternal life. Jesus told him to love God with his whole being and to love his neighbor as himself. Insincerely, the lawyer then asked Jesus who his neighbor was. Jesus told him who his neighbor was, and added, "Go and do likewise" (Luke 10:25-37). That's the usual sequence: find out what is good, then do what is good. Know the truth, then do the truth.

But sometimes it works the other way: do the truth so you can know the truth. That's what Paul was driving at when he prayed for Philemon: "I pray that you will be active in sharing your faith, so that you will have a full understanding of every good thing we have in Christ" (Philem. 6). Philemon already knew a lot about the faith, but there were things he could understand only by doing—like forgiving his former slave and receiving him back as a brother in Christ.

In the Bible, knowledge involves so much more than the mind. It involves one's whole being. When Adam knew his wife Eve, she got pregnant. Their knowledge consisted in getting their bodies together, not just their brains. Like the lawyer in his encounter with Jesus, Philemon needed to *do* the truth so he could really *know* the truth.

We can pray for others to have their eyes opened to know the truth by acting on it. We can pray this prayer for ourselves, too. Nothing is more critical for the growth of justice in a society than that people begin to see others as God sees them. There is no better view than the view you get when you serve and are reconciled to those you have hurt and who have hurt you.

PRAYER: *Lord, teach me and strengthen me to pray only for things to be done that I am willing to do. Holy Spirit, unite my heart with my mind and my body.*

Introduction to Hebrews

DAY 330: APPROACH THE THRONE OF GRACE WITH CONFIDENCE

"Let us then approach the throne of grace with confidence" (Heb. 4:16).

In C.S. Lewis's story, *The Last Battle*, the heroes have been transported from the land of Narnia to Aslan's Land. (Aslan's Land is to Narnia what heaven is to earth.) What strikes the characters, however, is how much like Narnia Aslan's Land is—yet different, too. They can see familiar landmarks—mountains, rivers, and towns—but in Aslan's Land these features of Narnia can only be described as "more like the real thing." In fact, they conclude that Aslan's Country is the real Narnia. The old Narnia was "only a shadow or copy of the real Narnia, which has always been here and always will be here." In his excitement, one of the characters speaks for them all when he says, "I have come home at last! This is my real country! I belong here. This is the land I have been looking for all my life, though I never knew it till now. The reason we loved the old Narnia is that it sometimes looked a little like this."[1]

The book of Hebrews makes a similar pronouncement on the relation of Christ to the laws, sacrifices, and prophets of the Old Testament. Two Greek words for "better" and "superior" occur fifteen times in the book—all in relation to Jesus. All that came before him was a copy or shadow of the real thing. Jesus is the real thing, the fulfillment of the old. The reason the old was so good was that it was a little like the new. "In the past God spoke to our forefathers through the prophets at many times and in various ways, but in these last days he has spoken to us by his Son, whom he appointed heir of all things, and through whom he made the universe. The Son is the radiance of God's glory, and the exact representation of his being" (Heb. 1:1-3).

The portrayal of Jesus as the perfect high priest makes Hebrews perhaps the most important book in the New Testament on prayer. One of the great challenges to biblical faith has always been access to God. How can sinful people come into the presence of a holy God? The answer, under the Old Covenant, was through sacrifices and the ministrations of the priesthood. The message of Hebrews is that these things were only copies and shadows of Jesus—the perfect priest and sacrifice. Jesus opened the way to God, and because he still lives to intercede for us, we may come into God's presence with confidence (Heb. 7:25; also 2:17-18; 4:15-16; 6:19-20; 10:19-25).

PRAYER: *Father in Heaven, give me the faith and vision to live by the unseen realities.*

DAY 331: HE WAS ONE OF US

Hebrews 2:5-18

"For this reason he had to be made like his brothers in every way" (Heb. 2:17).

One way to approach this marvelous text is by opening a book on childcare and scanning the index. Try reading the list of childhood diseases and behavioral issues knowing that Jesus was fully human. Preface each reference with something like, "Jesus was susceptible to…" Then read, whooping cough, colic, measles, mumps, colds. Consider that "Jesus may very well have…" sucked his thumb, been curious about dangerous objects, or clung to his mother around strangers. The purpose of this suggestion is not to be irreverent (or to imply that the infant Jesus was sinful), but to explore the rich meaning of the phrase, "he had to be made like his brothers in every way" (Heb. 2:17). True, the writer is speaking of much more than childhood issues. He has in mind the whole range of things that make up what it means to be a human being. Jesus was one of us.

The point is, if you find it hard to pray because of shame or fear of judgment, this passage is good news for you. Jesus is your brother. He knows what it means to be a human being (Heb. 2:14). He knows what it's like to be afraid and tempted and weak. Because he was made like you in every way, he understands your vulnerability. Though Jesus himself never gave in to temptation, he is inclined toward mercy, not censure (Heb. 4:15).

Jesus is also your high priest. In Old Testament times, the high priest was the one who went into the holy place, stood before God on behalf of the people, and interceded for them by offering a sacrifice—first for his own sins and then for the sins of the people (Heb. 5:1-3). By offering the sacrifice, the priest provided a "bridge" between the people and God. Jesus, the better high priest, made himself this bridge! As a human, Jesus prays for us with great sympathy because he has experienced our weakness and the temptations we encounter. As God's sinless Son, he speaks to God on our behalf as no earthly high priest ever could (Heb. 7:25). Put away shame and fear when you come to Jesus. He knows all there is to know about you, and he will be merciful.

PRAYER: *Jesus, you know me inside and out; and you still love me and sympathize with my weaknesses. Thank you!*

DAY 332: STUNNED CONFIDENCE

Hebrews 4:14-16

"Let us then approach the throne of grace with confidence" (Heb. 4:16).

There are different kinds of confidence. There is the cocksure confidence of the athlete who has never been challenged, or the thrill of the daredevil who loves heights and danger. There is the foolish confidence of one who is blissfully ignorant of what is at stake—like a toddler blithely waddling into rush hour traffic. Then there is the rare and wonderful confidence of one stunned, amazed, and trembling at what he is doing—like the novice fighter pilot on his first solo flight. This is the confidence of a man or woman who realizes the miracle and utterly undeserved privilege of entering the presence of God. Such confidence is described in verse 16: "Let us then approach the throne of grace with confidence, so that we may receive mercy and find grace to help us in our time of need."

This is the second time the author of Hebrews has spoken of Jesus' great sympathy with our weaknesses. He reminds us of Jesus' sympathy to encourage fearful believers to approach God with confidence. You should ask yourself questions like, "Do I need that reminder? Or does it seem self-evident to me? Am I so accustomed to the gift that it seems no longer a gift, but an entitlement? Is my confidence cocksure or foolish?"

We must not forget that it is a wonderful privilege to enter the presence of a holy God and address him as Father. Philosopher Peter Kreeft speaks a corrective to the cocksure and foolish:

> *We appreciate how incredible this intimacy is only after we have learned the opposite lesson, God's awesomeness and infinite otherness, the distinctively Jewish revelation of God as transcendent Creator. Only after we are Jews can we be Christians; only after we know God in awe can we know God in intimacy. "The fear [awe] of the Lord is the beginning of wisdom" and filial intimacy is the end.*[1]

When you pray, pray boldly—as one stunned and amazed at the privilege.

PRAYER: *O Holy One! How kind of you to open wide the doors of communion through the precious blood of Jesus. May I never tire of thanking you or grow callous to the gift.*

DAY 333: TAKE MY LIFE

Frances Havergal (1836-1879)

"Therefore I urge you, brothers, in view of God's mercy, to offer your bodies as living sacrifices, holy and pleasing to God" (Rom. 12:1).

By most standards, the young Miss Frances Havergal was an exceptional Christian. By age twenty-two, she had memorized large portions of Scripture including all four Gospels, all of the Epistles, the Book of Revelation, Psalms, and Isaiah. In later years she also learned the Minor Prophets by heart. It was common for her to pray three times a day.

She was also very beautiful and gifted with a lovely voice that had her performing before large audiences. Furthermore, she was a talented poet and hymn writer. At age nine, Frances was already composing long letters to her friends in perfect rhyme.

But there was something missing in her life. She so longed to know more of Christ and to be more fully consecrated to him that she was restless in spirit and often disconsolate. A hymn she wrote at age twenty-two touched on the source of her yearning. In the lyrics, Jesus questioned her:

I gave My life for thee,
My precious blood I shed,
That thou might'st ransomed be,
And quickened from the dead;
I gave, I gave My life for thee,
What hast thou given for Me?[1]

It seemed to Frances that such immense love on Christ's part demanded an equal measure of love and dedication, or consecration, from her. This consecration is the effect of a deeper understanding of the vast dimensions of a love that surpasses knowledge (Eph. 3:18-19).

This realization came to her on Advent Sunday, December 2, 1873. Frances described it to her sister Maria as the day, "I first saw clearly the blessings of true consecration. I saw it as a flash of electric light, and what you see, you can never unsee. There must be full surrender before there can be full blessedness."[2] Her famous hymn, "Take My Life and Let it Be" grew out of that defining spiritual experience. It was her lifelong prayer, and it has become the prayer of all those who know that surrender is the path to blessedness.

PRAYER: *As a simple prayer, pray this line from Havergal's hymn, "Take my life and let it be consecrated, Lord, to Thee."*[3]

DAY 334: LOUD CRIES AND TEARS

Hebrews 5:7-10

"During the days of Jesus' life on earth, he offered up prayers and petitions with loud cries and tears" (Heb. 5:7).

When his disciples asked him to teach them to pray, they probably didn't have this part in mind: "During the days of Jesus' life on earth, he offered up prayers and petitions with loud cries and tears" (Heb. 5:7). They eventually began to learn this part of prayer too, as all who enter Christ's school of prayer will. Gethsemane and the cross still lay ahead, as they do in their many forms for all believers.

But what on earth does it mean that "he learned obedience from what he suffered" (Heb. 5:8)? Was it that Jesus had a few lessons to learn? Was he a little disobedient when he arrived on earth but got that straightened out before he left? No, not at all. It was that his obedience was completed when he carried out his mission to the full extent. What he "learned" was not to obey, but where his obedience would take him, experientially. He made himself nothing and humbled himself and became obedient to death, even death on a cross (Phil. 2:7-8). Jesus knew what would happen before he came to earth, and he was committed to it. In this sense, he had no obedience to learn. But in another sense, he had much to learn—in the same way a traveler learns what is on the map by traveling the roads. We, of course, have much *more* to learn. And learn it we will in Christ's school of prayer. Where our Master goes, we will too.

"He was heard because of his reverent submission" (Heb. 5:7). Though he was a Son, Jesus learned obedience. Because he was a Son, he was heard. The distinguishing mark of our Lord's Sonship was more than his unique relationship to God; it was his reverent submission to the will of God. At bottom, this is what it means to pray in the name of Jesus. It is to wrap all our petitions in adoration and reverent submission to our Father in the same way our Savior and brother prayed. This is what it means to pray like Jesus.

PRAYER: *Lord Jesus, blessed Savior and brother, thank you for the way you prayed and obeyed. Teach us to pray that way: confident in our relationship to the Father, deeply dependent, reverent, and obedient.*

DAY 335: THE ANCHOR

Hebrews 6:13-20

"We have this hope as an anchor for the soul" (Heb. 6:19).

There are some things that will never change, and this is one of them. Jesus "has become a high priest forever, in the order of Melchizedek" (Heb. 6:20). (We'll get to the Melchizedek part.) Do you know what Jesus is doing right now, this very moment, and will be doing forever? Hint, jump ahead in Hebrews and read 7:25: "he always lives to intercede." Right now, Jesus is praying for you. These things will never change—God will never lie, and Jesus will never leave his side or stop praying for us. Delight in the fact that Jesus is praying for you. Better yet, start praying. This is likely one of the things Jesus is praying for you to do!

The Old Testament Melchizedek (Gen. 14:18-20) is seen here as a prefigure of Jesus—a picture that helps us understand who Jesus is and what he came to do. Melchizedek seems to come on the scene out of nowhere. There is no mention of parents, children, birth, or death. What makes him significant is that he is both a priest and a king. Like Melchizedek, Jesus is also both king and priest—but unlike Melchizedek, he stands as king and priest forever.

This hope—that Jesus stands as king and priest forever—serves as an anchor for the soul. It's probably a little confusing to visualize, but imagine an anchor thrown out to secure a ship in its place. Similarly, Jesus has gone behind the curtain of the Holy of Holies and stands there as high priest, for us. Nothing can move him from that place, and therefore nothing can move us from the hope we have in Christ (Rom. 8:38-39). We are anchored in it by Jesus himself. Early Christians appreciated this truth so much that the anchor (along with the fish and a ship) was one of its favorite symbols of the church.

There is great comfort in this anchor—and great encouragement to pray. We may feel tossed about by life's storms, but we are anchored in faith by Jesus. We may be distracted and anxious in prayer, but we are anchored in hope. We may lose all speech and lie mute in grief, but our anchor holds, and our high priest lives to pray for us. We are anchored in him.

PRAYER: *Son of God and great High Priest, you are my anchor in heaven, my confidence, and my hope. Hear my prayers and answer me according to your mercy.*

DAY 336: PRAYER, ENCOURAGEMENT, AND THE FAMILY OF GOD

Hebrews 10:19-25

"Let us encourage one another" (Heb. 10:25).

Prayer is decidedly a family matter, a community activity. It is so much more than "me and God." It is, above all, "we and God." "No Christian is an only child."[1] Count the plurals in this text, the times words like "we," "you," "house" (read, "household"), and "brothers" appear. There are eighteen occurrences in just four sentences. What follows in chapters 11 and 12 reminds us that this family is very, very, big. It stretches out not only over space, but back in time. We live our life of faith before a great "cloud of witnesses" (Heb. 12:1) who came before. The Apostles' Creed calls the life of this family, "the communion of saints."

There is a direct link between the privilege of prayer and the responsibility of living together as a family. It's based on the "Therefore" in verse 19: "Therefore, brothers, since we have confidence to enter the Most Holy Place by the blood of Jesus... and since we have a great high priest over the house of God" (Heb. 10:19, 21). To come into the presence of the living God is always to come with a host of other people who, like you, have been given the same privilege. To ignore them is to reject the gift. "Prayer is an act, indeed the act of fellowship," wrote Peter Taylor Forsyth. "We cannot truly pray for ourselves without passing beyond ourselves and our individual experience.... Even private prayer is common prayer."[2]

A healthy church has a culture of encouragement and prayer. People consider how they may "spur one another on toward love and good deeds" (Heb. 10:24). The word translated "spur" is used usually in a negative sense, as in goading someone to fight. But here it is used of positive, proactive efforts we should make to produce love and goodness in one another. Since the privilege of prayer is the basis of the communion of saints, the encouragement to pray should sustain the communion. Tell a brother or sister in Christ that you are praying for them. Better, ask a fellow believer to pray with you.

PRAYER: *Dear Lord, I am thrilled and encouraged to know that I may pray to the God of Abraham, Isaac, and Jacob; to the God of Paul, Augustine, and Luther; to the God who unites me with all believers everywhere. Make me an encourager to all your family and a force for united prayer with all believers everywhere.*

DAY 337: PRAYER AND AWE

Hebrews 12:25-29

"Our 'God is a consuming fire'" (Heb. 12:29).

Here is a sobering item in the biblical view of time: One day, everything that can be shaken will be shaken. That "everything" is all things in heaven and earth (Heb. 12:26, 27). All that can be shaken will be removed, and only unshakable things will remain. God is a consuming fire, and the only unshakeable reality is the kingdom of God. Another way of saying this is: "The world and its desires pass away, but the man who does the will of God lives forever" (1 John 2:17). To be in this unshakeable kingdom is to be "part of the permanent."[1]

What things keep you from prayer? Know this: whatever they are, they are always shakable things that will pass away. Don't let the impermanent keep you away from the permanent.

Instead, be thankful and filled with reverence and awe that you can pray. That is part of what it means to "worship God acceptably" (Heb. 12:28). Gratitude is what must follow grace—like thunder follows lightning. What an incredible grace we have been given to be welcomed to a kingdom that is eternal. Neither death nor calamity nor demons can separate us from our King and our place in his kingdom (Rom. 8:31-39). So be grateful and pray, for prayer is the most important act of gratitude.[2]

You experience awe and reverence when you know how enormous the stakes are. The kingdom is a matter of life and death, heaven and hell. You have been saved as one snatched from certain death. Pray as one who knows this. The way to God has been opened to you. Enter boldly but don't swagger in or saunter as one who has forgotten the gravity and greatness of the gift.

Lastly, pray for others to be rescued from their slavery to things that will be shaken. Ask God to bring them into the kingdom that cannot be shaken (Col. 1:13). When you gather to worship, remind others that God is the lover of our souls, a tender father, but also a consuming fire—not a God to trifle with.

PRAYER: *Holy Father, give me such a vision of your holiness and tenderness that I will see no conflict between love and fear, but only feel a trembling awe and joy that I belong to a God as great as you.*

DAY 338: A SACRIFICE OF PRAISE

Hebrews 13:15

"Through Jesus, therefore, let us continually offer to God a sacrifice of praise—the fruit of lips that confess his name" (Heb. 13:15).

This simple sentence tells us a lot about who we are and how we are to live. If you are a Christian, that is if you confess Christ as your savior, you are a member of what the Bible elsewhere calls a holy priesthood: "You also, like living stones, are being built into a spiritual house to be a holy priesthood, offering spiritual sacrifices acceptable to God through Jesus Christ" (1 Pet. 2:5). In the Old Testament, priests were to reflect God's holiness, intercede for people before God, and represent God before people.

But what priests were most known for was the offering of sacrifices. The sacrifices were usually animals like lambs or goats, and they had three things in common. First the sacrifice was to be precious, the best that one had. Second, the sacrifice was to be total because death is total. Nothing could be held back. A sacrifice was, by definition, given with total abandon. Third, the sacrifice was to give life, symbolically. The point of a sacrifice was not death, but life, released through death. "For the life of a creature is in the blood" (Lev. 17:11). When blood was spilled, life was given, symbolically.

Because Christ is the complete sacrifice, the perfect atonement for our sins, the only sacrifice that can now have any legitimacy is a living sacrifice of praise on our part (Rom. 12:1-2). This is the sacrifice that pleases God. This is the fruit of lips that confess his name.

Try to imagine giving praise as sacrifice. Do you hold anything back? Of course not! Is your whole person involved—spirit, mind, and body? Absolutely! Does God get your best? Is your mind engaged, your emotions engaged, your attention total? Is your sacrifice of praise precious, total, and life-giving like Christ's sacrifice on the cross? Such extravagant grace calls for extravagant praise.

Poet George Herbert said humankind is the world's high priest.[1] We can offer what no other creature can: eloquence of words, clarity of thought, and depth of feeling unparalleled in the creation. How tragic if we refuse to offer what only we can offer, and the stones must cry out by (Luke 19:40).

PRAYER: *Holy Spirit, summon from my heart, mind, and body the best I have that I may truly offer a sacrifice of praise.*

DAY 339: PRAYER FOR ALL YOU REALLY NEED

Hebrews 13:20-21

"May the God of peace equip you with everything good for doing his will" (Heb. 13:20-21).

All you ever really need to desire and to ask for in life is in verse 21: "everything good for doing his will." The only one you ever need to ask is described in verse 20: "the God of peace, who through the blood of the eternal covenant brought back from the dead our Lord Jesus, that great Shepherd of the sheep."

Let's start with the only one you ever need to ask. Have you ever stood at a construction site for a giant building and watched the builders excavate the foundation? Deep holes are dug for massive pilings of concrete and steel upon which the great structure will be secured. The bigger and stronger the foundation, the greater the building will be. Spiritually speaking, great hopes for great things are guaranteed in great foundations. We have the greatest foundation for the greatest prayer in these three things:

> *The name of God: He is the God of peace, the one who has forgiven us and reconciled us to himself in Christ. Will he not also give us everything else that we need (Rom. 8:32)?*
>
> *The risen Shepherd: Jesus Christ is the Good Shepherd who laid down his life, and whom God raised from the dead. Nothing can separate us from his love (Rom. 8:37-39).*
>
> *The everlasting covenant. God has placed himself under major obligations and guaranteed his promise with his Son's blood. He will do nothing less than give us new hearts (Jer. 31:31-34; Ezek. 36:26-27).*

To change the metaphor, a threefold cord is not easily broken (Eccles. 4:12). This is the strongest of three: the name of God, the risen Shepherd, and the blood of the eternal covenant. Give God thanks! Praise his name!

Now, ask this God for what you need according to who he is. Ask him to give you and others, "everything good for doing his will." Everything. Don't be timid; ask him to work in you everything good for doing his will. Let your aspirations be as high as his purposes. Don't insult him by praying only little prayers. Pray the big prayers. Let your petitions rise as high as their foundation is deep.

PRAYER: *"My hope is built on nothing less that Jesus' blood and righteousness. I dare not trust the sweetest frame, but wholly lean on Jesus' name. On Christ the solid rock I stand, all other ground is sinking sand" (from the hymn, "My Hope is Built on Nothing Less," by Edward Mote).*

Introduction to James

DAY 340: PRACTICAL CHRISTIANITY

"The prayer of a righteous man is powerful and effective" (James 5:16).

The book of James is known for its espousal of "practical Christianity." The epigram, "faith without deeds is dead" (James 3:26) is a sharp rebuke to those who would divide faith and action. We are saved by faith, not by deeds, true. But real faith does something. With biting sarcasm, James says faith without deeds is the faith of the Devil whose knowledge of the facts about God is thoroughly orthodox. But, of course, the Devil does not want any part of doing what knowledge of God demands. "You believe that there is one God? Good! Even the devils believe that—and shudder" (James 2:19).

How significant that a book which is so practically-minded and action-oriented should have such strong passages about prayer. The wisdom we need to survive the rigors of the Christian life are to be had through prayer (James 1:5-8). Prayer is the one thing that "fits all sizes" or situations in life—trouble, joy, sickness, and reconciliation (James 5:13-18). The secularization of our culture may have us acting as though prayer has little practical power, but James knows better. Faith without works is dead; and prayer is one of the chief works of a robust faith. Prayer is practical and is the basis of all action under God. "You can do more than pray, after you have prayed," wrote A. J. Gordon. "But you can never do more than pray until you have prayed."[1]

PRAYER: *Father in Heaven! Let my prayers and my actions be one.*

DAY 341: WISDOM: DO YOU REALLY WANT IT?

James 1:2-8

"If any of you lacks wisdom, he should ask God" (James 1:5).

The Christian life is hard. You'll need a lot of help from God to live it, and he will give his help generously. But take note—the help you want may not be the kind of help he'll give.

The hard part of the Christian journey is that the road to heaven is uphill. There will be trials along the way—guaranteed (Acts 14:22; 2 Tim. 3:12). The even harder part is that you should regard the trials with "pure joy" because of the wonderful things they will do for your character. "The testing of your faith develops perseverance. Perseverance must finish its work so that you may be mature and complete, not lacking anything" (James 1:3-4). Harder than the trials themselves is the way the Lord wants us to respond to them! Most of us would be glad to just get through difficulties. But God wants us to get through them with pure joy and emerge from them "mature and complete, not lacking anything." For that we will need wisdom.

What is this wisdom? It is not so much knowing what to do as how to be. It is described in some detail in James 3:17 as qualities of character and perspective. These qualities include being "pure… peace-loving, considerate, submissive, full of mercy and good fruit, impartial, and sincere." This is the wisdom God gives to get through trials with pure joy. To understand the strength of this wisdom, think of its opposite qualities. These include being impure, combative, inconsiderate, rebellious, and vindictive. People like this will never get through trials with pure joy—pure rage and resentment maybe, but not pure joy. The wisdom God gives makes us teachable. It gives us a mind and a heart that will be shaped into the image of Christ. God is more concerned about what we become as we suffer than he is that we be free from suffering.

Pray for wisdom, but ask yourself, "Do I really want this kind of wisdom in my trials? Or do I just want to get out of them?" God will give wisdom generously but only to those who do not doubt. The word translated doubt means literally to be of "two minds." The idea is that you need to be of one mind about God's wisdom to receive it. Do you really want it, or do you just sort of want it? Ambivalence and a divided heart will not make you wise.

PRAYER: *"Have Thine own way, Lord! Have Thine own way! Thou art the Potter, I am the clay. Mold me and make me after Thy will, While I am waiting, yielded and still" (from the hymn "Have Thine Own Way, Lord" by Adelaide A Pollard).*

DAY 342: SWEET DELIGHT IN GOD

Jonathan Edwards (1703-1758)

"Now to the King eternal, immortal, invisible, the only God, be honor and glory for ever and ever. Amen" (1 Tim. 1:17).

As a young man, Jonathan Edwards had a profound experience of the goodness of God that shaped his ministry and spirituality for the rest of his life:

> *The first instance I remember of that sort of inward, sweet delight in God and in divine things, that I have lived much in since, was on reading these words, 1 Timothy 1:17: "Now unto the King eternal, immortal, invisible, the only wise God, be honor and glory for ever and ever. Amen." As I read the words, there came into my soul, and was as it were diffused through it, a sense of the glory of the Divine Being; a new sense, quite different from any thing I ever experienced before. Never any words of scripture seemed to me as these words did. I thought with myself, how excellent a Being that was, and how happy I should be, if I might enjoy that God, and be rapt up to him in heaven, and be as it were swallowed up in him forever!*[1]

Edwards is considered by many to be the greatest theologian and philosopher America has produced. Were it not for his "sweet delight" in God, Lyman Beecher (a great preacher of a later generation) believed Edwards' powerful intellect might have been tempted to do evil. In 1830, Beecher wrote his son George at Yale:

[Edwards'] vigor of intellect, compass of thought, patience of investigation, accuracy of discrimination, power of argument, knowledge of the Bible, and strength of holiness, stand unrivalled. But for his piety, he might have been a skeptic more dangerous than Hume or Voltaire.... But the attractions of his heart to God kept him in orbit.[2]

In his classic, *Religious Affections*, Edwards' powerful intellect combined with his "sweet delight in God" to interpret and defend the revival known as the Great Awakening that swept through the American colonies in the mid 1730s. In his *An Humble Attempt*,[3] Edwards proposed a plan for strategic, synchronized prayer that transcended denominations—a true "Concert of Prayer." *An Humble Attempt* was widely circulated in America and had a profound effect on the hundreds of "prayer societies" formed in both England and America.

PRAYER: *Father, send your Spirit to so kindle in me a delight in your perfections, that I may love you passionately with my whole being; heart, soul, and mind.*

DAY 343: PURE MOTIVES

James 4:1-3

"You do not have, because you do not ask God" (James 4:2).

Taken by itself, the line, "You do not have, because you do not ask," is one of the most encouraging words for prayer in all of Scripture. The only thing standing between you and receiving what you need, is your failure to ask. It's taken right out of the Sermon on the Mount (Matt. 7:7-8). And it's good advice, so ask that you may receive.

But there's more to it than that. One's motives in asking are all-important: "When you ask, you do not receive, because you ask with wrong motives, that you may spend what you get on your pleasures." The first three petitions of the Lord's Prayer—"hallowed be your name, your kingdom come, your will be done"—are a reminder to wash our requests in the pure water of God's holiness and in light of his kingdom and his will. Without these considerations, our desires can easily be the kind of desires condemned in the text—pleasure-seeking and self-centered. In fact, the Greek word for "desires" is the very word behind our English word, *hedonism*, which means the pursuit of pleasure or self-indulgence.

There is something else we must not miss about proper asking. We must pray with proper motives, and we must also pray in a loving community. A church of individuals driven by selfish desires will be a church whose members are at war with each other (James 4:2). Right relationships in the church are one of the fundamentals of answered prayer. Jesus prayed that we would be one as he and his Father were one (John 17:20-23). How can we expect our prayers to be heard by the Father, if we are, in our relationships with one other, working against the prayer his Son prayed for us? There is a direct relationship between our motives in prayer, our relationships, and answered prayer.

PRAYER: *"Thee will I love with all my power in all my works and Thee alone, Thee will I love till sacred fire fills my whole soul with pure desire" (from the hymn, "Thee Will I Love, My Strength," by John Wesley).*

DAY 344: ALWAYS THE RIGHT THING TO DO

James 5:13-18

"The prayer of a righteous man is powerful and effective" (James 5:16).

In the United States, most people tend to stay away from church services when they are sick. In some African countries and in other parts of the world, church is the first place Christians want to be when they are sick. Western Christians think of containing the disease while many others think of healing the disease—largely because of this passage from James. "Is any one of you sick? He should call the elders of the church to pray over him and anoint him with oil in the name of the Lord. And the prayer offered in faith will make the sick person well; the Lord will raise him up" (James 5:14-15).

There is also a hint here of the relationship between prayer and medical care. The oil of anointing was probably more than a symbolic gesture pointing to the presence of the Holy Spirit. It was an ancient practice to use oil for healing. The picture here appears to be one of prayer and medicine, not prayer or medicine. Both, under God, are legitimate collaborators in working his mercy in the world.

There are other wonderful things this passage touches on about prayer. It is always appropriate to pray. Are you in trouble? Pray. Are you happy? Pray. Are you sick? Pray. It is never rude or inappropriate or uncouth to pray. God is the God of all situations and seasons, "for from him and through him and to him are all things" (Rom. 11:36). Since God is the God of all seasons, prayer is the act for all seasons. Because all life is lived under God, all life is enriched and transformed by prayer. Prayer affects everything. It enhances joy, lightens trouble, heals sickness, and effects reconciliation and forgiveness.

The book of James begins with the assertion that hardship is a big part of the Christian pilgrimage, and it calls the church to pray for the special wisdom God gives in hardship. The book ends as it began: There will be suffering, we must be patient (James 5:7-12)—and pray, pray, pray.

PRAYER: *Father, there is so much to do each day and there are so many different situations; remind me to pray in all of them! Help me to acknowledge you in all my ways, that you may direct my steps.*

Introduction to 1 and 2 Peter

DAY 345: PRAYER IN A HOSTILE WORLD

"The eyes of the Lord are on the righteous and his ears are attentive to their prayer" (1 Pet. 3:12).

Clarence Jordan, the remarkable man who founded the first interracial farming community in the Deep South, was visiting a church. The pastor gave him a VIP tour of the church's new sanctuary, pointing with pride at the rich wood of the imported pews and the elegance of the decorations. He saved the best for last. Darkness was falling as he led Jordan outside to the front lawn of the church. A spotlight illumined a huge cross perched atop the church steeple. Beaming, the pastor said to Jordan, "That cross alone cost us $10,000."

"You got cheated," said Jordan. "Times were when Christians could get them for free."

There was indeed a time when Christians were quite literally nailed to crosses, like Jesus was, because of their faith in him. It still happens today. But where there are no literal crosses, there are cross-equivalents. Some analysts believe that in the twentieth century, more Christians died because of their faith than all the other centuries combined. But then, as now, persecution did not destroy the church. In fact, in some ways, it has made the church stronger. As someone has said, "Christians are like nails; the harder you hit them, the deeper they go."

This realty is the backdrop against which Peter wrote his two epistles. Much of what he said was to encourage believers to live faithfully in a hostile world. Added to this external pressure was the internal threat of heresy addressed in 2 Peter. Peter the pastor-shepherd had his hands full as he wrote. But he was carrying out his Master's command to feed his sheep (John 21:15-17). His two letters provide a wealth of material to help us pray through the pressures and enticements of a world that is no less hostile today.

PRAYER: *Father in heaven! Let me know the blessedness of suffering faithfully and joyfully for your great name." (Matt. 5:10-12)*

DAY 346: THE GIGANTIC SECRET

1 Peter 1:3-9

"In this you greatly rejoice" (1 Pet. 1:6).

G. K. Chesterton wrote, "Joy, which was the small publicity of the pagan, is the gigantic secret of the Christian."[1] What he meant was the mass of people in the world without Christ must be sad about the really big things and happy about only the little things. Death and eternity—the big things—are terrors to be denied or faced stoically. All there is to be happy about are the little things like health, money, friends, houses, and vacations. The best the pagan can do in this miserable state of affairs is to make much ado about the little things and create a "publicity" of the small and insignificant. These things carry big price tags and command big advertising campaigns—or social media posts.

The Christian, on the other hand, may have much to be sad about: persecution and death may be at hand, as they were for Peter's readers. But these are small things compared to the forgiveness of sins, and the prospect of an eternity of joy in the presence of God. Joy is indeed "the gigantic secret of the Christian." How gigantic? It is so big that it filled these believers "with an inexpressible and glorious joy" (1 Pet. 1:8). This is truly amazing, because their joy came from a love and a faith in someone they had not seen. This must have delighted Peter since he had seen the Lord and they had not.

Are you a Christian? Does your faith bring you this kind of joy? If it doesn't, you need to dig deeper channels in your soul for the joy to flow into. There is no better way to do this than to pray this great passage, and others like it, often. Make it personal by changing "us" to "me" and "you" to "I." Get a good commentary or Bible dictionary and soak in the meaning of Peter's theological vocabulary. Words and phrases like "new birth," "living hope," "resurrection," and "an inheritance" that can't fade, will make room in your heart and mind for more truth and, with it, "an inexpressible and glorious joy."

PRAYER: *My heart is narrow and my capacity for joy is shrunken. Dear Lord, open my eyes to see your gigantic goodness and expand my heart to sing your praise—with inexpressible and glorious joy.*

DAY 347: PRAY FOR YOUR CHURCH

1 Peter 2:4-12

"You are a chosen people" (1 Pet. 2:9).

How does your experience of church square with Peter's description of the church in this text? His language couldn't be loftier—and, perhaps, sound more unrealistic to some. The church is a spiritual house, a holy priesthood, a holy nation, and a chosen people. The church is central to God's purposes in the world. Is that what you think of when you go to church and look at those worshiping together with you?

In C. S. Lewis's, *The Screwtape Letters*, the senior devil Screwtape urges the junior devil named Wormwood to weaken the faith of a new Christian by highlighting the disparity between what the church looks like and what the Bible says it is.

> *When he gets to his pew and looks around him, he sees just that selection of his neighbors whom he has hitherto avoided. You want to lean pretty heavily on those neighbors. Make his mind flit to and fro between an expression like the "body of Christ" and the actual faces in the next pew. It matters very little, of course, what kind of people that next pew really contains.... Provided that any of those neighbors sing out of tune, or have boots that squeak, or double chins, or odd clothes, the patient will quite easily believe that their religion must therefore be somehow ridiculous.* [1]

The devil has great insight here. It is but a small step from thinking the church to be ridiculous to believing the faith of the church to be ridiculous. Though usually unstated, this can also lead us to see Jesus, the head of the church, as foolish. This text gives us much to pray for a local church and its members. You can begin by praising God for the church. Celebrate with gratitude and wonder that somehow, in his infinite wisdom, God chose to create a community of weak and foolish people like us to "offer spiritual sacrifices acceptable to God through Jesus Christ" (1 Pet. 2:5). Intercede for the church—your church—that it would faithfully "declare the praises of him who called you out of darkness into his wonderful light" (1 Pet. 2:9).

PRAYER: *Pray for your church following the guidelines suggested in the above paragraph.*

DAY 348: A MARRIAGE THAT CAN PRAY

1 Peter 3:7

"So that nothing will hinder your prayers" (1 Pet. 3:7).

It is one thing to pray to have a good marriage. It is another thing, equally important, to have a marriage that *can* pray. That's what Peter means when he tells husbands to love their wives in such a way, "so that nothing will hinder your prayers." How one treats a spouse has a lot to do with how God hears prayer. We must pray to have good and godly marriages. We must pray that marriages will be good and godly so we can pray!

This touches on a profound reality, developed more fully by Paul in his letter to the Ephesians (Eph. 5:21-33). Marriage, for the Christian, is defined christologically; that is, in terms of our relationship to the Lord Jesus. The relationship of Christ to his church is pictured in marriage. Wives are to submit to their husbands as the church submits to Christ. Moreover, husbands are to love their wives as Christ loved the church. The upshot of this is that there is more going on in a marriage than the mere coming together of two people to love and cherish each other. As important and wonderful as that is, the significance of marriage is much greater: In God's miraculous calculus, two become one, and in the loving reduction multiply love exponentially. One of the ways this shows itself is in the ability of a husband and wife to pray.

Marriage is therefore yet another arena in which Christians must live out their vocation to serve Christ. Dietrich Bonhoeffer once spoke to a love-struck couple in a marriage homily: "In your love you see only the heaven of your happiness, but in marriage you are placed at a post of responsibility towards the world and mankind." What greater way to stand at that post, and to live out that responsibility, than to have the kind of marriage that can pray powerfully. We do nothing in this life unto ourselves alone. Even a happy marriage is not only for the happiness of husbands, wives, and children; it is for God's glory in the world.

PRAYER: *Dear God, you created marriage for our happiness and welfare, and to display your glory. Strengthen the bonds of love between husbands and wives so they can better pray and stand at a post of responsibility for future generations.*

DAY 349: PARTICIPATING IN THE DIVINE NATURE

2 Peter 1:3-11

"He has given us his very great and precious promises" (2 Pet. 1:4).

Peter says you have everything you need to participate in the divine nature (2 Pet. 1:4). Pause and try to wrap your mind around this staggering declaration! Then pray for it, starting with something small. What would you like to be, on a lesser scale? A great athlete or artist or musician, perhaps? Imagine if God told you he had given you everything you need to be just what you've always have wanted to be—and he guaranteed you would become it. If your desire was to be a great distance runner, would you respond, "Good. I'll be a great distance runner; it's in me. Since it is a given, I'll spend all my time watching television and eating fatty foods." That would be ridiculous and unthinkable. If you really wanted what God had given and promised, then you'd "be all the more eager" (2 Pet. 1:10) to pursue it. The guarantee would stimulate effort, not smother it.

What does it mean to participate in the divine nature? It means to be as full of God or godliness as a human can be and still be a human. It is to be what Paul prayed the Ephesians would be: "filled to the measure of all the fullness of God" (Eph. 3:19). Does that appeal to you? Read the list of the fruit of the Spirit in Galatians 5:22-23. Is God love? Yes, perfectly and infinitely so. Would you like to participate in this kind of love, as fully as a human being can? Or in his joy? Or his peace and patience and kindness?

The possibilities are breath-taking. Do you perceive the glory of the promise of 2 Peter 1:3-4? It is a promise to become divinely human, or humanly divine. It is the restoration and fulfillment of what was short-circuited in the Fall—to be all that God made us to be when he made us in his image. Pray for this promise by praying for the things we are told to make every effort to have in verses 5-11: faith, goodness, knowledge, self-control, perseverance, godliness, brotherly kindness, and love. Because God has given us such "great and precious promises… be all the more eager to make your calling and election sure" (2 Pet. 1:4, 10).

PRAYER: *Strengthen me, Oh Lord, by your Spirit, to grow in faith, goodness, knowledge, self-control, perseverance, godliness, brotherly kindness, and love. Fill me to the measure of all the fullness of God.*

DAY 350: PRAY FOR THE COMING OF THE LORD

2 Peter 3

"You ought to live holy and godly lives as you look forward to the Day of God and speed its coming" (2 Pet. 3:11-12).

At the entrance of the fossil museum at the La Brea tar pits in Los Angeles, California, is a painting of an 85-foot ribbon. It represents five billion years of the earth's history. Guess how much space on that ribbon belongs to the history of humanity, from cave man to astronaut... less than one-half inch! Looking at that ribbon, one wonders what God was doing the other 84 feet 11 ½ inches. Whether you think creation existed before humans for billions of years or for most of a week, it highlights how small we are and how little we know. What was God's purpose for all those bizarre and extinct creatures who roamed the earth? What was God thinking? Only he knows. One thing we do know is the truth of what Peter wrote: "With the Lord a day is like a thousand years, and a thousand years are like a day" (2 Pet. 3:8).

But Peter wrote what he wrote not to speculate about the mysteries of God's sense of time. These are implicit in what he said, but the point is to encourage us not to lose our focus and interest in the coming of the Day of the Lord. During the early years of the church, Christians were very animated by thoughts about the end of all things as we now know them. They were eager for the day when the old order would disappear and the "new heaven and earth, the home of righteousness" would appear (2 Pet. 3:13). As time passed, and persecution increased, some were tempted to lose heart and wondered if that day would ever arrive. Peter wrote to strengthen their hope by reminding them that God's sense of time is not like ours. More importantly, whatever may seem like a delay to us is really God's mercy and patience at work. He does not want, "anyone to perish, but everyone to come to repentance" (2 Pet. 3:9).

But here is the really encouraging thing: "You ought to live holy and godly lives as you look forward to the day of God and speed its coming" (2 Pet. 3:11-12). We don't know when that day will come, but we can influence how soon! The way Christians live—and pray—in this world has a direct impact on the history of the world (see devotions on Rev. 8:1-5 and 22:20).

One of the Christian community's earliest calls to worship was the prayer, "Maranatha!" It meant, "Come, Lord!" Hope in the coming of Christ will make us live holy and godly lives, and pray holy and godly prayers.

PRAYER: *Maranatha! Come, Lord Jesus! And until you do, work in me by your Spirit the will and the power to live a holy and godly life.*

DAY 351: ENFOLDED IN LOVE

Julian of Norwich (1342-1413)

"For I am convinced that neither death nor life, neither angels nor demons, neither the present nor the future, nor any powers, neither height nor depth, nor anything else in all creation, will be able to separate us from the love of God that is in Christ Jesus our Lord" (Rom. 8:38-39).

The time in which Julian of Norwich lived were as bloody and sordid as any in human history. From 1337 to 1453, England and France were locked in the so-called "Hundred Years War," a catastrophe that devastated medieval society top to bottom. The bubonic plague struck twice, 1348-49 and 1361, cutting the population of Europe by a third. Yet, at a time when God's love might have been seriously in question, this medieval mystic is remembered for her "Revelations of Divine Love."

No one knows her baptismal name. She is called Julian because of the years she spent in solitude in her cell at the church of St. Julian and St. Edward at Carrow, England. The "Revelations," or "shewings" as she called them, came to her on May 8, 1373. Her writings on these revelations are the result of her twenty-year meditation on them.

Julian's revelation of the immense and sovereign love of God strengthened her faith that nothing can separate us from the love of God (Rom. 8:35-39). Even though we may not see that this is so now, we will in heaven. She wrote,

> *When judgment is given and we are brought up above, then we shall see clearly the secrets now hidden from us. In that day not one of us will want to say, "Lord, if it had been done this way, it would have been well done." But we shall all say with one voice, "Lord, blessed may you be, for it is so, and it is well. And now we see truly that all things were done as it was ordained before anything was made."*[1]

Indeed, as she said famously: "All shall be well and all shall be well, and all manner of things shall be well."[2] Because God does all things well, sometimes despite appearances, Julian counseled praise as the way to strengthen the heart when spiritually dry or apathetic or assaulted by temptation, doubt, and fear. She believed that praise and thanksgiving were powerful acts of faith that teach the heart to joyfully beat with God's great heart of love. Through praise and thanksgiving we are assured that:

> *We are enfolded in the Father, and we are enfolded in the Son, and we are enfolded in the Holy Spirit. And the Father is enfolded in us, and the Son is enfolded in us, and the Holy Spirit is enfolded in us: almightiness, all wisdom, all goodness: one God, one Lord.*[3]

PRAYER: *"God, of your goodness, give me yourself, for you are sufficient for me. I may not ask for anything less, to be worthy of you. If I were to ask anything less, I should always be in need, for in you alone do I have all."*[4]

Introduction to 1, 2, and 3 John

DAY 352: WHAT HAPPENS TO YOU WHEN YOU SPEND TIME WITH JESUS

"This is the message you heard from the beginning: we should love one another" (1 John 3:11).

Mary and Don (not their real names) were both very old and senile. The years had whittled them down to their core, and all that was left was what had been essential to their character through their whole life. Mary couldn't remember names, or what day it was, but when asked to pray, her face beamed beatifically. Her prayer was the prayer of one who had long known Jesus and was conversing with him in that moment. She ended her life the way she had always lived it. Don, on the other hand, had chased money his whole life. It was sad and pathetic to hear him drone and babble about the money he had made in his lifetime. It was worthless to him in his final years, but he had become trapped in his life's pursuit.

John is the youngest of the disciples when we first meet him in the gospels, and he is something of an ambitious firebrand (Mark 10:35-45; Luke 9:54). But he describes himself as the one Jesus loved (John 20:2; 21:7). As we meet John again though his epistles, he is a very old man near the end of his life, and probably the only disciple to die of natural causes. What is left of him are the effects of having been loved by Jesus all those years. It is touching to read his repeated, grandfatherly encouragements for his people to love one another (1 John 3:11, 15, 16, 23; 2 John 5; 3 John 4). John's gospel was an intimate look at Jesus, and his epistles give us an intimate look at what Jesus made of John. He had become the apostle of love. The best thing you will ever have to give to others is what you become in the time you spend with Jesus in prayer, letting him love you.

PRAYER: *Turn Jesus' words in John 15:5 into your prayer. Say, you, Lord, are the vine. I am but a branch, and apart from you I can do nothing. Help me to remain in you, that I may be fruitful.*

DAY 353: GOOD FOR THE SOUL AND THE CELL

1 John 1:5—2:2

"If we confess our sins, he is faithful and just and will forgive us our sins" (1 John 1:9).

A writer invented a creative and illuminating title to a meditation on this text. It was, "Confession is good for the cell." The word "cell" sounds just enough like the word "soul" in the older, more familiar saying to catch our attention. Both are true: confession is good for the soul and for the cell. The cell is the darkness that imprisons our soul if we do not confess. That is the message here: God is light, sin is darkness—the two cannot coexist. But sin's greatest darkness is the refusal to admit its own existence. God forgives sin, but he will not forgive sin that is denied. Denial deceives and imprisons us and insults God. "If we claim to be without sin, we deceive ourselves and the truth is not in us.... If we claim we have not sinned, we make him out to be a liar and his word has no place in our lives" (1 John 1:8, 10).

Confession of sin is a "must" and a "may." We *must* confess or lose fellowship with God—and with each other (1 John 1:6-7). If we say we have no sin, we say Christ died for nothing. The good news, however, is that we *may* confess without fear of condemnation because God "is faithful and just and will forgive our sins and purify us from all unrighteousness" (1 John 1:10). There are few prayers more liberating than honest prayers of confession. This is because confession takes us straight to the heart of the gospel.

When Satan tempts me to despair,
And tells me of the guilt within,
Upward I look and see him there
Who made an end to all my sin.

Because the sinless Savior died,
My sinful soul is counted free;
For God, the just, is satisfied
To look on him and pardon me.[1]

PRAYER: *Holy One, I have chosen darkness over light. I have not loved you with my whole being and my neighbor as myself. I have left undone things I should do, and I have done things I shouldn't do. Forgive me and restore me, that I may live in your light.*

DAY 354: PRAYING ACCORDING TO GOD'S WILL

1 John 5:14-15

"This is the confidence we have in approaching God: that if we ask anything according to his will, he hears us" (1 John 5:14).

This sounds simple enough: ask God for what he already wants to give, and he will hear and answer. But what's the point? We learn two things. First, God wants to give us something wonderful. Second, we become wonderful when we pray for what he wants to give. Consider what God wants to give. The petitions of the Lord's Prayer alone take one's breath away. To ask that God's kingdom come—that he will rule the world in peace and justice and love—is to ask for the fulfillment of the dreams of billions of people, even if they don't realize God is the source of what they desire. Most people would follow any leader who could deliver these things. God not only *wants* to give these things, he is able to give them, and he promises to bring them about if we ask. Our pulse rate should go up every time we pray for the things God wants to give.

Consider what we become when we pray for the things God wants to give. Jesus said he will give the Holy Spirit to those who ask him (Luke 11:13)! What could be better than to be filled to the measure of all the fullness of God (Eph. 3:19)? Can anything match the beauty and power of the fruit of the Holy Spirit flourishing in your life—love, joy, peace, patience, kindness, goodness, faithfulness, gentleness, and self-control (Gal. 5:22-23)?

It stretches the imagination to appreciate what is being offered here. This may help: In May 1982, astronomers saw a solar flare shoot out from the sun so powerful that their instruments couldn't measure it. They estimated that in twenty minutes it released more energy than is produced by the entire earth in one year. An object anywhere near that flare would be consumed. Imagine that light and heat compared to a candle. Then imagine a love so rich and deep that it is to all human love what that solar flare was to that candle. Or a joy that is to all earthly joys what that solar flare was to a flashlight. Get the picture? No eye has seen, no ear has heard, no mind can imagine the glory of what God will give to those who ask according to his will!

The greatness of what John promises in this passage is not that we may convince God to give us what we want, but that we can come to want what he wants. Just as we become what we worship, we become what we pray to the one we worship.

PRAYER: *Come, thou fount of every blessing, tune my heart to sing and pray for your grace. Give me your Spirit, make me like Christ, and so rule over me that in me you are all in all.*

DAY 355: PRAYING FOR AN OLD MAN'S JOY

2 John 5

"I ask that we love one another" (2 John 5).

This letter and the next are first century equivalents of an office memo or an e-mail. Of course, no communication traveled with that kind of speed in those days. But the situation called for a brief note from the apostle to address a troubling situation—itinerant heretics in the first note and a despotic pastor (Diotrephes) in the second. The people he wrote to—"the chosen lady and her children" and Gaius—are trustworthy, and John is confident they will follow through on what needs to be done.

Regarding prayer, what comes through (almost between the lines) is the kind of man who wrote these notes. His overriding concern for "the chosen lady and her children," whom he loves in the truth (2 John 1), is that they have a love that honors the truth. "It has given me great joy to find some of your children walking in the truth, just as the Father commanded us" (2 John 4). For love to truly desire and bring about what is best for those it loves, it must know what is true. Blind love is not love at all. What good is the love of a parent for a child if the parent doesn't understand that it is bad for child to eat poison? If the child dies, there will be no comfort in the thought that the parent meant well. Paul showed the same concern in his prayer for the Philippians. He prayed that their love would "abound more and more in knowledge and depth of insight, that [they] may be able to discern what is best and be pure and blameless until the day of Christ" (Phil. 1:9-10).

Think of those you love and pray for wisdom to love and pray well. What could be better than to ask the Holy Spirit to give a love that is wise and faithful to the truth? A person with a tender heart, a keen mind, and a strong backbone of integrity is a beautiful thing to behold. The world needs people like that.

PRAYER: *Father, give me, along with all your people, a love that is wise and faithful to the truth. Give us tender hearts, keen minds, and genuine integrity, to the praise of your glory.*

DAY 356: FELLOWSHIP WITH GOD AND WITH OTHERS

3 John 11

"Do not imitate what is evil but what is good" (3 John 11).

Love needs the truth to have a backbone (see devotion on 2 John 5). A concern for the truth will determine the proper boundaries between what is consistent with faith and what is not. Love needs the support of sound doctrine to be effective. By itself, mere passion can be foolish or destructive. The proper order in the life of the church is "ready, aim, fire," not "ready, fire, aim."

But truth needs love, too. John's concern in this memo is that the church be loving and hospitable, "so that we may work together in the truth" (3 John 8). Let the emphasis here fall on the word "together." Jesus said the greatest argument for the truth of the gospel would be the unity of his people (John 17:23). Note that he didn't say the greatest argument for the truth would be an argument! Beyond words and powerful rhetoric (as important as they are) is the love of Christ manifested in Christ's people. The truth is credible only when we proclaim it by the way we live together. That's why Diotrephes is such a dangerous man. He "loves to be first" and will have nothing to do with other Christian leaders. He is a gossip (3 John 9-10). That means he is more than an irritant in the church; he is an enemy of the truth.

Pray for your church. Pray that the truth of Christ will be commended to outsiders by the way you live together. Shun absolutely gossip and slander or backbiting and competition, so you can pray and work together.

Introduction to Jude

DAY 357: CONTEND FOR THE FAITH

"Contend for the faith that was once for all entrusted to the saints" (Jude 3).

"I love to sin, God loves to forgive; it's a marvelous arrangement." That saying, attributed to Voltaire, is a good summation of the kind of false teaching that beleaguered Jude's readers. There was nothing new here; the issue appears again and again throughout the New Testament epistles. Some people find salvation by grace through faith alone too good to be true. Others find it merely a good deal, in the sense of Voltaire. And they manage to sound very "spiritual" as they exploit God's grace.

The forerunners of a yet more virulent Gnostic heresy to come later, Jude's readers reasoned that the spirit was good and the body was bad (or of no account). What one did with one's body had no bearing on the state of one's spirit. They argued that true religion is spiritual, not physical. Since sexual behavior is physical and irrelevant to the spiritual life, they could do whatever they wanted. Jude roundly condemned this heresy and gave his readers some very good advice: "But you, dear friends, build yourself up in your most holy faith and pray in the Holy Spirit" (Jude 20). Prayer again is a key element in walking the straight and narrow in a crooked world.

PRAYER: *Holy Spirit, give me a sober and vigilant mind that discerns truth from error, good from evil.*

DAY 358: PRAY IN THE HOLY SPIRIT

Jude 20

"Build yourselves up in your most holy faith and pray in the Holy Spirit" (Jude 20).

The strength of slogans is that they are easy to remember. The weakness of slogans is that they oversimplify things. But as slogans go, this verse would make a good one. The Christian life comes down to two things: "Build yourself up in the faith and pray in the Holy Spirit." It is worthy of calligraphy on parchment—or a laminated card.

"Build yourself up in the faith." By *faith*, Jude doesn't mean the subjective sense of trust in Christ by which we stake our lives on his faithfulness. That kind of faith is, of course, critical; but what Jude has in mind is its flipside. He means faith in an objective sense—a body of doctrine or a set of propositions. Jude is talking about the Christian Faith, as opposed to the Muslim Faith or Hindu Faith. This is the faith mentioned in verse 3, "once for all entrusted to the saints," for which we are to contend.

This objective faith is critical, also. It reminds us that our subjective faith is not built on something we have made up, but on something we have received. The object of our faith was there before we came on the scene, and it will be there after we leave the scene. Further, faith has been entrusted to us. We are stewards of something that we adhere to, but we do not own it as a private possession to do with whatever we wish. We must give an account for what we did with the body of truth that was entrusted to us.

"Pray in the Holy Spirit." This is prayer that is prompted and empowered by the Holy Spirit. Prayer in the Holy Spirit is related to faith, the way breath and blood and the central nervous system are related to a skeleton. There can be no body without a skeleton (objective faith), but the body can have no life without breath (subjective, personal faith). We can be right theologically, but dead unless the life of God courses through our veins. Doctrines can stay locked up in the head until the Holy Spirit writes them on the heart (Ezek. 36:26-27). If we are to have desires and behavior worthy of the great doctrines we hold to, we need the Holy Spirit to blow in us the way a smoldering fire is fanned into flame by fresh air.

PRAYER: *Holy Spirit, make me courageous to hold to the most holy faith. Give me desire and prompt me to obedience that is worthy of that great faith.*

DAY 359: THE SMALL WOMAN

Gladys Aylward (1902 -1970)

"By the grace of God I am what I am, and his grace to me was not without effect. No, I worked harder than all of them—yet not I, but the grace of God that was with me" (1 Cor. 15:10).

When a Hollywood movie is made of the life of a woman who was an English parlor maid, it's usually a rags-to-riches, Cinderella tale. Gladys Aylward went from poverty and obscurity to international fame, and a movie was made about her life, *The Inn of the Sixth Happiness*, starring the renowned actress, Ingrid Bergman. However, rags-to-riches hardly describes her story. Miracle of God's sovereign grace comes closer.

Gladys Aylward heard God's call to go to China as a young woman. But her poor educational background had not prepared her for the rigors of the China Inland Mission's missionary training classes, and she flunked her exams. Deemed unqualified for service, she went back to her life as a parlor maid. Meanwhile, her passion for China and the gospel wouldn't go away, and when she heard that Jeannie Lawson, an elderly missionary in China needed help, she wrote and asked her if she could come and assist her. Lawson answered that she was welcome to come, but that she couldn't pay travel expenses for Gladys. With no money and no backing, she felt herself slipping into depression. Gladys emptied the contents of her pocketbook upon her Bible. Three copper coins fell out. She prayed, "Oh, God, here's my Bible! Here's my money! Here's me! Use me, God!"[1]

With only her meager savings, Gladys booked passage to China by the most dangerous route possible. As an undeclared war between Russia and China raged, she rode the Trans-Siberian Railway across Russian to China. She lived a life of such unbelievable courage and miraculous providence, that when a Newsweek film critic reviewed the movie about her life, some readers thought it was a work of fiction. A letter to the editor complained, "In order for a movie to be good, the story should be believable!"[2]

For instance, during the Japanese invasion of China in 1938, with a price offered on her head by the invaders, this little woman led 100 Chinese orphans on a perilous 27-day journey across the mountains to safety. At the end of her life all she could say about herself was, "My heart is full of praise that one so insignificant, uneducated, and ordinary in every way could be used to His glory for the blessing of His people in poor persecuted China."[3]

PRAYER: *With your Bible open, place your wallet or pocketbook on its pages and pray with Gladys Aylward: "Oh, God, here's my Bible! Here's my money! Here's me! Use me, God!"*

Introduction to Revelation

DAY 360: THE PRAYING IMAGINATION[1]

"The smoke of the incense, together with the prayers of the saints, went up before God from the angel's hand" (Rev. 8:4).

There is a widely told story about seminary students who were playing basketball one evening in a church gym. As they played, the night custodian sat on the sidelines and read his Bible. One evening, a student noticed that the custodian was reading the book of Revelation. Knowing the many difficulties of the book, he asked him, "Do you understand what you are reading?"

The custodian surprised him and said, "Yes, I do."

The student arched his brows and replied, "What do you think it means?"

"It means, Jesus is gonna win," the custodian answered.

Whether or not the story is true, the point of the tale is. Amid all the controversies that have surrounded the interpretation of this wonderful and puzzling book, there remains the central truth: "Jesus is gonna win"—or more accurately, "Jesus has won, and Jesus will win."

Jesus introduces himself in the book saying, "I am the First and the Last. I am the Living One; I was dead, and behold I am alive for ever and ever! And I hold the keys of death and Hades" (Rev. 1:17-18). This is the one to whom we pray!

Great praying requires a great imagination, not in the sense of fanciful or wishful thinking, but in the sense of seeing with the heart the burning realities that lie beyond our five senses. John's visions may tax our minds, but they will fire our hearts to pray with fervor and faith to the One who has conquered—"who was, and is, and is to come" (Rev. 4:8).

PRAYER: *Thank you, Sovereign Lord, that my prayers, along with all the prayers of all your people, though unheard by the powers of this world, go straight to your throne in heaven.*

DAY 361: PRAISE THE CREATOR

Revelation 4

"Holy, holy, holy is the Lord God Almighty" (Rev. 4:8).

When John says he stepped through a door opened in heaven, he means he has stepped into the control room of history and the entire cosmos. What he sees there is of immense comfort—he sees a throne. The word for "throne" is used in the New Testament 62 times, and John uses it 47 of those instances. His readers were familiar with earthly thrones, particularly Caesar's. Earthly thrones and powers were threats to the church. The comfort is that there, in the control room of history, is a throne above all these other thrones, and it is occupied by the King of kings and Lord of lords! Earthly powers do not have the last word, God does.

There is more to John's vision. Encircling the throne is a rainbow, the sign of God's promise to preserve his creation (Gen. 9:12-16). No matter how bad things may seem on earth, God is still in control, he still remembers his promise, and he still loves the world. That is why he is worshiped. Nothing has changed, he is the still the Creator God. He is the same yesterday, today and forever: "Holy, holy, holy is the Lord God Almighty, who was, and is, and is to come.... You are worthy, our Lord and God, to receive glory, honor, and power, for you created all things, and by your will they were created and have their being" (Rev. 4:8, 11). The last book of the Bible reaffirms and celebrates what the first book celebrates (Gen. 1:1-31).

These verses provide great words to pray, and they have been sung and prayed throughout the history of the church. As when they were first written, they still bring peace and comfort to troubled hearts. You could pray these words now, and it would honor God and be good for your soul. As you pray, remember that the same kind of praise is going on in heaven—right now, day and night (Rev. 4:8a, 9a). Whenever you praise God, you join the citizens of heaven in singing something that never changes. Sing along.

PRAYER: *"Holy, holy, holy is the Lord God Almighty, who was, and is, and is to come.... You are worthy, our Lord and God, to receive glory, honor, and power, for you created all things, and by your will they were created and have their being" (Rev. 4:8, 11).*

DAY 362: PRAISE THE SAVIOR

Revelation 5

"Then I saw a Lamb, looking as if it had been slain" (Rev. 5:6).

A new player is added to the ensemble around the throne of God. God holds in his right hand a sealed scroll. In it are written his decrees, purposes, and judgments in history—everything he will do to save and redeem his world. But someone needs to open the scroll for these things to be carried out, someone who is "worthy" to do so (Rev. 5:2). John wept bitterly because he looked everywhere and could find no one. In a moment of high drama, one of the elders of heaven, announces that there is one who is worthy, "the Lion of the tribe of Judah, the root of David" (Rev. 5:5). All heaven stands on tiptoe to see the lion appear, but what they see is a lamb, "looking as if it had been slain" (Rev. 5:6)! The creature that symbolizes royalty, ferocity, and strength is embodied in a creature that symbolizes meekness, vulnerability, and sacrifice. The lion is a lamb; the lamb is a lion. He is the Lamb of God who takes away the sins of the world (John 1:29). The Lamb will be the controlling image of Christ throughout the remainder of the book of Revelation. He stands in a position of equality, on the throne, at God's right hand.

Now the Creator is also worshiped as Savior: "You are worthy to take the scroll and open its seals, because you were slain, and with your blood you purchased men for God from every tribe and language and people and nation. You have made them to be a kingdom and priests to serve our God, and they will reign on the earth.... Worthy is the Lamb, who was slain, to receive power and wealth and wisdom and strength and honor and glory and praise" (Rev. 5:9-10, 12)!

The church has sung and prayed these words for centuries—to God's glory and for the church's comfort and encouragement. You may sing too, remembering that you never do so alone. You join all the citizens of heaven (Rev. 5:8, 11, 13, 14). Be thrilled to know this! That "you have come to thousands upon thousands upon thousands of angels in joyful assembly, to the church of the firstborn, whose names are written in heaven. You have come to God, the judge of all men, to the spirits of righteous men made perfect, to Jesus the mediator of a new covenant" (Heb. 12:22-24a).

PRAYER: *Worship God with the multitudes of heaven. Change the pronouns in Revelation 5:9, 10, to personally involve you and your church. Where the text says "men" and "them," say "us."*

DAY 363: PRAY FOR THE PERSECUTED CHURCH

Revelation 6:9-11

"I saw under the altar the souls of those who had been slain because of the word of God" (Rev. 6:9).

This is a jarring passage. For one thing, the kind of prayer being prayed is not what one would expect in heaven. The prayers come from the souls of martyrs crying out from under the altar, the place where the blood of sacrificial animals was poured in the Old Testament temple. The martyrs plead, "How long, Sovereign Lord, holy and true, until you judge the inhabitants of the earth and avenge our blood?" (Rev. 6:10). Even in heaven, they are longing for justice.

God's answer is equally unsettling. "They are told to wait a little longer, until the number of their fellow servants and brothers who were to be killed as they had been was completed" (Rev. 6:11). More followers of Jesus will die to "complete" their number. The victory comes through sacrifice. Satan, the accuser of the God's people is hurled down and overcome by the blood of the Lamb and his martyrs: "They overcame him by the blood of the Lamb and by the word of their testimony; they did not love their lives so much as to shrink from death" (Rev. 12:11).

Vernard Eller, in his commentary on Revelation, underlines the significance of God's answer to their prayer: "As clearly as can be stated, we are told that the human activity upon which the outcome of history depends, the action by which progress toward the kingdom is marked, is not the piling up of good deeds, not our winning of men to Christ, not our consolidating power for the good, not our taking over and building up anything. No, we contribute to the coming of the kingdom by making like the Lamb, being willing, in love, to give ourselves, even to the slaughter."[1]

How should we pray for the persecuted church? We should pray as the persecuted church in heaven prays—for justice! We should pray knowing that God's chief method of doing his work is by the blood of the Lamb. It is no coincidence that the Greek word for "witness" and "martyr" is one and the same. We should also pray, therefore, for the church to remain faithful and courageous and full of the hope that one day all be well—not in spite of its sufferings, but through them.

PRAYER: *Pray the words the souls under the altar pray and add the names of the places in the world where the church is suffering. Say, "Sovereign Lord, holy and true, do not delay! Act swiftly to bring justice in (name specific places—like North Korea, Afghanistan, etc.). Strengthen my brothers and sisters there with hope, so that they will remain faithful and courageous until the day of Christ.*

DAY 364: HEAVEN'S VIEW OF PRAYER

Revelation 8:1-5

"The smoke of the incense, together with the prayers of the saints, went up before God" (Rev. 8:4).

Try asking a group, perhaps a congregation on Sunday morning, to be silent for half an hour. Or try it yourself at home. It's not only hard to do, but it creates a tremendous sense of expectancy. Ears and eyes begin to strain, to lean into whatever will be next. That is the scene in heaven. There has been silence for about half an hour, and all heaven is eager to hear what will come next. Then seven angels are given seven trumpets! Watch out! Hands move to cover ears, and people move to the edge of their seats. The first sound will be a trumpet blast! Anticipation becomes electric as another angel, with a golden censer, moves to the altar before the throne of God. In the censer, mixed with the incense, are the prayers of God's people. The smoke of their prayers goes up before God. Then the angel scoops, with the censer, fire from the altar, and hurls it down to earth. The first sound heaven hears is louder and more startling than trumpets: "there came peals of thunder, rumblings, flashes of lightning and an earthquake" (Rev. 8:5).

Sometimes prayer can feel so impotent. Have your words ever seemed to dribble off your tongue and pool on the floor? That is an earthly view of prayer. Heaven's view is powerful! With thunder, lightning, and earthquakes, the prayers of the God's people move the whole earth. The future belongs to the intercessors, says New Testament scholar Walter Wink. It pleases God to give this power to prayer for the same reason it pleased him to save the world through the "foolishness" of the cross and to perfect his strength through human weakness: "so that no one may boast before him" (1 Cor. 1:18-29; 2 Cor. 12:9-10). When we pray, God gets all the glory, and we get the joy of seeing him work wonders. Prayer truly changes things. Kings and those in authority are affected, unknowingly, and churches stand firm and mature in hope (1 Tim. 2:1-2; Col. 4:12-13).

PRAYER: *Take time to pray about things that seem to be really frightening and intractable issues in the world. Declare them to the Lord, one at a time, and pray: Come, Lord! Save us, Lord! May the kingdoms of this world become the kingdom of Christ. May your will be done on earth as fully as it is done in heaven.*

DAY 365: MARANATHA!

Revelation 22:7-21

"Whoever is thirsty, let him come" (Rev. 22:17).

The first and last words of the Bible are of grace. Here, grace comes in the form of a benediction: "The grace of the Lord Jesus be with God's people. Amen" (Rev. 22:21). In the beginning it came without the actual word, but by an awesome act of grace. Freely and sovereignly, entirely on his own initiative, God spoke the universe into existence. No one made him do it, no one asked him to do it, he did it simply because it was his gracious pleasure. It pleased him to create in the same way it later pleased him to save—freely, by grace.

The first and last words of the Bible are of blessing. Here it is, "Whoever is thirsty, let him come; and whoever wishes, let him take the free gift of the water of life" (Rev. 22:17). In the beginning, it was God delighting in everything he made, pronouncing it all very good and blessing humankind with the command to be fruitful (Gen. 1:29, 31). Why did God bless? Why does he bless? Not because he must, for he is free; but because it is who he is. It pleases him.

In between the first and last words of the Bible is the story of the Bible. On the one hand there is the human debacle: our irrational and inexplicable refusal to be graced and blessed. But on the other hand, there remains the divine freedom to grace and bless. Again and again we see God's dogged determination to say "Nevertheless" to our sin. So, the Bible ends with another promise and appeal. Three times Jesus says, "Behold, I am coming soon" (Rev. 22:7, 17, 20)! Then he adds, "Whoever is thirsty, let him come" (Rev. 22:17). The message is, "I am coming. Will you come, too? Everything depends on it, life or death, heaven or hell."

What is there left for us to do but pray, "Amen. Come, Lord Jesus" (Rev. 22:20)? The early church made this prayer a standard call to worship with an Aramaic word that has found its way into our vocabulary, "Maranatha!" When it was prayed, the church sincerely believed the prayer would be answered, and Jesus would come, if not physically, then spiritually. Will you pray it now with the church throughout the ages—one more time, or for the first time? "Amen. Maranatha!" He will come because he is coming.

PRAYER: *Amen! Come, Lord Jesus! We are thirsty; we crave the water of life. So come and save us and gather us to yourself. We pray these things in the name of the Father and of the Son and of the Holy Spirit.*

Notes:

Introduction

1 Andrew A. Bonar, *Robert Murray M'Cheyne: Memoir and Remains* (London: Banner of Truth Trust, 1966).
2 Bingham Hunter, *The God Who Hears* (Downers Grove, IL: Inter varsity Press, 1986), 12.
3 C. S. Lewis, *The Weight of Glory* (Grand Rapids, MI: Eerdmans, 1977), 1-2.
4 Charles Spurgeon, *Spurgeon's Expository Encyclopedia*, vol. 4 (Grand Rapids, MI: Baker Book House, 1978), 329.
5 George Herbert, "Prayer," *George Herbert, The Complete English Works*, edited and introduced by Ann Pasternak Slater (London: David Campbell Publishers, Ltd., 1995), 49.
6 P. T. Forsyth, *The Soul of Prayer* (London: Independent Press Ltd., 1954), 14.
7 Source unknown. I copied these words from a magazine article more than 40 years ago.

Day 1: Created to Pray

1 From Augustine, *The Confessions*.

Day 2: The Face in Front of the World

1 From G. K. Chesterton, *The Man Who Was Thursday: A Nightmare (1908)*.

Day 3: When All Else Fails

1 Frederick Buechner, *Wishful Thinking* (New York: Harper and Row Publishers, 1973), 88.

Day 4: Living by Unseen Realities

1 Luci Shaw, "The Foolishness of God," from *A Widening Light* (Wheaton, IL: Harold Shaw, 1984), 134.

Day 6: Finding out about Prayer

1 A widely circulated sermon illustration on prayer.

Day 8: For Life or Death

1 This quote is widely attributed to Luther but is not found in his existing writings.

Day 10: Wrestling with God

1 P. T. Forsyth, *The Soul of Prayer* (London: Independent Press, Ltd., 1954), 92.

Day 11: An Elder's Prayer

1 Karl Barth, *Church Dogmatics* 3:4, ed. G. W. Bromiley and T. F. Torrance (Edinburgh: T & T Clark, 1978), 615.

Day 12: God Intends It for Good

1 *The Heidelberg Catechism*, Questions 27 and 28 (Grand Rapids, MI: CRC Publications, 1988).

Day 13: Night of Fire

1 Blaise Pascal, *Pensees*, "The Memorial," A. J. Krailsheimer, trans. (Penguin Classics: New York, 1966), 309.

Day 16: Honest Complaining or Mere Grumbling

1 The question mark, exclamation point metaphor comes from Old Testament scholar, Tremper Longman.

Day 19: On the Pure Love of God

1 From the hymn "My God, How Wonderful Thou Art" by Frederick William Faber.
2 A line from, *For the Time Being*, by poet W. H. Auden.
3 Told by Peter Kreeft, in *Three Philosophies of Life* (San Francisco: Ignatius Press, 1989), 94-95.

Day 25: A Long Obedience

1 Augustine, *Confessions*, VII, xxi. Quoted by C. S. Lewis, in *Surprised by Joy* (New York: Harcourt, Brace and World, 1955), 230.

Day 28: Outrageous Grace

1 From Owen Collins, *2000 Years of Classic Christian Prayers* (Maryknoll, NY: Orbis Books, 1999), 185-186.

Day 30: Remember!

1 Questions 2 and 116 of the *Heidelberg Catechism* (Grand Rapids, MI: CRC Publications, 1988).

Day 34: From Social Butterfly to Saint

1 Drummond, Lewis and Betty, *Woman of Awakenings* (Grand Rapids, MI: Kregel Publications, 1997), 69-70.
2 Ibid.
3 Foster, Richard and James Bryan Smith, ed. *Devotional Classics* (Harper, CA: 1993), 323.
4 Drummond, 77.

Day 39: The Perennial Need

1 Earle Cairns, *An Endless Line of Splendor* (Wheaton, IL: Tyndale House Publishers, 1986), 19.

Day 41: Fie on Fleeces!

1 John White, *The Fight* (Downers Grove, IL: Intervarsity Press, 1976), 165-167.

Day 42: Father, Make of Me a Crisis Man

1 Elisabeth Elliot, *Shadow of the Almighty* (New York: Harper and Brothers, 1958), 53, 247-249.

Day 44: Prayer in the Worst of Times

1 From Thomas Hobbes, *The Leviathan* (1651).

Day 45: Prayer Changes Things

1 Virginia Stem Owens, "Prayer–Into the Lion's Jaws," *Christianity Today* (November 19, 1976), 17-21.

Day 49: The Dignity of Causality

1 C. S. Lewis, *Surprised by Joy* (New York: Harcourt, Brace and World, Inc., 1955), 229.
2 The following is a summary of the essay, "Work and Prayer," from *God in the Dock* (Grand Rapids, MI: William B. Eerdmans, 1970), 104-107.

Day 53: Open My Eyes, Lord

1 Annie Dillard, *Pilgrim at Tinker Creek* (New York: Harper's Magazine Press, 1974), 11-12.

Day 55: When Our Eyes are Opened

1 Alexander MacLaren, *Expositions of Holy Scripture, 2 Samuel* (1904).

Day 56: Seeing Through

1 George Herbert, "The Elixir," *The Complete English Works*, Ann Pasternak Slater, editor (London: Everyman's Library, David Campbell Publishers, Ltd., 1974), 180.

Day 57: No Higher Calling

1 *The Prayers of Susanna Wesley*, Edited and arranged by W. L. Doughty (Grand Rapids, Michigan: Clarion Classics, Zondervan Publishing House, 1984), x.
2 Drummond, Lewis and Betty, *Women of Awakenings* (Grand Rapids, MI: Kregel Publications, 1997), 80.
3 W. L. Doughty, 17.

Day 58: Deadly Pride

1 C. S. Lewis, *Mere Christianity* (New York: Macmillan Publishing Company, 1960), 94, 96.
2 Lewis, 96-97.

Day 60: Whatever You Want

1 C. S. Lewis, *The Weight of Glory* (New York: The Macmillan Company, 1965), 2.

Day 63: Breathe on Them, Breath of God

1 George Herbert, "Prayer (1)," *The Temple* (1633).

Day 64: The 7.5-Million-Dollar Man

1 Quotations in this sketch are taken from Basil Miller's, *George Mueller, Man of Faith and Miracles* (Minneapolis: Bethany House Publishers, 1983).

Day 68: Indiscriminate Thanks

1 Virginia Stem Owens, *The Trees Clap Their Hands*, quoted in *Disciplines for the Inner Life*, by Bob Benson and Michael W. Benson (Waco, Texas: Word, Incorporated, 1985), 334.

2 George Herbert, "Gratefulness," *The Complete English Works*, Ann Pasternak Slater, editor (London: Everyman's Library, David Campbell Publishers, Ltd, 1974), 120.

Day 70: "Man's Extremity Is God's Opportunity"

1 This sketch is taken from Norman Grubb's *Rees Howells Intercessor: The Story of a Life Lived for God* (Fort Washington, PA: CLC Publications, 1973).

Day 76: No One is An Island

1 John Donne, "Meditation XVII," *John Donne, Selections from Divine Poems, Sermons, Devotions and Prayers*, John Booty, editor, *Classics of Western Spirituality* (New York: Paulist Press, 1990), 270.

Day 77: The Sacrament of Geometry

1 This sketch is based upon the writings of Simone Weil.

Day 79: A Choreography of Coincidences

1 See the chapter on Esther in *An Introduction to the Old Testament*, Raymond B. Dillard and Tremper Longman III (Grand Rapids, MI: Zondervan Publishing House, 1994), 189-198.

2 See devotional on Day 2: "The Face in Front of the World."

Day 82: A Humble and Grateful Guide

1 Søren Kierkegaard, *Edifying Discourses* (London: Collins Publishers, 1958), 78-80.

Day 84: Little Left to Lose

1 This prayer and the story of Polycarp are told in *The History of the Church from Christ to Constantine* by Eusebius.

Day 90: The Pleasure of God's Company

1 Quoted by Phillip E. Howard, in his introduction to *The Life and Diary of David Brainerd*, Jonathan Edwards, editor (Grand Rapids, MI: Baker Books, 1989), 14.

Day 92: The Glory and Power of God's Word

1 Gerard Manley Hopkins, "God's Grandeur," *Poems of Gerard Manley Hopkins* (1918).

Day 101: Hunger for God

1 *The Poems of George Herbert*, George Herbert, Ann Pasternak Slater, editor (London: Everyman's Library, Random House, 1974), 156.

Day 102: Whom Have I in Heaven but You?

1 Frederick Buechner, *Wishful Thinking* (New York: Harper and Row Publishers, 1973), 2.

2 Alexander MacLaren, "Psalm 73," *Expositions of Holy Scripture* (Grand Rapids, MI: Baker Book House, 1977), 104.

Day 104: Inner Health Made Audible

1 C. S. Lewis, *Reflections on the Psalms* (New York and London: Harcourt, Brace, Jovanovich, 1958), 94-95.
2 Henry Scougal, *The Life of God in the Soul of Man* (Grand Rapids, MI: Christian Classics Ethereal Library).

Day 105: The Son of These Tears

1 This and previous quotes taken from Saint Augustine, *The Confessions*, translated by R. S. Pine-Coffin (New York: Penguin Books, 1961), 69-70.
2 From the Gelasian Sacramentary, based on a prayer by Augustine, quoted in *2000 Years of Classic Christian Prayers*, edited by Owen Collins (Maryknoll, New York: Orbis Books, 1999), 27.

Day 108: Road Songs

1 The themes in the following list are taken from Eugene Peterson's, *A Long Obedience in the Same Direction* (Downers Grove, IL: Intervarsity Press, 1980).

Day 112: Saying No to Say Yes

1 Saint Augustine, *The Confessions*, translated by R. S. Pine-Coffin (New York: Penguin Books, 1961), 100-101.

Day 116: Wisdom is Supreme

1 Taken from choruses in *The Rock*, a 1934 play by T. S. Eliot.

Day 119: Two Towers

1 Blaise Pascal, *Pensees*, translated by A. J. Krailsheimer (New York: Penguin Books, 1966), 434, 133.

Day 120: Sink or Swim

1 Retold from Robert O. Bakke, *The Power of Extraordinary Prayer* (Wheaton, IL: Crossway Books, 2000).

Day 123: "Meaningless, meaningless...utterly meaningless!"

1 Quoted in Robert Raines, *Creative Brooding* (London: the Macmillan Company, 1969), 76.

Day 125: Too Much but not Enough

1 Quoted from Pascal's *Pensees*.

Day 127: Take the Time

1 Taken from Andrew Murray's *Waiting on God* and other writings.

Day 128: A Good Youth and a Good Death

1 Peter Kreeft, *Love is Stronger Than Death* (San Francisco: Harper and Row, 1979), 104-105.

Day 129: Part of the Permanent

1 J. B. Phillips, *The New Testament in Modern English* (London: Geoffrey Bles, 1960), 502.
2 Quoted by Derek Kidner, *The Message of Ecclesiastes* (Downers Grove, IL: Inter-Varsity Press, 1976), 110.

Day 130: Love is Stronger than Death

1 David Hubbard, The Communicator's Commentary, *Ecclesiastes, Song of Solomon* (Dallas, TX: Word Books, 1991), 267-270.

Day 133: God Guides

1 This sketch is taken from Mary Geegh's *God Guides* (Missionary Press).

Day 135: Holy Terror

1 C. S. Lewis, *The Problem of Pain* (New York: Touchstone Books, 1996), 45, 41.

Day 137: Drink, Thank, Pray, and Proclaim

1 Karl Barth, *Church Dogmatics: The Doctrine of Reconciliation* (London: T&T Clark, 2004) 41-42.
2 John Piper, *Let the Nations be Glad* (Grand Rapids, MI: Baker Book House, 1993), 11.

Day 138: On This Mountain

1 John Donne, "Death Be Not Proud," *Holy Sonnets* (1633).

Day 141: A Candle Burning Brightly

1 Further information about Robert Murray M'Cheyne can be found in Andrew Bonar's biography *Robert Murray M'Cheyne* (Banner of Truth, 1960).

Day 145: The Lord's Watch

1 A paraphrase of a statement by theologian Donald Bloesch.

2 Blaise Pascal's description of why God lets us act on him in prayer.

Day 146: Come Down, Lord!

1 The prayer begins at 63:12 and continues through Isaiah 64 to the end of the chapter.

Day 147: Wrestling with God

1 P. T. Forsyth, *The Soul of Prayer* (London: Independent Press, 1954), 11.

2 Ibid., 88.

3 Ibid., 92.

Day 149: Divine Constraint

1 C. S. Lewis, *The Lion, the Witch and the Wardrobe* (New York: The Macmillan Publishing Company, 1950), 64.

Day 152: Run with the Horses

1 Robert Atwan and Laurence Weider, *Chapters into Verse: Poetry in English Inspired by the Bible* (Oxford: Oxford University Press, 1993), 412.

Day 155: God Plus One

1 Quoted in Basil Miller, *Mary Slessor* (Minneapolis: Bethany House Publishers, 1974), 130, 138.

Day 158: Make Memory a Good Servant

1 John Bunyan, *The Pilgrim's Progress*, Part 1: Section 8.

Day 159: When Things Go Badly

1 George Herbert, "Gratefulness," from *The Temple* (1633).

Day 162: SDG

1 George Herbert, "The Elixer," from *The Temple* (1633).

Day 166: A Model Prayer

1 George Herbert, "Prayer (1)," from *The Temple* (1633).

2 Quoted by Ronald Wallace, *The Message of Daniel* (Downers Grove, IL: Inter-Varsity Press, 1979) 155. This devotion owes much to Wallace's insights.

Day 167: Prayer and Powers

1 "There are two equal and opposite errors into which our race can fall about the devils. One is to disbelieve in their existence. The other is to believe, and to feel an excessive and unhealthy interest in them. They themselves are pleased by both errors and hail a materialist or a magician with the same delight." From the preface to C. S. Lewis, *The Screwtape Letters*.

2 Cited by Ronald Wallace, *The Message of Daniel*, 160.

Day 168: The Redemption of Work

1 This quote and the sketch are taken from Brother Lawrence's *Practice of the Presence of God* (https://ccel.org/ccel/lawrence/practice/practice.i.html).

Day 169: A Marriage Made in Heaven

1 Anders Nygren, *Agape and Eros* (1939).

Day 176: So That You May Know Me

1 The quotations and information for this sketch can be found in Elisabeth Elliot's *Through Gates of Splendor* (Harper & Brothers, 1957).

Day 177: The Mystery of Prayer

1 George Herbert, "Providence," from *The Temple* (1633).

Day 179: Family Feud

1 William Shakespeare, *Romeo and Juliet*, Act II, Scene II.

Day 182: Through a Mighty Strength

1 Translation taken from Thomas Cahill, *How the Irish Saved Civilization* (New York: Doubleday, 1995), 212.

Day 187: Holy Jealousy

1 Peter Kreeft, *Fundamentals of the Faith* (San Francisco: Ignatius Press, 1988), 194.

Day 188: The Righteous Shall Live by Faith

1 Raymond B. Dillard and Tremper Longman III, *An Introduction to the Old Testament* (Grand Rapids, MI: Zondervan, 1994), 409.

Day 190: Men of Prayer

1 Quotation and sketch drawn from E. M. Bounds, "Power Through Prayer," *The Complete Works of E. M. Bounds on Prayer* (Grand Rapids, MI: Baker Book House, 1990), 447.

Day 193: The Sins of the Afternoon

1 Quoted by Earl Palmer, *Alive from the Center* (Waco, TX: Word, Incorporated, 1982), 7.
2 Ibid.

Day 194: Misplaced Priorities

1 Andrew Murray, *With Christ in the School of Prayer* (New Kensington, PA: Whitaker House, 1981), 236.

Day 197: The Imitation of Christ

1 Thomas A Kempis, *The Imitation of Christ*, trans., Leo Sherley-Price (New York: Penguin Classics, 1952), 98.
2 *Prayers from the Imitation of Christ*, Ronald Klug, ed. (Minneapolis, MN: Augsburg, 1996), 24.

Day 203: The Sum of All Prayers

1 These wonderful metaphors come from Peter Kreeft, *Fundamentals of the Faith* (San Francisco: Ignatius Press, 1988), 190-191.

Day 204: Forgive as You Have Been Forgiven

1 Richard Cecil, *The Memoirs of Rev. John Newton* (1838).

Day 205: Always Ready to Listen

1 Quoted in John Blanchard, *The Complete Gold* (Darlington, England: Evangelical Press, 2006), 446.

Day 209: Know Yourself

1 John Calvin, *Institutes of the Christian Religion*, vol. 1 (Philadelphia: The Westminster Press, 1977), 35, 37.

Day 215: Then Help Me, Lord

1 Retold from Corrie ten Boom and Elizabeth and John Sherrill, *The Hiding Place* (Grand Rapids, MI: Baker Publishing Group, Chosen Books, 2006).

Day 222: Why Have You Forsaken Me?

1 From the hymn "O Sacred Head Now Wounded" by Bernard of Clairvaux.

Day 223: By Prayer Alone

1 This quote and the content of the devotional are taken from *The Autobiography of Hudson Taylor, Missionary to China* by J. Hudson Taylor.

Day 226: Holy Exaggeration

1 G. K. Chesterton from the biography of *St. Thomas Aquinas* (first published 1933).

Day 228: If You Are Willing

1 From Charles Spurgeon's sermon "His Name—The Mighty God."

Day 230: Being and Doing

1 From *Faust* by Johann Wolfgang von Goethe (Part 1 published in 1808; Part II in 1832).

2 Widely attributed to Dr. A. J. Gordon (1836-1895), founder of Gordon College.

Day 232: Persistence and Humility in Prayer

1 From the biography *Martin Luther* by Herman Selderhuis (Wheaton, IL: Crossway Books, 2018).

Day 233: Batter My Heart

1 John Booty, editor, *John Donne: Classics of Western Spirituality* (New York: Paulist Press, 1990), 82.

Day 237: Into Your Hands

1 William Barclay, *The Gospel of Luke* (Philadelphia: The Westminster Press, 1956), 301-302.

2 Charles Spurgeon, *Spurgeon's Expository Encyclopedia*, vol. 4 (Grand Rapids, MI: Baker Book House, 1978), 329.

Day 239: Of the Father's Love Begotten

1 William Barclay, *The Gospel of John,* vol. 1 (Philadelphia: The Westminster Press, 1955), xv.

2 Earl Palmer, *The Intimate Gospel* (Waco, TX: Word Books, 1978).

Day 240: It's All in the Family

1 Thomas Wilson, quoted in 2000 *Years of Classic Christian Prayers*, Owen Collins, ed. (Maryknoll, NY. Orbis Books, 1999), 126.

Day 242: Blessed Are the Peacemakers

1 This quote and the content of the sketch can be found in *Blood Brothers: The Dramatic Story of a Palestinian Christian Working for Peace in Israel* by Elias Chacour and David Hazard (Grand Rapids, MI: Baker Books, 1984).

Day 244: Drinkable Light

1 C.S. Lewis. *The Voyage of the Dawn Treader* (New York: The Macmillan Company, 1952), 193, 196.

Day 248: Maximum Love, Not Minimum Love

1 See Palmer, *The Intimate Gospel*, for an excellent discussion of the scene, 115-118.

Day 249: The Power of the Name

1 Dante Alighieri, *The Divine Comedy*, Charles Eliot Norton, trans. (Chicago: Encyclopedia Britannica, 1952), 157.

Day 250: Of Fruit and Prayer

1 Quoted in Earl Palmer, *The Intimate Gospel*, 129.

Day 251: With His Dying Breath

1 The story of Blind Chang was originally recounted by Rosalind Goforth, *Blind Chang: Missionary Martyr of Manchuria* (Toronto: Evangelical Publishers, 1940).

Day 252: The "Real" Lord's Prayer

1 Attributed to English economist and historian, R. H. Tawney (1880-1962).

Day 253: The Continuing Words and Deeds of Jesus

1 John Stott, *The Spirit, The Church and the World*, The Message of Acts (Downers Grove, IL: InterVarsity Press, 1990), 34.

Day 254: Being a Prayer Meeting

1 Widely attributed to Armin R. Gesswein (1908-2001), founder and director of Revival Prayer Fellowship, Inc. and Minister's Prayer Fellowship.

Day 259: "The Most Dejected and Reluctant Convert"

1 C. S. Lewis, *Surprised by Joy* (New York: Harcourt and Brace, 1955), 228-229.
2 From P.T. Forsyth's *The Soul of Prayer* (Grand Rapids, MI: Christian Classics Ethereal Library online).
3 Lewis, 229.

Day 260: A Castle and a Garden

1 *The Study of Spirituality*, edited by Cheslyn Jones, Geoffrey Wainwright, Edward Yarnold, SJ (New York: Oxford University Press, 1986), 366.
2 *2000 Years of Classic Christian Prayers*, edited by Owen Collins (Maryknoll, NY: Orbis Books, 1999), 71.

Day 262: The Fuel and the Goal of Missions

1 John Piper, *Let the Nations be Glad* (Grand Rapids, MI: Baker Book House, 1993), 11.

Day 264: "The Chief Part of the New Testament"

1 John Calvin, *The Epistles of Paul the Apostle to the Romans and to the Thessalonians*, trans by Ross Mackenzie, ed by David W. Torrance and Thomas F. Torrance (Grand Rapids, MI: William B. Eerdmans, 1960), 5.
2 Quoted in John Stott, *Romans, God's Good News for the World* (Downer's Grove, IL: InterVarsity Press, 1994), 19.

Day 265: Paul, The Praying Activist

1 Widely attributed to Dr. A. J. Gordon (1836-1895), founder of Gordon College.
2 Andrew Murray, With Christ in the School of Prayer (New Kensington, PA: Whitaker House, 1981), 236.

Day 266: A Model Prayer

1 Haldane, Robert. *Exposition of the Epistle to the Romans: With Remarks on the Commentaries of Dr. MacKnight, Professor Moses Stuart, and Professor Tholuck.* (New York: Robert Carter & Brothers, 1849), 37

Day 268: Crying and Groaning and Learning to Pray

1 James Montgomery Boice, "The Reign of Grace, Romans 5-8," *Romans*, vol. 2 (Grand Rapids, MI: Baker Book House, 1992), 892.

Day 269: Passion for One's People

1 From the hymn "And Can It Be That I Should Gain" by Charles Wesley.

Day 270: The True Seminary

1 This story is retold from *A Biography of John Sung* by Leslie T. Lyall (London: China Inland Mission Overseas Missionary Fellowship, 1954).

Day 279: The Joy of a Melancholy Man

1 From *The Diaries of David Brainerd*, Edited by Jonathan Edwards (Grand Rapids, MI: Baker Book House, 1989), 170.

Day 280: Spiritual Discipline

1 Quoted in *Devotional Classics*, A RENOVARE Resource for Spiritual Renewal, Richard J. Foster and James Bryan Smith, eds. (Harper: San Francisco: 1993), 16.

Day 283: Love, the Heart of Prayer

1 J. B. Phillip's paraphrase of 1 Cor. 13:13 (available as *J.B. Phillips New Testament* on BibleGateway.com).

Day 285: The God of All Comfort

1 Joseph Medlicott Scriven, "What a Friend We Have in Jesus," *The Hymnal* (Waco, TX: Word, Inc., 1986), 435.

Day 288: The Worldview of Prayer

1 Retold from *Orthodoxy* by G.K. Chesterton (originally published in 1908).

Day 289: A Diary of Private Prayer

1 John Baillie, *Christian Devotion* (New York, Scribner, 1962), 62.
2 John Baillie, *A Diary of Private Prayer* (New York: Scribner, 1949), 25.

Day 290: Spiritual Warfare

1 From a sermon on 2 Corinthians 10:4-5, by Alexander Maclaren, *Expositions of Holy Scripture*, vol. 14, (Grand Rapids, MI: Baker Book House, 1977), 61.

Day 295: Praying for the Fruit of the Spirit

1 Quoted in John Stott, *The Contemporary Christian* (Downers Grove, IL: InterVarsity Press, 1992), 156.

Day 299: A Prayer for Illumination

1 Retold from *The Sickness Unto Death* (1849) by Søren Kierkegaard.

Day 300: The Fulfillment of All Desire

1 C. S. Lewis, *The Weight of Glory* (Grand Rapids, MI: Eerdmans, 1977), 1-2.
2 From the poem "Andrea del Sarto" by Robert Browning. Published in *Men and Women* (1855).

Day 303: Grateful, Joyful Prayer

1 Karl Barth, *Church Dogmatics: The Doctrine of Reconciliation* (London: T&T Clark, 2004), 41-42.
2 Patterned after a prayer by George Herbert: "Thou that hast given so much to me, /Give one thing more, a grateful heart." *George Herbert, The Complete English Works*, Ann Pasternak Slater, ed. (Everyman's Library; Alfred A. Knopf, New York, London, Toronto, 1995), 120.

Day 306: A Demonstration of the Spirit's Power

1 Samuel Chadwick, "How I Became a Missioner," *Prevailing Intercessory Prayer* (https://www.path2prayer.com) accessed January 25, 2024.
2 Samuel Chadwick, "Praying in the Spirit" (http://www.heraldofhiscoming.com) accessed January 25, 2024.
3 Chadwick, "How I Became a Missioner."
4 Chadwick, "Praying in the Spirit."
5 Samuel Chadwick, "The Way to Pentecost" (http://www.heraldofhiscoming.com).

Day 308: The Point of Convergence

1 Story told by Earl Palmer in *Alive from the Center* (Waco, TX: Word Incorporated, 1982), 19.
2 A.T. Robertson, *Paul and the Intellectuals: The Epistle to the Colossians* (New York: Doubleday, Doran and Company, 1928).

Day 310: The Still Point in the Turning World

1 T.S. Eliot, "Burnt Norton," from *Collected Poems* (New York: Harcourt, Brace & World, 1963).

Day 311: Muscular Prayer

1 From Billy Graham's sermon "Witnessing Boldly," September 16, 1963 (Billy Graham Evangelistic Association archives: https://billygraham.org/audio/witnessing-boldly/).

Day 312: Prayer and the Parousia

1 *Parousia* is a Greek word in the New Testament used to refer to Christ's second coming.

Day 314: Prayer, Praise, and Perfection

1 Quoted by Robert Llewelyn in *Our Duty and Our Joy* (London: Darton, Longman and Todd, Ltd, 1993), 1.
2 William Law, *A Serious Call to a Devout and Holy Life* (first published 1729), chapter 15.

Day 318: Guilt, Grace, and Gratitude

1 Excerpt from *The Prayers of Kierkegaard*, Perry De. LeFevre, ed. (Chicago: University of Chicago Press, 1996).

Day 321: Fan the Flame

1 This account was included in a speech by Barth scholar, Martin Rumscheidt, in 1968. Quoted in a Patheos blog by Roger Olson (https://www.patheos.com/blogs/rogereolson/2013/01/did-karl-barth-really-say-jesus-loves-me-this-i-know/).

Day 322: God's Breath in Man Returning

1 From P.T. Forsyth, *Positive Preaching and the Modern Mind* (1949).
2 George Herbert, "Prayer (1)," *The Complete Works* (Everyman's Library: Alfred A. Knopf: New York, 1995), 49.

Day 323: Finishing Strong

1 Martyn Lloyd-Jones, *Twenty Centuries of Great Preaching,* vol. 11 (Waco, TX: Word, Inc., 1971), 296.

Day 324: A Great and Humble Mind

1 *The Oxford Dictionary of Quotations* (Oxford: Oxford University Press, 1980), 275:36.
2 Ibid, 274:8.
3 Ibid, 90:15.
4 Elton Trueblood, ed., *Dr. Johnson's Prayers* (New York: Harper and Brothers, 1947), x-xi.
5 *Oxford Dictionary*, 275:3.
6 *Dr. Johnson's Prayers,* 5.

Day 330: Approach the Throne of Grace with Confidence

1 C.S. Lewis, *The Last Battle* (New York: The Macmillan Company, 1956), 160, 162.

Day 332: Stunned Confidence

1 Peter Kreeft, *Fundamentals of the Faith*, Essays in Christian Apologetics (San Francisco: Ignatius Press, 1988), 193.

Day 333: Take My Life

1 Frances Havergal, "I Gave My Life for Thee," *The Hymnal for Worship and Celebration*, Tom Fettke, Senior Editor (Waco, TX: Word Music, 1986), 453.
2 J. Gilchrist Lawson, *Deeper Experiences of Famous Christians* (Uhrichsville, OH: Barbour Publishing, Inc., 1999), 268.
3 Frances Havergal, "Take My Life and Let it Be," *The Hymnal for Worship and Celebration*, 379.

Day 336: Prayer, Encouragement, and the Family of God

1 Eugene Peterson, *A Long Obedience in the Same Direction* (Downers Grove: InterVarsity Press, 2000), 175.
2 P. T. Forsyth, *The Soul of Prayer* (London: Independent Press, 1954), 11.

Day 337: Prayer and Awe

1 J. B. Phillips, *The New Testament in Modern English* (London: Geoffrey Bles, 1960), 502.
2 The Heidelberg Catechism (Grand Rapids, MI: CRC Publications, 1988), question 116.

Day 338: A Sacrifice of Praise

1 Paraphrased from George Herbert, "Providence," *The Temple* (1633).

Day 340: Practical Christianity

1 Widely attributed to Dr. A. J. Gordon (1836-1895), founder of Gordon College.

Day 342: Sweet Delight in God

1 Quoted in *The Life and Diary of David Brainerd*, edited by Jonathan Edwards (Grand Rapids: Baker Book House, 1989), 14.
2 Quoted in *The Study of Spirituality*, edited by Cheslyn Jones, Geoffrey Wainwright, Edward Yarnold, SJ, (Oxford: Oxford University Press, 1986), 474.
3 This is an abbreviation of the full title, *An Humble Attempt to Promote Explicit Agreement and Visible Union Among God's People, in Extraordinary Prayer for the Revival of Religion, and the Advancement of Christ's Kingdom on Earth, Pursuant to Scripture Promises and Prophecies Concerning the Last Times.*

Day 346: The Gigantic Secret

1 G. K. Chesterton, *Orthodoxy* (San Francisco: Ignatius Press, 1986), 365.

Day 347: Pray for Your Church

1 C.S. Lewis, The Screwtape Letters (New York: Macmillan, 1982), pp. 12-13.

Day 351: Enfolded in Love

1 Quoted in *Our Duty and Our Joy*, Robert Llewelyn (London: Darton, Longman and Todd, 1993), 25.
2 Quoted in *Devotional Classics*, edited by Richard J. Foster and James Bryan Smith (San Francisco: Harper San Francisco, 1993), 68.
3 Owen Collins, ed., *2000 Years of Classic Christian Prayers*, (Maryknoll, NY: Orbis Books, 1999), 44.
4 Ibid., 67.

Day 353: Good for the Soul and the Cell

1 Charitie Lees Bancroft, "Before the Throne of God Above," quoted by David Jackman, *The Message of John's Letters* (Downers Grove, IL: Intervarsity Press, 1988), 40.

Day 359: The Small Woman

1 Catharine Swift, *Gladys Aylward* (Minneapolis, MN: Bethany House Publishers, 1989), 15.
2 James E. Kiefer, "Biographical sketches of memorable Christians of the past," Anglican Resource Collection, Justus.Anglican.org, 3 January, 1970, http://justus.anglican.org/resources/bio/73.html.
3 "Gladys Aylward's 'Impossible Mission' to China," *Glimpses,* Issue #6: http://www.gospelcom.net/chi/GLIMPSEF/Glimpses/glmps006.shtml.

Day 360: The Praying Imagination

1 This phrase is taken from the subtitle of Eugene Peterson's book, *Reversed Thunder* (HarperOne, 1991).

Day 363: Pray for the Persecuted Church

1 Vernard Eller, *The Most Revealing Book of the Bible* (Grand Rapids, MI: Eerdmans, 1974), 93.

About the author

Reverend Ben Patterson was the campus pastor at Westmont College in Santa Barbara, California from 2001 until his retirement in 2018. He was responsible for organizing the college's chapel program, mentoring students, counseling, and encouraging every person in the Westmont community to grow toward their full maturity in Christ.

Ben has contributed to *Christianity Today* and *Leadership Journal*. Previously he was a contributing editor and editorial writer with *The Wittenburg Door*. Ben has written several books, including *Serving God: The Grand Essentials of Work & Worship; Waiting: Finding Hope When God Seems Silent; Deepening Your Conversation with God; The Prayer Devotional Bible;* and *He Has Made Me Glad*. Ben's most current work, which was released in November 2008, is *God's Prayer Book: The Power and Pleasure of Praying the Psalms*.

Ben served at New Providence Presbyterian Church of New Jersey from 1989 until his appointment as dean of the chapel at Hope College in 1993. From 1975 to 1998 he served as the founding pastor of Irvine Presbyterian Church in California. Ben was also minister of youth and adult education at La Jolla Presbyterian Church in California. Previous to that he was assistant minister to college students at First Baptist Church of Pomona, California, working with the Claremont Colleges.

Ben earned his bachelor's degree from La Verne University and his master of divinity from the American Baptist Seminary of the West. Ben and his wife, Lauretta, have four adult children: three married sons, a daughter, and a grandson.